Oligarchy

For centuries, oligarchs were viewed as empowered by wealth, an idea muddled by elite theory in the early twentieth century. The common thread for oligarchs across history is that wealth defines and empowers them, and inherently exposes them to threats. The existential motive of all oligarchs is the defense of wealth. Their pursuit of wealth defense varies with the threats they confront, including how directly involved they are in supplying the coercion underlying all property claims, and whether they act separately or collectively. These variations yield four types of oligarchy: warring, ruling, sultanistic, and civil. Democracy does not displace oligarchy but rather fuses with it. Moreover, the rule-of-law problem in many societies is a matter of taming oligarchs. Cases studied in this book include the United States, ancient Athens and Rome, Indonesia, the Philippines, Singapore, medieval Venice and Siena, Mafia commissions in the United States and Italy, feuding Appalachian families, and early chiefs *cum* oligarchs dating from 2300 B.C.E.

Jeffrey A. Winters specializes in oligarchy and elites in a range of historical and contemporary cases, including Athens, Rome, medieval Europe, the United States, and several countries in Southeast Asia. His research, publications, and teaching focus on the areas of comparative and international political economy. Themes in his work in addition to oligarchy include state-capital relations, capital mobility and the structural power of investors, human rights, authoritarianism and democratic transitions in postcolonial states, and the World Bank. He has conducted extensive research in the region of Southeast Asia, especially Indonesia, Vietnam, Thailand, the Philippines, Malaysia, and Singapore. He is the author of *Power in Motion: Capital Mobility and the Indonesian State* (1996). He coedited *Reinventing the World Bank* (2002, with Jonathan Pincus). He has also published two other books in Indonesian. Professor Winters has received grants and scholarships from the John D. and Catherine T. MacArthur Foundation, the National Science Foundation, the Rockefeller Foundation, the Sawyer-Mellon Foundation, the Henry R. Luce Foundation, the J. M. Kaplan Fund, and a J. William Fulbright Senior Specialist Grant.

Oligarchy

JEFFREY A. WINTERS
Northwestern University

CAMBRIDGE
UNIVERSITY PRESS

CAMBRIDGE
UNIVERSITY PRESS

32 Avenue of the Americas, New York NY 10013-2473, USA

Cambridge University Press is part of the University of Cambridge.

It furthers the University's mission by disseminating knowledge in the pursuit of education, learning and research at the highest international levels of excellence.

www.cambridge.org
Information on this title: www.cambridge.org/9780521182980

First published 2011

A catalogue record for this publication is available from the British Library

Library of Congress Cataloguing in Publication data

Winters, Jeffrey A. (Jeffrey Alan), 1960–
Oligarchy / Jeffrey A. Winters.
  p.   cm.
Includes bibliographical references and index.
ISBN 978-1-107-00528-0 (hardback) – ISBN 978-0-521-18298-0 (paperback)
1. Oligarchy.   I. Title.
JC419.W56   2011
321'.5–dc22   2010045994

ISBN 978-1-107-00528-0 Hardback
ISBN 978-0-521-18298-0 Paperback

In memory of Gordon Bishop

Contents

List of Figures and Tables

Figures

Tables

Preface

When Michael Bloomberg was running for his third term as mayor of New York, he was compared unfairly in the media to the Roman oligarch Marcus Licinius Crassus, who had "deployed his wealth in the service of his political ambitions" (Hertzberg 2009, 27). Drawing on a fortune estimated in 2010 at $18 billion, Bloomberg had "spent more of his own money than any other individual in United States history in the pursuit of public office." It is true that both men are oligarchs. However, the comparison is misleading because it fails to recognize important changes in oligarchy over the centuries. When oligarchs like Crassus spent their resources to become consul, it was one of the most important things they could do politically to secure their core oligarchic interests. For modern American oligarchs like Bloomberg, buying public office with private funds is driven more by vanity than motives of oligarchic survival.[1] Unlike in Rome, oligarchs in America enjoy strong property rights enforced by others, and thus do not need to rule to pursue their core interests. When they do hold office, it is neither *as* nor *for* oligarchs. It is unlikely that Bloomberg the billionaire would do anything differently as mayor had his political career been entirely funded by donations or public resources.

If direct rule is much less vital for American oligarchs than for their Roman counterparts, why even label someone like Bloomberg an oligarch? This book argues that the answer lies in the very different ways that oligarchs defend their wealth in a civil oligarchy like the modern United States. A clearer insight into Bloomberg's oligarchic behavior was provided a year later in an exposé (Roston 2010) detailing how the Bloomberg Family Foundation had moved hundreds of millions of dollars into "various offshore destinations – some of them notorious tax-dodge hideouts."[2] Hiding wealth, restructuring it to evade

---

[1] Steen (2006) studies self-financed candidates and finds that the vast majority of them lose their bids for office. There is no hint of oligarchic inclinations among the few who prevail.

[2] Funds from the Bloomberg Family Foundation had been transferred to The Caymans, Cyprus, Bermuda, Brazil, Mauritius, Japan, Luxembourg, and Romania. In an interview, Bloomberg

taxation, and designing complex tax shelters are high-priced services provided to American oligarchs by a sophisticated Income Defense Industry. The very existence of this industry is an expression of oligarchic power and interests. When individual oligarchs hide and defend their money, causing an estimated $70 billion in annual losses to the Treasury according to Senate investigations, it is referred to by the professionals as "cross-border abusive tax avoidance transactions and schemes" – something not only unknown to Crassus, but as unnecessary for ensuring his oligarchic interests in Roman times as governing is for ensuring Bloomberg's today. This study traces what oligarchs in different eras have in common, but also how oligarchy has evolved as the circumstances confronting oligarchs have changed.

There are many important cases, from the ancient to the contemporary, in which available explanations of the politics of minority power and influence over majorities are either unpersuasive or poorly theorized. Continuing the focus on the United States for a moment, consider the problem of decades of rising inequality. In 2004, an American Political Science Association (APSA) task force tried to explain why a vibrant American democracy was becoming increasingly unequal with regard to wealth, despite real progress overcoming inequalities in other areas like race, ethnicity, gender, sexual orientation, and disability. The task force framed the matter as a classic problem of democratic participation.

The argument is familiar. With overwhelming numbers on their side, the poor have potential power based on votes. However, participation, skills, resources, and information all increase as one moves up the wealth ladder. With these advantages comes government responsiveness. The theory is founded on the notion that underparticipation by the poor and full participation by the rich results in policies that leave the poor behind. This pluralist-democratic optic would be plausible except for one major problem: on closer inspection, the data on wealth and income in the United States show that the lion's share of the gains causing the yawning wealth gap accrued to a sliver of the population far too tiny to account for such exaggerated power and responsiveness on democratic participation grounds alone. The largest gains went to 1/10th and even 1/100th of the top 1 percent of households. The drop-off beyond that was steep.

Starting from the 95th percentile downward, incomes and wealth were stagnant or negative for the decades covered by the APSA study. Even more problematic for the theory is that the very wealthiest fraction of a percent at the top managed to shift tax burdens downward – not to the middle class or poorest segments of society, but to households in the 85th to 99th percentile income

stated that "the first rule of taxation is, you can't tax too much those that can move" (Roston 2010). In his capacity as mayor, Bloomberg is as aware of this fact as Mayor Daley of Chicago, a man of modest wealth. However, as an oligarch, Bloomberg has a far greater appreciation than Daley of precisely *how* the rich move their money and defend against taxation – and equally important, he has enough money to hire the services to do it.

range. It is one thing for the poor, despite their numbers, to lose in the game of democratic participation. However, democratic theory would predict that Americans in the "mass affluent" income range ought to have the votes, skills, and resources to prevent a vastly smaller stratum at the very top from grabbing a much larger share of the wealth pie while avoiding commensurate tax burdens.

A key problem with the APSA study is that the analytical framework it employs is incapable of treating concentrated wealth and the influence it confers as a distinct basis of minority power for excluding or dominating majorities. The political inequalities that arise from wealth inequalities are qualitatively different from others that have been effectively addressed in recent decades through democratic participation and social movements. Indeed, the APSA study was prompted by the worrying fact that the distribution of wealth was becoming more unequal during the same decades when all the other indicators of injustice were showing significant improvements. The case study presented in Chapter 5 offers a more plausible explanation of how American oligarchs, under inviolable protections of private property and assisted aggressively by an Income Defense Industry propelled by fees from oligarchs, achieve this outcome. The evidence is clear both from U.S. history and from European comparisons (including Scandinavia) that when inequality is reduced through government transfers to the poor, the wealthiest fraction of a percent at the top consistently deflects the tax burdens downward to those whose wealth is insufficient to buy an effective defense.

Oligarchic theory explains how and why this occurs. The starting premise is that concentrated wealth in the hands of individuals empowers them in ways that produce distinct kinds of oligarchic politics that are not captured within a generic pluralist framework. In place of viewing ultrawealthy actors as one among many competing interest groups (in this case "the rich"), the theory developed in this work argues that whatever other forms of power may exist in society, extreme wealth has a profound influence on the capacities of oligarchs to defend and advance their core interests. The unusual aspect of oligarchic politics is that massive fortunes produce both particular political challenges – the need to defend wealth – and the unique power resources for pursuing that defense. This approach helps explain why those most able to pay are also the ones most empowered to avoid doing so, and why ordinary democratic participation is an ineffective antidote.

Recognition of this fact does not amount to a denial of pluralist democratic politics across a range of issues in contexts like the United States, nor to claims that electoral democracy is a sham. It is, rather, an acknowledgment that under conditions of extreme economic stratification, there is also an oligarchic realm of power and politics that engages different power resources and merits separate theorization. This separate realm of minority power and politics involving concentrated wealth is unusually resistant to remedies based on widening participation.

Oligarchy in Varying Contexts

"I'll tell you, sometimes I feel like funding a revolution," an exasperated oligarch in Southeast Asia told me. It was a classic expression of oligarchic power that would be immediately familiar to Crassus. Instead, it was spoken late in 2007. After a quick calculation, the oligarch realized that it would only cost him about $20 million to $30 million to put 100,000 demonstrators on the streets of his capital for a month – a sum he considered cheap. In this instance, the oligarch did not rent a regime-destabilizing crowd. He was merely venting his frustration. Nevertheless, what is striking – and what this book helps explain – is how he could reasonably make such a calculation in the first place. For most of us, this would be an absurd exercise. To get demonstrators to pour into the streets and remain there for a month, one would have to lead a mass movement, the followers would have to be organized, and they would have to believe in the cause. Although some money would be needed for basic logistics, it certainly would not be paid as a *per diem* to the protesters. Only oligarchs have sufficient private resources to muse about such political actions.

Sometimes they do more than muse. A world audience was provided a glimpse in the spring of 2010 of what happens when ruling oligarchs clash in the streets. Dramatic broadcasts from Thailand showed government troops breaking through barricades and violently clearing thousands of "Red Shirt" demonstrators from Lumpini Park in the heart of Bangkok. Reporters explained that "Yellow Shirt" protesters were on the other side of the struggle. However, beyond this chromatic shorthand, the details of the political conflict were fairly murky. Missing from the story was the fact that this battle of shirts was also a titanic fight involving Thailand's most powerful oligarchs, including members of the royal family. Thaksin Shinawatra, a telecommunications mogul and Thailand's richest billionaire, was a master at buying Thai electoral outcomes. He became prime minister in 2001. With the support of poorer voters in the Northeast, his corrupt party won a landslide victory for a second term in 2005. Agitated oligarchs in Bangkok, each as corrupt as Thaksin, repeatedly failed to outflank him at the polls.

Sondhi Limthongkul, a media tycoon and former Thaksin ally, took it personally when several government decisions threatened his business. Combining cash from his private fortune with resources from his media empire, Sondhi launched a series of politically destabilizing protests in the same Lumpini Park at the end of 2005. His yellow shirts were eventually enjoined by Thaksin's red shirts. Various other political themes like corruption, democracy, and the dignity and rights of the downtrodden came and went as the conflict unfolded. However, these two oligarchs had engineered the eruption of Thailand's shirted proxy war through massive outlays drawn from enormous personal riches. In the event, Sondhi did not fund a revolution, but the faux "people power" attack he launched was profoundly destabilizing and resulted in Thaksin being ousted in a bloodless military coup in 2006. Sondhi, meanwhile, was repaid in typical ruling oligarchic fashion. One April morning in 2009, his car was riddled with a hundred rounds of automatic rifle fire from AK-47s and M-16s. Somehow he escaped with only a few shrapnel fragments lodged in his skull.[3] Oligarchic theory is indispensable for making sense of these events.

It is also useful for explaining certain important puzzles. The perception is widespread in Indonesia, for instance, that things have changed radically since Suharto's fall in 1998, and yet somehow barely changed at all. In 2009, Indonesia was ranked as the most democratic *and* the most corrupt nation in Southeast Asia. The country is beset by chronic political and economic problems that seem to have grown worse since the democratic transition. These are generally interpreted as the birth pains of democracy itself. However, the interpretation presented in Chapter 4 argues instead that there were two transitions in 1998: the obvious one from dictatorship to democracy, but also a separate and quite different transition from a sultanistic oligarchy tamed by Suharto to a ruling oligarchy that has been untamed since he was deposed. It is this second transition, no less important than the first, which is the source of many of Indonesia's difficulties. Why this is so is only explicable through a theory capable of discerning the power and politics of oligarchs. Often misinterpreted as a "quality of democracy" problem, the result in Indonesia has been the emergence of a "criminal democracy" in which oligarchs use their wealth both to compete unfairly for office and to defeat the rule of law when they get in trouble for things like corruption or causing environmental disasters.[4] This book argues that the specific manner in which democracy has been captured and distorted since Suharto's fall is best explained by a materialist oligarchic theory.

The case of Singapore poses a similar problem but in inverted form. Instead of being a criminal democracy, the city-state is an enduring example of "authoritarian legalism" characterized by the strong rule of law without democracy. Oligarchs in Singapore are well tamed by a reliable and impersonal system of laws and enforcement, but there are no liberal freedoms. Oligarchic theory predicts that strong safeguards in the realm of property and contracts, including arrangements that protect oligarchs from each other, can and do coexist

---

[3] The use of oligarchic resources in postcolonial societies is not restricted to major battles like the one that caused Thailand's democracy to collapse. An Indonesian oligarch happened to mention in an interview that he had just met with a group of nine other oligarchs to discuss how much each must contribute to a pool of funds to be paid in cash to members of parliament to break a logjam on key tax and labor legislation. The amount needed was $500,000 each. "All ten agreed to chip in?" I asked. "Done" was the reply. Confidential interview in Jakarta with Oligarch "C," August 12, 2008.

[4] The reference is to Indonesian oligarch Aburizal Bakrie's role in the May 2006 Lapindo mud-flow disaster in East Java, Indonesia. Wantchekon (2004) writes on the equally surprising phenomenon of "warlord democracy." On the "quality of democracy" argument, see O'Donnell 2004. Criminal democracy adds to the list that Collier and Levitsky (1997) compiled of more than 550 examples of "democracy with adjectives."

with democratic freedoms. However, Singapore shows in a different way from Indonesia that there is no necessary relationship between law and democracy, and even that the same court system can consistently uphold impartial justice in matters of property while repeatedly trampling the human rights of political opponents. Authoritarian regimes are not supposed to have strongly institutionalized and independent infrastructures of law. Oligarchic theory helps account for why they sometimes do.

In addition to the critical issues raised in these examples, another that receives sustained theoretical attention across all the cases discussed in this book is the important relationship historically among oligarchs, the pressures to defend their concentrated wealth from an array of threats, and the locus of the coercion indispensable for this defense. A theory of oligarchy that emphasizes material power and places at its center the challenges of wealth defense is especially helpful in explaining not only the shift in coercive roles between oligarchs themselves and property-guaranteeing states, but also why oligarchs seem to appear and disappear. This has important implications for a range of literatures in the social sciences, but especially for analyses in the New Institutional Economics tradition.

Architecture and Cases

A few words are needed about what is and is not attempted in this book. First, oligarchy is approached through oligarchs, understood as individuals empowered by wealth. A fuller explanation of this is presented in Chapter 1, but to avoid confusion, it must be emphasized here that collectivities like corporations do not play a central role in defining oligarchs or oligarchic theory. Oligarchs can be sole or controlling owners of corporations and can use them as personal instruments of power. Under these conditions, corporations serve as vehicles to amplify the interests of the oligarchs who command them. There are periods in history when this has been the dominant pattern. However, corporations can also be owned in ways that are highly diffuse and impersonal, and they can be run by managerial strata that sometimes include workers or the state. Oligarchs existed long before corporations appeared, and they continue to exist despite the rise of managerial capitalism and state (or worker) ownership of firms. Corporations do not stand alone within oligarchic theory, but instead should be seen as potential instruments of oligarchs.[5]

A second point concerns the international dimension, which historically concerns the broader matter of oligarchs crossing territories and boundaries. The cases examined in this book include many instances in which oligarchs

---

[5] Mizruchi (2004) discusses the managerial transformation within firms dating back to the pioneering work by Berle and Means. *Citizens United v. Federal Election Commission* (U.S. Supreme Court 2010) allowed unlimited, secret spending by organizations, including corporations, during election campaigns. This enabled oligarchs using 501(c) nonprofit organizations as fronts to anonymously deploy tens of millions to sway political outcomes in the 2010 elections.

operate (usually violently) far from home. They have most often done this as collectivities – for instance, as commanders of invading armies from nearby warring or ruling oligarchies. Nothing in this study precludes analyses of how oligarchs in modern times interact, project their power (as individuals or collectively through corporate instruments), or defend their interests transnationally. Attempting such an analysis is, however, a major undertaking and beyond the scope of this book. One point that can be said with regard to international relations theory (which focuses far more on states and organizations than on persons) is that it is unlikely that a theory of oligarchs and oligarchy designed to illuminate the power and motives of actors at the level of the individual (including when they cooperate) can be applied without major modifications to the interplay of states (each of which would presumably contain numerous oligarchs and yet would somehow have to be treated as a unitary actor).

In writing a book on oligarchy, case selection is a daunting prospect. Cases were chosen for this study based on both analytical and practical grounds. With regard to the first, cases were selected that could inform and expand important aspects of oligarchic theory and could offer useful comparisons and contrasts. Cases were also deliberately chosen to demonstrate the historical and contextual reach of the approach. The claim is not that oligarchs in ancient Rome are interchangeable with oligarchs in the United States or modern Philippines. Rather, it is that oligarchs in all the cases studied are empowered by wealth and intensely focused on wealth defense, and that they pursue wealth defense in different ways and in highly variable contexts. The cases were chosen and organized in a manner that casts these differences and variations in the sharpest possible relief. The result is a sometimes-jolting but entirely intentional juxtaposition of materials.

On the practical side, cases were selected because the author could discuss them with a reasonable degree of confidence (and even then, with some obvious unevenness). After setting aside several cases because of space limitations, the book ends with major discussions of the United States, ancient Athens and Rome, and Indonesia. It has slightly more abbreviated (but still detailed) comparative discussions of the Philippines, Singapore, and the medieval Italian city-states, especially Venice and Siena. It also includes shorter discussions of Mafia Commissions in the United States and Italy; feuding Appalachian families in nineteenth-century Kentucky; and early chiefs, warlords, and oligarchs dating from around 2300 B.C.E.

As for the architecture of the book, it opens with a theoretical chapter establishing the material foundations of oligarchy. The important concept of wealth defense is also introduced. The theory chapter closes with a typology of four kinds of oligarchy that have predominated throughout history: warring, ruling, sultanistic, and civil. A chapter is devoted to each of these types, with additional theoretical discussions and case material presented in each. The chapters could have been presented in any order. The key reason this order was chosen is that in warring oligarchies, the actors are most personally engaged in rule and coercion and operate in the most fragmented manner. In civil oligarchies, at the other extreme, oligarchs are fully disarmed, do not rule, and submit to the property-defending laws of highly bureaucratic institutional states. The other two forms in the middle – ruling and sultanistic – exhibit certain hybrid characteristics. Despite the appearance of an evolutionary progression across these types (and especially the decidedly late appearance of the civil form), there is no easy linearity to the history of oligarchy.

Studies structured around typologies can sometimes be static. There are, however, highly dynamic elements built into the cases presented, and major transformations are tracked and explained in several of them. That said, a unifying theory of oligarchic change from one type to another (assuming such a theory is possible) is beyond the scope of this book. The last chapter offers a brief conclusion addressing selected issues and comparisons not developed in the other chapters. It also discusses how oligarchic theory intersects with important literatures and themes in the social sciences. A key theme running throughout the book is that oligarchs and oligarchy result from extreme concentrations of wealth (and wealth's power) in private hands. This implies that where such stratification is absent, oligarchs and oligarchy are also absent.

Acknowledgments

In researching and writing this book, I have benefited enormously from conversations with and generous criticisms and input from many scholars, students, family, friends, and even some accommodating oligarchs who agreed to be interviewed (only one of whom took offense at being so labeled). There are several scholars and political observers I would like to thank by name, who read parts or all of this book and provided important insights, suggestions, and corrections. They include the late Arief Arryman, Edward Gibson, Roger Haydon, Chris Howell, Richard Lachmann, Sara Monoson, Ben Page, Jonathan Pincus, Rizal Ramli, Arthur Stinchcombe, Benny Subianto, and Herman Widodo. I also want to thank the anonymous reviewers for the very careful read they gave to this book. I was not able to incorporate all of their thoughtful and constructive suggestions, but their input greatly improved the arguments I attempt here. I also want to extend my appreciation to Lewis Bateman and the excellent staff at Cambridge University Press.

I have benefited from discussions and debates with many colleagues during the research and writing of this book. I especially want to mention and thank the late Gordon Bishop, Teri Caraway, Bruce Cumings, Mary Dietz, Jim Farr, Thomas Ferguson, Michael Hanchard, Bonnie Honig, Paul Hutchcroft, Michael Loriaux, Mark Mizruchi, Will Reno, Richard Robison, Joan Tronto, and Meredith Jung-en Woo. Some individuals who made major contributions to the development and arguments of this book have asked to remain anonymous. I thank them for their patience and generosity during our extended discussions and interviews.

I presented early versions of this work at several conferences and talks, including at the Harvard Business School in March 2006; Oberlin College in October 2006; Northwestern University's Buffett Center for International and Comparative Studies in November 2007; the "Chieftancy Working Group," also at Northwestern, in 2008; the Harvard Kennedy School in 2010; and Columbia University's "Working Group on Elites and Inequality," also in 2010. I received valuable feedback at all of these forums, and I want to thank Jordan Siegel, Marc Blecher, Harlan Wilson, Ben Schiff, Tim Earle, Shamus Khan, and Dorian Warren for making these important opportunities possible. I am indebted to the many Northwestern undergraduate and graduate students who took my seminar on oligarchy and elite rule, as well as to Ngurah Karyadi and the students and colleagues at Udayana Law School in Indonesia. My profound gratitude goes to Nelly Paliama and the Fulbright program for making the semester at Udayana possible. I want to offer my warm appreciation to Tirta, Miriam, and Ariel for their kindness and tolerance during my sabbatical months in the mountains of West Java where major parts of this book were drafted. Finally, I want to thank my family – Diane, Julie, Chris, Ralph, and Barbara – for their unconditional love and engaging political conversations.

For the many ways in which these individuals and others strengthened this book, I am sincerely grateful. As for its weaknesses and errors, all responsibility is mine.

1

The Material Foundations of Oligarchy

Oligarchy ranks among the most widely used yet poorly theorized concepts in the social sciences. More than four decades ago, James Payne (1968) declared the concept a "muddle." More recently, Leach (2005) applied the updated label "underspecified."[1] The *International Encyclopedia of the Social Sciences* defines oligarchy as "a form of government in which political power is in the hands of a small minority," adding that it "derives from the Greek word *oligarkhia* (government of the few), which is composed of *oligoi* (few) and *arkhein* (to rule)" (Indridason 2008, 36).[2] References to oligarchs and oligarchy abound, and yet the theoretical perspectives employed across cases and historical periods have very little in common. There is, for instance, minimal

---

[1] Leach's 2005 article – "The Iron Law of What Again?" – captures the conceptual disarray surrounding oligarchy and provides a useful review of the literature. Her definition of oligarchy centers on the degree of legitimacy and turnover in the leadership of an organization or community. For Leach, oligarchy is defined as the "concentration of entrenched illegitimate authority and/or influence in the hands of a minority, such that de facto what that minority wants is generally what comes to pass, even when it goes against the wishes (whether actively or passively expressed) of the majority" (2005, 329). Illegitimacy and entrenchment are what matter in this definition. For there to be illegitimacy, in Leach's view, community members under oligarchic domination must believe they are oppressed – the indicator of this being resistance of some kind – and the oppressors need to hold on anyway. Chen's (2008) definition of oligarchy closely follows Leach's social movements emphasis: "When organizational survival and leader interests displace an organization's goals, an organization experiences oligarchy." These approaches provide important insights into minority power, but should be viewed as elaborations of elite rather than oligarchic theory.

[2] As Schmidt (1973, 10) points out: "Since Plato and Aristotle, most writers who discuss oligarchy fail to define the concept, apparently because they assume the word is understood in the light of its Greek etymology (the rule of a few)" [quoted in Leach 2005, 315]. The *Oxford Concise Dictionary of Politics* (McLean and McMillan 2003, 381) emphasizes the "logically exclusive categories of government by the one, the few, or the many" in its definition. Scruton's (1982, 332) *A Dictionary of Political Thought* defines oligarchy as rule by the few, and then adds in befuddlement: "Quite what this means in practice is as difficult to determine as the meaning of democracy."

conceptual overlap in the application of the term to Filipino, Russian, and medieval oligarchs.

Mention of oligarchs is especially plentiful in the literature on postcolonial and postcommunist countries. However, the term occurs less frequently in advanced-industrial contexts, largely because oligarchy is generally thought to be overcome by electoral democracy. The dominant view among Americanists, for instance, is that pluralist democracies almost by definition cannot be oligarchic.[3] The literature examining the many dimensions of minority power and influence in the United States, even when oligarchs are mentioned, centers almost entirely on elite rather than oligarchic forms of power – an important distinction further explained later in the chapter.

The lack of clarity extends to discussions of oligarchy drawing on Aristotle (1996 [350 B.C.E.]) and Michels (2001 [1911]), two of the most prominent theorists cited in the literature. What undergraduate has not been introduced to Aristotle's famous typology in which forms of rule are defined by the one, the few, or the many? Yet, Aristotle's theoretical perspective on oligarchy is rarely presented fully or accurately except by political theorists. It comes as a surprise to many social scientists that the number of people ruling is not the primary foundation of Aristotle's theory of oligarchy or democracy. There is no less confusion about Michels's famous "iron law of oligarchy" – which, when examined closely, is not a theory of oligarchy at all, but rather an analysis of how elites eventually dominate all complex organizations. Most societies, but not all, are oligarchic, although not for the reasons Michels emphasizes.

The meaning of oligarchy is so incoherent that almost any political system or community that falls short of full and constant participation by its members arguably displays oligarchical tendencies.[4] A Soviet-style *nomenklatura* is an oligarchy, but so is the executive committee of the local Parent-Teacher Association or an influential group of elders in a commune.[5] Russian

---

[3] For the classic statement of the pluralist argument, see Dahl 1958 and 1961. For an alternative perspective, see Winters and Page 2009, Tronto 2007, as well as Chapter 5 focusing on civil oligarchy in the United States. The bulk of the American literature on minority power and influence spans from the 1950s through the 1990s and focuses almost exclusively on elites, starting with Mosca (1939 [1896]), Pareto (1935 [1916], 1968 [1901]), and Michels, and continuing through Mills (1956), Higley, Burton, and Field (1990), Domhoff (1990, 2002, 2006), and Wedel (2009).

[4] To cite just one example, Samons (1998, 117) writes that "'oligarchies' may be formed based on many different kinds of constituent elements (wealth, bureaucracy, birth, religion, physical attributes, social connections, political views); they are almost never completely closed to 'outsiders' and must, of course, consider the views or 'ideology' of the body they seek to dominate. That is, no hypothetical ruling 'elite' can ever be separated from the social matrix that spawned and sustains it." Notice that oligarchy not only applies to every conceivable kind of minority domination, but it is used interchangeably with "ruling elite." Cassinelli (1953, 779) defines oligarchy as "irresponsible leadership" because those in power enjoy "freedom from control," whereas Friedrich (1937, 462–5) moves ambiguously between formulations that focus on rule by the few, the wealthy, or both.

[5] The deinstitutionalized and radically participatory character of communes ought to render them paragons of democracy, but even these informal and consensus-based bodies are seen by some

billionaires are oligarchs, but so are Cardinals in the Catholic Church. The internal authority structures of corporate boards of directors are oligarchical (when they are not dictatorial), and even representative democracies in which the few are chosen by the many to set policy have been criticized as oligarchies. Meanwhile, figures of every stripe who wield exaggerated power, whether in or out of government, have been called oligarchs. Missing from this jumble of interpretations is the recognition that not all forms of minority power, influence, or rule are the same. It is meaningless to label as oligarchies every tiny subset of people exercising influence grossly out of proportion to their numbers. Minorities dominate majorities in many different contexts. What matters is how they do so and especially through what power resources.[6]

Despite all the confusion, oligarchy is – and oligarchs are – extremely important for understanding politics, whether ancient or contemporary, poor or advanced-industrial. The main problem is that the concept has defied clear definition. The solution lies in defining oligarchs and oligarchy in a manner that is precise, consistent, and yet still provides an analytical framework that is broad enough to be theoretically meaningful across a range of cases. "Rule by the few" simply will not do. Toward that end, this book seeks to clarify, sharpen, and apply the theory of oligarchs and oligarchy by emphasizing, as Aristotle did, the material foundations of the concepts. "The element of wealth was," for the earliest students of politics, "generally recognised as an essential condition of oligarchy" (Whibley 1896, 22). More than anything else, it is the conceptual drift away from this fundamental wealth-oligarch nexus that is the source of the chronic muddle.

As a first step toward defining oligarchs and oligarchy, two things matter. First is the basis of oligarchic minority power. All forms of minority influence are predicated on extreme concentrations of power and are undone through radical dispersions of that power. However, different kinds of power are more or less vulnerable to dispersion, and the political methods for achieving that dispersion vary widely. For instance, an exclusive lock by eunuchs on certain influential offices in China's imperial government can be challenged through a struggle mounted purely within the Chinese civil service and bureaucracy for reforms that redefine access to those offices. Exclusive access to civil rights by a dominant race or religious group can be challenged by the participation, mobilization, and resistance of excluded races or religions, thereby dispersing access and ending discrimination. Dominance of a territory or community by a violent subgroup, perhaps a gang or a mafia, can be undone by arming everyone

---

to be prone to oligarchy. Leach (2005, 318) cites the work of Staggenborg (1988) and Freeman (1975, 1984), who claim that collectivist organizations are inherently oligarchic because "without the constraints that bureaucracy places on informal power, a 'tyranny of structurelessness' results in which a minority with greater status will always come to dominate the group."

[6] Although not focused specifically on oligarchies, selectorate theory (Bueno de Mesquita, Smith, Siverson, and Morrow 2004) treats them generically as systems in which leaders are sustained in office by small "winning coalitions" that are a subset of a larger "selectorate" – those with a say in choosing leaders.

else to a level equal to or stronger than the dominant minority, or by cutting off their access to instruments of coercion. All of these cases involve different kinds of concentrated elite power and different means of dispersing or equalizing that power.

Oligarchs are distinct from all other empowered minorities because the basis of their power – material wealth – is unusually resistant to dispersion and equalization. It is not just that it is difficult to disperse the material power of oligarchs. It is that massive personal wealth is an extreme form of social and political power imbalance that, despite significant advances in recent centuries on other fronts of injustice, has managed since antiquity to remain ideologically constructed as unjust to correct. Across dictatorships, democracies, monarchies, peasant societies, and post-industrial formations, the notion that it is wrong to enforce radical redistributions of wealth is remarkably durable. The same cannot be said about attitudes toward slavery, racial exclusion, gender domination, or the denial of citizenship.

The second thing that matters is the scope of oligarchic minority power. An example will help make the point. An avid bowler may belong to a league that has been dominated for years by an exclusive group of tightly networked bowling fanatics who control all the important decisions for the league – nominating officers, scheduling bowling nights, setting drinking rules, controlling tournaments, and approving logos and colors for jerseys. Although this is certainly an odious case of minority power and influence, it is not an oligarchy because the bowler can easily leave the league and escape the reach or scope of the domination. If many bowlers were to do so, the exclusive group in charge might accept a major dispersion of power in response to signs of a mass exodus. In addition, if they resisted dispersion to the bitter end, the league and their minority power would collapse. An oligarchy is different in that the scope of oligarchic minority power extends so widely across the space or community that exit is nearly impossible or prohibitively expensive. Thus to be worthy of the name, oligarchic power must be based on a form of power that is unusually resistant to dispersion, and its scope must be systemic.[7]

An understanding of oligarchs and oligarchy begins with the observation that extreme material inequality produces extreme political inequality. This statement generates considerable confusion and controversy because most interpretations of democracy see political equality in terms of access to and participation in the political process. A nation becomes democratic and overcomes political inequality when it extends rights to all members of a community to participate freely and fully, to vote, speak, assemble, gain access to information, dissent without intimidation, and to hold office even at the highest political levels.[8] Material inequality among citizens is widely recognized as

---

[7] The systemic character of oligarchy does not preclude it from being manifested unevenly in different localities – for instance, a much higher engagement in politics and policies by local oligarchs in one city or region versus in another.

[8] This political equality does not require absolute equality of personal capacities. Some people are brighter than others, more ambitious, better organized, and more stubbornly determined in the

an important political issue, but not as a major source of unequal political power.[9]

In fact, massive wealth in the hands of a small minority creates significant power advantages in the political realm, including in democracies. Claiming otherwise ignores centuries of political analysis exploring the intimate association between wealth and power. In 1878, de Laveleye wrote that "the philosophers and legislators of antiquity knew well, by experience, that liberty and political equality can only exist when supported by equality of conditions."[10] The same basic nexus of material and political power was echoed more recently by Robert Dahl (1985, 4), who referred to the wealthy robber barons that arose in the United States in the second half of the nineteenth century as a "body of citizens highly unequal in the resources they could bring to political life." The simple claim is that the distribution of material resources across members of a political community, democratic or otherwise, has a profound influence on relative power. The more unequal the distribution is, the more exaggerated the power and influence of enriched individuals becomes, and the more intensely the material gap itself colors their political motives and objectives. The study of oligarchs and oligarchy centers on the power of wealth and the specific politics surrounding that power. This emphasis on the political implications of material disparities – on the "inequality of conditions" – makes oligarchic forms of minority power and exclusion different from all others.

Given that equating money with power is almost axiomatic in the study of politics, it is surprising that there is resistance to the proposition that gross inequalities in wealth generate massive inequalities in political power and influence within democracies. A political candidate who has a mountain of cash with which to campaign is exceedingly difficult to defeat. Political movements that are well funded are more influential than those with limited resources are. Government ministries with huge budgets enjoy exaggerated power. Yet, when equally massive material resources are held by citizens in a democracy, it remains a controversial notion to argue that they enjoy major political advantages or that they constitute a separate category of ultra-powerful actors with a core set of shared political interests linked to the defense of wealth. If money is power (and it surely is), then we need a theory for understanding how the unusually moneyed are unusually powerful. Such a theory must explain how concentrated wealth creates particular capacities, motivations, and political problems for those who possess it. And it also must be sensitive to how the politics surrounding wealth-as-power have changed over time and why.

pursuit of their goals. Such people will have personal advantages in a political system based on equal access to fundamental rights and procedures. However, these personal differences do not have the effect of making the system unfair or unjust because these individuals share no power resources in common. Moreover, there are no core policies or interests associated with their personal strengths that lend group coherence to these actors or point to a political agenda that necessarily excludes or disempowers others. The same cannot be said of wealthy oligarchs.

[9] Important exceptions are Goodin and Dryzek (1980), Bartels (2005, 2008), Solt (2008), and Hacker and Pierson (2010).

[10] See especially de Laveleye (1878), "Property at Rome," chapter 12.

Toward a Theory of Oligarchy

Most theories of oligarchy start by defining the term as some variant of "rule by the few," and then go in search of actual oligarchs. Here the perspective is reversed. The first task is to define oligarchs, with the specification of oligarchies to follow. Adapting power resource theory (Korpi 1985), oligarchs are defined in a manner that is fixed across political contexts and historical periods. *Oligarchs* are actors who command and control massive concentrations of material resources that can be deployed to defend or enhance their personal wealth and exclusive social position. The resources must be available to be used for personal interests even if they are not personally owned.[11] If extreme personal wealth is impossible or absent, oligarchs are also absent. Three points are immediately relevant. First, wealth is a material form of power that is distinct from all other power resources that can be concentrated into minority hands. Second, it is important that the command and control of the resources be for personal rather than institutional gain or operation. Oligarchs are always individuals, never corporations or other collectivities. Third, the definition of oligarchs remains constant over time and across cases. These factors are what consistently define oligarchs, what distinguish them from elites, and what set oligarchy apart from other forms of minority domination.

What of oligarchy? Before offering a definition, it is necessary to introduce the concept of wealth defense. As extremely rich actors, oligarchs face particular political problems and challenges that are directly linked to the material power resources they own and use in stratified societies. Ordinary citizens want their personal possessions protected from theft. However, the property obsession of oligarchs goes well beyond protecting mere possessions. The possession of fortunes raises property concerns to the highest priority for the rich.[12] Moreover, oligarchs alone are able to use wealth for wealth's defense. Throughout history, the massive fortunes and incomes of oligarchs have attracted a range of threats, including to private property as a concept or institution. The central political dynamic for oligarchs across the centuries turns on the nature of these threats and how oligarchs defend their wealth against them. Wealth defense for oligarchs has two components – *property defense* (securing basic claims

---

[11] The scale of wealth that crosses an oligarchic threshold varies across social formations, and therefore it can only be specified in concrete contexts. The scale of wealth to be a Russian oligarch in 2010 is not the same as that needed to be a Filipino oligarch in 1895. The key point is that there are particular powers, capacities, and threats that arise with extreme concentrations of wealth. The case for an oligarchic interpretation is strengthened when these factors are manifested. An example of defining oligarchs in this way is presented in the case material on the United States in Chapter 5.

[12] President Theodore Roosevelt (1910), in his "New Nationalism" speech, underscored this fundamental divide between modest possessions and concentrated wealth: "The really big fortune," he said, "the swollen fortune, by the mere fact of its size, acquires qualities which differentiate it in kind as well as degree from what is possessed by men of relatively small means."

to wealth and property) and *income defense* (keeping as much of the flow of income and profits from one's wealth as possible under conditions of secure property rights). The subject of wealth defense and the important distinction between property claims and property rights is touched on only briefly here, but is taken up in greater depth in a separate section later.

With a clear definition of oligarchs established and the notion of wealth defense introduced, it is now possible to define oligarchy. *Oligarchy* refers to the politics of wealth defense by materially endowed actors. The defense of riches by oligarchs involves specific challenges and capacities not shared by other forms of minority domination or exclusion. Oligarchy describes how that defense is pursued – a process that is highly variable across political contexts and historical periods. The definition of oligarchs is fixed, but oligarchies assume different forms. As already hinted, the most important source of oligarchic variation lies in the nature of the threats to wealth and property, and how the central problem of wealth defense is managed politically. Extreme material stratification in society generates social conflict. Highly unequal distributions of wealth are impossible without a firmament of enforcement, which means property claims and rights can never be separated from coercion and violence. Thus the variation across oligarchies is closely related to two key factors: first, the degree of direct involvement by oligarchs in providing the coercion needed to claim property, which is linked to whether oligarchs are personally armed and directly engaged in rule; and second, whether that rule is individualistic and fragmented or collective and more institutionalized.

Put differently, the direct political engagement of oligarchs is strongly mediated by a stratified society's property regime. The greater the need oligarchs have to defend their property directly, the more likely it is that oligarchy will assume the form of "direct rule" by oligarchs, with other power resources and roles, such as holding government office, "layered" on top of or blended with their material power substratum. It follows that being in a position of rule does not define an oligarch, only a particular kind of oligarchy. There are many paths to defending extreme material stratification, and the prominence of oligarchs changes with how wealth is defended and who or what is defending it.

In systems where property is reliably defended externally (especially by an armed state through institutions and strong property rights and norms), oligarchs have no compelling need to be armed or engaged directly in political roles. What changes with the shift from self-enforced property claims to externally enforced property rights is not the existence of oligarchs, but rather the nature of their political engagement. Oligarchs do not disappear just because they do not govern personally or participate directly in the coercion that defends their fortunes. Instead, the political involvement of oligarchs becomes more indirect as it becomes less focused on property defense – this burden having been shifted to an impersonal bureaucratic state. However, their political involvement becomes more direct again when external actors or institutions fail to defend property reliably. Thus, the property regime mediates the politics of wealth defense by making it more or less direct and by shifting the relative emphasis oligarchs give to property defense versus income defense – the latter suddenly looming in importance when the sole remaining threat to oligarchs is a state that wants to redistribute wealth through income taxes.

Oligarchy does not refer to everything political that oligarchs do with their money and power. It is not uncommon for oligarchs to engage their material resources across a range of political issues and battles about which they care deeply and yet have nothing to do with wealth defense and oligarchy. When they do so, their individual potency and power can easily match that of large collectivities of actors pursuing their agendas via interest group or pluralist politics. However, oligarchs are as likely as any other citizen to cancel each other's power in various struggles for and against issues ranging from abortion rights to better environmental standards to gun laws. Some oligarchs also choose to remain politically quiescent. Power held is not always power used.[13] Oligarchy refers narrowly to a set of wealth-defense issues and politics around which the motives and interests of oligarchs align, are shared, and cohere.

Oligarchs and Elites. A materialist perspective on oligarchs and oligarchy helps distinguish types of minority power and influence based on the different kinds of power resources minority actors have at their disposal. More will be said about this in the next section on power resources. However, oligarchic theory cannot advance until it is separated analytically from the much broader theory of elites. Ordinarily, the term *elite* serves as an umbrella concept for all actors holding concentrated minority power at the top of a community or state. From this perspective, oligarchs would simply be a special category of economic elites. Although it runs against the grain of ordinary usage and a mountain of scholarship in the social sciences to do so, that formulation is rejected here. Ever since the work of Pareto and Michels in particular, elite theorists have undermined the concept of oligarchy by obscuring the central role of material power in their studies. This is particularly evident in the work on elites in the United States that, however revealing of other aspects of unequal power, fails to illuminate what are specifically oligarchic aspects of power and politics.

Both elites and oligarchs exert minority power and influence. However, their ability to do so rests on radically different kinds of power. This fact has produced political outcomes that are profoundly divergent. One of the most fundamental divergences is that nearly all elite forms of minority influence have been significantly challenged through democratic struggle and change, whereas oligarchic power, because of its different nature, has not.[14] Elite theorists have

---

[13] The existence of oligarchy does not require that all oligarchs rule, even when all rulers are oligarchs. Many oligarchs are content to remain on the political sidelines as long as their vital material interests are secured. The emphasis in this discussion is on power capacities, or, as Isaac (1987) frames it in his critique of the faces-of-power debate, "power to" rather than "power over." Korpi (1985) also provides an important summary and critique of the faces-of-power debate. Key contributions include Bachrach and Baratz (1962) and Lukes (1974).

[14] The central conundrum in the study conducted by the Task Force on Inequality and American Democracy (APSA 2004) turned on precisely this issue – why was material inequality getting worse despite great successes achieved by pluralist politics and participation in challenging

no explanation for why the immense political power of oligarchs is highly resistant to all but the most radical democratic encroachments – precisely the ones existing democracies were deliberately designed to impede. Oligarchs can have elite forms of power stacked on top of or blended with their defining material foundation. This would make them simultaneously oligarchs and elites. But no elite can be an oligarch in the absence of holding and personally deploying massive material power.

It should be evident from these definitions that an oligarch is not necessarily the same as a capitalist, a business owner, or a corporate CEO. In emphasizing the ownership of the means of production, Marx's theory of the capitalist bourgeoisie focuses on the power of actors who deploy material resources *economically* with important social and political effects. In oligarchic theory, the focus is on the power of actors who deploy material resources *politically* with important economic effects. Both approaches are materialist, but in different ways. Neither oligarchs nor oligarchy is defined by a particular mode of production or surplus extraction. Nor is oligarchy defined by a particular set of institutions, which is why it is so resistant to institutional reforms. A feudal lord could be an oligarch but is clearly not a capitalist. A business owner could be a capitalist, and yet possess personally far too little material power to be an oligarch. A CEO of a large firm might deploy massive material resources on behalf of shareholders, but still receive a personal salary that falls far short of what he or she would need to wield oligarchic power. Such an individual is a member of the corporate elite, but not an oligarch. Similarly, high-ranking government officials (also elites) could daily allocate billions of dollars through the national budget, and yet have at their personal disposal only the resources of an upper middle-class citizen. Nevertheless, if those same officials were corrupt and amassed personal fortunes (however ill gotten), they would now be simultaneously elites in government *and* oligarchs capable of engaging in the politics of wealth defense.

The analytical emphasis in a Marxist framework is on the power of owning and investing classes rooted in their control of capital for investment and on the extraction of surpluses from direct producers. Nothing in the materialist approach to oligarchy developed here conflicts with this framework. Instead, there is a shift in emphasis to the politics of defending extreme material inequalities. The central premise that oligarchs are defined by their extreme wealth, and that extreme wealth is impossible without a means of defense, results in a theorization of oligarchy that asks how threats to wealth vary and how the political responses to defend wealth against those threats also vary. It is a perspective influenced as much by Marx's historical materialism as by Weber's

---

exclusion in so many realms of deep injustice? Lacking a theory to treat material concentration at the top by oligarchs as a distinct kind of power with unique political dynamics, the Task Force diagnosed the problem as one of insufficient participation. There is scant evidence that the concentration of wealth in the United States has fluctuated with levels of democratic participation.

emphasis on the locus of the means of coercion in his classic definition of the modern state.

Another difference between Marx's theory of the capitalist bourgeoisie and the theory of oligarchs and oligarchy offered here concerns the problem of fragmentation and coherence. A major problem in the theory of capitalists as a power group is that, depending on their sector, scale, or even nationality, their political interests as investors often clash or are crosscutting. A theory of oligarchs and oligarchy centered on wealth defense is prone to far less dissent and conflict on the core set of political objectives linked to securing property and preserving wealth and income. Oligarchs may disagree about many things, and, depending on the situation, they may even fight violently to grab each other's fortunes. Nevertheless, they still share a basic ideological and practical commitment to the defense of wealth and property, and, in the presence of some sort of state, to policies that advance their wealth-defense agenda.

A high concentration of material power in the hands of some actors is hardly new, but neither is it an artifact of the early modern era. The rise of contemporary institutions and politics, including the emergence of democracy, has neither eliminated oligarchs nor rendered oligarchy politically obsolete. This is because there are virtually no constraints built into electoral democracy that can effectively limit the material forms of power wielded by oligarchs. Indeed, it is in advanced-industrial democracies that some of the largest concentrations of material resources are personally controlled and politically deployed by extremely small minorities for oligarchic objectives. This means that even systems that are democratic in all other respects still contain major power asymmetries when massive material resources are concentrated into few hands. Thus, although its forms and character have changed significantly since the rise of the first materially stratified societies, oligarchy has persisted across historical periods and across forms of the polity as long as wealth has remained concentrated in a few hands.

A related point is that because oligarchy is grounded in material power, it is not deeply affected by nonmaterial reforms or political procedures. Political institutions can mediate oligarchy, temper it, tame it, and change its character – especially the degree to which oligarchs are directly engaged in the use of violence and coercion in defending their wealth. However, concentrated material power in the hands of a limited set of actors operates as a potent power resource under all manner of institutional arrangements. It is for this reason that whatever the form of the polity, extreme political inequality has been the conjoined twin of extreme material inequality. Oligarchs and oligarchy arise because some actors succeed in stockpiling massive material power resources and then use a portion of them for wealth defense – with important implications for the rest of the social formation. It follows that oligarchs and oligarchy will cease to exist not through democratic procedures, but rather when extremely unequal distributions of material resources are undone, and thus no longer confer exaggerated political power to a minority of actors.[15]

---

[15] Marx argued that suffrage and modern democracy could never be more than "political emancipation" as long as concentrated property and wealth were excluded from the

This last point helps explain why democracy is not zero-sum with oligarchy. Democracy and oligarchy are defined by distributions of radically different kinds of power. Democracy refers to *dispersed formal political power* based on rights, procedures, and levels of popular participation. By contrast, oligarchy is defined by *concentrated material power* based on enforced claims or rights to property and wealth. The nature of the political powers that get widened or narrowed as systems become more or less democratic is distinct from the political powers that can be dispersed or concentrated materially. This is why democracy and oligarchy are remarkably compatible provided the two realms of power do not clash. Indeed, democracy and oligarchy can coexist indefinitely as long as the unpropertied lower classes do not use their expanded political participation to encroach upon the material power and prerogatives of the wealthiest. This is precisely the equal-yet-unequal political arrangement that exists in all stable capitalist democracies. In addition, it explains why oligarchy is rarely disturbed by dramatic increases in popular participation or even universal suffrage: oligarchy rests on the concentration of material power whereas democracy rests on the dispersion of nonmaterial power.

The sections that follow develop these arguments. A key point of departure is that significant material inequalities in society produce frictions and conflicts. There are many ways these inequalities can be manifested. One ethnic or religious group might be dramatically richer than others might be, or the disparities might be regional. We enter the realm of oligarchs and oligarchy when the inequalities in question position a small number of rich actors against the masses that are much poorer (and, under certain circumstances, position oligarchs against each other). The friction and conflicts that arise generate significant political challenges for the wealthy. To sum up, a profound material gap creates a bounded minority of actors (oligarchs); it generates identifiable social and political conflicts that present specific challenges these actors must confront (wealth defense); and it simultaneously provides a stockpile of unique material power resources that get deployed politically to surmount the challenges (oligarchy). A key building block for oligarchic theory is the notion of power resources, to which the discussion now turns.

Power Resources

Power is a notoriously difficult concept to define. It changes with different circumstances. Some forms of power are brutally physical and directly expressed, whereas others are indirect or latent. Sometimes power has effects not because it is used, but because others anticipate its use. Some of the most subtle kinds

---

equalizing reforms. Political freedom via a state that outlaws property qualifications for democratic participation, and yet guarantees rights to asymmetric material wealth, means that people are free in an *"abstract, narrow, and partial way"* (Marx 1978 [1844], 32, emphasis in original). According to Marx, because property is a basic source of social and political power, real equality (including the elimination of what is here called oligarchy) can only be achieved if the material dimension of inequality is addressed.

of power operate structurally, culturally, or unconsciously. A power resource approach is especially useful for understanding oligarchs and oligarchy because it emphasizes particular capacities, instruments, or positions that individuals hold in varying concentrations or magnitudes and use for social and political influence. Oligarchs are defined by the type and scale of the power resources they control. This perspective relies on an assessment of power capacities at the level of the individual rather than of collectivities. It posits that every individual in a social formation has some magnitude of power, however small.

The task is to specify the kinds of power individuals have and estimate their relative endowments. Some power resources, especially those based on wealth, are more amenable to measurement and comparison than others are.[16] At least theoretically, if different power resources could be measured on a common scale, it would be possible to compute an *individual power profile* for each actor in society, and then rank each actor quantitatively from the least to the most powerful. The notion of an individual power profile is only a heuristic device that focuses attention on the relative power positions of individual actors rather than groups or classes. This method is crucial for specifying who oligarchs are and distinguishing them from other relatively powerful and powerless actors in the society.

According to this approach, presidents, leaders of mass movements, armed warlords, or oligarchs are dramatically more influential than the average person because their relative accumulation or distribution in one or more of the power resource categories is extremely high. Other individuals in the system would have much lower overall power profiles because their share of power resources is exceedingly small in some categories and possibly nonexistent in others. Whatever power individuals have – latent or manifest – is almost always magnified when actors mobilize into networks, associations, or movements that pursue common goals. However, mass movements as well as complex institutions (such as states) do not exist apart from the individuals that comprise them. For this reason, the collective power that derives from mobilization and networking can still be tracked from the perspective of the augmented power position of each mobilized individual.

It is useful to think of five main individual power resources: power based on *political rights*, the power of *official positions* in government or at the helm of organizations, *coercive* power, *mobilizational* power, and finally *material* power. This is hardly an exhaustive list of power resources, but it encompasses the lion's share of the types of power individuals can possess in politics and society.[17] By far the most important analytical payoff of the power resources

---

[16] All could agree that a unionized worker has more power than an unorganized laborer, but how might the relative magnitudes of their power be quantified? Similarly, a senator or a judge has substantially more individual power than the average nurse or schoolteacher. The differences in the individual power profiles for these actors are very real. However, no reliable method exists for measuring and comparing – much less summing up – the magnitudes of power for each.

[17] The most glaring omission from this list is ideological power. Ideas and frames of understanding are powerful and important. The main reason ideological power is not included is that it is

approach is that it sharpens the distinction between elite and oligarchic forms of minority power. The first four power resources, when held by individuals in a concentrated and exclusionary manner, produce elites. Only the last, material power, produces oligarchs and oligarchy. Each type merits brief elaboration.

Formal Political Rights. Under conditions of universal suffrage and few obstacles to political participation, formal political rights are the least scarce and most diluted power resource at the individual level. The rights and privileges that comprise liberal freedoms include one-person-one-vote, the ability to express views without repression, and the opportunity to gain access to the same information all others have in society. Setting aside the right to assembly, which is treated separately under mobilizational power, political rights only become truly significant across individuals as they become more exclusionary, whether formally or in practice. The great majority of people in so-called democratic Athens, for instance, were not citizens and thus had vastly lower individual power profiles than the minority of men who enjoyed citizenship. The same was true for propertied Caucasian males who had substantially higher individual power profiles for much of American history than did African slaves, women, or the unpropertied. Moreover, the asymmetries in power resources based on political rights and participation need not be formal. The individual power profiles of Caucasian Americans remained significantly higher than those of former slaves and their descendants for more than a century after the passage of the Thirteenth Amendment to the U.S. Constitution in 1865.

Throughout history, individuals have been excluded from basic political rights and participation on the basis of slave-citizen status, race, ethnicity, gender, religion, geography, and wealth (as a qualification to participate, not as a power resource). When this occurs, and especially when these bases of exclusion are layered on each other, major inequalities arise in individual power profiles related to this first power resource. In the absence of pronounced exclusions, this power resource is more dispersed and it largely washes out of the equation when comparing individual power profiles across a democratic society. The history of democratization shows that the spread and thus the equalization of power resources based on political rights and participation is highly responsive to agitation and struggle.

Official Positions. Holding high-ranking office in government, major organizations (secular and religious), or corporations (private and public) is a power resource that has a dramatic influence on the power profiles of a limited number of individuals. In the modern era, these organizations are rule-based bodies that concentrate power by pooling financial resources, networks of operation, and

---

not something that can be held or wielded as a power resource by individuals except perhaps when mobilizing actors create or make use of ideas and interpretive frames (and thus it is a key component in the mobilizational power category). The character of ideological or cultural power is systemic. They envelop members of a society and they tend to augment the power of groups more than of individuals. When they boost the power of individuals, it is linked to their role as mobilizers but not as a power resource they "hold."

groupings of members or underlings who can be led, engaged, or commanded through the institutions. Gaining high positions in these institutions allows certain actors to exert a highly concentrated form of power. Having these power resources is wholly contingent on holding the positions. Loss of office entails a loss of power. Before the rise of the modern state, the power of those holding high positions was not so limited or distinct. It was blended with (and mutually reinforced by) the other four power resources that they also possessed. In the modern era, however, there is much more separation of powers and roles, so that official positions confer particular powers with particular characteristics, and it is possible for individuals to hold high offices despite having no other power resources.

It is important in building a clear definition of oligarchs and oligarchy to emphasize that the small minority of actors who wield only the power resource of official positions constitute elites, not oligarchs. Existing as separate and impersonal from individuals, high offices are held but not owned. The powers associated with the positions are unique among all power resources in the speed at which they can increase or deplete an individual's power profile. The power of the individual holding the office of president of the United States, for instance, undergoes a sharp collapse in the space of a few minutes on January 20 every four or eight years. Actors who are elected or named CEO of a major corporation, head of a party, or leader of a national union experience a sudden and massive increase in their power profiles relative to all other persons in the system or community. They may have other power resources as well – the right to vote, for instance, or personal wealth. However, they have certain augmented powers that are tied to their office and that they wield only as long as they hold their positions.

These separations are important analytically. A general positioned at the apex of a military organization can deploy hundreds of thousands of soldiers as one armed force. Yet, this capacity is not because of the mobilizational power of the general, but rather because of the power resource intrinsic to the office he or she holds. It is also wielded in a temporary and contingent manner by the officer. Once the person is separated formally from the uniform and the office, the chain of command stretching down to the soldier will no longer obey. If they continue to obey anyway, it is not because of the power conferred by office or position, but rather because of the high mobilizational power resources of a charismatic warlord or rebel who used to be a general.

A similar situation applies to government officials whose decisions allocate huge sums of public money in official budgets, and to heads of corporations who deploy sizeable resources on behalf of their firms and its interests.[18] They

---

[18] These distinctions do not always apply perfectly. There are gray-area cases in which actors at the apex of corporations can deploy institutional resources for personal rather than corporate objectives. A good example is hedge funds in the United States and the tax treatment of so-called "carried interest." Hedge fund managers spent many millions of their company's resources on

may be personally wealthy actors (which involves material power resources to be discussed presently), but their capacity to deploy public or corporate money and capital is not due to their personal wealth, but rather to the power resource intrinsic to their official positions. Again, it is wielded in a temporary and contingent manner by the official or CEO. If the office is taken away, all the individual power they possessed to deploy the money or command the organization evaporates in an instant. This second power resource, especially in the modern era, is unique in that it tends to accumulate incrementally through career advancements, but also to evaporate suddenly and completely through retirement, firing, electoral loss, being pushed out, or term limits.[19]

Coercive Power. This power resource is one of the most difficult to discuss because its role as a component of individual power profiles has changed so radically over the course of civilization. Weber's most important insight was to focus on the role and social locus of coercion and violence as the defining feature of the modern state compared to all previous political forms. Before the rise of the modern state, coercive capacities were distributed among actors in society. Extreme asymmetries in individual capacities for violence meant that coercive power figured prominently in individual power profiles. The signal achievement of the modern state is the effective disarming of all individuals, or, in Weber's parlance, the state's ability to achieve a monopoly on the legitimate means of coercion. If a member of society harms someone and deserves punishment, it is the state and not the harmed individual that legitimately punishes the offender.

Coercion is particularly important in the discussion of oligarchy because the change in the locus of coercive power, from individual to state, is the single greatest source of transformation in the character of oligarchy in history. This is because of the links among violence, property claims, and wealth defense. How property claims are enforced, and by whom, has had a radical effect on oligarchs and oligarchy. This will be discussed further in the section dealing with wealth defense. The key point for the present is that coercive power has shifted from being a power resource that was a crucial element in the individual power profile of oligarchs, to being a form of *elite* power in the modern nation-state, with actors organizing violence based on professional office. Failed states, by contrast, are marked by the rise of "warlords," who combine elements of elite and oligarchic power.

Mobilizational Power. This power resource has two dimensions. It refers to the individual capacity to move or sway others – the ability to lead people, persuade followers, create networks, invigorate movements, provoke responses, and inspire people to action (including getting them to take risks and make

congressional lobbyists to make sure that the money they earned from the capital gains of their clients would be taxed as if they were capital gains on their own personal funds, rather than as fees or salary. This claim is developed more fully in Chapter 5.

[19] The "revolving door" from, say, senator to corporate board member can maintain an impressively high power profile for an actor, but it is one that is nevertheless interrupted by the shift from the powers of one office or position to the powers of another. Moreover, although such power-maintaining moves are common, they are not assured.

great sacrifices). These actors derive their extraordinary individual power from their capacity to activate the latent political power of others. Mobilizational power also refers to the often sharp change in the individual power profiles of actors who are in a state of mobilization for a given period. Starting with the first dimension, on a grand scale, some highly powerful actors have only limited formal political rights, hold no official positions, have no armaments or coercive capacities (sometimes even rejecting the sizeable coercive potential of the masses they lead), and no personal fortunes. Yet, they can use their personal charisma, status, bravery, words, or ideas to mobilize masses of otherwise powerless individuals into formidable social and political forces. On a lesser scale, writers, media figures, commentators, scholars, celebrities, and agitators can also sway significant numbers of people.

Examples of major figures with high concentrations of mobilizational power abound in history. Mohandas Gandhi, Ho Chi Minh, Mao Zedong, Martin Luther King, and Vaclav Havel all possessed high individual capacities to mobilize others. Other power resources they may have accumulated, such as official positions or command over coercive forces, were subsequently layered on top of their primary mobilizational power.[20] On a more modest scale, figures like scholar-activist Noam Chomsky, media agitator Rush Limbaugh, *New York Times* columnist Thomas Friedman, author Ayn Rand, Indonesian writer Pramoedya Ananta Toer, or celebrity Oprah Winfrey exhibit significant concentrations of mobilizational power because of their ability to shape the attitudes and sway the actions of actors far beyond their circles of personal associates. As was the case with the other power resources elaborated earlier, actors with high concentrations of mobilizational power fall into the category of elites, not oligarchs.

Mobilizational power is conditioned by the degree of formal political rights. Liberal freedoms to speak, organize, and assemble enhance the individual power of mobilizational figures as well as the individual and collective power of the mobilized. The most important aspect of mobilizational capacity (or being in a mobilized state) as a power resource, especially in the context of an analysis of oligarchs and oligarchic power, is that it requires a significant and sustained level of personal engagement by the actors involved for the power resource to be effective rather than merely latent. Mobilizational power is not delegative, but instead is necessarily direct, relying on personal commitments of time and participation (Piven and Cloward 1978, 2000).

Because political influence is based on direct involvement, the personal burdens and demands are significant and zero-sum with all other daily activities that mobilizational (or mobilized) actors might engage in. Being "political"

---

[20] Mobilizational religious figures constitute a special hybrid category of actors. Whether they mobilize congregations or followers on a local or a national (even international) scale, they do so based on their mobilizational power resources in combination with the power resource of holding official positions within established organizations (which tend to have official material resources and established institutional bodies). If they use their ministries for massive personal enrichment, which some clearly do, their individual power profile would include an oligarchic element as well.

requires ongoing investments of effort that compete directly with time that can be spent on work, family, and leisure.[21] The payoffs for this effort are likely to be small and long-delayed except in moments of crisis. This contrasts sharply with how oligarchs are able to deploy and manifest their power and influence, especially during the politically ordinary periods between crises.

One of the major criticisms of oligarchic theory is that to prove oligarchy exists, analysts must first demonstrate a high degree of active "cohesion" among oligarchs (see Aron 1950, Dahl 1958, and Payne 1968). Ironically, this precondition is one of the least important elements for oligarchic power. The greatest degree of cohesion is required of those whose primary power resource relies on mobilization, not on wealth. Cohesion and mobilization can augment the power and effectiveness of oligarchs, which is generally true for all actors, whether at the top or bottom of society. However, because of the nature of the material power resources that define oligarchs and make them formidable political actors, cohesion is a helpful but not a necessary part of oligarchic power. Another characteristic of mobilizational power is that the tremendous individual power of actors who influence and mobilize others is built up over long careers, but can be lost suddenly because of personal scandals, political miscalculations, or infidelity to the principles or ideologies on which these actors mobilize.

The duration and the degree of institutionalization of mobilized social forces vary with a range of factors. In general, mobilizational power in the sense of the augmented power of masses of actors is exceedingly difficult to sustain and requires draining commitments of personal time and energy. It also requires horizontal and personal networks on a scale oligarchs never need to match to be influential. On the other hand, there is no social force more overwhelming than mobilized masses. No matter how difficult they are to sustain, even "mobilizations of the last minute" are explosive enough to briefly trump all the other power resource categories combined. When masses of otherwise disempowered

---

[21] Referring to the salaried "machine men" employed by big political bosses in the United States and the "time such persons give to organization, to 'preparedness' in a political sense, to meetings, conferences," Yarros (1917, 393) vividly contrasts their determined political engagement with that of the average American citizen. "How can the man who neither seeks nor expects office," he asks, "who has to make a living and save for a rainy day, compete with the professional politician and their quasi-professional allies?" Writing ninety years later, Reed (2007) describes the intense personal commitments needed to build social movements from the ground up. Criticizing the hype among progressives surrounding Obama's 2008 presidential bid, Reed argues that mobilization according to a four-yearly electoral cycle is not "an alternative or a shortcut to building those movements, and building them takes time and concerted effort. Not only can that process not be compressed to fit the election cycle," Reed writes, "it also doesn't happen through mass actions. It happens through cultivating one-on-one relationships with people who have standing and influence in their neighborhoods, workplaces, schools, families, and organizations. It happens through struggling with people over time for things they're concerned about and linking those concerns to a broader political vision and program." Mobilizing and being mobilized for political change is a full-time, evening-weekend vocation on top of one's full-time day job – which helps account for the weaknesses and episodic character of many social movements. Also see Verba, Schlozman, and Brady (1995).

citizens are activated on a sufficient scale, even the formidable coercive power of the modern state is no match. Of course, mass mobilizations are not always targeted at people who hold minority power at the top of society. Oligarchs and elites try to harness the power of the mobilized for their own agendas, and often succeed in doing so. However, genuine People Power from below can be unpredictable and devastating to oligarchic and elite interests. Such moments are rare and transient, and minority power (oligarchic and elite) predominates during the long periods of what might be termed "the politics of the ordinary" – the long periods that fill the space between episodes of crisis and mobilization.

Material Power. Wealth is the power resource that defines oligarchs and sets in motion the politics and processes of oligarchy. Material power resources provide the foundation on which oligarchs stand as formidable political actors. Material resources in their varying forms (the most flexible being cash money) have long been recognized as a source of economic, social, and political power. Having no wealth does not make someone utterly powerless. One might still be empowered through the other power resources already discussed. Those lacking money and property might, for instance, be formally empowered to vote periodically in reasonably competitive elections or might hold influential offices themselves. However, large and concentrated sums of wealth in the hands of a small fraction of a society's members represent a power resource that is not only unavailable to the propertyless, but significantly more versatile and potent than formal or procedural power resources such as equal voting rights – particularly when measured at the individual level.

The sheer versatility of material power is what makes it so significant polit-ically. It is the power to buy wealth defense, whether in the form of coercive capacities or hiring the defensive services of skilled professionals. In addition, the magnitude of that power for oligarchs is limited only by the scale of the wealth they have at their disposal. The individual political influence of oli-garchs does not depend on how much of their own time and effort is directly consumed. Mobilizational power, by contrast, relies on the personal and coor-dinated activity of large numbers of people whose direct involvement is difficult to sustain because intensive political activity demands a high level of political engagement that is uncommon for most citizens, and it takes time and energy away from other important activities, not least of which is working for a living. Material power is unique in that it allows oligarchs to purchase the sustained engagement of others who require no personal commitment to the goals of the oligarchs they serve. Their only requirement is material compensation for their services.

Oligarchs are the only citizens in liberal democracies who can pursue their personal political objectives indirectly and yet intensively by exerting deter-mined influence through armies of professional, skilled actors (the middle and upper class worker bees helping produce oligarchic outcomes) who labor year-round as salaried, full-time advocates and defenders of core oligarchic interests. Their day job is wholly devoted to winning constant victories for oligarchs – and they compete vigorously to attract the payments oligarchs offer to defend their wealth and incomes. These professional forces and hired defenders require no ideological invigoration to keep going, and they are not prone to mobilizational fatigue, disorientation, or crosscutting agendas. They are paid handsomely to give their maximum effort year after year, decade after decade. No social or political force pursuing policies that threaten oligarchic interests can match this focus and endurance.

In countries or political communities where the rule of law and property rights are weak, these same material resources can be used to buy security forces (sometimes even militias or small armies); to maintain networks of officials on retainer; to pay off police, prosecutors, and judges; and even to fund masses of people to demonstrate in the streets as if they were genuine political mobilizations from below.[22] Oligarchs in places like Indonesia and the Philippines can and do calculate how much it would cost them to do things like amass hundreds of thousands of people for a period of weeks to destabilize a government, or to get legislatures to vote favorably on laws that impinge on oligarchic fortunes.

This is a form and scale of political power that is unimaginable for all but a handful of actors in societies throughout history. Elites with high mobilizational power, for instance, need masses of people built up via intensive social movements to actually agree with them before they will pour into the streets for direct political action. Oligarchs face no such constraints, and the crowds they can pay to assemble are often underemployed and desperate for the compensation oligarchs offer. The point is not that oligarchs deploying material power resources are so influential that they win every battle or are invulnerable to attacks, including confiscation of their property. During periods of severe crisis, oligarchic power is always vulnerable to surges in other kinds of power, especially massive mobilizations they are not funding and controlling. Rather, the point is that especially during "the politics of the ordinary," oligarchs constitute a set of actors who are tremendously powerful because they have at their disposal massive material resources that are unusually versatile and dwarf the power resources of atomized common citizens across society.

By way of illustration, Winters and Page (2009) estimate the relative material power of actors in the United States. Using wealth data, they calculate that the average American in the top 1/100th of 1 percent of the population has 463 times the material power resources of the average individual in the bottom 90 percent. One 1/100th of 1 percent would be an oligarchy of some 30,000 people, all of whom could fit comfortably in a modest football stadium. Were American oligarchs to be defined at a much higher material threshold, Winters and Page calculate that the richest 400 Americans could deploy on average about 22,000 times the material political power of the average member of the bottom 90 percent, and each of the top 100 or so has nearly 60,000

---

[22] A particularly sophisticated variant is when oligarchs use their material resources to catalyze mass protests that are genuine but unlikely to occur without oligarchic involvement. The key role oligarchs played in overthrowing Thaksin in Thailand in 2006 is a prime example.

times as much. It is the single most unequally distributed power resource in American society, and also the one most resiliently resistant to dispersion and equalization.

This is a measure of the power of individual actors in society. The same material power resources deployed by oligarchs exist also for every other citizen in the system, just at levels so low and crosscutting as to be individually insignificant. Collectively the material power of the lower, middle, and upper classes (the affluent, not the fabulously rich) is potentially enormous. Yet, it is inert and insignificant unless it can be deployed toward uniform rather than cross-purposes.[23] Material issues factor most intensely in the lives of those at the extremes – actors who have almost no material resources (even collectively) and actors who control almost unimaginable concentrations of wealth (even individually). Whatever else the rich may care about that divides them, they are united in being materially focused and materially empowered. For clarity of political purpose and the capacity to pursue it with maximum effectiveness, they rely less on cohesion, networks, and organization than any other actors in society. A shared commitment to wealth and property defense is the source of their cohesion as a set of political actors. It is the rare oligarch who uses material power to undercut their collective wealth-defense agenda. No other actors or groups have the focused interest or ability, without first being in a heightened and sustained state of mobilization, to match or counter this oligarchic power.

Although blurred since the end of the nineteenth century, this analytical emphasis on the material foundations of oligarchs and oligarchy has a lineage dating back to antiquity. It is important to trace this materialist perspective back to its ancient origins. However, before doing so, the next section develops the notion of wealth defense and the intimate link between unequal property and coercion.

Wealth Defense

Blomley (2003, 121) argues that property is inherently relational and thus "held against others." Economists view property rights as excludable in the sense that they can be held by one individual or institution against competing claims. However, exclusion also makes property prone to chronic contestation, which economists refer to as *enforcement costs*. The claim "all of this is mine" will constantly be confronted with the response "says who?" or "says

---

[23] Citizens across a pluralist democracy like the United States who are concerned with any of a thousand issues can each write a check for $25 or $50 from their relatively limited stock of material power resources for Greenpeace, Amnesty International, or the National Rifle Association. As material power, the *collective* sums may be substantial. However, they nevertheless rely on networking and mobilization to be operationalized; they are dispersed across issue areas that cancel each other; and more to the point, they are rarely directed in concert against the core wealth defense agenda of oligarchs.

what?" The threats posed by such challenges increase as the scarcity of property increases, as the number of people making claims and counterclaims rises, and as the scale of property claimed by a few becomes increasingly unequal.[24] Claims, counterclaims, exclusion, and inequality explain why property cannot be sustained without a means of enforcement. The need for effective coercive capacities rises as the inequality of the property claimed increases. This creates profound political challenges for the rich both as individuals and as a group. It is for this reason that wealth defense is the core political dynamic and objective for all oligarchs.

A consistent pattern in human history is for very small minorities to amass great wealth and power.[25] However, because of the conflicts just mentioned, material domination by the few has never been easy. "Concentrated economic power," observed the New Deal liberal Adolf Berle (1959, 98), "raises at once the question of 'legitimacy.'" People persist in asking, "Why should this man, or this group, hold power...?" For long stretches of history, that question was answered with a shocking degree of naked violence. This does not mean that other means have not also been employed. Brute force alone can be a costly and unreliable instrument for maintaining stable economic domination. "If a few Great Ones had title to every last penny in the world, would they feel secure?" asked Charles Merriam (1938, 858). If these same wealthy few "commanded an army containing every able-bodied man and woman in a given state, would they be or feel more secure – or shiver a little as they reviewed their own?" Ideological hegemony thus plays an important role for oligarchs in defending their material dominance. There is, according to Berle, "no instance in history in which any group, great or small, has not set up some theory of right to power." Yet, there should be no illusions. All such theories, ideologies, and norms serving to secure property claims – including "trust," the benign-sounding obsession of formal theorists – are erected ultimately on coercive capacities.[26] Property and violence are inseparable.[27]

---

[24] Will and Ariel Durant, authors of *The Story of Civilization* spanning eleven volumes, describe wealth concentration and the challenges to it as an almost Polanyian double-movement: "We conclude that the concentration of wealth is natural and inevitable and is periodically alleviated by violent or peaceable partial redistribution. In this view, all economic history is the slow heartbeat of the social organism, a vast systolic and diastole of concentrating wealth and compulsive recirculation" (quote in Judson 2009).

[25] On the material foundations of the transformation from "primitive democracy" to a persistent "inequality of condition," see de Laveleye (1878).

[26] When theories about rights to property work well, extreme material inequalities get constructed as justified, dampening threats to oligarchs from the poor who vastly outnumber them. This ideological success allows a highly unequal society to achieve a stable peace without the richest actors, always a dangerous group if provoked, having to resort to extreme violence. When right-to-riches theories fail and ideological hegemony falters, materially privileged minorities have unleashed fierce oppression to defend their claims. For an especially illuminating discussion of the relationship between theories of right and domination, see Foucault (1980).

[27] Blomley's (2003) exploration of this relationship is especially illuminating.

In the study of oligarchs and oligarchy, it is important to draw a sharp distinction between a property *claim* and a property *right*. Property is a fluid thing, its status shifting throughout history between claims and rights, with the two sometimes mixed in the same system.[28] Both are secured by violence and coercion. However, the distinction arises in the locus of enforcement – that is, who or what provides the coercion that makes a property claim or right secure. There are two broad possibilities: property can be enforced personalistically *against* the community; or it can be enforced impersonally either *by* the community (when distribution is fairly equal), or *in the name of* the community (when distribution is highly unequal). The first is a property claim; the second two are property rights. The first is enforced individually and personalistically; the second two through collectivities.

Property claims are always enforced by oligarchs themselves (separately or jointly) or personalistically by a sultanistic ruler who is invariably a leading oligarch.[29] Property rights are enforced externally by an impersonal state via laws. Thus, state enforcement through the law is only one means by which property can be secured, and not even the most prevalent in the long history of property claims and rights. On this view, Jeremy Bentham (1978 [1843], 52) was mistaken when he wrote: "Property and law are born together, and die together. Before laws were made there was no property; take away laws, and property ceases."[30] This is true only with reference to property rights, not property claims. Long before there were modern states and laws – and including where these once existed but later collapsed – oligarchs and sultanistic rulers have been aggressively and effectively enforcing property claims personalistically. Smith (1993, 170) makes the point concisely: "Private property... precedes the state."

The challenge for the wealthy is how to maintain their fortunate material position against an array of threats to their property claims or rights. Indeed, the story of oligarchy is written in the ways this challenge has been met over the millennia. The larger the property and wealth claimed, the more numerous the horizontal and vertical threats (counterclaims) become, and the greater the need for reliable defenses. When the scale of claimed property is

[28] Ellickson (1993, 1365) argues that the earliest property in land resulted from "forceful self-defense." Property takes on a juridical-legal meaning only when it is defended impersonally via laws and states. Under all other conditions, one's property refers to the totality of one's wealth that is claimed and successfully defended as "mine and under my control." This distinction is important because there are many societies around the world and throughout history where property in the Western sense does not exist. My thanks to Arief Arryman for his insights on this point.

[29] Under a sultanistic regime, the ruler cannot adjudicate every matter great and small throughout society. Thus, there are often laws and procedures that operate in a routine and systemic fashion. Yet they do so in a context where the wishes and preferences of the ruler are well understood. When major conflicts arise and there is intervention from the top, the laws bend to the ruler, not the ruler to the laws. Chapter 4 examines this point in depth.

[30] Olson (1993, 572) makes the same error of failing to distinguish between property claims and rights when he declares: "There is no private property without government!"

modest, wealth itself plays no role in wealth's defense. However, on a much larger scale, wealth becomes a power resource for property and income defense. In other words, at a sufficient level of accumulation and concentration, wealth and property become material power. The relationship between individual property claims and the means to enforce them – between material and coercive power resources – is central to oligarchy and its different forms.

Both dimensions of wealth defense – property defense and income defense – are essential to the existence and persistence of oligarchs. However, the relative weight of each and the degree to which oligarchs are directly engaged in the politics of property and income defense varies tremendously. Each dimension merits elaboration. Property defense refers to the effort by oligarchs or some external guarantor to ensure that their riches are not taken by those who covet them. "Taking" can be vertical, as when the poor attack the rich from below and redistribute their property, or when a state or autocratic ruler seizes property from above. Taking can also be horizontal, as when one oligarch encroaches on the holdings of another. As subsequent chapters will show, claimants have often played a central and direct role in the coercion required to establish and maintain their wealth against vertical predations or laterally from other armed and wealthy oligarchs.

It is important to note that property defense for oligarchs is quite distinct from the ordinary defense of personal property, which is an obsession shared by the rich and poor alike. A lock on one's house, a fence to protect bicycles and toys, or an alarm system to keep burglars from taking a plasma TV or golf clubs – these are individual efforts to defend personal effects. For many people, their personal possessions constitute the entirety of their wealth. Yet, this is not the case for ultra-rich actors, and their personal effects are not relevant to wealth defense. For much of history, property defense for oligarchs has referred to securing vast landed estates, or an individual's control over a community's irrigation system or most of its livestock. This has entailed major personal investments in coercive capacities to defend against violent counterclaims.

As the history of medieval Europe demonstrates, a sharp increase in an oligarch's fortune always required substantial new investments in greater defenses – walls, fortresses, castles, towers, vassals, knights, militia, mercenaries, and costly alliances against enemies. Failing to do so would invite ruinous attacks as there was no reliable state or external authority to offer defense and security. The situation is very different for disarmed oligarchs who benefit from property rights that are strongly defended externally and impersonally by a coercive state. If a contemporary oligarch worth billions of dollars suddenly earned additional billions in a given year, she would not feel compelled to expend a significant part of her new wealth to physically safeguard her enlarged fortune. Nor does she bother to double the security system on her mansion, as this is not where the new wealth is located, nor where a threat would be manifested.

When U.S. hedge-fund managers like Paulson, Soros, and Simon enjoyed single-year increases in income of between $1 and $3 billion in 2007, there is no evidence that they had to hire coercive defenses, erect fortifications, or supplement the state's armed capacities. The truly revealing fact is that it would not have mattered if their annual gains in personal income had been $1 billion or $30 billion each. None would have felt a need to form an armed militia to defend against the masses of the poor, nor against predatory oligarchs who might attack and plunder the wealth if they sensed personal defenses were lacking. The contrast between this happy arrangement and most of the rest of the history connecting rising wealth to rising defenses is profound.

It is taxation on new wealth that poses the greatest threat to contemporary oligarchs who are already partially secured by states that guarantee strong property rights. The establishment of secure property rights shifts the emphasis within wealth defense from property to income defense. The rise of bureaucratic states and the reliable enforcement of property rights through impersonal legal regimes solve the threat of taking and encroachment by punishing anyone who attacks the wealth and property of others. One of the most remarkable aspects of this defense is that it is scale-blind. Property rights to a mind-boggling fortune – a constant source of social tension throughout history – are defended using the same methods and principles as property rights to lawn chairs. In return for the state providing this "public" service, oligarchs are willing to disarm. However, now the armed state poses threats and makes demands of its own in the form of taxes on wealth and income.

Wealth defense under the modern state system no longer involves oligarchs arming themselves and fighting to defend property claims, or deploying material resources to hire the coercive capabilities of others. Income defense, by contrast, involves hiring very different kinds of capacities to prevent valued resources from being taken. The struggle for oligarchs shifts to deploying material resources to specialized professionals (lawyers, accountants, tax avoidance consultants, lobbyists) to keep as much of their wealth and income as possible out of state hands, thereby shifting the costs of the state and even of property defense for oligarchic fortunes to poorer actors in the system. This burden falls particularly hard on the middle and upper-middle classes, whose material resources are large enough to fund the state (including welfare policies),[31] but not large enough individually to purchase the armies of professionals needed to shift the financial burdens upward to oligarchs.

The character of oligarchy is inseparable from the nature of the property defense regime. When property rights are weak and threats to property claims are high, oligarchy becomes more visible because oligarchs engage directly and personally in the coercion needed to defeat threats to their fortunes. Oligarchy has a very different character under conditions where fortunes are not only highly secure, but defended institutionally by a state that maintains a permanently organized apparatus for violence and holds a reliable monopoly on the means of coercion. This shift in the locus of property defense from

---

[31] For evidence of the wealthiest strata shifting tax burdens downward in the rich democracies, see Kenworthy (2009a).

wealthy individuals to an external guarantor dramatically changes the character of oligarchy, but does not eliminate oligarchs or oligarchy itself. Oligarchy becomes less visible as the political engagement of oligarchs, freed from the heavy burden of property defense, shifts away from direct rule and coercive-martial functions to the gentler problem of income defense – how much of one's growing wealth one may keep. It is a shift from the materialist core of wealth defense to its margins: from avoiding confiscation to avoiding redistribution.

A more genteel form of oligarchy does not imply its absence. There are two reasons for this. First, although income defense is far less politically spectacular than property defense and direct rule by oligarchs, it remains a realm in which the sums of money being withheld from the treasury are massive and the political-economic stakes for oligarchs are high. This will be particularly evident in Chapter 5 when examining oligarchs and the Income Defense Industry in the United States. Since ancient times, taxation has always been a central and conflictual matter in political economy. It has links to important notions of justice, fairness, morality, legitimacy, and citizenship.

The second reason is that property defense is a settled issue most of the time in the rich democracies. The separation of property defense from oligarchs, and the fact that the state defends the modest possessions of the barely propertied in like manner, creates the appearance that property defense is no longer a core oligarchic issue. Indeed, the absence of the more frontal and visible aspects of oligarchy lead to the mistaken impression that there are no longer any oligarchs – only ordinary citizens who happen for the first time in history to enjoy politically neutral fortunes. This illusion is shattered the moment the state falters in its defense of property. There is a direct correlation between the visibility and directness of oligarchic engagement in political systems and in violence on the one hand, and the settled or unsettled state of property rights and claims (and who or what is enforcing them) on the other.[32]

When the property regime in modern states has been disrupted by serious threats to oligarchs and their wealth, and all options for capital flight to safety have been exhausted (Winters 1996), the character of oligarchy reverts to its more martial form. The evidence of this is seen in cases in the twentieth century whenever democratic systems produced political results that threatened basic property rights.[33] In some instances, such as in contemporary Brazil under

---

[32] Wealth defense was a chronic problem for Russia's new oligarchs in the chaotic and violent period after the USSR collapsed. Confronted with a state that was incapable of securing property, oligarchs used their material resources to hire their own coercive forces for defense. Gans-Morse (2010) traces how this direct oligarchic role in coercion declined as state capacities for defending property improved, leading to a growing use of lawyers and the court system by wealthy Russians (or their firms) to settle property and contract disputes between firms or between oligarchs.

[33] Polanyi (2001 [1944], 199-200) argues that coercion was the immediate response (and fascism the more gradual one) to radical threats to property from organized workers in democratic

President Luiz Inácio Lula da Silva and in Paraguay under President Fernando Armindo Lugo Méndez, oligarchs in the countryside who were threatened by what they term peasant "land invasions" first appealed to the state to defend their property rights. When that failed, they rearmed, formed murderous militia, and commandeered local police forces to enforce their property claims (Hetherington 2009). In other cases, such as Chile under Allende, the government was violently overthrown by right-wing movements when property was threatened by electoral outcomes that were unacceptable to oligarchs.[34]

Oligarchy and the Elite Detour

A material definition of oligarchs and oligarchy may be jolting to contemporary analysts, but prior to the rise of elite theory and its focus on other power resources, materially-centered analyses of oligarchs had been the dominant approach since antiquity. Elite approaches eventually became preponderant in the scholarly literature, particularly in twentieth-century work on the United States and other advanced industrial societies. The turning point came with the work of Mosca, Pareto, and Michels – all of whom remain strongly associated with oligarchic theory despite their pivotal role in the shift to elite perspectives. However, much of the conceptual confusion surrounding oligarchs and oligarchy evident today can be traced to a misreading of the materialism of the Ancients and a careless blending of oligarchic and elite theory. The point merits brief elaboration.

It was mentioned earlier in this chapter that the generic definition of oligarchy, "rule by the few," relies on a familiar typology reproduced endlessly in undergraduate texts in political science and derived loosely from Aristotle's *Politics*. Along one axis is the number of actors who rule (the one, the few, or the many), and along the other is for whom each rules (in their own self-interest or in the common interest – meaning everyone's interest rather than just that of the majority). Figure 1.1 reproduces the standard typology.

The boxes in the typology have generally been viewed as discrete forms of government, implying movement from one box to another – for instance, from monarchy to oligarchy to democracy (or the reverse). The problem with this widely used framework is that it is not even supported by Aristotle's own arguments and logic. Indeed, he abandons the axes of the typology almost as soon as he mentions them. When discussing rule by the few or the many, Aristotle immediately shifts the emphasis away from the number of actors exerting

Germany. The period following World War I, he writes, "showed conclusively that in an emergency the working class, its trade unions and parties, might disregard the rules of the market which established freedom of contract and the sanctity of private property as absolutes." Polanyi continues: "Not the illusory danger of communist revolution, but the undeniable fact that the working classes were in the position to force possibly ruinous interventions, was the source of the latent fear which, at a crucial juncture, burst forth in the fascist panic."

[34] Schryer (1986) examines violent oligarchic responses to the Mexican state's failure to enforce property rights against peasant land invasions in the 1970s and 1980s.

		Number of Rulers		
		One	Few	Many
Rule for	Self Interest	Tyranny	Oligarchy	Mobocracy
	Common Interest	Monarchy	Aristocracy	Democracy

FIGURE 1.1. Aristotle's Typology.

influence over the system of government to what explains their numbers – their material position, the few rich and the many poor. He writes: "Whether in oligarchies or in democracies, the number of the governing body, whether the greater number, as in a democracy, or the smaller number, as in an oligarchy, is an *accident due to the fact that the rich everywhere are few, and the poor numerous*" (III viii 1279^{b}35–9, my emphasis).

Recasting his original quantitative categories now in explicitly materialist terms, Aristotle writes that "oligarchy is when men of property have the government in their hands; democracy, the opposite, when the indigent, and not the men of property, are the rulers" (III viii 1279^{b}17–20). Rejecting a focus on the number of rulers as a "misapprehension of the difference" between democracy and oligarchy, Aristotle emphasizes instead the relative riches and the material interests of those in power. "For the real difference between democracy and oligarchy is poverty and wealth," he states. "Wherever men rule by reason of their wealth, *whether they be few or many*, that is an oligarchy, and where the poor rule, that is a democracy" (III viii 1280^{a}1–3, my emphasis).

For Aristotle, plutocracy is a redundant term. Oligarchy always refers to the nexus between wealth and power.[35] Moreover, Aristotle never takes seriously the divide between the virtuous motives of ruling for the common interest versus self-interested rule. He expects whomever is ruling to do so in their own interest, and the political problem at the heart of *Politics* is how to manage the inevitable clashes this produces between the rich and poor. Extreme material inequalities produce a situation in which "the poor and the rich quarrel with one another, and whichever side gets the better, instead of establishing a just or popular government, regards political supremacy as the prize of victory, and the one party sets up a democracy and the other an oligarchy" (IV xi 1296^{a}28–32). Analytically, Aristotle is the original materialist and realist.

---

[35] Xenophon uses the more precise term plutocracy where most of the other ancients simply used oligarchy to mean the same thing. In the *Republic*, Plato states that oligarchy exists when "the rich rule and the poor man has no share," while in the *Politicus*, he defines oligarchy as government by the rich. However, Plato never develops the material aspects of oligarchy to the degree seen in Aristotle's work. Whibley (1896, 9) notes that "Plato's description of actual constitutions in the *Politicus* is incidentally introduced to show how worthless they are in comparison with the rule of the perfect statesman," which was his primary focus. For an important interpretation of Plato, see Monoson (2000).

He also grapples with the core oligarchic problem of wealth defense. Political equality enjoyed by all citizens of Athens coexisted with material inequality favoring the wealthy few. Aristotle recognizes the material foundations of the political conflicts that plagued most Greek cities. "But strikingly," Stalley (1995, 356) observes, "he does not suggest that they should be dealt with by economic reform." This is partly because Aristotle understood that threatening the property of oligarchs is dangerous and destabilizing. It is evident throughout *Politics* that he considers their power to be formidable even when they are not ruling directly. "The regulation of property is the chief point of all," he writes, "the question upon which all revolutions turn" (II vii 1266ª37–9). The solution to the conflict, for Aristotle, lies in blending oligarchy and democracy in the hope that the wealthy few will not be overly oppressive and the many poor will not threaten and provoke the rich.[36]

The analytical link among wealth, wealth defense, and oligarchy established by Aristotle endured through the Middle Ages and into the modern era. Niccolò Machiavelli's *Discourses* in the early 1500s sought to devise institutional means to limit the overwhelming power of the wealthy.[37] The rise of the modern state in the seventeenth and eighteenth centuries ushered in the single most dramatic transformation in the long history of oligarchy. It marked the first time oligarchs were disarmed and no longer ruled directly. The notion that property defense could be reliably guaranteed by a state instead of oligarchs doing the job themselves was untested and generated considerable anxiety.

Although not theorists of oligarchy and elite rule, writers like James Harrington (1656), John Adams (1854 [1776]), Adam Smith (1776), James Madison (1787), Thomas Jefferson (1950 [1785]), and Alexis de Tocqueville (2007 [1838]) grapple in different ways with the tensions inherent in having the formal arrangements of equal power in democracies overlaid on extreme inequalities of material power in society. Harrington observes that "where there is inequality of estates there must be inequality of power; and where there is inequality

---

[36] A "polity" or "constitutional government" is a "fusion of oligarchy and democracy" (IV viii 1293ᵇ34–6), which is based on an "admixture of the two elements, that is to say, of the rich and poor . . . " (IV viii 1294ª22–4). The key to success is in combining the two so that observers are never certain which it is. "There is a true union of oligarchy and democracy when the same state may be termed either a democracy or an oligarchy," Aristotle writes (IV ix 1294ᵇ16–17). "In a well attempted polity," he adds, "there should appear to be both elements and yet neither" (IV ix 1294ᵇ35–6). de Montesquieu (1748) echoes Aristotle when he defines a just democracy as one whose legislature protects the few rich against the many poor by allowing the rich to "form a body that has a right to check the licentiousness of the people."

[37] McCormick (2006, 147) notes that thinkers prior to the eighteenth century were far more likely than later analysts to ask: "What institutions will prevent wealthy citizens from dominating the political process?" He adds: "Unless formally restrained, the richest citizens tended to use their privilege to molest fellow citizens with impunity and direct the workings of government toward their own benefit rather than toward the general citizenry. Wealthy individuals and families would often subvert popular governments, maneuvering them in more narrowly oligarchic or autocratic directions, even, on occasion, going so far as to deliver them over to foreign powers."

of power there can be no commonwealth." The predominant form of wealth at the time was landed estates, and Harrington argued that because the source of the inequality was material, only a material solution could address it. He supported enacting laws that would limit the amount of property any one person could own, so that "no one man or number of men, within the compass of the few or aristocracy, can come to overpower the whole people by their possessions in land."

Harrington's arguments had a major influence on democratic thinkers in the seventeenth and eighteenth centuries, including John Adams (1854 [1776], 376), who observes that "the balance of power in a society, accompanies the balance of property in land."[38] This same association between concentrated wealth and exaggerated power was central to de Tocqueville's (2007 [1838]) analysis of democracy in the United States, except in inverted form. It was the absence of extreme material inequalities that gave democracy in America a grounding and vitality rarely seen in a more economically stratified and aristocratic Europe.

As democracy reemerged in the modern era, the emphasis shifted back to Aristotle's concern with the dangers that inequalities of property and wealth presented to the rich if political power is shared with the poor. "Wherever there is great property there is great inequality," Smith (1776) writes. "The affluence of the rich excites the indignation of the poor, who are often both driven by want, and prompted by envy, to invade his possessions." For Smith (Book V), there was no more compelling explanation for the rise of the state than wealth defense – the oligarchic need for a guarantor of highly unequal distributions of riches in society. "Civil government, so far as it is instituted for the security of property," Smith notes, "is in reality instituted for the defence of the rich against the poor, or of those who have some property against those who have none at all."[39]

In his writings on factions, Madison (1787) is partly concerned with political conflicts based on religion. However, the two factions that most trouble him are the rich and the poor: "The most common and durable source of factions has been the various and unequal distribution of property. Those who hold and those who are without property have ever formed distinct interests in society."

---

[38] "Harrington has shown that power always follows property," Adams (1854 [1776], 376) argues. "This I believe to be as infallible a maxim in politics, as that action and reaction are equal, is in mechanics." Despite this materialist interpretation of political power, Adams (1875, 121) remained conservative with regard to private property. He argued, with Harrington, that only those with property should be able to vote.

[39] Smith (1776, Book V) focuses on the pressing need to secure against the constant threats facing the wealthy: "It is only under the shelter of the civil magistrate that the owner of that valuable property, which is acquired by the labour of many years, or perhaps of many successive generations, can sleep a single night in security. He is at all times surrounded by unknown enemies, whom, though he never provoked, he can never appease, and from whose injustice he can be protected only by the powerful arm of the civil magistrate continually held up to chastise it. The acquisition of valuable and extensive property, therefore, necessarily requires the establishment of civil government."

The most alarming faction of all for Madison is the majority of poor citizens who will abuse a pure or direct democracy by passing policies injurious to the rich minority. Allowing people too much direct participation in democracy is a formula for disaster because "such democracies have ever been spectacles of turbulence and contention; have ever been found incompatible with personal security or the rights of property."[40]

If Madison's main fear is that too much direct democracy will threaten to unleash a majority "faction" of poor citizens against the rich, Jefferson and de Tocqueville worry that a particular kind of wealthy stratum of society will subvert American democracy. Their concern is narrow and historically proximate in that it focuses exclusively on the danger of having a European-style landed nobility take root in the United States. They pay virtually no attention to the broader threat to democracy posed by an ultra-wealthy minority, landed nobility or otherwise, that has the motivation and the means to defend their material interests against institutional arrangements of power-sharing. The challenge, as Jefferson (1950 [1785], 589) sees it, is to avoid the specific *transgenerational* pattern of concentrated wealth prevalent in Europe. "I am conscious that an equal division of property is impracticable," he writes to Madison. "But the consequences of this enormous inequality producing so much misery to the bulk of mankind, legislators cannot invent too many devices for subdividing property." Like Jefferson, de Tocqueville was obsessed only with the European version of oligarchy based on birth and continuing across generations. He lauded the finality and genius of abolishing primogeniture, which acts automatically to subvert aristocracies of wealth that plagued Europe for centuries.[41]

The remedies and safeguards put in place by figures like Jefferson worked well to block what they were narrowly designed to prevent – a European oligarchy that had a particular kind of cohesion because it spanned generations – but did nothing to halt the rise of an American oligarchy grounded on concentrated material power that is deployed to great effect in the present without the necessity of spanning generations. Just fifty years after de Tocqueville's work appeared, the United States of the late nineteenth century had already entered a fully matured Robber Baron era marked by an extreme "inequality of condition" for a small number of wealthy Americans. This rising stratum of citizens, although not European-style aristocrats, nevertheless ended the

---

[40] As Polanyi notes, English oligarchs pushing for constitutional protections initially focused all of their attention on arbitrary acts against property by the Crown. A century later, the fear would shift to the potential threats to property from a rising class of laborers if they were allowed to vote. The challenge of democracy, Polanyi (2001 [1944], 234) writes, was to "separate the people from power over their own economic life."

[41] "When the legislator has once regulated the law of inheritance," de Tocqueville (2007 [1838], 30) writes, "he may rest from his labor. The machine once put in motion will go on for ages, and advance, as if self-guided, towards a given point. When framed in a particular manner, this law unites, draws together, and vests property in a few hands: its tendency is clearly aristocratic. On opposite principles its action is still more rapid; it divides, distributes, and disperses both property and power."

relative balance of material power in society that undergirded de Tocqueville's image of American democracy.

Elite Theory. Just as the Robber Baron period was reaching its peak in countries like the United States, theories of minority power and influence turned away from an emphasis on material power in the hands of oligarchs and focused instead on a range of nonmaterial power resources held by elites (Higley, Burton, and Field 1990; Higley et al., 1991; Higley and Gunther 1992; Dogan and Higley 1998; Cammack 1990 offers a trenchant critique). The result was to blur the concept of oligarchy by conflating things like executive committees, representative government, and a range of elite forms of minority dominance (based on education-information, organizational complexity, ethnicity, exclusive networks, etc.) with the unique and specific kind of power and political interests centered on the defense of concentrated wealth. The downplaying of material power resources occurred partly as a reaction to Marx, but also drew on the earlier and quite explicit elitism of the French socialists that influenced Marx. From the middle of the nineteenth century onward, Marx's class analysis had displaced all earlier analytical frameworks for discussing the relationship between material and political power.

The first elite theorists – Mosca, Pareto, and Michels – acknowledge a place for material power, but seek in their writings to shift the analytical attention to other aspects of minority power among influential actors at the helm of governments and empires. Although all three discuss oligarchs and oligarchy, they use these terms interchangeably with elites, aristocrats, governing elites, and ruling classes. This diffusion of meaning and mixture of terminology commenced the loss of clarity and precision surrounding the materialist conceptualization of oligarchs and their power resources.[42]

As elite theory evolved in the twentieth century, material forms of power received less attention than other bases of minority influence. For C. Wright Mills (1956, 3–4), the "power elite" are a minority of actors at the top of society who are influential because they hold positions in major organizations. He writes:

> The power elite is composed of men whose positions enable them to transcend the ordinary environments of ordinary men and women; they are in positions to make decisions having major consequences. Whether they do or do not make such decisions is less important than the fact that they do occupy such pivotal positions: their failure to act, their failure to make decisions, is itself an act that is often of greater consequence than the decisions they do make. For they are in command of the major hierarchies and organizations of modern society. They rule the big corporations. They run the machinery of the state and claim its prerogatives. They direct the military establishment. They occupy the strategic command posts of the social structure, in which are now centered the effective means of the power and the wealth and the celebrity which they enjoy.

---

[42] The differences between these theorists and Marxist scholars focusing on class have been well analyzed (Bottomore 1964; Domhoff and Ballard 1968; Etzioni-Halevy 1997; Lachmann 2003).

Mills's definition of a power elite fits squarely within the second of the five power resources – that based on official positions in government or at the helm of major organizations. The power elite are explicitly not an oligarchy or class that derives power from wealth. Mills begins instead with powerful institutions and organizations. Particular actors become members of the power elite because they hold commanding positions within them.

Although elite theory played a significant role in undermining the precision and utility of oligarchic theory, and especially the centrality of material power, it nevertheless has produced a literature that is rich in insights about various forms of minority power and influence.[43] What that scholarship does not do effectively is account for the unique power of those who control high concentrations of wealth. They remain powerful whether or not they are the best at what they do, organizations are complex, or they hold any formal offices. Indeed, what is striking about oligarchs is that their power is substantial no matter how organized or institutionalized a social formation is, including contexts where institutions and organizations are rudimentary or absent.

The argument thus far has redefined oligarchs and oligarchy by focusing on material power resources and the central problem of wealth defense. It has traced the long lineage of this material focus and emphasized how it differs in important ways from elite theory. One of the key points advanced early in this chapter is that the definition of oligarchs remains constant across time and social formations, but oligarchies vary. In the final section of this introduction, attention turns to the presentation of a typology that describes fundamental differences in the major kinds of oligarchy that have existed throughout history.

Types of Oligarchies

All oligarchies can be categorized according to four major characteristics: the extent to which oligarchs are directly engaged in supplying the coercion that undergirds their claims or rights to property and wealth; whether oligarchs are also directly engaged in rule or governing; whether that engagement in coercion and rule is fragmented or collective; and finally, whether oligarchs are wild or tamed (with external taming being both more common and more stable than self-taming). The most significant historical line of demarcation among oligarchies divides those before and after the rise of the modern nation-state. The dominant form of oligarchy prior to the rise of the state saw oligarchs as coercive actors that ruled. How fragmented or collective their rule was changed in tandem with the rise and collapse of empires.

---

[43] Field and Higley (1980) take the classical elite theorists as a starting point, but offer a substantial restatement of the elitist paradigm that downplays the determinacy the classical theorists assigned to elites. They emphasize instead how elites are checked and limited by nonelites, and how they must make appeals for support to nonelite groupings. Lachmann (2000) offers an important elite conflict approach that incorporates material bases of power and interests. Carlton (1996) presents a typology of elites.

No matter how collectively or individually oligarchs ruled in the pre-modern era, they were at no time fully disarmed. What varied was whether they were martial specialists themselves or used their material resources to hire guards, militia, or armies. Even so-called gentlemen consuls in Athens and senators in Rome played a direct role in financing the state's coercive apparatus. They played an even more direct role in deploying the means of coercion to defend claims to their considerable agricultural holdings and slaves in the countryside. From the Dark Ages through the feudal period, oligarchy was more fragmented and oligarchs tended to fight alongside the mercenary forces they purchased or could assemble as needed through vassal obligations.

The truly dramatic transformation of the modern nation-state was the change it represented in the regime of property defense. Oligarchs always struggled mightily with the dangers and burdens of defending their claims, and they accepted being fully disarmed once centralizing states demonstrated both the ability and commitment to provide this crucial aspect of wealth defense. The long and violent struggles and negotiations that resulted in this new form of government have been well analyzed and do not need to be recounted here.[44] The important point for present purposes is that this change in the form and function of the state marked a major change in oligarchy, but not its end.

The period stretching from the medieval era when a new class of wealthy actors arose in the urban interstices of the feudal order to the contemporary world where states successfully defend property, demonstrates repeatedly that oligarchs are content to use their resources for the income aspects of wealth defense. Having oligarchs no longer personally engaged in rule or government almost always means they are no longer directly engaged in property defense. The notable exception is when conditions in the state are such that the property of oligarchs is defended generally but threatened selectively. In such situations, oligarchs are often disarmed in the sense that they do not hire coercive forces to secure their property. Instead, they deploy material resources in the form of payments to officials to ensure that the state's formidable coercive capacities are not used against them individually. Chapter 4 focuses on this widespread method of wealth defense by examining the case of modern Indonesia.

A typology of oligarchies based on these characteristics is presented in Figure 1.2. The x-axis describes how directly oligarchs are involved in the provision of coercion for property defense. At the far left, their role is high and their involvement in the violence is more personal. Moving to the right along the x-axis indicates a less direct and less personal role in coercion by oligarchs. In the middle of the x-axis, oligarchs use material power to hire others to supply coercion for property defense. At the extreme right side of the x-axis, oligarchs are completely disarmed and property defense has been surrendered to an external, higher authority.

---

[44] See Anderson (1974b) and Greif (2005, 2006) for two very different perspectives on the same period.

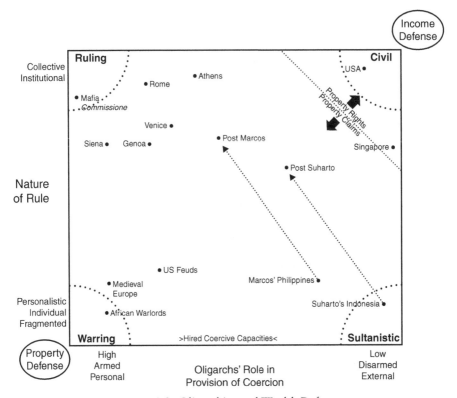

FIGURE 1.2. Oligarchies and Wealth Defense.

The *y*-axis describes whether the system of rule or government is personal-individual-fragmented or more collective-institutionalized. At the intersection of the *x*-*y* axes, rule is highly personal and fragmented, and oligarchs are directly engaged in the provision of coercion. Moving up the *y*-axis to the top left corner, oligarchs are still engaged in the violence of property defense, but rule is more collective and institutionalized. The bottom right corner of the diagram refers to situations in which a single oligarch with a formidable state coercive apparatus (sometimes supplemented with private militia) rules individually and personalistically, and defends the property claims of fully disarmed oligarchs. The extreme top right area of the diagram describes a situation in which oligarchs are fully disarmed, do not rule directly, and government is thoroughly institutionalized and collective rather than personalistic. As one moves diagonally from the bottom left to the top right, the political engagement by oligarchs shifts from a preponderant focus on property defense to an almost exclusive focus on income defense. This typology yields four ideal types of oligarchy: warring, ruling, sultanistic, and civil.[45]

---

[45] Ideal types are abstractions of highly complex realities for purposes of explanation. Selective simplification is their strength, not their weakness. See Hodgson (1998, 174.)

Warring Oligarchy. At its most extreme, this is the realm of the warlord (Reno 1998). Fragmentation among oligarchs is at its maximum. Alliances are unstable in a context of violent competition that shifts constantly. Any superior authority figure that emerges among oligarchs enjoys only temporary dominance. Conflict and threats are predominantly lateral between warring oligarchs and claims to enriching territory, resources, and subordinate populations are overlapping and contested. Rapid accumulation is mostly by conquest, although warring oligarchs also extract surpluses from primary producers. Coercive and material power resources are so intertwined for warring oligarchs as to be essentially coterminous. Coercive capacities exist for wealth defense and wealth is deployed to sustain coercive capacities.

Ruling Oligarchy. When oligarchs retain a high and personal role in the provision of coercion, and yet rule collectively and through institutions marked by norms or codes of conduct, the result is a ruling oligarchy. An assembly of fully armed and dangerous oligarchs is highly unstable and has rarely existed in its pure form except for brief periods. The clearest examples are the Mafia Commission in the United States and the Italian *Commissione*, a council of mafia dons that adjudicated conflicts among the families and sometimes meted out sanctions. Gambetta (2000, 165 n10) uses the term "confederation" to describe the organization across mafia "clusters," each headed by a boss or don.[46]

The classic examples of ruling oligarchies appeared in a more mild form in the Greco-Roman consuls and senates of antiquity. The Italian *magnati*, the violent noble clans and families that dominated medieval city-states, could also be categorized as ruling oligarchs. These examples of collective government by ruling oligarchs were more enduring mainly because the oligarchs involved played a less personal role in the provision of violence for wealth defense – hence being positioned more to the right along the x-axis than the Mafia Commissions. Ruling oligarchs divide their expenditures on coercive forces between those they hire and deploy themselves (particularly in the countryside outside the capital) and those hired and deployed with their collective consent by the quasi-state apparatuses through which they govern directly. These are also the first forms of oligarchy in which urban merchant and financial oligarchs begin to share power with, and eventually displace, landed feudal oligarchs.

Sultanistic Oligarchy. A sultanistic form of oligarchy exists when a monopoly on the means of coercion is in the hands of one oligarch rather than an institutionalized state constrained by laws (Chehabi and Linz 1998). Patron–client relations predominate with certain norms of behavior and obligation associated with them. However, the rule of law is either absent or operates as a personalistic system of rule *by* law. Authority and violence are the exclusive or overwhelming preserve of the ruler, whose stability at the apex of the regime, and especially over the powerful oligarchs immediately below, depends vitally on providing property and income defense for oligarchs as a whole. Failure to do so or frontally threatening oligarchs are key catalysts for destabilization and overthrow. Sultanistic rulers either disarm oligarchs or effectively overwhelm

---

[46] Ruling oligarchies have also arisen among the Japanese Yakuza and Chinese Triads.

their individual coercive capacities, usually by deploying state instruments of violence or blending these with the ruler's private means of coercion. Disarmed oligarchs defend their wealth by investing part of their material resources as payoffs to the ruler to deflect individualized predations. Property threats laterally from other oligarchs are managed strategically by the sultanistic ruler at the top. The ruler also defends oligarchic wealth and property against threats from the poor below.

Civil Oligarchy. As in a sultanistic oligarchy, oligarchs in a civil oligarchy are fully disarmed and do not rule directly (except sporadically as individual political figures, not in an oligarchic capacity). The difference in a civil oligarchy is that in place of a single individual serving as an external provider of coercion, and thus defender of oligarchic property, there exists an institutionalized collectivity of actors highly constrained by laws. In a ruling oligarchy, oligarchs surrender a major part of their power to a collectivity of oligarchs. Oligarchs as a group are more powerful than any single member. In a sultanistic oligarchy, they surrender a major part of their power to a single individual. One oligarch is more powerful than the rest.

In a pure-form civil oligarchy, oligarchs surrender a major part of their power to an impersonal and institutionalized government in which the rule of law is stronger than all individuals. With property defense well provided by the state, wealth defense in a civil oligarchy is focused on income defense – the effort to deflect the potentially redistributive predations of an anonymous state. The further one moves along the diagonal stretching from a warring oligarchy at the intersection of the *x-y* axes toward civil oligarchy in the upper right corner, the more likely it becomes that oligarchy will be mixed with democracy in an Aristotelian fusion. It is important to recognize that there is no necessity for a civil oligarchy to be electorally democratic. The United States and India are procedurally democratic; Singapore and Malaysia are soft-authoritarian. All are civil oligarchies.

Tamed and Wild Oligarchs. Of the four major characteristics mentioned at the outset of this section, the first three are captured in the typology just elaborated. The fourth concerns whether oligarchs are wild or tamed. This is an extremely important characteristic of oligarchies, but it does not vary according to the axes in Figure 1.2. The extent to which oligarchs are tamed refers to whether the system of rule is powerful enough to control the behavior of oligarchs by imposing costs on their most pathological social behaviors. The ability of a government or regime to tame oligarchs does not depend on whether oligarchs are directly engaged in rule, whether the government is personalistic or collective-institutional, nor does the disarming of oligarchs guarantee that they will be tamed – although it is certainly easier to tame disarmed oligarchs. Even if they play no coercive role, oligarchs are capable of having a tremendous social and political influence simply from the deployment of their enormous material resources.

There are examples of both tamed and wild oligarchs across all the forms of oligarchy except the warring type. Warring oligarchs are by definition in almost constant and often violent conflict with each other, and they are masters of their own territory unless displaced. Ruling oligarchies range from those in which oligarchs are semi-armed to fully disarmed. As the Roman case illustrates in Chapter 3, the ability of oligarchs to tame themselves collectively depends on whether formidable collective instruments of coercion and control can be used to limit the behaviors of individual oligarchs (or cabals). A ruling oligarchy can fail in a general way to constrain the pathological behaviors of oligarchs without individuals or small groups being able to challenge or displace the collectivity. Thus they might engage in disruptions of the peace at the center of the empire (agitating groups on the basis of class or citizenship or other divisive forms of identity), destabilizing political intrigues within the ruling oligarchy itself, self-enriching military campaigns in the provinces and beyond ("misusing" the collective coercive apparatus), or extreme corruption. As long as the debilitated ruling oligarchy persists, these are evidence of wild rather than tamed oligarchs.

When circumstances are reversed and an individual oligarch or a cabal manages not only to capture the collective coercive apparatus of the ruling oligarchy and turn it against the group, but also to stabilize and possibly institutionalize this narrower form of domination, this is an example of a transition from a wild ruling oligarchy to a tamed sultanistic one. This occurred under Caesar in Rome and under Marcos in the Philippines, although as Chapter 4 illustrates, with a more limited capacity for taming the oligarchs in the Marcos case. The end of authoritarian rule in the Philippines in the 1980s and Indonesia in the 1990s was widely heralded as a transition to democracy. However, what this study reveals clearly is that there was another equally important transition that occurred – from relatively tamed oligarchies under sultanistic domination to wild oligarchies under democratic governments that lacked the capacity to constrain oligarchs.

Indonesia's Suharto, a sultanistic oligarch, successfully tamed the rest of the country's oligarchs for decades. Yet, Indonesia's legal system has been unable to constrain the nation's oligarchs during the period of electoral democracy following Suharto's removal in 1998. The transition from authoritarian to democratic rule in Indonesia has received considerable analytical attention. However, this second transition – from an oligarchy tamed by a sultanistic ruler to a wild oligarchy unconstrained by the rule of law – is no less important in its impact on the country's political economy. Indeed, transitions back and forth between tamed and untamed oligarchies are not well explained in either the democratic transitions literature or the work done on the rule of law.[47]

---

[47] The literature on transitions to democracy, for instance, pays considerable attention to the role of elites, including "elite pacts" (O'Donnell and Schmitter 1986) and "elite settlements" (Burton and Higley 1987). However, the central focus is on the decline of authoritarian rule, the rise of procedural democracy (or this process in reverse), and the role powerful actors or classes play in how events turn out. An emphasis on transitions between tamed and wild oligarchies shifts the focus to fundamental changes in the *degree and nature of constraints* on oligarchs, whatever the form of the polity.

Once the two types of transition are separated, it becomes possible to account for situations where there is a dramatic transition from authoritarian rule to electoral democracy and an equally dramatic transition from a tamed to a wild oligarchy.[48] The fall of a dictator who had successfully tamed a nation's oligarchy frequently produces both a transition to democracy and a transition to wild oligarchy, in which the formal institutions of law and punishment that were deliberately weakened during the authoritarian period prove too feeble to constrain oligarchs when electoral democracy displaces dictatorship.

The Indonesian case under Suharto makes clear that a strong legal system is not necessarily needed to tame oligarchs – just an authority stronger than they are. It also suggests that in discussions about the need for the rule of law, the most relevant matter is not necessarily the systemic failure of the legal system, but the narrower question of whether the legal regime is stronger than the strongest actors – both the oligarchs and elites. This might be termed the "high" rule of law to distinguish it from situations where the legal system functions reasonably well for crimes and disputes involving ordinary citizens (the "low" rule of law), who have neither the coercive power to intimidate the legal infrastructure nor the material resources to buy outcomes. Hendley (2009) refers to these in the Russian context as "mundane cases" to distinguish them from "telephone law" cases involving interventions from powerful actors in the Kremlin.

A key theoretical contribution of this book is the argument that the taming of oligarchs is an extremely important political phenomenon that has nothing to do with democratization. Ruling and sultanistic oligarchies are consistently nondemocracies, but they also range widely from being tamed and untamed oligarchies. Meanwhile, civil oligarchies are by definition systems with an impersonal government under a legal regime that is stronger than individual oligarchs. Civil oligarchies successfully punish oligarchs who engage in pathological behaviors.[49] However, as Chapter 5 shows, civil oligarchies can be electorally democratic as in the United States or undemocratic as in Singapore.

Conclusions

This chapter raises several key points about oligarchs and oligarchy that go a long way in addressing some of the muddle and confusion mentioned in the

---

[48] This separation of democratic and oligarchic transitions is useful in analyzing patterns of continuity of oligarchic power (even if that power is highly dynamic), adaptations of oligarchs to electoral democratic politics, as well as the surge in a broad range of political, economic, and social pathologies that often accompanies democratic transitions.

[49] The system-damaging ponzi scheme perpetrated by Bernie Madoff shows the tremendous power of oligarchs on the one hand, but also that he could be successfully tried and jailed on the other. The point is not that a civil oligarchy manages to detect all pathological activities oligarchs are capable of, but rather that the power resting in the judicial system is sufficient to punish any oligarch it ensnares. By contrast, in all civil oligarchies the power resources of oligarchs enable them routinely to defeat such legal systems as exist. Indeed, the larger the oligarch, the more likely it is that he or she will succeed in subverting the legal system through the use of payoffs or hiring means of intimidation.

opening pages. The theoretical claims presented here are firmly grounded in materialist arguments that extend back at least to ancient Greece, but probably much further in thought even if not in written form. This theory narrows the concept of oligarchy rather significantly and separates it sharply from elite approaches. Some scholars might object vehemently to this narrowing, but it gives an unwieldy and nearly meaningless concept much more clarity and utility for analysis. The reader is invited to judge the validity of that claim in the evidence, cases, and interpretations presented in the remaining chapters of the book.

Although at various times in history oligarchs have ruled directly, they are not defined by a role in government or by a position of rule. Oligarchs can rule, but there is no necessity that they do so. In addition, because ruling is not an element in what constitutes an oligarch, the absence of oligarchs in ruling roles has no effect on the existence of oligarchs and oligarchy. Oligarchs are actors defined by specific power resources they possess and control. They constitute a form of minority power and influence because of the material power resources they have accumulated personally and seek to retain and maintain.

The relevant and defining political motivations of oligarchs are defensive and existential. Once constituted, an oligarch's paramount objective is to secure, maintain, and retain his or her position of extreme wealth and power against all manner of threats. This does not preclude a desire to accumulate more wealth, particularly when such accumulation is spurred by the rising costs of wealth defense. Otherwise, the drive to enlarge one's material fortune is a secondary characteristic of oligarchs and has varied widely based on the historical period, the mode of production, the property regime, and the degree of economic competition. Put another way, accumulation motives do not define oligarchs but have played a major role in some of the specific forms oligarchy has assumed.

Oligarchy does not refer to a system of rule by a particular set of actors. It describes the political processes and arrangements associated with a small number of wealthy individuals who are not only uniquely empowered by their material resources, but set apart in a manner that necessarily places them in conflict with large segments of the community (often including with each other). Oligarchy centers on the political challenges of defending concentrated wealth. The oligarchies that have existed since the dawn of settled human history and that continue to exist today differ according to how those political challenges have been met.

The next four chapters examine in greater detail the four types of oligarchy presented in the typology in Figure 1.2 – warring, ruling, sultanistic, and civil. The discussion begins with a brief treatment of warring oligarchies, the form that is the most simple and violent. The chapters exploring the more complex forms of ruling, sultanistic, and civil oligarchies present case studies that are considerably more detailed.

2

Warring Oligarchies

In a recent debate over warlords, Jackson (2003) and Marten (2007) argue that the concept accurately describes cases stretching much further back in history than the period covered by the contemporary African cases around which the warlord literature developed (Reno 1998; 2002). They suggest that the term *warlord* applies as readily to early twentieth-century China and feudal barons in medieval Europe as it does to the violent figures operating in Somalia, Sierra Leone, and Liberia in the 1980s and 1990s. This effort to free warlord theory from the analytical constraints imposed by the modern state system is a useful corrective, but much too timid. Reaching back to medieval Europe does not address the equally limiting notion that warlords emerge from the disintegration of some prior central authority.[1] Looking much further back than the medieval period highlights the crucial role warlords play in founding stratified societies in the first place, and especially in the earliest efforts to claim private property and concentrate individual wealth – which is to say, become oligarchs. And it is for this reason that the debate over warlords provides a useful entry point for an examination of warring oligarchies.

The historical record confirms that warlords have repeatedly arisen out of the detritus of broken empires and disintegrated states, only to recede again when new kingdoms and centralized regimes are formed. The problem is that this emphasis on breakdown ignores the long period of warlordism that predates the appearance of the first kingdoms. The true zenith of warlordism is seen not in the *intermezzos* of empire, but rather in the unbroken centuries of warring oligarchies that existed before the first empires ever appeared. Wealth-accumulating warriors do not merely capture fragmented power from crumbling kingdoms or states. They play a crucial role in solidifying the first conquest

---

[1] Jackson (2003, 131) argues that warlords have "periodically emerged whenever centralised political-military control has broken down"; Marten (2007, 48) states that warlordism exists when "armed men take advantage of the disintegration of central authority to seize control." Johnson (1997) examines oligarchy in medieval China.

societies on which kingdoms and states are built. Warlords were pioneers at the crucial historical intersection of violence, property, and wealth in the genealogy of oligarchy and empire.

This longer view does not deny that there are important differences between contemporary warlords and those of the late Neolithic period or in medieval Europe. Prehistoric warlords operated in a social milieu barren of economic and political institutions or ideologies. Indeed, they helped forge the first such artifacts of civilization. Whether operating on a scale great or small, early warlords were rarely embedded within larger political and economic systems with which they might engage. However, the most important differences between then and now lie in the social institutions and technologies of violence and warfare at a warlord's disposal. Individual capabilities for destruction and coercion have risen exponentially, allowing contemporary warlords to control much larger territories and populations. In addition, although modern warlords represent the negation of the institutional state, their rule has tended to mimic a range of modern state forms.[2]

What is far more striking than these differences, however, are the similarities across warlords. Although it would be an exaggeration to construe the most ancient warlords as oligarchs, the more successful among them evolved from being chiefs into warring oligarchs. The defining characteristics of these actors include personally controlling or owning massive wealth, controlling the means of violence, engaging in direct and personal relations of dominance over a stratum of warriors, and holding positions of direct rule and control over the broader communities they lead. Among prehistoric warlords, the relationship among coercion, property, and wealth was often blurred – although becoming a truly powerful warlord depended on economic success that eventually elevated the importance of material and mobilizational power resources over purely coercive ones. In all instances, warlords – and the warring oligarchs they sometimes became – competed and clashed in a context marked by endemic fragmentation and parcelized, personal sovereignties.

The case material presented in this chapter begins in the prehistoric era, moves to medieval Europe, and ends with feuding Appalachian clans in nineteenth-century America. The juxtaposition of such disparate examples of warring oligarchy is deliberate. The cases emphasize that there are certain basic characteristics common to the warring type, but that their occurrence is not limited to a particular historical era. Warring oligarchies arise from a specific combination of coercion by oligarchs and fragmentation among them as they engage directly in efforts of wealth defense. Despite radically different contexts, these conditions existed five thousand years ago and they continue to occur in the twenty-first century. This suggests that the warring form has not been made obsolete by other oligarchic solutions to the challenges of wealth defense. In

---

[2] One of the reasons states and even the international system figure so prominently in the scholarship on warlords in Africa is precisely because of the remarkable engagement between warlords and institutions at the national and international level.

oligarchic theory, the history of state building and the rule of law is inseparable from the oligarchic imperative to secure fortunes against threats. When
states and legal regimes break down – and this sometimes happens because of
oligarchic behaviors – warring forms of oligarchy will always be one of the
alternatives for wealth defense. This chapter traces how warring oligarchs first
emerged and explores other forms of warring oligarchy that arise when they
have reemerged after a period of absence.

Chiefs, Warlords, and Warring Oligarchs

To understand the genealogical connections between the earliest warlords and
the first warring oligarchs, it is essential to trace how chiefs came to power.
Chiefdoms arise as a superior social technology for communal property defense,
but quickly become instruments for individual wealth concentration. It is at
this crucial tipping point that warlord-chiefs, defined predominantly by their
coercive power resources, become warring oligarchs defined increasingly by
material power resources. All subsequent human history from that juncture
until the end of the medieval era, when civil oligarchies first emerge, was
marked by the rise and decline of warring, ruling, and sultanistic forms of
oligarchy. When strong empires or states existed, they were either ruling or
sultanistic oligarchies, sometimes moving back and forth between these forms.
When central or shared authority collapsed, warring oligarchs reappeared amid
the wreckage of empire. The historical record permits no simple progression in
which, for instance, warring oligarchies give way to personalistic rulers, who
then yield to more collective forms of oligarchic rule. If there is any consistent
pattern, it is that the most important arbiter of change in this long history of
oligarchic flux centers on changes in how wealth and property are threatened,
and the shifting form and locus of coercion for their defense.

Individual power based on highly concentrated wealth, which distinguishes
oligarchs from elites, presupposes the emergence of complex societies and especially material stratification within them. Prehistoric chiefdoms were the earliest
social forms to exhibit these characteristics, and thus were the incubators of the
first oligarchs. Compared to kingdoms, empires, and states, these communities never encompassed wide territories or controlled large populations. Many
never evolved beyond what Earle (1997, 105) describes as "the strategic use
of naked force."[3] However, a few managed to become complex and powerful
entities capable of conquest over neighboring chiefdoms. The key was whether

---

[3] This section on the earliest evidence of material stratification draws liberally on Earle's work
comparing three emerging chiefdoms spanning four thousand years of history. He examines
the Thy region of Denmark between 2300 and 1300 B.C.E., the Andean highlands of Peru
between 500 and 1534 C.E., and Hawaii between 800 and 1824 C.E. "These societies were
chiefdoms, polities organized in the thousands, or at most tens of thousands, with emergent
political leaders and some measure of stratification" (Earle 1997, 15). Although the terms
warlord-chief and warring oligarchs are mine, they are consistent with Earle's treatment of more
complex chiefdoms, especially the "paramount chiefs" that arose in Hawaii.

the coercive power of chiefs, initially deployed to defend communal claims to land or other valued resources, could be used to concentrate wealth in a manner that enriched and strengthened the leaders, who defended and controlled first their own group and eventually others they engulfed around them.

It is important to recognize that there was neither a single geographic location nor a particular historical period in which chiefs and warlords built stratified societies and transformed themselves once and for all into warring oligarchs. Until quite recently, the world contained numerous compartmentalized populations at widely varying levels of social development. The struggles to build complex societies were repeated many times in many places over several millennia, and often with limited intervention from outside communities or civilizations (Diamond 1999). One cannot, therefore, study the "original" or "definitive" cases that served as the models others would emulate or that set the trajectory for all communities that came afterward. In place of such origins there are instead dominant patterns of social transformation that were repeated countless times throughout history, with the greatest source of variation among them being traced to ecology and geography.

Material and economic resources played a central role in the emergence of the earliest social stratifications. Examining the rise of chiefs in prehistory, Earle (1997, 75) notes that "in all cases, economic power was in some sense basic to the political strategies to amass power." Mann (1986, 83) emphasizes irrigation and fixed claims to land in tracing the rise of economically powerful strata in Mesopotamia around 3100 B.C.E. Although material power would eventually become concentrated in individual hands, it was initially organized into "collective social power" because it was based on village, small-clan, and family property, the preparation and protection of which was "collectively organized."[4]

The early collective character of property casts a long shadow into the modern era as village and clan property gradually became more differentiated into propertied individuals and families that formed a wealthy nobility. With time, concentrated material resources were personally rather than collectively owned. Although long stretches of history are marked by pitched conflict among warring oligarchs, the early modern period saw a basic oligarchic cohesion emerge among those making claims to massive personal property within increasingly institutionalized systems. This pattern became so entrenched that for centuries oligarchy (and its softer cousin, aristocracy) was defined as direct rule by an exclusive and cohesive set of wealthy noble families. The emergence of powerful families, clans, and nobilities is a historically important, but by no means necessary, form of oligarchic power and influence. In other words, networking and cohesion had been an important aspect of oligarchy for centuries, but oligarchy is neither defined by nor reliant on such cohesion.

---

[4] Mann (1986, 83) adds that the prominent role of collective property in the formative years of permanent hierarchy renders "absurd" liberal theories of stratification that try to "locate the stimulus in interpersonal differences in ability, hard work, and luck."

The theory of "environmental circumspection" offers the best explanation for these dominant patterns of social transformation in early human history – particularly how chiefs and warlords became warring oligarchs as they successfully concentrated wealth and stratified their societies. The theory holds that as population pressures increased, communities began closing off areas containing valuable subsistence resources – with some areas being more valuable than others. These original claims to property were made by groups rather than individuals. That is, the claims were initially more "ours" than "mine." They tended to focus on land, although sometimes the valued property was livestock, as in the Early Bronze Age region of Thy in the north of today's Denmark, or among the ancient Irish Celts.

Aggressive counterclaims to the same valuable resources by outsiders provoked defense responses.[5] In primitive societies, these defenses followed two broad patterns. One was without specialization. Clastres (1999) refers to these as societies "with warriors," in which all males fight when the community is threatened. Sastre's (2008) examination of the Castro Culture on the Iberian Peninsula in the Late Bronze and Early Iron period suggests that this less stratified form of defense can persist for long periods. The second pattern is "warrior societies," which have a subset of males whose superior coercive power resources make them fighting specialists who maintain prestige by continually pursuing battles. Communities quickly discovered that defending their property claims proved more effective when led by skilled warriors. These defensive advantages in warfare had the inevitable effect of also increasing capacities for attack. Intergroup warfare necessitated "strong leaders to defend a group's resources against hostile neighbors, and a society with strong military leaders can expand laterally to bring new lands and their people under dominion. Warfare thus results in the rise of state organizations when circumspection has defined limited resources needed for subsistence and controlled by warrior might" (Earle 1997, 108).

Successful property defense at home, augmented by the conquest of neighboring lands and other valuable goods, had two important effects. First, warrior-led communities had the potential of becoming markedly richer. Second, warlord-defended societies rapidly became warlord-dominated ones as chiefs discovered that coercive capacities directed initially against external threats and targets could also be used internally, enabling them to claim a greater share of the group's wealth and power. In other words, what began as claims of "ours" yielded to claims of "mine." Warrior-chiefs became enriched personally, which enabled them to recruit still more warriors – although now for the defense of personal as well as communal property. "As complex societies emerge," Earle (1997, 108) points out, warlord-chiefs "use war to seize

---

[5] Warfare is "never autonomous and self-regulating," write Otto, Thrane, and Vandkilde (2006, 9). "War always forms part of something else." On violence and warfare in prehistory, see Clastres (1999), Guilaine and Zammit (2001), Otto, Thrane, and Vandkilde (2006), Sarauw (2007), and Sastre (2008).

and defend the most productive agricultural lands and facilities. Leaders then control these most productive lands as their basis for political power."

Early proto-states arose in tandem with powerful families controlling land, followed by the rise of imperial regimes typically with a lead oligarch as monarch. For thousands of years in Sumer, the temple was the locus of the first state while priests assumed the roles of secular land administrators and irrigation managers. "Access to land came to be monopolized by a unified but still representative elite," Mann writes (1986, 86–7), "which controlled the temples and large estates and held priestly, civil, and military office." The first permanent political form was likely part democracy and part "a loose and rather large oligarchy consisting of the heads of the more important families and, perhaps also, of the territorial wards of the town."[6]

This evolving social complexity, marked by increasing wealth stratification and the coercion needed for defense against internal and external threats, produced the earliest warring oligarchs. The violent systems that resulted were unstable, and life for pioneering warlord-oligarchs tended to be short and consumed with dangers from other warlords and ambitious subordinates. "The warrior is constantly competing with himself and others, which necessarily leads to his death," Sastre (2008, 1025) writes. "In fact, in many cases the warrior mentality may even destroy the unity of the society." Chiefdoms are characterized by "endemic warfare, and the rise to power is always implicitly military at its roots," Earle (1997, 8) argues. "The paramount chiefs of Hawai'i rarely died in bed; they were killed in battles of rebellion and conquest or were assassinated by their close affiliates."[7]

Not all chiefs proved able to build complex systems over which they could rule as warring oligarchs. Being an effective warrior was only a minimum qualification (Sastre 2008). Becoming an oligarch required that enough surplus wealth was available in the community to permit significant increases in material stratification. In the cases Earle examines, the warlord-chiefs in the Thy region of Denmark and the Andean highlands of Peru never mustered enough concentrated personal wealth to become warring oligarchs, whereas those in the Hawaiian Islands succeeded. The challenge for warlord-chiefs with oligarchic ambitions was to convert capacities for violence into instruments of

---

[6] Mann (1986, 98) adds: "Along with the state grew a stratum of leading families with private landholdings: Along with monarchy and despotism grew aristocracy."

[7] "To be an aging warrior chief was rather unusual," Earle (1997, 140) observes. "Only the strong survived, but often in a rather gruesome state." Wealth and coercive prowess were a volatile mix. "Military might is in fact a highly problematic source of social power. Warriors are an instrument of fear by which an emerging chief asserts political domination over a region. But at the same moment the chief must fear those warriors, whose power and rage can turn on him. Rebellion, betrayal, and intrigue fill the Icelandic sagas, the narratives of the Hawaiian ruling lineages, and the accounts of Andean lords. While leaders depend on their warriors to extend political power, they must always be on the lookout for treachery. Ultimately warrior might is a destabilizing and divisive power in institutions of leadership; it is only effective as long as it can be reigned in and directed strategically" (Earle 1997, 6).

control over the basic economic factors on which the community thrived, so that all access to current and new wealth could be dominated by the self-enriching warlord. "Economic power is based on the ability to restrict access to key productive resources or consumptive goods," Earle (1997, 7) argues. Control over production and distribution is the key to amassing power beyond the limitations of force and coercion.[8]

Some dominant actors are adept at using force but fail to direct their coercive power resources toward amassing material power. Beginning in 2300 B.C.E. and lasting for one thousand years, the Neolithic and Early Bronze Age chiefdoms in the Thy region of Denmark valued herding and cattle, "a source of movable wealth within a prestige-goods exchange system" (Earle 1997, 103). Population growth had been rapid for centuries, but then stagnated once warlords emerged and focused on herding for their own aggrandizement rather than an intensification of subsistence farming. The shift to herding "ultimately destabilized long-term staple production, but it increased elite control over long-distance exchange." There was constant warfare among chiefs over grazing areas and trade routes, but few investments were made in fixed assets like irrigation and land, to which access could be selectively given and taken away by consolidating chiefs (Kristiansen 1999).

Based on evidence of apprenticeship in the crafting of flint daggers, Apel (2001) finds indications in the region of institutionalization within families and clans. However, this was limited, and the typical Thy warlord excelled at grabbing and taking rather than at channeling or building. "His military prowess helped seize cattle and control wealth obtained through long-distance exchange" (Earle 1997, 141). Yet roaming cattle on unbounded fields present limited opportunities for erecting kingdoms. Thy warrior-chiefs "relied on no in-place fortification; rather, they must have met opposing forces on the open field, where individual skill and personal weapons won the day." Sarauw (2007, 78) notes that "no extremely rich graves indicating concentrations of wealth and power and thereby social inequality have been found in Denmark." Differentiated in burial by little more than the bronze swords they took to their graves, Thy warlords enjoyed elevated status but never became significantly richer than other members of the community, and thus never became oligarchs of the warring type.

---

[8] Analyses focused on power, coercion, and warfare – and how these intersect with property, wealth, and the rise of complex communities and the oligarchs who dominate them – contrast sharply with perspectives, such as New Institutional Economics discussed in Chapter 6, that emphasize cooperation and voluntarist equilibria. Earle (1997, 68) makes the point nicely: "Voluntarist, adaptationist theories follow an ancient rationalist tradition in western thought. Social systems are seen as evolving through a process of improvement, the gradual development of better solutions to the problems of existence and excellence. According to such theories, leadership in human society evolved to create efficient solutions to individual and group problems of survival." The evidence suggests that violence and coercion played a fundamental role, including in causing cooperation. "This vision of chiefdoms as coercive and fundamentally warlike," Earle (1997, 109) continues, "contravenes earlier models, broadly accepted by a generation of researchers, of chiefdoms as kin-based societies, voluntarist, peaceful, and religious."

Warring oligarchs also failed to emerge in the Andean highlands of today's Peru. Beginning in 500 C.E. and stretching for a thousand years, the Wanka warlords of the Mantaro Valley perfected a system of entrenched and bellicose redistribution among themselves (D'Altroy and Hastorf 2001). The endemic warfare ended only with the onset of the Inca and Spanish conquests. Earle argues that the goals of warfare were economic – "seizing land, animals, and women. Leaders were warriors, with their authority legitimized by success in battle. Chiefdoms appear to have been fairly small spatially, typically focused on a single dominant settlement." Wanka leaders made only modest investments in irrigation systems compared to the coastal areas of Peru. Their geographic positions were more fixed than the mobile warlords of Denmark, but the Wanka warlords also failed to control economic factors in a manner that concentrated wealth either in communal or individual hands. The result was centuries of standoff and stagnation. "Politics were fragmented into small hill-fort chiefdoms, and warfare became focused on in-place defense that proved insurmountable by available military technology" (Earle 1997, 116, 141). Although significantly more hierarchical than the Iberian Castro warfare (Sastre 2008), the Wanka warlords were unable to convert coercive power into economic control and concentrated wealth. Thus, the warlords of the Andean highlands, like their counterparts in Denmark, also failed to become warring oligarchs.

Warlordism was no less prevalent among the Hawaiian chiefs than among those in ancient Denmark and pre-colonial Peru. And yet, of the three cases, only the consolidating Hawaiian chiefs managed to use military power to create chiefdoms that yielded sufficient wealth concentration to produce warring oligarchs. Warfare in ancient Hawaii was a "primary tool for political centralization," argue Kolb and Dixon (2002, 515). "High chiefs sought to expand territorial control, eliminate rivals, and integrate current holdings whenever feasible," they write. "Their desire was to increase their productive resources by subsuming the agricultural fields and commoner labor pool of rivals, thus strengthening the financial foundations of their territory."[9]

The key difference setting Hawaii apart from Denmark and Peru was that the ecology in the Hawaiian Islands offered more opportunities for warring chiefs to refashion the mix between coercive and material power resources so that wealth could be concentrated upward, transforming generic warlord-chiefs into "paramounts" – warring oligarchs. They were able to build and then control a system of agricultural irrigation. Followers who were permitted by warring Hawaiian oligarchs to tap into the controlled flows of water enjoyed major gains in farming yields. Paramount chiefs used their coercive power not just to fight other chiefs, but to enforce their control over when the irrigation spigot was turned on or off. "In Hawai'i, community chiefs allocated to commoners

[9] Hommon (1995, 14) argues that conquest warfare had become "a standard political technique for enhancing the prosperity of ruling chiefs." It entailed "the capture of entire productive units (often districts of islands), complete with resident commoners, and the elimination (often by human sacrifice) of the defeated chiefs."

their subsistence plots in the chief's irrigated farmlands in return for corvée work on chiefly lands and special projects," Earle (1997, 7) writes. "By owning the irrigation systems, and thus controlling access to the preferred means of subsistence, chiefs directed a commoner's labor."

The logic behind these arrangements served the aggrandizing interests of the rising oligarchs. However, the benefits to the communities they dominated were modest. By 1400, when the massive new irrigation systems had been built and paramount chiefs had extended their rule over all vassals on the major islands of Hawaii, Maui, Oahu, and Kauai, population growth had stopped even as the power and wealth of the emerging oligarchs continued to rise. "The irrigation systems were created not to feed more people," Earle (1997, 66) points out, "but to mobilize a surplus of subsistence goods used to finance the chiefdoms' expansions." The warring oligarchs that this more sharply stratified system produced were strong actors compared to the leaders in northern Denmark and the Andean highlands, but each proved to be only strong enough to control his own island. It was not until the introduction of new weapons from the West that this fragmentation typical of warring oligarchies was overcome and a single king was able to establish a more sultanistic oligarchy over all the islands.

This section on chiefs and warlords concludes with the example of the successful rise of warring oligarchs among the ancient Irish Celts. The case is important for two reasons. First, it demonstrates that valued property in the form of livestock can form a basis for stratifying wealth and building a more complex society, as long as the prized animals are strongly linked to land and place (a factor absent in Denmark). Second, the granting of cattle by chiefs to subordinates in exchange for service was likely the earliest form of vassalage, predating the rise of medieval feudalism by many centuries. Before examining how livestock could also form the basis of wealth for warring oligarchs, it would be instructive to begin with some etymologies.

Some of the most basic modern legal and economic vocabulary can be traced to cattle and related domesticated animals. The words "capital" and "chattel" derive from *capitāle*, which refers to a head (*caput*) of cattle.[10] From *pecus*, which refers to cattle and sheep, come the words *peculium* (private property) and *pecunia* (money and wealth). Earle (1997, 100) notes that: "The Old Norse word for wealth (*fé*) was cattle." In addition, de Laveleye (1878) points out that the English word "fee," which refers to remuneration and honorarium, is "the same as the Dutch *vee* and German *vieh*, signifying cattle." He adds that the same words mean both remuneration and cattle because among the ancient Celts, "cattle were formerly given for services rendered."[11] The word *od* meant land. Thus, the term "fe-odal" originates in the transition from an oligarch granting remuneration in cattle to remuneration in land.

---

[10] This section draws on de Laveleye (1878), especially chapter 17, "The Origin of Inequality in Landed Property."

[11] "Among the Irish Celts, as among the Germans, tribute, penalties, and compositions for crimes were originally paid in cattle" (de Laveleye 1878, chapter 17).

In the ancient Irish Brehon Laws, there are numerous references to chiefs who – based on their control over cattle, the pastures they grazed, and the agricultural lands the animals helped to till – used their concentrations of material and coercive power resources to become warring oligarchs complete with networks of dependent vassals. de Laveleye (1878, chapter 17) writes that "the chief of the clan, besides his private property, enjoyed a domain attached to his office, together with certain rights over the unoccupied lands of the commune. He could, therefore, feed more cattle than the others." He continues:

> In his capacity as military chief, he obtained a larger share in the spoil; which chiefly consisted of herds, the only capital they could take from the vanquished. Thus the chief often had more cattle than he required, while the rest were in want of them; and to attach his companions to himself he granted them beasts under certain conditions. In this way, the free man became the vassal *ceile* or *kyle* of the chief, to whom he owed homage, service, and payments.

The cattle were on loan, and the more animals a "stock tenant" received, the greater his obligations and the lower his status. The warring oligarchies that arose among the Celts were stratified systems built on concentrated wealth in the form of cattle and land, combined with enlarged coercive capacities (including the aid of dependent vassals owing military service) for taking yet more livestock and territory.

These early, and in some instances prehistoric, cases of warring oligarchy highlight the central place of wealth defense in the political and economic dynamics that unfolded. Chiefs and warlords could arise as skilled fighters with highly concentrated coercive power resources. However, the question was, could they direct these capacities to the task of establishing control over key economic resources of the community, and then convert that control into highly concentrated personal wealth? It was this last step – the active enforcement of material stratification – that transformed warlord-chiefs into warlord-oligarchs.

In the cases recounted here, personal capacities for violence play a central role in both the creation and maintenance of stratification. Warring oligarchs were personally armed actors who, if successful, used their wealth and control over economic resources to recruit additional fighting forces. A warring oligarch who gained major new wealth and yet failed to invest a significant portion of the added riches in stronger capacities for defense risked becoming an enticing target of conquest. Moreover, an oligarch who failed personally as a warrior would lose not only his wealth and property to his subordinates or competing oligarchs, but often his life. Finally, these warring oligarchies were consistently marked by a lack of cohesion and cooperation among the competing oligarchs. They were armed actors who ruled their communities directly and faced the challenges of wealth defense personally in a context of high fragmentation and frequent outbreaks of violence.

Attention now turns to an examination of evidence of warring oligarchy from medieval Europe, where the emphasis is on how the scale of wealth and property claimed by oligarchs proved far too great for them to defend effectively. Their response was to subcontract the task of wealth and property defense to lesser oligarchs, which exacerbated the fragmentation and lateral violence of the oligarchic structure. The novel contribution of oligarchic theory for the medieval period lies precisely in the centrality of the problem of wealth defense.

Warring Oligarchs in Medieval Europe

The roughly ten centuries stretching from the collapse of the Roman Empire in the west to the rise of absolutist kings at the end of the medieval era saw a profound transformation in the character of oligarchy. Warring oligarchs thoroughly dominated the landscape until at least the eleventh century. During the next four hundred years of conflict and competition, rising "absolutist" monarchs oversaw the transformation of the warring oligarchies into ruling and even limited sultanistic oligarchies. The changes this process of centralization brought to the organization of oligarchs are discussed in Chapter 3. The focus for the present remains on the warring oligarchies of the Middle Ages and medieval period, and the highly fragmented manner in which armed actors ruled personally and engaged directly in the enforcement of their claims to concentrated wealth.

By the time Rome had collapsed, the world had already witnessed the ascent and decline of countless kingdoms and empires. The warlords in Thy, who were just getting started at the end of the Neolithic era, were unaware that the first cities had already arisen twelve centuries earlier in southern Mesopotamia around 3500 B.C.E. Nor could they have imagined the kingdom of the world's first emperor, the Akkadian King Sargon of Sumeria (2310–2273 B.C.E.), who fielded a massive standing army that rivaled the 20,000 men assembled centuries later by the New Kingdom Egyptian pharaohs, and the 100,000 soldiers comprising the Assyrian army in the first millennium (Ferguson and Mansbach 1996, 80).

Unlike the warlord-chiefs in the north of Denmark or in the Andean highlands, the warlords of the Middle Ages and medieval era were not geographically isolated social pioneers struggling to fashion novel combinations of violence and property in an effort to secure their local positions of dominance. They were fully formed warring oligarchs embedded within matured systems of material stratification left over from Rome. Their political objective was to survive within and remain atop complex and violent social formations already marked by extremes of wealth and improved means of coercion. Empires and states supply a reliable overarching authority and coercive apparatus to defend oligarchic claims to property and wealth. It is precisely this apparatus of property defense that breaks down when empires collapse. To meet the rising threats to property that inevitably follow, oligarchs rearm and become more personally engaged in wealth defense and more directly engaged in rule. The result is a reversion to complex warlordism, which is to say warring oligarchies.

Although a long and complicated process, the fall of the western half of the Roman Empire is generally viewed by historians to have occurred by 476 C.E. The next ten centuries were marked first by a severe weakening of Europe's kings (especially the Merovingian, the Carolingian, and finally the Capetian dynasties), followed by a period of deep fragmentation and the rise of warring oligarchies, and finally ending with a reassertion of centralized power in the hands of absolutist kings by the sixteenth and seventeenth centuries. There are many illuminating angles from which to view this period, and the historical, economic, and political literatures are unusually rich. In placing oligarchs at the center of the analysis, this study emphasizes the evolving difficulties and challenges of wealth and property defense in a context of shifting threats to powerful medieval actors trying to enforce their claims to wealth – which in Europe during this period meant landed property and the surplus that could be extracted from agriculture.

This emphasis underscores the fundamental political question at the heart of oligarchic theory: how do actors making claims to concentrated wealth defend their property and realize the fruits of their fortunes? The compact answer is that the fragmented feudal response at the dawn of the Middle Ages and throughout the medieval period was provoked by massive and violent threats to the established property defense regime of the late Roman Empire. It was then a different set of threats in a more parcelized system of wealth and property claims that account for the warring contestations throughout the feudal warlord period. It was yet a third set of threats – initially from below and later externally via war – that pushed fragmented and violent feudalism into absolutist monarchical consolidations.

Feudalism came into existence as great landed nobles were forced to out-source the heavy burdens of wealth defense they could no longer bear themselves. In effect, they "hired" coercive capacities by a process of subcontracting. Lacking sufficient funds to purchase mercenary forces for extended periods, the nobles paradoxically ended up trying to defend their property by giving it away "temporarily." Lords and barons at the top of the social formation laid claim to vast territories whose perimeters they could not defend against invading tribes and bands, and whose wealth they could not effectively extract from direct producers. Feudalism began as limited and contractual land grants to armed vassals to assist in the defense of the overlord's realm. A feudal fief was "not just a grant of land to a warrior follower," Critchley (1978, 37) argues, "but a conditional grant." These contingent grants quickly hardened into strong transgenerational claims by the vassals themselves to the wealth and land they increasingly ruled locally and regionally. The baronial motive of wealth defense had resulted instead in a pandemic of wealth fragmentation.

Feudalism produced a fractured pattern of smaller but better enforced claims to property. The warring oligarchs on the landed estates were personally armed and militarily engaged in property defense. They ruled directly over the territories they defended. They collected taxes and dispensed justice, including *haute justice* – the legitimate power to kill by hanging. In addition, they were intimately engaged in the extraction of agricultural surpluses from direct producers on the land. Anderson (1974b, 19) describes the feudal pyramid starting from its base in the village, where wealth was extracted and the coercive capacities of the warring oligarchs found their most mundane expression. "The institution of serfdom as a mechanism of surplus extraction fused economic exploitation and politico-legal coercion at the molecular level of the village," he writes. "The lord in his turn typically owed liege-loyalty and knight-service to a seigniorial overlord, who claimed the land as his ultimate domain." It was precisely because the overlords' property claims were so indefensible in the first place that they participated actively in creating a feudal structure that would, as the centuries unfolded, severely undermine overlord property claims.

The vassals and viscounts of the feudal era not only locked horns with their *de jure* feudal overlords for dominance, but battled laterally with each other while wrestling with the next stratum of vassals and knights immediately below them. They also had to contend with resistance, rebellion, and flight by peasant farmers on the land. These multidirectional conflicts were bloody and constant, but they were never as nakedly violent or anarchic as those among the Thy chiefs in Denmark or the warlords in the Andean highlands. As Hegel notes in the *Philosophy of Right*, sovereignty in medieval Europe had a dual character. Inwardly the fragmentation was so great that there was no meaningful sovereign state to mediate among the powerful warring oligarchs. Overlords were incapable of establishing an internal monopoly on the means of coercion.

However, there existed an "outward state" that claimed and enforced sovereignty vis-à-vis other states in times of war. Failing to achieve "sovereignty at home," kings and lords who were incapable of controlling the maelstrom of conflicts among warring oligarchs within their kingdoms managed to "present a unified front in their external relations" (Nederman 1987, 505).[12] This was because oligarchs were well equipped to defend their claims to wealth and territory against each other and against the serfs below. They were no match individually, however, against a massive external attack by a neighboring kingdom bent on conquest. Warring oligarchs would be overrun separately if they ignored the king's call to defend the realm as a whole. Once the external threat disappeared, the weak monarchs on the throne during the centuries from 800 to 1300 C.E. could do little to prevent Europe's warring oligarchs from resuming their violent, local, and particularistic political economies of wealth and property defense until the next external threat arose.

Wealth defense was a full-time job for warring oligarchs, and cohesion in the medieval era – although more prevalent than that seen among the warlords of Thy, the Andes, and Hawaii – remained limited. Except when united for external defense or conquest, warring feudal oligarchs fought each other individually or in constantly shifting alliances that arose for immediate

---

[12] The phrases "outward state" and "sovereignty at home" are Nederman's (1987, 504–7, especially note 7), although they are well supported by the Hegelian passages he cites.

purposes and collapsed when the purposes changed. The kings tried to manipulate the conflicts within the upper reaches of the feudal pyramid to their own advantage, but doing so was risky. "It was possible for the feudal monarch to use the vassals of a great or middling great lord against him for the purpose of centralizing more power in the king," Myers (1982, 158) writes, "but this was dangerous business and apt to alienate the support of the feudal nobility as a whole. Often a less overt policy of letting the territorial lords vent their jealousy toward each other or against too successful feudal newcomers would benefit the monarchy equally well in the long run."[13]

A significant increase in wealth for warring oligarchs during the feudal era was impossible without fighting each other, whether individually against neighboring estates, in shifting alliances regionally, or under the banner of the king in major "outward" attacks. It is not that agricultural productivity and trade were completely stagnant during these centuries. Yet, as Anderson (1974b, 31) argues, their growth was very slow "compared with the sudden and massive 'yields' afforded by territorial conquest." The social definition of the wealthy warring oligarch was military. "The economic rationality of war in such a social formation is a specific one: it is a maximization of wealth," Anderson states. "The nobility was a landowning class whose profession was war: its social vocation was not an external accretion but an intrinsic function of its economic position."[14]

Because the historical record is incomplete, there is no precise date demarcating the start of the feudal age. It is believed to have commenced sometime between 700 and 900 C.E. It reached its high point in the year 1000 and continued in varying forms until at least the early 1600s. Although feudalism existed across Europe, its epicenter was on the continent in the area roughly equal to modern France – bounded by the Alps, the Pyrenees, and the Rhine. The rise of feudal warlordism is often associated with the collapse of the Carolingian Empire toward the end of the ninth century. "Empire" is a grand word conjuring up images of great authority. However, even at their strongest, kings in the Middle Ages and medieval period exerted only a modest degree of actual control over the broad realms they claimed. Poly and Bournazel (1991, 9–10) describe the Carolingian Empire as "a mosaic of disparate territories, more or less firmly

---

[13] William the Conqueror pursued a preventative strategy, keeping the oligarchs "from holding large, compact fiefs of a type which made figures like the duke of Aquitaine of the margrave of Flanders so formidable on the Continent" (Myers 1982, 215).

[14] The horizontal violence endemic among warring oligarchs is linked to the fact that throughout history, they are almost always defending land, a region, a province, a hacienda, or, in the case of Mafiosi or warring urban gangs, a "turf." Anderson's (1974b, 31) comparison of this mode of wealth accumulation and defense with that under capitalism is instructive and worth quoting at length. "The normal medium of intercapitalist competition is economic, and its structure is typically additive: rival parties may both expand and prosper – although unequally – throughout a single confrontation, because the production of manufactured commodities [or the supply of services] is inherently unlimited. The typical medium of interfeudal rivalry, by contrast, was military and its structure was always potentially the zero-sum conflict of the battlefield, by which fixed quantities of ground were won or lost. For land is a natural monopoly: it cannot be indefinitely extended, only redivided."

held, more or less well controlled, concentric circles where Frankish influence became increasingly weak as it neared the borders, the marches, beyond which lay barbarism." With the collapse of empire, they continue, "tyrants or petty kings set themselves up to build their own dynasties. These princes now had their own territories." There ensued a cascading shift of power downward, until even "the stewards of the great fortresses, refused to obey and in turn established an almost autonomous power."

At the end of the late Roman period, landed estates across Europe varied in scale, with the largest ones existing in France and more modest versions in England – with the obvious exception of the demesne of William the Conqueror, who, together with his half-brothers in 1066, "owned directly nearly half the land of England after the Norman conquest, and what was not carefully granted as fiefs remained crown land" (Myers 1982, 162). Not all land was outsourced into fiefs. Manors were independently owned by great lords and barons who differed from kings only in the scale of their demesne, with the royal demesne, the "fisc," being held by the lord among lords, the "suzerain." It was the king's vast demesne that was most thoroughly carved into feudal parcels, given first to margraves and counts, and then divided as fiefs and feuds held by vassals. Some vassals accumulated so much land that their estates became nearly as large as some manors. From an oligarchic perspective, feudal fragmentation in the form of proliferating warring oligarchs reflected a process of wealth and property defense moving socially downward to levels that were finally effective.

In the face of various armed incursions, it was the Emperor Charlemagne who began the process of granting large territories of his realm to be secured by margraves and counts. However, it was Charles the Bald – responding in alarm to invading Vikings, "barbarian" Germanic tribes, and Saracens – who issued broad decrees that accelerated the transfer of lands to nobles and vassals in a vain effort to strengthen the kingdom's defenses. By the end of the ninth century, the "insolence of the margraves" was accelerating as these former commanders of the marches, the border counties of the realm, moved up in status and began referring to themselves as royalty (Poly and Bournazel 1991, 12). Starting first at the fringes of the Frankish kingdom, and gradually moving toward its weakening center, rising oligarchs increasingly began to call themselves *princeps* – princes – and, in so doing, demarcated new territorial "principalities."

The signs of the shift in power downward and outward were symbolic as well as substantive. For generations the *vassi* had been expected to show fealty and pay homage in person to the king, never by proxy.[15] However, by the end of the tenth century, the more common pattern was for vassals to communicate

[15] All of this sounds more hierarchical than it was. The asymmetries were far more pronounced between the rulers and the ruled, than among the rulers themselves (Critchley 1978, 101). This includes the subservient-sounding vassals. In the Merovingian period, the earliest vassals began as an utterly dependent group who relied on lords for food and clothes. "The actual term vassal derived via the Latin *vassus* from the Celtic *gwas*; it meant 'boy' and had the same derogatory association in adult relationships which American blacks object to. No man would be another

with the kings via envoys (Poly and Bournazel 1991, 17). Even the vassal's oath to render homage and service to his lord deteriorated. Initially, once a warring oligarch agreed to be contracted as a vassal, "a supporting oath of fealty or fidelity was then sworn to on relics of a saint or on Holy Writ." Reflecting the growing dangers vassals posed to their lords as warring oligarchs proliferated, "oaths survive in which the vassal promised no more than to abstain faithfully from doing his lord any injury" (Myers 1982, 155).[16]

Critchley (1978, 56–7) argues that "feudalism means above all the decentralisation of power" marked by "defiant" vassals who consistently "appropriate their fiefs." Thus feudal government "implies disorder and political fragmentation." The territories ruled by barons and the most powerful vassals were zones in which "the king's agents were forbidden to enter," and in some instances royal officials were "required to swear an oath to respect them." Critchley adds: "Royal proclamations had no force within a baron's lands without his consent; or, if the king's men were allowed in, the baron would claim all or a proportion of any fines or confiscations they imposed."[17]

Changes in power relations governing the distribution of property, as well as claims to and the defense of the economic surplus, were evident in the rising wealth of the vassals and the concomitant capacity of these warring oligarchs to hire mercenary fighting forces. "The most obvious social reason for the mercenary phenomenon was," Anderson (1974b, 30) wryly notes, "the natural refusal of the noble class to arm its own peasants wholesale." The transformation was also visible in the proliferation and design of castles and

man's 'boy' in this sense if he could help it in Merovingian Gaul" (Myers 1982, 150). The decisive feudal innovation under the Carolingians was to blend the notion of vassal service with the ancient and respectable Germanic institution of *comitatus* (armed retainership, which in the Middle Ages survived as *antrustiones*), and then combine these service and military components with a property element in the form of the *benefice* – a land grant on favorable terms given previously to the church, but now made available to laymen. The new vassals this produced, the *vassi dominici* (vassals of the king), were a stratum of proud and armed oligarchs forming the first and most direct line of defense over the property and wealth of the vaguely formed kingdom "above." See Myers (1982, 152).

[16] The declining symbolism of fealty and homage could be quite comical. Myers (1982, 155) writes that "in the late twelfth century, the English King Henry II granted a manor and a fully equipped mill to a lesser vassal in return for the service '... of keeping a white hound with red ears and delivering it to the king at the end of the year and receiving another puppy to rear.' In a similar spirit, Edward III later granted a manor for the annual service of having his chessmen counted and returned to their proper places when he finished his games on Christmas Day."

[17] The earliest known example of this feudal tendency toward disintegration occurred in Egypt around 2300 B.C.E. "The overmighty officials in this case were known to the Greeks as nomarchs, the governors of the provinces, nomes, of old Egypt. It is alleged that these officials became more and more powerful as the pharaohs of the fourth and subsequent dynasties granted them land... and allowed them to establish hereditary rights to their offices. Inscriptions of the nomarchs show them to have become practically independent rulers." The nomarchs not only converted their access to control over the land into permanent claims and permanent power, but chipped away at the kings even at the symbolic level. "The nobles also usurped the power to become Osiris after their deaths. This was to be achieved by magic spells and in the Old Kingdom only the kings could do it" (Critchley 1978, 70–1).

other fortifications. The changes in "encastellation" were dramatic as the feudal era evolved, reflecting the rise of warring oligarchs and the specific challenges of wealth and property defense they faced. At the end of the Roman era and even as late as the middle of the Carolingian period, castles scattered across the European landscape were large and positioned on rocky plateaus. "They evolved in order to protect large populations in times of danger," write Poly and Bournazel (1991, 26), "and do not appear to have been inhabited on a regular basis."

Around the year 1000, there was an explosion in the number of castles.[18] These fortifications were smaller, more reinforced, secured narrower areas, and were far more likely to be inhabited by a warring oligarch and his forces. The *castrum* were directed primarily at ongoing control over the countryside rather than serving as a locus of occasional defense or refuge against raiding invaders.[19] The new castles provided the architectural infrastructure for the emergence of the *bannum*, the institutional innovation for the intensification of noble rule and extraction on their estates. "These military structures were not only aimed at ensuring peace in the countryside," Poly and Bournazel (1991, 28) write, but "also aided the lord of the castle in extending his *bannum* and making it more profitable."

As the effective reach and power of the feudal kings was eroded, it was replaced locally and regionally by the prerogatives of the "banal" lordships enforcing their property claims from fortified residences at the heart of their estates. The *bannum* referred to "the rights exercised by the lord – or those he claimed to exercise – over everything that lived in the shade of his castle" (Poly and Bournazel 1991, 29). These rights included proclaiming rules and levying fines, arresting and punishing criminals (including execution), and collecting taxes in kind and currency (which was increasingly minted locally).[20] Going far beyond mere taxation, warring oligarchs employed these powers to squeeze value from the production on their lands. These new modes of extraction came to be known as *banalités*.

> At the end of the eleventh century the first *banalités* begin to appear. It was forbidden to grind one's corn anywhere but in the lord's mill, to cook in any other oven but his, to sell wine just before the new harvest in order that the lord might empty his own barrels, or to open a tavern without his permission. In Catalonia, people might not use any grindstone but the one in the lord's forge or store grain anywhere but in his loft. In Provence, the lord had the monopoly

---

[18] "In Provence, there were a dozen castles in the first half of the tenth century, several dozen a little before 1000, and a good hundred around 1030" (Poly and Bournazel 1991, 27).

[19] "This growth in the number of castles, as also the increase of smaller fortresses," argue Poly and Bournazel (1991, 27), "cannot be related to the need for defense against invaders – the Viking raids north of the Loire ceased around 930 and in the Midi the Saracens of Freinet were wiped out in 972."

[20] "Everything became an excuse to put pressure on the peasants. The public carting duties became obligatory duties on the lord's estate; the transfer of property was taxed; in Catalonia even the meeting of a couple wishing to marry was taxed" (Poly and Bournazel 1991, 31).

on buying and selling vermillion. Although the system of *banalités* did not apply equally everywhere, it nevertheless indicates the increasingly strong grip of banal lordship on every aspect of peasant life (Poly and Bournazel 1991, 31).

Imitating the strategies of the kings and barons, warring oligarchs also out-sourced some of the burdens of property defense and surplus extraction to the armed actors on the next rung of the coercive hierarchy of the *bannum*.

> His concern with income often induced the lord to involve his *milites* in these new profits. In Catalonia the *castla* and his men generally received an aggregate portion. Elsewhere the *milites* shared out the rights accompanying strips of land. In the eleventh century a new kind of official of the lord was to appear, the provost or bailiff, who was to ensure that the profits of the estate came to the lord. This accounts for the decline and sometimes disappearance of peasant allods (Poly and Bournazel 1991, 31).

The treatment of peasants at the lowest level of the system was degrading and brutal. "From the lord's point of view," Turner (1948, 87) writes, "the laborer was a work animal 'exploitable at will,' not different from livestock." The balance of power overwhelmingly favored the warring oligarchs. "The feudal warriors possessed weapons against which the laborers were unable to contend successfully," Turner adds. Between the tenth and twelfth centuries, violent resistance by serfs was mostly local and sporadic – except in the areas only recently brought under feudal control, whose inhabitants asserted themselves with greater ferocity. According to Turner, "outbreaks in which lay lords and their families were murdered and their habitations burned were more or less continuous throughout northern Europe from Brittany to Saxony." He adds that these uprisings "lacked both organization and program," and "were put down with great brutality."[21]

Everyday forms of resistance by direct producers – "the muted but obstinate resistance of all those men written off in the documents as very poor and very humble" (Poly and Bournazel 1991, 259) – were far more pervasive than violent revolts and much harder for feudal warlords to remedy. The apparatus of feudalism was a sophisticated instrument of wealth defense, but it was not immune to subversion. As Poly and Bournazel note, "it came up against those spontaneous tendencies that have always given life to the collective action of oppressed peasantries: the sabotage of forced work, flight, and incessant dealing in land or goods stolen from under the nose of the master and his stewards."

Compared to the limited control barons and kings could exert, the out-sourced vassal system was far superior in its capacities to penetrate to the village and even family level, enforce the property claims of the estate, and forcibly shift surpluses upward to fund the coercive apparatus centered at the

---

[21] Turner (1948, 87–8) concludes: "The lasting effects of three centuries of life under this system of labor control seem to have been a deep hatred of the lords of the land, both lay and ecclesiastical, by the laborers and, as a counterweight, a conviction among the lords that the laborers, tricky and never to be trusted, were to be governed only by terror."

castle. However, these superior capacities were only a matter of degree and never fully effective in countering peasant resistance, which was constant even if it was only rarely organized and violent. The weak underbelly of the feudal system was that it was only strong and effective over the territories it could command directly: feudalism was a fragmented system of rule over a geography that was porous.

As long as peasants preserved allodial lands in the interstices of the system, they could bleed feudal oligarchs of human resources. "Above all, the presence, greater or smaller but universal, of groups of allodial peasants who were partly able to escape the embrace of the estates made it difficult for the lord to control his own dependents. Freedom is an inconvenient neighbor for servitude and there were too many villages where *coloni* and serfs escaping from the *bannum* could take refuge" (Poly and Bournazel 1991, 259–60). Erecting a more impermeable structure to counter peasant flight would have required warring oligarchs to make a far higher investment in their apparatus of coercion "to suppress these islands of safety and to extend the manorial system in order to encompass completely the peasant masses." It would have also demanded that "the differences separating noble groups of different cultures had to be resolved and the masters united into a single aristocracy," and "a section of the peasantry itself would have to participate actively, even militantly, in this process." Neither condition could be met under the fragmented and endemically conflictual context created by Europe's warring oligarchs.

The efforts by oligarchs to gain dominance in all directions extended upward through the social hierarchy to a remarkable degree. In addition to using the *bannum* as a mode of wealth control and extraction over the peasantry, the vassals stripped even the relatively rich and free landowners outside the oligarchy of their independence. Early in the feudal era, the *mallum*, a kind of public tribunal chaired by the count or the viscount, had been an assembly of "the *boni homines*, free and wealthy landowners," men who were "sufficiently rich in inherited property to prevent them from being subject to anything except public judgment" (Poly and Bournazel, 1991, 18). As warring oligarchs grew stronger and their fortifications proved more effective, semi-rich landowners saw the *mallum* become an instrument completely dominated by the count. "Free men in the country, or at least those of them who had managed to avoid servitude or dependence, now lost the main center of their collective social life," write Poly and Bournazel (1991, 25). "A more effective and also more grasping power forced them to bow their heads; a narrower framework restricted them. The castles . . . became threats."

By this point in the history of complex human societies, the ideas and concepts of status, hierarchy, and authority were extremely advanced. The notion of king and sovereign ruler of the realm was not new. The warring oligarchies scattered across medieval Europe arose not because a vacuum in authority structures in the abstract, but instead because of a collapse of one of the most basic pillars of that structure – the coercive capacities to defend royal claims to wealth and property and to extract the latent surplus constituting royal fortunes. Pyramids of patron–client relations can function with a high degree of stability when the flows upward and downward though the system that sustain them are primarily in the form of goods, wealth, or positions of status. When a key element of the pyramid is the outsourcing by patrons of wealth defense to armed clients, the patron–client system is prone to extreme fragmentation. The notion of warring oligarchy provides a useful optic for understanding why feudalism arose and how oligarchy itself changed as the solutions to the formidable challenges of wealth and property defense evolved.

Attention turns now to an examination of warring oligarchs in North America. It is a jolting shift. However, an oligarchic perspective on feuding families in Appalachia highlights the range of contexts in which warring oligarchs have arisen, and how they can persist within states whose legal regimes and coercive capacities are insufficient to overwhelm powerful actors who defend their wealth and property directly and violently.

Appalachian Feuds

Feuds in the Appalachian Mountains hold a prominent position in American folklore. During the nineteenth century, the eastern counties of Kentucky – dubbed the "Corsica of America" (Blee and Billings 1996, 671) – were the main battleground, although feuding occurred as far west as the California coast. Inhabiting a "dark and bloody ground," the feuding Kentucky mountaineer of the late 1800s was portrayed in *New York Times* dispatches as "a backward, drunken killer." The Appalachian feudist continues to conjure up images of "an uncouth hillbilly with a slouch hat and overalls, full beard, rifle, whiskey jug, and a demeanor characterized as 'dull when sober, dangerous when drunk'" (Kleber 1992, 315). Sonnichsen (1949, 83) writes that "the mere mention of the word 'feud' brings up a picture of Kentucky hillbillies starting a war of extermination over a razorback hog."

The reference is to a dispute over a pig that supposedly triggered the most famous of Appalachian feuds, between the Hatfields and McCoys. Conforming to the "Lil Abner Yokum" stereotype, the common belief is that the feuds flared up over trivial matters and amounted to little more than petty bickering (MacClintock 1901). Folklore has it, for instance, that the bloody "Clay County War" began when "one man called another's dog a cur" (Kleber 1992, 315). Dominant impressions of the violence emphasize irrationality, stupidity, and senseless mendacity. Feuds in the United States have been blamed on traditional attitudes or categorized as "mountain violence," which amounts to rampant lawlessness among an uncultured stratum of hot-tempered Scotch-Irish immigrants on the wild American frontier.[22] Feuding Appalachians are dismissed as cartoon characters who take a swig of moonshine one moment and engage in

---

[22] Analyses of feuds in the United States have theorized that the conflicts resulted from "isolation, or strong family ties, or partisan politics, or moonshine whiskey, or the absence of religion and education, or the Civil War's effects" (Blee and Billings 1996, 672, n1).

"reasonless deeds of hate" the next. As Blee and Billings (1996, 672) point out, "feuds were seen to result from poverty, ignorance, and isolation, as having been triggered by the most trivial of incidents, prolonged by primitive clan loyalties and tolerated because of the ineffectiveness of, or hostility toward, legal institutions in mountain society."

These are profoundly distorted images, and they miss the most important aspects of the warring oligarchs of Appalachia. Nearly all the lead feudists were, by local and sometimes by national standards, wealthy and privileged. Much of the fighting centered on wealth defense for the oligarchs leading the feuds. Poorer members of the community who got drawn into the "clan" violence were unemployed workers or farmers hit hard by the severe economic downturns of the nineteenth century. In case after case, the hillbilly trivialities of Appalachian feuds prove unfounded. In the Hargis–Cockrill feud, James F. Hargis was a merchant, politician, and a county judge.[23] Other major participants in the feud included a judge, a governor, and a mayor who was also a University of Kentucky trustee. The feud was linked to the elections of 1901 and had important economic and political implications.

In the bloodiest feud of the period, between the Tollivers and the Martins (also known as the "Rowan County War"), the violence could be traced back to a circuit judge race and a pitched struggle over control of county politics and key mining resources. The French–Eversole feud was fought between rival merchant forces, and the Turner–Howard feud started with the killing of the son of the Democratic county chairman and involved the profitable trade in illegal whiskey. The Roach–Belcher feud in Monterey, California, was played out between William Roach, founder of a political clique that gained him several public offices including sheriff, and Lewis Belcher – the "Big Eagle of Monterey" – who held large land grants in Carmel Valley and in Santa Clara and Stanislaus counties. At stake in this feud was a fortune in gold and control over a vast landed estate made up of several southern California ranches previously owned by José Mariá Sánchez – worth more than $300,000, a princely sum in 1850 (Parker 1950).

If a razorback hog was the proximate cause of the feud between the Hatfields and the McCoys, the deeper sources of tension were material – particularly disputes over land titles. Clark (1948, 427) describes Hatfield, whose family owned major timbering operations, as a "mountain feudal lord." Contrary to the country-bumpkin mythology surrounding these two families, "each of the leaders died a natural death and was interred in regal fashion befitting a respected chieftain," Ambler (1949, 698) writes. "An Italian-executed statue costing about $3,000 marks the resting place of Hatfield." The Hatfields and McCoys produced an array of professional offspring, including doctors, lawyers, a governor of West Virginia, and a U.S. senator. As the "patriarch and political leader of Logan County," Hatfield enjoyed the protection of the governor of West Virginia, who blocked his extradition to Kentucky to face

[23] The brief descriptions of these feuds are from Kleber (1992, *passim*).

criminal charges related to the feud. Hatfield was the "staunchest Democratic [Party] bastion" in the areas of West Virginia over which he exerted oligarchic influence.[24]

In her authoritative history of the feud, Waller notes that the Hatfields and McCoys were leading and prosperous families in the region, and it was the rising wealth of the Hatfields in particular that was a source of conflict in the community. She also refutes the notion that clan and kin relations (and thus blood vengeance) were the driving motive behind the violence – fully 84 percent of the "Hatfield Gang" had economic ties to "Devil Anse" Hatfield, whereas less than 50 percent were kin (Waller 1988, 79). Further weakening the clan argument is the fact that members of both families could be found on both sides of the conflict. There were also predatory oligarchs from outside the region who played a role in the plunder of the eastern counties. The considerable timber and mineral wealth along the eastern Kentucky border attracted industrialists to the region, such as Perry Cline, who viewed Hatfield's grip on the timbering industry as an obstacle to their business plans. Fanning the feud, Cline manipulated the head of the McCoy clan as a surrogate in his effort to displace Hatfield and reap the economic gains. Meanwhile, Hatfield and his gang – termed the "regulators" by contemporaries – fought to set and control the terms of economic access to the local resources (Waller 1988, 170). The conditions were far more complex than those faced by warring Hawaiian oligarchs, but the basic struggles over rich resources and for wealth defense were similar.

By far the largest and longest of all the Appalachian feuds was the Clay County War, also known as the Garrard–White feud and the Baker–Howard feud.[25] This extended and highly structured conflict offers an illuminating example of how warring oligarchs pursued their objectives of wealth defense by blending direct armed engagement with the capture or intimidation of emerging governing and legal institutions. The Appalachian oligarchs sometimes held posts in government, although a more common pattern was to use their coercive and material power resources to place family members or dependents in office, or exert control over whomever got elected or appointed. Because the conflicts were mainly over direct control of fixed assets like timber, mines, or salt works, the jurisdictional struggles tended to unfold at the geographic scale of the county rather than at the city or state level.[26]

When county governments were well captured or thoroughly intimidated, feuding oligarchs made extensive use of the county's institutional capacities, including its courts. When county governments tried to operate independently

---

[24] Williams (1976) quoted in Blee and Billings (1996, 690.)

[25] The most authoritative studies of this feud are by Blee and Billings (1996, 2000). The oligarchic optic employed in this study does not appear in their work, but is fully consistent with it.

[26] "Feuding is an extreme manifestation of elite conflicts within clientistic states," Blee and Billings (1996, 700) write. "Feuding was not uncommon in the Kentucky mountains in the 19th century – erupting in as many as 18 counties between 1874 and 1895." This warring form of oligarchy was intimately linked to the resource-extractive economies of the Appalachian region.

or were captured by an opponent, warring oligarchs directed their violence not only at their opponents in the feud, but against the formal governing institutions – especially the instruments of enforcement like the sheriff's office and the courts. The office of sheriff – which enforced the law, collected taxes, and oversaw the sale of land in tax defaults – was an important cog in an oligarch's wealth defense apparatus and a key nexus of patronage. It was not uncommon for sheriffs and judges to be murdered, or for prisoners or witnesses in cases involving feuding oligarchs to be assassinated through the windows of the county jail. On several occasions, governors deployed state militia to defend the courthouses against the armed forces of warring oligarchs. The capture of county-level governing apparatuses by oligarchs was so chronic that one desperate response by states in the Appalachian region was to consider breaking up or eliminating certain county jurisdictions.

The Clay County War in eastern Kentucky was a complex, transgenerational conflict that began during the economic stress of the 1839–42 national depression, well before the Civil War, and finally ended in a formal truce in 1901 (although related incidents of local violence are said to have reverberated until 1932). The sophisticated warring oligarchs at the center of the feud were anything but moonshine hillbillies. The key actors were the Garrards and the Whites.[27] Both families were highly educated and politically connected.[28] Blee and Billings (2000, 126) note that these oligarchic dynasties produced "numerous county magistrates, judges, sheriffs, legislators, state officials (including a secretary of state), and members of Congress (including a speaker of the United States House of Representatives)."

Power resources rooted in the holding of office were combined with private and personal coercive power, both of which were layered on top of a base of massive material power. Blee and Billings (2000, 126) demonstrate that these warring oligarchic families "were immensely wealthy and controlled Clay County's economy from its earliest years." James Garrard, the founder of the dynasty, was the second governor of Kentucky and owned 45,000 acres of land, including in Clay County. His son Daniel Garrard established the family's profitable salt works and furnaces and added thousands of acres of land to their holdings before 1860. General Theophilus Toulmin ("T. T.") Garrard was Daniel's son and emerged as the lead oligarch of the clan during the second half of the nineteenth century. General Garrard, wealthy grandson of a governor, had fought in the Civil War and served in the state legislature as well as in the U.S. Congress.

James White was the founder of the opposing dynasty of Clay County. The Whites came to Kentucky from Virginia. When James died in 1838, his

---

[27] The feud also involved the Bakers (allies of the Garrards) and the Howards (allies of the Whites).

[28] Education was prized by both warring families. According to Blee and Billings (2000, 126), the dynasties "expended great efforts to educate their children in the nation's finest schools. Laura White, daughter of feud leader Daugherty White, for example, was one of the first female graduates of the University of Michigan." She pursued advanced degrees at MIT and the Sorbonne in Paris, where she studied architecture.

estate was worth two million dollars, ranking him among the wealthiest Americans of the era. The Whites established deep economic roots across the same Appalachian terrain occupied by the Garrards. Blee and Billings (2000, 126) argue that they began "purchasing land and manufacturing salt in Clay County," and by the outbreak of the Civil War, "the White family owned more than twenty thousand acres of land in Clay and other mountain counties."

> From the settlement of the county in the first years of the nineteenth century, the two families competed for control of the county's industry and commerce, first as salt manufacturers in antebellum times, and later as merchants and timber and coal developers. Economic competition fueled conflict over control of the county's political machinery, which alternated between the Whites and Garrards through much of the nineteenth century (Blee and Billings 2000, 122).[29]

As the salt works industry declined, the Whites and Garrards adapted to new economic opportunities. Focusing on land, timber, and coal resources, the Whites "served as land agents for the massive real estate speculation of the New York and Kentucky Land Company in the 1890s, while the Garrards made staggering sums by selling land to outside timber and railroad companies" (Blee and Billings 2000, 129).[30]

Although the competition and tensions between the two oligarchic group-ings were constant, violence in the form of murder and property destruction was more episodic. In the periods when the attacks intensified, governing insti-tutions were crippled and citizens across the region felt threatened. "Conditions in the county [in early 1898] became so strained that even the neutral families felt they were in danger . . . [and] began to go armed at all times. If men had to be away from home overnight they arranged for armed neighbors to protect their families. Both sides armed themselves for war."[31]

While the feuds turned on the antagonisms between the county's most pow-erful and wealthy families, they inevitably drew much larger segments of the community into the battle. This was a reflection of the sizeable material power resources the warring oligarchs possessed to hire foot soldiers for their wealth

---

[29] They add (2000, 126): "The Whites and Garrards, along with a few other families, thus established economic and political dynasties in Clay County based on slave labor, salt man-ufacturing, commerce, and large-scale farming that persisted throughout the antebellum and early postbellum periods and, in some cases, even into the modern era."

[30] The two families competed across Clay County for dominance in a context marked by significant economic strains. "In their roles as landowners and manufacturers, and later as local boosters, lawyers, and indigenous agents of outside capital in the exploitation of local labor, land, timber, and coal resources, the two families prospered immensely from the increasing commercialization of Clay County. At the same time, economic contradictions of low accumulation, population increase, intergenerational farm division, soil depletion, and land shortages produced great strain in the subsistence farming system. [. . .] Economic and political power in the county was contested frequently by the two families and their allies, but no faction was able to exert enduring control over county affairs" (Blee and Billings 1996, 675).

[31] Richardson (1986) quoted in Blee and Billings (1996, 676).

defense apparatus, as well as the "economic dependency that compelled alle-
giance to these families from the rest of the populace." Pools of unemployed
and uneducated citizens of Clay County provided the Whites and Garrards
with "dependent and readily deployable human resources for lethal battles"
(Blee and Billings 1996, 128, 675).

The use by the oligarchs of the county courts and the filing of an endless
torrent of civil suits against each other was an extension of the feud rather
than an alternative method for settling conflicts. Blee and Billings (1996, 682)
show that the feuding families were "consistent, and intense, litigators," always
filling up between a fifth and a third of the circuit court docket with suits and
countersuits against each other. There was no "remoteness of the law" as the
Garrards and Whites hired some of the best lawyers in the state to battle over
land, titles, mining and timber use rights, and forced tax sales of properties.
However, the struggles in the courtroom did not substitute for other forms
of oligarchic conflict. On the contrary, the use of the courts intensified in
tandem with the violence in the courtyard and on the court steps (literally, in
many instances). The gangs of dangerous citizens hired by the oligarchs and
assembled inside and outside the courthouse constituted intimidating "armed
parties of supporters to insure 'fair' trials." Blee and Billings (1996, 689) argue
that the lawsuits filed by the feuding families did not signify a willingness to
compromise or a respect for higher institutions of legitimate authority, but
rather reflected "the tactical use of courts for harassment."

The mythology surrounding feuds in the United States suggests a kind of
primitive warlordism in which "low" people fought petty wars of vengeance
over small stakes in a social milieu desperately in need of civilizing influences.
A more accurate analysis of the feuds reveals that the parties to the violent
battles were wealthy and educated. Their engagement in direct rule was intense
locally and extended upward to the state and national levels. The violence itself
was a key element in a strategy of wealth and property defense in a climate
of mutual intimidation and pitched struggles over the offices and institutions
that impinged directly on the security of property claims. The actors at the
center of these conflicts were warring oligarchs *par excellence*, and prominent in their mode of political-economic interaction with each other was open
warfare.

Conclusions

This chapter has presented a range of examples of warring oligarchies that are
not limited to a single historical period, do not arise from a consistent set of
political developments (such as the breakdown of a preexisting order), and are
not confined to circumstances where overarching authority is entirely absent or
alternative means for settling disputes are unavailable. Warring oligarchies represent a particular solution to the basic oligarchic challenge of wealth defense.
Like all other oligarchs, warring oligarchs are defined fundamentally by their
high concentration of material power resources.

However, warring oligarchies are distinguished from ruling, sultanistic, and civil oligarchies by three things: the oligarchs involved are directly armed and personally engaged in the violence and coercion of wealth defense, they have an unusually high degree of involvement in rule over the community (in Appalachia the oligarchs exerted a high degree of control over those in government when immediate family members were not in office), and they pursue their objectives of wealth defense in a manner that is highly fragmented as opposed to collective-institutionalized, much less provided externally by a sultanistic figure or an impersonal state. Whatever the differences that exist across the varied examples presented in this chapter (and there are too many to list), all of them share these essential characteristics of warring oligarchies. Attention turns now to a consideration of ruling oligarchies.

3

Ruling Oligarchies

The differences among the four types of oligarchy described in this study reflect the changing nature of the threats oligarchs face to their property and wealth, and how they act to solve these wealth defense challenges. It matters enormously whether the primary threats are from the have-nots "below," laterally from other oligarchs, from a sultanistic ruler or state from "above," or from some combination of these. The nature of the responses is as important as the sources of the threats. Oligarchs can defend their property and wealth either separately or collectively. As they do so, they can be fully armed, hire coercive capacities and partially disarm, or exchange full disarmament for reliable guarantees of wealth and property provided by a higher authority. Chapter 2 examined these factors and variables in the context of warring oligarchies.

The focus in this chapter is on ruling oligarchies. The key difference between a warring oligarchy and a ruling oligarchy is the higher degree of cooperation among oligarchs in the latter. When successful, such cooperation is closely related to modifications in the role oligarchs play in the provision of coercion for wealth defense, which reduce one of the greatest dangers oligarchs have faced since the emergence of the earliest stratified societies – lateral attacks from each other, whether by individual predatory oligarchs locally or collectivities of oligarchs attacking from abroad.

In a ruling oligarchy, oligarchs still play a direct role in defending their wealth and in ruling over a community or society. However, they do so collectively rather than as individuals. In most cases, collective rule is institutionalized in a governing body populated almost exclusively by oligarchs (although not all oligarchs need to rule). Ruling oligarchies span a fairly broad spectrum, ranging from those that are highly unstable and meet infrequently for limited purposes, to those that are stable, meet on a regular basis, and govern the entire community or empire. The most important internal factor affecting the stability of a ruling oligarchy is the degree to which oligarchs insist on remaining personally armed and dangerous, or accept partial disarmament, using their wealth and positions to hire the coercive capacities of others (whether as individuals, or through their collective institutions of rule, or some combination of both).

In its most extreme and least successful form (the top left corner of Figure 1.2), a ruling oligarchy would consist of warring oligarchs who somehow manage to cooperate despite being fully armed and in violent competition with each other over landed wealth or some other zero-sum domain. Such oligarchies are exceedingly rare because the centrifugal forces among armed actors make it difficult for them to convene peacefully for extended periods. In the few cases where they have done so, it is usually not to govern a community or empire as a whole, but rather for the limited objective of managing potentially explosive conflicts among themselves or to confront temporary external threats. It is for this reason that the vast majority of ruling oligarchies in history are comprised of oligarchs who are still deeply engaged in wealth and property defense, but in a manner that involves a less personal role as enforcing warriors.

In these more stable and enduring ruling oligarchies, oligarchs usually live and rule together in urban settings or at the center of an empire. The coercive capacities that oligarchs hire often operate along two tracks and in different spaces. At the center of the state or empire, oligarchs rule directly and share the expenses of hiring *public* means of coercion to defend the realm they mostly own. This is an especially effective arrangement for deterring attacks from other ruling oligarchies seeking to absorb wealth and property by conquest or subjugation. However, the obvious challenge is to create rules and mechanisms to secure the collective oligarchy against a rogue local oligarch who might try to turn these formidable public forces against the group.

Particularly when oligarchic wealth remains tied to agricultural surpluses, oligarchs maintain a second track of defense by hiring their own *private* coercive forces to protect their estates, haciendas, and *latifundia*. These separate forces, even if raised in the provinces, can be a source of instability if they become large and are deployed to the capital to settle intra-oligarchic battles through violence. The reduction or elimination of these private forces, and the temptations and threats they create, is a key reason ruling oligarchies are more likely to arise and be stable as the sources of oligarchic wealth and accumulation move away from property and income in land, become less zero-sum, and derive increasingly from trade, manufactures, or services. These points are further developed through an examination of several ruling oligarchies, beginning with the Mafia "Commissions" in the United States and Italy, followed by the oligarchies of the Greco-Roman period, and in the late medieval Italian city-states of Siena and Venice.

Mafia Commissions

What is the result when armed oligarchs, driven by a need to manage the constant dangers and threats to wealth and property (and persons) that they pose to each other, attempt to overcome their fragmentation and form a ruling oligarchy – but do so while remaining fully armed? The rise of the "Commission" among mafia organizations in the United States in the 1930s, and the related emergence of the *Commissione* (or *Cupola*) in Sicily in the 1950s, provide a rare glimpse of this most extreme form of a ruling oligarchy.[1] Dons at the head of crime families enjoy a high concentration of personal wealth, rule their territories directly (in Sicily the territories are practically mapped onto Italian provinces), and play a personal role in the violence of wealth and territoral defense.[2] Although mafia dons do not govern whole societies or communities, they can usefully be viewed as individual warring oligarchs operating in an illegal political economy that parallels the legal system.[3]

The predominant threat to mafia dons is from other Mafiosi. Such threats as there are from "below" arise within the separate mafia organizations, from ambitious capos and underbosses who seek to obtain the greater wealth and power of the bosses and dons they serve. Cooperation among dons is of limited utility in managing such challenges. Meanwhile, threats from "above" are external, in the form of state efforts to crush organized crime. Although this external threat was not a motive for creating the Mafia Commissions, they eventually addressed relations with the state, mainly in the form of trying to control collectively whether a don or boss could murder politicians, judges, or members of law enforcement. The most important driving force behind establishing the Commissions was the need to forge a collective solution to the dangers warring mafia oligarchs posed to each other.

These attempts at creating a ruling oligarchy constituted, in essence, a wealth defense strategy to mitigate the problem of lateral predation and conquest among chronically fragmented oligarchs. However, the Commissions were limited in scope and highly unstable precisely because the dons refused to disarm, except in the limited sense of leaving one's weapons, hit men, and soldiers outside the Commission meeting room. The efforts by individual mafia oligarchs to dominate the Commissions and exercise greater control over the other dons tilted these bodies toward becoming sultanistic oligarchies. Yet the fact that the dons remained armed and directly engaged in the violence of property and wealth defense frustrated the transition to a sultanistic form.

---

[1] There were similar attempts to form associations of warring oligarchs in medieval Europe, especially by the French regional estates, but the centrifugal forces proved too strong and no lasting or significant ruling oligarchies arose.

[2] Santino (2003, 83) describes Sicilian mafia organizations using language emphasizing governance, jurisdictions, and territory: "There isn't a monarchy, a Number One, in the organized crime world, but there are many republics that variously interact," he writes. "Mafia is a form of totalitarian State and its peculiarity is the territorial control (*"signoria territoriale"*), from the economy to politics, to private life." Linked to the specific manner in which southern Italy emerged from feudalism, the Italian mafia originated in the late Middle Ages but assumed its modern form at the beginning of the nineteenth century. Existing neither as fragmented warring oligarchs nor united under a single ruler able to monopolize violence, mafia are characterized by organizations that combine feudal and capitalist forms. Capturing the nexus between property defense and violence, Franchetti (1974 [1876]) described the Sicilian mafia as an *"industria della violenza."*

[3] On the American and Sicilian mafia, including extensive analysis of the Commissions, see Arlacci (1986), Bonanno (2003), Catanzaro (1992), Gambetta (1993, 2000), Hess (1973), and Paoli (2003).

Gambetta (2000, 164) firmly establishes the material and territorial foundations of mafia oligarchs. He argues that their "single most important activity is the enforcement of monopolies over the largest possible number of resources in any given territory." In the absence of externally defended property rights by a coercive state, armed mafia oligarchs enforce their own property claims. "Each Mafioso is either a monopolist or the acolyte of a monopolist," Gambetta writes, and *Cosa nostra* literally means that "the thing is ours, *not* yours; it stresses inclusion, and inclusion can only subsist by simultaneously postulating exclusion." The wealth that mafia oligarchs defend is substantial. In 2001, the estimated annual value of the organized crime economy globally, especially drug trafficking, was between $500 and $700 billion (Santino 2003, 83). The United Nations estimated the cash assets of these groups to be $322 billion in 2005 (Flynn and Cinelli 2009).

The sophistication and organization of mafia clusters has increased over the decades, but unifying and organizing mafia dons and bosses into a stable collectivity or a single monopoly has proven difficult. According to Gambetta (2000, 165) the mafia "has not managed to reach a stage at which stable cooperation can be sustained for any length of time." Despite the fragmentation and conflict among warring mafia oligarchs, the mafia persists. "The characteristics of its persistence," Gambetta notes, "suggest those of a turbulent equilibrium."

American Mafia Commission. A turbulent equilibrium nicely captures what resulted when armed mafia oligarchs sought to erect a ruling oligarchy through the formation of Commissions. The first Mafia Commission was established in Atlantic City, New Jersey, in 1931 (Federal Bureau of Investigations 2009). In that year, the bloody "Castellammarese War" had just ended with the murder of Giuseppe Masseria, whose violent efforts to rule the mafia nationally had damaged profits for the Italian organizations and made them vulnerable to Irish mafia oligarchs. Masseria was killed by the powerful Salvatore Maranzano, assisted by Masseria's own top soldier, Charles "Lucky" Luciano. For the next six months, Maranzano was the richest and most powerful mafia oligarch in North America – the *capo di tutti capi*, the "boss of all bosses." However, just as Maranzano was making plans to form a Commission to provide more order and reduce the threat of warring mafia oligarchs killing each other, Lucky Luciano turned once again and engineered Maranzano's murder, together with that of nearly forty other mobsters in a two-day bloodbath in September 1931 (Magnuson 2001). It was in the wake of this turbulence that Lucky Luciano and the warring New York mob families "found a peaceful way of solving their grievances" – a ruling oligarchic Commission (New York Times 1986).

Joseph Bonanno was the boss of one of the five New York families that formed the first Mafia Commission. Emphasizing a need for collective rule, he described how the dons of the 1930s "opted for a parliamentary arrangement" with "leadership by committee." The Commission would meet infrequently – sometimes only once in five years – and it would make only major decisions intended to regulate lateral conflicts among the mafia oligarchs. The goal was to prevent open warfare over mafia markets and exclusive economic zones, and to minimize threats to each oligarch's rich material base. Dutch Shultz was likely the first casualty of Commission-endorsed discipline. In 1935, he came before the body seeking permission to assassinate U.S. Attorney Thomas Dewey. Appearing not to accept the ruling oligarchy's denial of his request, Schultz was assassinated that same year on Commission orders to prevent a potentially devastating government backlash. During the remainder of the twentieth century, the ratio of major mafia killings not approved by the Commission to those approved has been roughly 2:1.[4]

By the 1950s, the mafia-ruling oligarchy's Commission had expanded from its East Coast base to incorporate the entire United States. In 1957, police broke up what turned out to be a Commission meeting of ruling oligarchs from around the country who had gathered in the small upstate New York town of Apalachin (Federal Bureau of Investigations 2009). By 2001, the existence of the Commission itself became the focus of prosecutions intended to weaken the mob. Assistant U.S. Attorney Michael Chertoff "charged flatly that the Mafia is run by a coordinating Commission" (Magnuson 2001). Referring to the eight mafia bosses on trial, Chertoff added:

> "What you will see is these men," he said, "these crime leaders, fighting with each other, backstabbing each other, each one trying to get a larger share of the illegal proceeds. You are going to learn that this Commission is dominated by a single principle – greed. They want more money, and they will do what they have to do to get it."

The prosecution presented evidence that the Commission had arranged the murder of the Bonanno boss Carmine Galante and two associates in 1979 because he was attempting an unapproved and disruptive conquest of the Gambino family. Downplaying this violent side of the mafia's ruling oligarchy, Samuel Dawson, defense attorney for the dons and bosses, claimed that the purpose of the Commission was merely to arbitrate disputes and "to avoid – avoid – conflict" (Magnuson 2001).

Prosecutors also showed that the Commission's functions included coordinating economic activities that generated significant wealth for the mafia oligarchs and defended them against competitors. The bosses in the Commission controlled the major concrete companies in New York City, and they cooperated in rigging the bidding process on all construction projects worth more than $2 million. The oligarchs decided among themselves whose turn it

[4] A partial list of assassinations not approved by the Commission would include: Benjamin "Bugsy" Siegel (1947), Vincent Mangano (1951), Philip Mangano (1951), Frank Costello (1957, attempted), Alberta Anastasia (1957), Anthony Carafano (1959), Santo Perrone (1964, attempted), William Devino (1970), Joe Colombo (1971), Joey Gallo (1972), Tommy Eboli (1972), Dominic Napolitano (1981), and Anthony Spilotro (1986). Commission-approved killings include: Dutch Schultz (1935), Willie Moretti (1951), Frank Scalice (1957), Sam Giancana (1975), Salvatore Briguglio (1978), Carmine Galante and two associates (1979), Paul Castellano (1985), and Thomas Bilotti (1985).

was to submit the lowest bid, and the dons took a 2 percent cut of all contracts. "Any [construction] company that disobeyed the bidding rules might find itself with unexpected labor problems, and its sources of cement might dry up" (Magnuson 2001).

Italian Mafia *Commissione*. The mafia in the United States traces its origins to European immigrants transplanted to major cities. The territories these rising oligarchs carved up were largely urban commercial markets. The mafia in Sicily, by contrast, has its origins in persistent semifeudal relations in the countryside that lasted until the middle of the nineteenth century. Absentee landowners outsourced the control of their large estates and extraction from farmers to *gabelotti*, who evolved toward the end of the century into mafia families. From the outset their character was more rural, agricultural, and territorial in a manner that more closely followed the boundaries of official jurisdictions, particularly at the provincial level (Gambetta 2000).

The *Commissione* did not arise organically in Sicily, but instead was transplanted there by the same Lucky Luciano who played a leading role in establishing the American Mafia Commission after he turned on Masseria and Maranzano in 1931. Although he had been incarcerated for several years, Luciano was deported to Italy in 1957 in return for assistance he provided to the United States and Allied forces from his jail cell during World War II. The *Commissione* in Sicily had two main functions: to mediate conflicts among the Mafiosi and to regulate when violence could be used. According to Paoli (2003, 55), no mafia ruling oligarchs could order the murder of government officials, police, journalists, or members of other mafia families without the *Commissione*'s approval. She also notes an additional power exercised by the Italian version of a mafia ruling oligarchy not evident in the U.S. counterpart: the authority to suspend leaders of a mafia family and appoint a temporary replacement or *reggente*.

Another difference was the compartmentalized and hierarchical nature of the Italian bodies. Reflecting the strength of regional jurisdictions in the Sicilian mafia structure, a *Commissione* arose in each province. These were then linked and governed by *Commissione Interprovinciale* typically with the head of the Palermo *Commissione* playing a hegemonic role over the more informal interprovincial body. This role was particularly evident in the 1970s and 1980s when two powerful dons from Palermo, Salvatore "Totò" Riina and Bernardo Provenzano, took over the *Commissione* for all of Sicily and used their *Corleonesi* coalition to transform the body into a personal instrument of domination.

The *Commissione* in Sicily was even more fragmented and unstable than its American counterpart. Despite the best efforts of the *Commissione*, major conflicts among Mafiosi in Italy continued to erupt. The most spectacular example involved Michele Cavataio, a boss from Palermo. He became enraged when he lost a profitable turf battle. Strongly opposed to the *Commissione*, Cavataio initiated a series of assassinations and bombings that sparked the Mafia War of 1963 among the ruling oligarchs. When Cavataio was murdered in 1969, the interfamily composition of the hit squad suggested it was a clear example of *Commissione* enforcement (Schneider and Schneider 2003, 65–6).

The limited capacities and instabilities of these Mafia Commissions help account for why such extreme forms of ruling oligarchy are so rare. Except when taken over by a single mafia oligarch, the Commissions were weak. In addition, even when dominated by a single hegemonic actor, the centrifugal tendencies of the Commissions produced repeated fragmentation. There was a constant oscillation between extreme democracy among the oligarchs, marked by consensus decision making, and extreme hierarchy when efforts at leadership briefly became sultanistic. The Commissions had no equivalent of a standing army or independent means of coercion. Whenever they enforced collective rules or disciplined renegade dons or bosses, they did so through the joint deployment of separate oligarchic coercive capacities temporarily on loan to the Commission.

Other examples of ruling oligarchies abound in history, but the predominant form involves a significant change in the nature of coercive capacities among the oligarchs seeking to cooperate. The next section examines the Greco-Roman cases from antiquity, both of which were ruling oligarchies based on the violent exploitation of slaves. The first case is that of Classical Athens, where ruling oligarchs formed a partnership or association rather than a "state," and where the distribution of wealth and property in the social formation was stratified but moderate. This is followed by an examination of Republican Rome, where the collective institutions of oligarchic rule were more developed and where the distribution of wealth and property in society was vastly more stratified. The stability and longevity of both ruling oligarchies was profoundly affected by the changing coercive capacities of oligarchs.

Greco-Roman Oligarchies

Arguably the single most important debate among ancient historians during the last century has been over how democratic or oligarchic Athens and Rome were. The discussion commenced with the now classic works of Matthias Gelzer 1969 [1912] and especially Ronald Syme (1939). The latter opened his groundbreaking analysis by declaring that "in all ages, whatever the form and name of government, be it monarchy, republic, or democracy, an oligarchy lurks behind the façade" (1939, 7). By the late twentieth century, historians had presented compelling evidence that the politics of these two empires contained considerably more democratic substance than had been acknowledged previously.[5] This vital and illuminating debate is mentioned not because it will be joined in earnest, but rather because it will be mostly avoided.

There are two reasons for sidestepping the controversy. The first is that this author is fluent in neither Greek nor Latin, nor trained as a historian of the Classical era, and thus can unearth nothing new from the ancient texts. The second is related to the differences in how the relationship between democracy

---

[5] For an overview of the debate see Samons (1998).

and oligarchy is treated in this book compared to most of the literature at the heart of the great debate. Syme's image of oligarchies lurking behind various governmental façades, including democracy, is based on an underlying notion of oligarchy as essentially zero-sum with other forms of government.[6] Syme implies that oligarchs are truly in power and democracy is mostly a sham. Whether explicitly or not, much of the literature responding to Gelzer, Syme, and the generation of scholars they influenced has sought to prove that during key centuries of the Greco-Roman era, democracy was not a sham.[7]

The perspective advanced in this book is that oligarchy and procedural democracy, especially in the representative form that had evolved by the early nineteenth century, barely conflict at all. The two kinds of politics are derived from different kinds of power and involve different kinds of political engagement. The politics of oligarchs is focused on defending wealth. Meanwhile, the practices and procedures of democracy evolved and widened in lockstep with the creation of daunting protections for oligarchic property against the potential threats that poor majorities, left unchecked, could pose. No protections, no democracy.[8]

[6] The idea that democracies and oligarchies displace each other is ubiquitous, as for instance when Lyttkens (1994, 62, n1), referring to Classical Athens, asserts that "democracy was replaced by oligarchy in 322." This creates the mistaken impression that there was no significant oligarchy during the "democracy" years from 508/7 (or perhaps 461) B.C.E. until the "replacement."

[7] Apart from having to disprove the view that oligarchs were in charge of everything that mattered, the "no sham" perspective for Athens struggles with another problem also raised by conditions in early American history: what does it mean to have democracy among a segment of society juxtaposed to massive exclusion for the many (slaves, women, nonpropertied, noncitizens)? In the late 1980s, there was an illuminating campus debate at Yale University between the *Nation* magazine and the *National Review* regarding South Africa. Defending the white South Africans, who enjoyed a vibrant but exclusionary democracy and economy among themselves, a woman from the *National Review* noted with admiration how the Afrikaners had "created an oasis in a desert." Christopher Hitchens, a formidable debater representing the *Nation*, approached the microphone and asked, "Did I understand her to say that the white South Africans had created an oasis *and* a desert?" As Hitchens sat down and the audience roared with delight, the sentiment in the room was clear: there is something deeply flawed about a social formation that is democratic and yet broadly exclusionary. On Athenian democracy, Mosca (1939 [1898], 52) remarked: "What Aristotle called a democracy was simply an aristocracy of fairly broad membership." This goes too far. It is nonsense to lump farmer-thetes in with the Three Hundred as aristocrats. Although privileged and free, many thetes lived simple and even poor lives. Anderson (1974a, 33) prefers to categorize democratic Athens as an "extended oligarchy." He never defines what "extended" means (a bigger oligarchy that includes smaller oligarchs, or oligarchs plus those they co-opted?). He does write, however, that "the direct popular democracy of the Athenian constitution was diluted by the informal dominance of professional politicians over the Assembly, recruited from traditionally wealthy and well-born families in the city (or later from the newly rich)" (1974a, 39). My own characterization would be: an exclusionary slave democracy heavily dominated by a ruling landed oligarchy. For a defense of the democratic substance of the *polis* despite its admitted flaws, see Josiah Ober (1993, 2007).

[8] This counterfactual is supported by four observations. First, the historical record is clear that wealth-defense measures were indeed erected securing the property of oligarchs as democracy was emerging. Chapter 1 showed that constitutional framers and political thinkers fretted openly about the need to protect the property of the rich as they argued for, designed, and voted into place the institutions and procedures that would do just that. Second, we have no examples

A wealth defense agenda admittedly has wide implications. In addition, it is certainly the case that if oligarchs are ruling directly (meaning they personally hold the bulk of key governing positions), their influence on decisions will extend well beyond core oligarchic concerns. However, the obverse is also true – that as oligarchs become less engaged in direct rule and the coercion necessary to defend their wealth, and as others in society play a greater role in government, the range of issues influenced by oligarchs as a whole narrows dramatically to a set of core policies directly related to wealth defense. When this happens, and democracy takes root, there exists a broad spectrum of important policies around which oligarchs *qua* oligarchs play no vital role in setting the political agenda or shaping the outcomes. It is for this reason that it was argued at the outset that electoral democracy, except under exceedingly rare and extreme circumstances, does not encroach on or significantly diminish oligarchy as it has been defined here.

Thus the relevant consideration for present purposes is not how much democracy there was in antiquity, or whether it was a façade or a sham – important as this obviously is. The focus, rather, is on establishing that oligarchs existed and were significant in both Greece and Rome, on exploring the nature of the threats posed to their substantial wealth, and on specifying the ways oligarchs in the two cases responded individually and collectively to form a ruling oligarchy to defend their fortunes. As for popular forces, they enter the picture in two key ways. One is as a threat to oligarchs from below – although this was felt far more often in the streets, on the agriculture estates from slaves, or even in the stadium than in the popular assemblies. The other is as an element in intra-oligarchic conflict – both as a potential force oligarchs manipulated for attacks against other oligarchs, and as a mediator in instances of potentially explosive oligarchic standoffs in the senate and other deliberative bodies.

Both Athens and Rome fall squarely in the category of ruling oligarchies. However, they differ from the Mafia Commissions in that collective rule was much more stable and enduring, and the instruments and institutions of government encompassed policies well beyond the task of managing the threats oligarchs posed to each other. Lateral dangers among oligarchs remained, but they were moderated by the terms and norms of collective rule – especially through the partial disarmament of the oligarchs themselves. Forming a ruling oligarchy with diminished oligarch-to-oligarch predations enhanced capacities

of meaningful democracy arising or enduring in nations where fundamental oligarchic property protections, however they are achieved, were not in place. Third, there is abundant evidence that strong property protections established prior to democracy's rise or built into the procedures and practices of the democracies themselves (or typically some combination of both) work remarkably well. In long-term and stable democracies, majorities of the nonpropertied, via their representatives, virtually never see policies initiated – much less passed – that would frontally threaten oligarchic property. And fourth, in the instances when such policies have been passed, democracy itself has consistently been the first casualty of such democratic hyperfunctionality. This yields the additional formulation: failed protections, failed democracy.

for confronting threats from below and from outsiders. In fact, so effective was the hired and jointly managed coercive apparatus of the oligarchs that it was neighboring political communities that had to contend with the threat of extracted tribute or conquest that Athens and Rome now represented.

Before examining the Greco-Roman ruling oligarchies, it is useful to recall the broad historical outlines of the era. Archaic Greece spanned the years 800 to 500 B.C.E., during which urban patterns had begun to emerge and cities were developed by tribal landed oligarchs who had deposed local kings. Important developments preserving small and medium farmers during the Archaic period set the stage for the more familiar era of Classical Greece, which extended across the fifth and fourth centuries B.C.E.[9] After the collapse of democratic Athens at the hands of the Macedonians, a more authoritarian Hellenistic period arose from 322 to 146 B.C.E., the year Greece was absorbed by Rome. In the middle of the fifth century B.C.E., the population of Athens and the nearby countryside was slightly more than 300,000.[10] The voting population of adult male citizens numbered around 38,200. This excluded women, foreigners, and slaves who together constituted around 87 percent of the population. Despite these exclusions, the Athenian *polis* during the fourth and fifth centuries was vastly more "democratic" and participatory than Rome in any century.

Turning to the Italian empire, there were two great periods of Rome: the Republic and the Empire. The Roman Republic stretched from 508 to 27 B.C.E. The Roman Empire[11] consisted of two major parts: first the Principate, sometimes characterized as an enlightened absolutism, which began in 27 B.C.E. after the rise of Augustus, and continued through 235 C.E. under the emperor Diocletian; and second the more authoritarian Dominate, starting in 235 C.E. and ending in 476, the year the western part of the Roman Empire collapsed and fragmented into feudal Europe, and the eastern part carried on as the Byzantine Empire until 1453. The scale of Rome and its empire dwarfed anything

[9] Anderson (1974a, 29–32) offers an excellent overview of the Archaic period and its important role in laying the foundation for the *polis* that followed. Following arguments first advanced by Thomson (1949), Runciman (1982, 361) offers a description of the earliest origins of Athenian landed oligarchs, who begin in a condition of "Neolithic self-sufficiency followed by the introduction of metal and therefore the extraction of surplus value placed in the hands of chiefs who, by waging wars of conquest with superior weapons and tilling their demesne lands with captured slaves, arrive at the stage of a landed aristocracy."

[10] The total population is difficult to estimate with precision because no census of slaves was ever taken. Estimates of the slave population range wildly from 75,000 to 300,000. Based on fragmentary indications of slave holdings at all levels of the citizenry, a reasonable number is 120,000. The number of foreigners, or *metics*, was around 25,000, including family. The wives and children of the 38,200 adult male citizens are believed to have totaled around 120,000. These elements yield an approximate total population of 305,000 at its height. Anderson writes that the population never exceeded 320,000. These proportions and totals draw on Anderson (1974a, 38) and Engen (2004).

[11] "Roman Empire" will refer specifically to this historical period, while "Roman empire" will refer to the capital and the territories in Italy and beyond under domination during various time periods.

seen in Greece. During the Roman Republic, the population reached just under 10 million. With the conquests of the Roman Empire period, that figure jumped to between 45 and 65 million spread across a vast swath of Europe.

Although the great mass of oligarchic wealth during the Greco-Roman era was in the countryside, the oligarchs lived in and personally ruled from the urban areas. The economy made up of the countryside estates and smaller farms on the periphery of Athens and Rome, even as late as the fourth century C.E., was roughly twenty times the economy of the capital cities. "The classical world was," as Anderson (1974a, 19) points out, "massively, unalterably rural in its basic quantitative proportions." He describes this imbalance as an "anomalous supremacy of town over country" (1974a, 23). This was a striking inversion of the feudal arrangement that would arise centuries later in which warring landed oligarchs resided on the lands that were the source of their wealth, and that they defended separately and ruled personally. Meanwhile, the weaker towns and cities of the feudal era struggled desperately to maintain such independence as they enjoyed (being quite high in Italy and almost nonexistent in Germany).

Oligarchs of the Greco-Roman era migrated to the cities to form "urban congeries of landowners" (Anderson 1974a, 19). The pressing analytical question is how this was possible. Anderson emphasizes the important role of slave estates that "permitted a permanent disjuncture between residence and revenue" (1974a, 24). Slavery provided the "economic hinge that joined town and country together, to the inordinate profit of the *polis*" (1974a, 25). There is no denying slavery was crucial, and its role is explored later. However, at least as important as slavery on the land were major adaptations that had to be made among oligarchs themselves. They had to ensure the defense of their immense agrarian-derived fortunes against threats, while also ruling collectively despite living in close physical proximity in Athens and Rome. There was no separate, impersonal state to which they could appeal for property defense. The ruling oligarchs were "the state" – its legislators, its executives, its administrators, its penal enforcers, and the leaders of its armies, legions, and naval forces.

Oligarchs could not establish and maintain a system of collective rule without significant changes in the organization of coercion. As Chapter 2 on warring oligarchies showed, one of the greatest threats armed oligarchs face is from each other. This problem seriously weakened the attempts by Mafiosi to form a workable ruling oligarchy from their essentially warring elements. There were several factors in Greece and Rome that combined to make collective oligarchic rule much more sustainable. The first dealt frontally with the destabilizing problem of lateral oligarchic threats. When physically in Athens and Rome – as opposed to when they were on their estates in the countryside or leading military campaigns – the ruling oligarchs were partially disarmed.

The disarmament was partial in the sense that throughout antiquity, the landowners populating the ruling bodies remained martial figures within martial societies. The disarmament was also partial in the sense that within the city, ruling oligarchs still had the personal resources to hire threatening coercive forces to achieve political outcomes or settle conflicts they could not manage by argument, persuasion, or alliances. Finally, it was partial in that the relatively disarmed oligarchs at the center of empires who had jointly created and commanded significant *public* coercive instruments, especially in Rome, nevertheless utilized *private* coercive means in the countryside to grab land, control slaves, extract debts and taxes from tenant farmers, and defend the boundaries of the lands that were the firmament of their wealth and power in the *polis*.

A second factor enhancing the stability of collective wealth defense was a set of elaborate arrangements, rules, norms, and punishments to safeguard oligarchs from aggressive peers who might try to deploy a fighting force in the capital, or later, especially in the case of Rome, from oligarchs holding military commands who might use their "public" troops to settle personal intra-oligarchic conflicts in the capital. The third factor concerns how slavery and exclusionary laws of citizenship throughout the Greco-Roman period shaped the behaviors of a significant middle stratum of free citizens, who were objectively oppressed but subjectively grateful not to be either slaves or exploited noncitizens in the cities or the provinces. This meant that threats from below, whether via democratic participation or violent rebellion, were dampened by the differentiation of status and extreme stratification among the multitudes of nonoligarchs. To elaborate these points, attention turns first to Athens.

Athens

Both the Athenian and Roman empires contained wealthy landed oligarchs. However, the scale and concentration of wealth and property in Rome was many magnitudes greater than that seen in Athens, where middle and small farmers remained firmly rooted and owned three-fourths of the land until the eclipse of the democratic period. The pattern in Athens was for the wealthy to own multiple smaller farms rather than the immense estates known in Rome as *latifundia*. Even during the Hellenic period when ruling oligarchs based in Athens began to form larger estates across Attica (the largest never exceeding 1,000 acres), they were still modest compared to their Roman counterparts. Anderson (1974a, 38) offers a concise summary:

> By Hellenic standards, big landed property was an estate of 100–200 acres. In Attica there were few large estates, even wealthy landowners possessing a number of small farms rather than concentrated *latifundia*. Holdings of 70 or even 45 acres were above average, while the smallest plots were probably not much more than 5 acres; three-quarters of the free citizenry owned some rural property down to the end of the fifth century.

The overall wealth contours of Athenian society were shaped rather like a spired umbrella. The long thin handle represents the mass of propertyless slaves at the bottom. Near the top of the social formation, all property was distributed in the rough shape of an open canopy, with wealthy ruling oligarchs forming a tall spire at the top. Table 3.1 provides a rough idea of the distribution of wealth

TABLE 3.1. *Wealth and Material Power in Classical Athens*

	Average Wealth (drachmae)	% Share Citizen Property	% Share Population	Material Power Index
1,200 Trierarch-Oligarchs				
Top 10	486,300	5.3	0.003	2,432
Next 290	20,470	6.5	0.095	102
Lower 900	12,000	11.8	0.295	60
Hoplites				
Upper 8,200	4,245	38.2	2.7	21
Lower 4,800	2,250	11.8	1.6	11
Thetes				
All 24,000	1,000	26.3	7.9	5
Slaves				
± 120,000	200	0.0	39.0	1

and the associated concentration of material power in Athens.[12] The approach adopted to produce the estimates in the table was deliberately conservative. The picture that emerges shows a relatively flat social formation with a substantial concentration of wealth into a few oligarchic hands at the very top.

The crucial message in this table is contained in the last column – the Material Power Index (MPI). However, before discussing the significance of the MPI, the other elements of the table merit elaboration.

Slaves. Table 3.1 is best understood when read from the bottom left, starting with the slaves of Classical Athens. Slaves and the population outside citizen-families formed a broad underclass. A relatively conservative number of 120,000 slaves is used. Far more important is the figure of 200 drachmae cited as the average "wealth" of a slave. Obviously, slaves were themselves chattel property and their wealth was zero. Yet some way must be found to represent the material position of a median individual – indisputably a slave – in the Athenian social formation, so that the relative material position and power of the citizens and especially the oligarchs at the top can be estimated. As a

---

[12] Table 3.1 relies mainly on Jones (1955, 1958), whose work on Athenian society focuses more on the fourth than the fifth century. He states that the distribution of wealth did not change significantly across these two centuries (Jones 1955, 145). His estimates have been adapted without changing proportions. The total population used to calculate the percentages in the fourth column is 310,000. The foreigner-*metics* tended to be better off financially than most, and some were extremely wealthy merchants – qualifying them as oligarchs according to the definition in this study (a radical departure from other analyses that locate the most powerful actors only among the citizenry). Except for some ultra-rich *metics* mixed into the 1,200 trierarchs at the top, the table does not present data on their wealth, little of which was in the form of agricultural land. The total value of property captured in Table 3.1 is 91.2 million drachmae, or 15,200 talents. The following conversions applied in ancient Athens: 1 talent = 60 minae; 1 mina = 100 drachmae; and 1 drachma = 6 oboloi.

proxy for an average slave's "wealth," a year's allowance for a public slave is used, and it is assigned a unit value of 1.0 as the basis for estimating an MPI for Classical Athens in the last column. Public slaves were paid an allowance of 3 obols a day, or 183 drachmae a year, assuming no days off. For simplicity, this is rounded up to 200 drachmae in the table – an estimate that is generous because most slaves were private and thus paid nothing (Jones 1955, 145).[13] The ratio of slaves to citizens for Athens and the surrounding countryside was roughly 3:1, and they constituted nearly 40 percent of the total population.

Thetes. Moving up the social and material stem of the umbrella, the largest and poorest element among the citizens of Athens were the farmer-thetes. They numbered roughly 24,000, of whom some 12,000 were rowers in the Athenian navy who were paid 6 obols per day, or 1 drachma, for 240 days of work per year (Jones 1958, 7; Anderson 1974a, 38). Of the remaining 12,000 thetes, roughly 5,000 at the bottom were landless and received wages of 6 to 9 obols a day. Assuming ideal conditions that rarely applied (9 obols, 6-day weeks, and employment year-round), this is 2,800 obols a year, or 470 drachmae (Jones 1955, 144–5). Thetes were a residual category, defined as free citizens whose total property was valued below the 2,000 drachmae threshold needed to qualify as a hoplite.[14] In Table 3.1, the net worth of a thete's property is estimated as 1,000 drachmae. According to Jones (1955, 145), thetes "earned their living by working on very small holdings of 5 acres downwards, or as skilled craftsmen or shopkeepers, with from five slave assistants downwards, or as casual labourers." The estimate of 1,000 drachmae for all thetes represents the midpoint between having no property at all and reaching the hoplite threshold of 2,000 drachmae, and is likely conservative given 5,000 thetes are known to have been landless. Thetes made up 63 percent of all citizens, just under 8 percent of the total population, but owned roughly a quarter of all citizen property in Athens.

Hoplites. Owning property worth at least 2,000 drachmae qualified a citizen to be a hoplite. Classical Athens had approximately 13,000 of these somewhat richer farmer-hoplites. Wealthy enough to supply their own weapons and equipment for war, they formed the backbone of the heavily armed infantry of the Athenian phalanx. By citizen standards, they ranged from quite poor to

---

[13] It is exceedingly difficult to make meaningful comparisons between ancient and contemporary currencies (Shelton 1988, 459). Engen (2004) states that "one drachma could buy enough food for 16 days for one person." Monsivais and Drewnowski (2007) estimate that a low-income American in 2007 spent $4 per day on food. Sixteen days of food equals $64. As a conversion factor, this number should be viewed as a very rough estimate at best. Jones (1955) makes the important point that despite the obstacles to converting values, it is still possible to make illuminating comparisons of *relative* stratification – for instance, the gap in income between a common Roman legion soldier and a centurion versus an American enlisted soldier and a modern Lieutenant Colonel. Also see "The Current Value of Old Money," http://projects.exeter.ac.uk/RDavies/arian/current/howmuch.html.

[14] This threshold, equivalent to 20 minae, was roughly equivalent to 5 acres, a farmhouse, and some livestock. One could also purchase six or seven skilled slaves with 2,000 drachmae (Jones 1955, 144).

comfortable. At 3,500 drachmae, the wealth of an average hoplite was more than 50 percent higher than that of a typical thete. Jones (1955, 147) writes that the line dividing hoplites and thetes was "an arbitrary one, and there must have been many hoplites just over the line, who were relatively poor men." Thucydides (Book III, Chapter IX) wrote that during the Peloponnesian War, which ended in 404 B.C.E., a hoplite and his squire each earned 1 drachma per day. Hoplites made up a third of all citizens, slightly more than 4 percent of the broader population, but owned fully half of all citizen property in Athens. If it were not for these 37,000 thetes and hoplites – most of whom owned a few acres of land that, combined, amounted to three-quarters of all citizen property, and who provided a vital self-armed defense of the *polis* – it is inconceivable that the slave-based society of Athens, comfortably ruled by oligarchs, would have contained such a tenacious, if decidedly conservative, democratic element.

Athenian citizens with assessed property values of at least 2,500 drachmae were obligated to pay the *eisphora*, a regressive property tax for wars or emergencies paid in equal shares by the richest citizens (Jones 1955, 147). It is clear from available records that the total number of citizens paying the war tax included not only all the oligarchs at the top, but a significant number of hoplites as well. This means that a substantial number of hoplites must have satisfied not just the 2,000 drachmae threshold, but also the *eisphora* minimum wealth of 2,500 drachmae. This information makes it possible to separate hoplites into "lower" and "upper" strata in Table 3.1.

"Lower" Hoplites. This group numbered around 4,800 citizens and had an estimated average wealth of 2,250 drachmae, which is barely over the hoplite threshold. They typically owned "a farm with house and stock of from 5 to 6 acres" (Jones 1955, 147). Some of the lower hoplites appear to have had severe liquidity problems. Jones writes that "Mantitheus, when his deme assembled for the muster, found that many of his poorer fellow hoplites could not even raise their journey money, and organized a subscription to provide them with 30 drachmae each." Although the lower hoplites made up less than 2 percent of the Athenian population, they constituted 13 percent of the citizen class of Athens and owned an almost equal share of all citizen property.

"Upper" Hoplites. This group numbered around 8,200 citizens and were better off than the lower hoplites because they met the 2,500 drachmae threshold for the *eisphora*. The average wealth entered in Table 3.1 for these upper hoplites is 4,245 drachmae, which would roughly equal $270,000 in 2007 using a conversion of $64 per drachma.[15] Of this group, Jones (1955, 147) writes: "We have the evidence – for what it is worth – of Demosthenes, that many of these were relatively poor." Among them were "farmers who pinch and scrape,

[15] Extrapolating from Jones's (1955, 147–8) estimates for the fourth century, a proportional total assessed property value for the *eisphora* for Classical Athens (with 38,200 citizens) would be 9,400 talents or 56,400,000 drachmae. Jones argues that the average wealth among 1,200 trierarchs is 3 talents, or 21,600,000 drachmae. This leaves 34,800,000 drachmae for the 8,200 upper hoplites, or a round figure of 4,245 each.

but who owing to the cost of bringing up their children, and domestic expenses and other public demands, have fallen into arrears of *eisphora*." He adds that there are indications that some of the *eisphora* payers "could not even afford to buy a single slave girl to help in the house."[16] The upper hoplites were more representative of the hoplite stratum overall. One in five citizens was an upper hoplite, although they accounted for only 2.7 percent of the broader population. They were the single largest landowning group, with just under 40 percent of all citizen property.

Trierarch-Oligarchs. These were the wealthiest citizens of Athens. Jones (1955, 148) writes that they "roughly corresponded with the 1,200 persons on the trierarchic register: there was no property qualification for trierarchic service, and the list was supposed to include the 1,200 richest Athenians." The trierarchy was the name given to the ultra-rich citizens obliged to command and outfit a *trireme*, an Athenian naval vessel. Based on an average wealth of 3 talents (about $1.15 million) for each trierarch, the total property for the entire trierarchy was 3,600 talents, or 21,600,000 drachmae (about $1.38 billion).[17] As with the hoplites, the trierarchy had an upper and lower element. Reproducing a pattern evident in nearly all materially unequal societies, the greatest stratification existed not between the average citizen and the merely rich, but rather among the rich at the very top. The richest segment in Athens was known as the "Three Hundred," 290 of whom were, on average, about twice as wealthy as the 900 oligarchs below them. However, the ten richest oligarchs out of the Three Hundred were, on average, forty times as wealthy as the lower 900. The single richest oligarch among the top ten owned 150 times the wealth of the average oligarch in the lower segment of the trierarchy, and 9,000 times that of the median member of the population – a public slave. The trierarchs made up slightly more than 3 percent of all citizens, but jointly they owned around one quarter of all citizen property. At just over one-third of 1 percent of the overall population, they constituted a tiny sliver of the Athenian social formation.

Lower 900 Trierarch-Oligarchs. To approximate the average wealth of this group, it is useful to note that "middle-level fortunes" in Classical Athens were in the range of 2 to 5 talents, or 12,000 to 30,000 drachmae (Jones 1958, 89). Consistent with the effort to err on the side of conservative estimates in the table, the more modest level of 2 talents, or 12,000 drachmae, is used as an average wealth for the lower 900 trierarch-oligarchs.[18] This would be a net worth of perhaps $770,000 in 2007.

---

[16] Jones (1955, 148) also mentions: "It must follow that in the lower half or two-thirds [of those designated "upper" hoplites] . . . the average fortune must have been well below 1 talent [6,000 drachmae]; a large group must have owned between 25 and 30 minae (half a talent [3,000 drachmae]) each, and these are probably the poor farmers whom Demosthenes describes."

[17] The collective wealth of the bottom 1,190 was 16,737,000 drachmae (2.8 talents), which is equal to the overall wealth of the trierarchy (21,600,000 drachmae) minus the estimated wealth of the top ten (4,863,000 drachmae).

[18] Collectively, the wealth of these 900 oligarchs accounts for 10,800,000 drachmae of the 16,737,000 drachmae owned by all but the top ten individuals in the trierarchy.

The 290 of the "Three Hundred." The top ten oligarchic fortunes are examined separately, leaving 290 members of the Three Hundred. These 290 enjoyed
an average fortune of 20,470 drachmae each, or about $1.3 million.[19] If the
wealth of the top 10 and the next 290 are combined, the average fortune of the
oligarchs in the Three Hundred is 36,000 drachmae (roughly $2.3 million), or
6 talents, which is almost three times the average for the lower 900 trierarchs.
These figures comport with Jones (1955, 148), who suggests that "5 talents
[30,000 drachmae] must have been well above the average trierarchic estate,"
which was "only 3 talents [18,000 drachmae]." Jones adds that "the majority
must have owned less than this amount, since a few are known to have owned
considerably more."[20] The three hundred richest oligarchs earned an *annual*
income on their property greater than the entire wealth of an average hoplite.

Top 10 Trierarch-Oligarchs. These individuals are a sample of the very
richest people living in Athens.[21] The average value of their fortunes was a
staggering 486,300 drachmae, or about $31.1 million. The largest and smallest
of the ten were 1,800,000 and 84,000 drachmae, or $115 million and $5.4
million, respectively. "Although fortunes such as these were quite exceptional,"
Jones (1955, 149) observed, "it does nevertheless seem to have been true that
there was a heavy concentration of wealth at the extreme top of Athenian

[19] This figure is reached by taking the wealth of the entire trierarchy (21,600,000) and subtracting
the wealth of the top ten oligarchs and the lower 900. This leaves 5,937,000 drachmae divided
among the 290.

[20] Jones (1955, 147–8) admits that the wealth of these richest oligarchs is "likely to be an underes-
timate" because when tax-based records are used "it was the exception rather than the rule that
an Athenian taxpayer declared the whole of his property. Land and houses were however difficult to conceal, and these were probably the main items. Slaves might be underestimated both in
numbers and value. Cash and loans could be concealed altogether. But there were sycophants,
and one of the reasons for the reign of terror which they are alleged to have exercised over
the wealthy may well have been that most wealthy men knew that their *eisphora* assessments
would not bear investigation."

[21] The list, which includes a few *metics*, was compiled from Jones (1955, 1958), de Ste. Croix
(1989), and Low (2008). When ancient sources mention two estimates of total wealth for
an individual, the lower figure is used (but the higher figure is included here in brackets).
Total wealth is reported in drachmae. These oligarchs lived over a period of almost two centuries. This creates a danger of overstating wealth at the top if they are listed as if they were
contemporaries. For instance, a distorted picture of the wealth concentrated in the hands of
the wealthiest U.S. oligarchs would result if the fortunes of Buffett, Gates, and Walton were
listed as existing alongside those of Rockefeller, Ford, Carnegie, and Getty. To compensate
for this problem, the first eight names are treated as contemporaries and their full fortunes
are counted. The next two names lived in different generations, and so their fortunes are discounted by 50 percent. The last name cited, Pasion, is listed for reference but his fortune is
not counted at all because he lived in an era too distant in time from the others. All estimates are from Jones (1955) unless otherwise noted. The ten representative oligarchs used
for the first entry in Table 3.1 are: 1. Epicrates 1,800,000 [3,600,000]; 2. Nicias 600,000;
3. Oionias 489,000 (Low 2008, 26); 4. Euthycrates 360,000 (Jones 1958, 60); 5. Conon
240,000; 6. Ischomachus 120,000 [420,000]; 7. Demosthenes 90,000; 8. Lysias 84,000
[600,000]; 9. Hipponicus 1,200,000 discounted to 600,000 (de Ste. Croix 1989, 118);
10. Diphilus 960,000 discounted to 480,000; 11. Pasion 480,000 (not counted).

society, in a small group of approximately 300 families." Because the sources mention them explicitly, scholars know these oligarchs by name, but they should be viewed as representative of oligarchic wealth at the very top and not as an ancient *Forbes* list. Jones (1958, 57) writes that 15 talents, or 90,000 drachmae, is the threshold Demosthenes said would "qualify a man to be called really rich." All but one of the ten meet that threshold.

Material Power Index. Based on these estimates of wealth across Athenian society, it is possible to discuss the concentration of wealth and power in greater depth. The last column of Table 3.1 presents the MPI that describes the intensity of wealth-power at each level of the social formation. The basic unit for calculating the MPI is the average material position of the mass of slaves at the bottom. Thus the last column is equal to the average wealth figures in column two divided by that of an average slave, 200 drachmae, who forms a base point with an MPI of 1.0. Using slaves rather than citizens as a basis for comparison is not the norm in analyses of the Athenian social formation. Citizens or not, however, they were the average or typical member of the Athenian society and economy. Slaves are central to any meaningful political-economic discussion of Athens, and setting them aside because they were debased as property and limiting the discussion only to citizens would be grotesque.[22] Thus, the MPI provides an indicator of wealth for each stratum of the social formation as a multiple of the most numerous median member, the slave.

Two aspects of the MPI figures stand out. The first is a rough multiplier pattern of 4 or 5 across the major social strata. Thetes with an MPI of 5 were roughly five times better off than the mass of slaves below them. With an MPI of 21, upper hoplites were roughly four times wealthier than the average thete. And the majority, the Three Hundred, with an MPI of 102 was about five times as wealthy as an upper hoplite. This is a relatively flat, open-umbrella pattern of stratification, and it helps account for many aspects of Athenian society – including the fact that most hoplites could afford to own a few slaves, and also why members of the Three Hundred rarely had more than a dozen slaves each (a modest complement of human property by Roman standards).

The second aspect is the intensity of wealth concentration at the very apex of the society. With an MPI of 2,432, the top ten oligarchs were not only thousands of times more wealthy than the average person at the base of the community, but almost twenty-five times the average member of the lower 290 of the Three Hundred. This spire atop the socioeconomic canopy of Athens probably extended downward to include the top fifty families as well. Their substantial wealth, and that of the Three Hundred and the remaining 900 of the trierarchy, gave the oligarchs of Athens the resources and power needed to dominate the country's affairs by populating all the top offices of their ruling oligarchy.

---

[22] A disturbing number of books and articles on Classical Athens focus almost exclusively on free citizens and mention slaves only in passing.

Davies (1971) describes as "property-power" the influence these oligarchs exerted on public affairs in Athens through the use of their personal wealth. He combed through the available records to compile a list of the richest and most powerful individuals and families. For the period spanning 600 to 300 B.C.E., Davies identifies "779 recognizably distinct Athenians may be identified as the wealthy, representatives of those families who owned large-scale property and thus possessed property-power in Athens. Many were important generals and politicians but many others remained *privati*, political nonentities" (Lenardon 1974, 380). And some, like Lysias and his brother Polemarchus, were even foreigners (*metics*).[23] This confirms that from the perspective of Athenian oligarchs, the rulers must all be wealthy, but there is no pressing need in a collective ruling oligarchy for all the wealthy to rule. A few were sufficient to safeguard the core wealth defense interests of the entire stratum.

That the social formation was stratified is not in serious dispute. There was an extremely small number of individuals who personally funded the apparatus of the *polis*, took turns outfitting the impressive Athenian naval forces, and subsidized the naval rowers with daily allowances together with the otherwise self-financed hoplite infantry. There was a sharp sense of rich and poor in society and clear hierarchies of prestige and privilege – all of which had wealth at its foundation.[24] However, it must also be said that the pattern of wealth concentration, even with the extreme position of the oligarchs toward the top of the Three Hundred, was very flat by Roman and modern capitalist standards. Jones's (1955, 150) observation that "even the richest Athenians were relatively modest men" is well supported by the evidence. "This social structure," writes Anderson (1974a, 38), "with its acknowledged stratification but absence of dramatic crevasses within the citizen body, provided the foundation of Athenian political democracy."[25] The small and medium farmers demanded and received a voice in the system because they met and maintained a certain minimum wealth threshold that, in turn, permitted them to play a vital role in the defense of the *polis*. Had there been a more fierce inequality of condition, it is far less likely that oligarchy and democracy could have achieved this remarkable fusion in Athens.

---

[23] The two brothers "may have been among the richest men in late-fifth-century Athens, and in 404 they are certainly said to have owned the largest number of slaves which can be reliably credited to any Greek of the Classical period, but in Athens they were *metics* (resident foreigners) and enjoyed no political rights" (de Ste. Croix 1989, 92).

[24] de Ste. Croix (1989, 115) points out that although thetes and hoplites were acknowledged as citizens, they still had to work part of the year to live, and therefore rich oligarchs looked down on them. Prestige attached to those who had enough property that they never worked at all, and thus could "live the good life, as the Greeks saw it, a life not constrained by the inescapable necessity of working for one's living, a life which could be devoted to the pursuits considered proper for a gentleman: politics or generalship, intellectual or artistic pursuits, hunting or athletics."

[25] This pattern was not limited to Athens. According to Anderson (1974a, 58): "Even the most oligarchic Greek *polis* of the classical epoch basically rested on a median body of propertied citizens, and precluded extreme economic disparities of wealth and poverty."

Threats to Oligarchs. Given this social structure and the arrangements of collective rule among the oligarchs of Athens, what were the threats they faced in defending their wealth? To answer this, it is necessary to provide a clearer sense of what the *polis* was like as a political system. To call it a state would be a gross distortion. There was no standing army, virtually no bureaucracy, and not even a regular police force. Borrowing from Aristotle, Berent (2000, 266) refers to Athens as "an association or partnership." This is an apt description of what results when a group of wealthy and powerful oligarchs form a relatively rudimentary cooperative system of rule and defense, augmented and strengthened by incorporating a significant stratum of medium and smaller propertied males. As benign as the label "association" sounds, there was great violence and conflict coursing through the veins of the system at all times. Berent (2000, 266) stresses that it "does not mean, of course, that the *polis*'s economy was not based also upon the appropriation of surplus production of the slaves (or the 'poor' in general), but that exploitation and slavery could exist in stateless conditions."

With no state or sultanistic ruler above them, the potential threats to the ruling oligarchs of Athens could only come from other oligarchs or from those lower down in society. The lateral threats could assume three forms – attacks from within the Athenian oligarchy by an individual or cabal; collective attacks from external oligarchies in Greece or nearby Persia; or some potent combination of these two. The structure of collective rule in the *polis* was an effective instrument for confronting the first and second, and less able to defend against the third. Starting with the purely internal threat, the partial disarmament among the ruling oligarchs so reduced the capacity of individuals or small groups to threaten the whole that there are almost no examples of it being seriously attempted. In addition, by allowing a middle class of propertied small farmers to serve as the bulk of the armed forces, individual oligarchs were robbed of the opportunity to turn mercenary forces ostensibly hired to defend Athens against the ruling oligarchy at the helm.[26]

External threats were a different matter. Anderson (1974a, 37) writes that the Greek cities were engaged in a "constant rivalry and aggression against each other." These attacks are an analog to the lateral predations for conquest conducted by warring oligarchs, only now they are conducted in a collective form. Property defense for any individual Athenian oligarch depended entirely on arrangements for territorial defense by the group. To meet the lateral danger from outside, reductions in individual coercive capabilities at home were converted into conjoined capacities to project tremendous violence outward.

---

[26] In *Politics*, Aristotle (V vi 1306ª20–36) warns that when one oligarch commands mercenary forces, "he frequently becomes a tyrant," and when several oligarchs are in command, "they make themselves a governing clique." These dangers favor raising forces from within in exchange for political participation. "Fear of such consequences," Aristotle reasons, "sometimes forces an oligarchy to employ a popular force, and thus to give the masses some share in constitutional rights."

This cooperative coercion was explicitly for external use, raised only as needed, and micromanaged by the ruling oligarchy. Moreover, a significant share of each oligarch's fortune was allocated to the creation and maintenance of these defense forces, and they benefited the most materially when, as the aggressors, they seized or subjected to tribute the lands of vulnerable neighboring oligarchies.

The third threat – domestic oligarchic *putsches* assisted by external oligarchs – posed the greatest danger of all. *Stasis* is the Greek word for sedition. *Stasis* on the part of the poor or slaves was widespread in Athens before and after the democratic centuries, but not during them (although they continued in an unbroken pattern elsewhere in Greece).[27] Instead, the key source of *stasis* during the fifth and fourth centuries was actually from within the oligarchy. Lewis (1980, 78) notes that "*staseis* were mainly within the upper classes" and the ambitions and confidence of predatory oligarchs was "conditioned by their foreign associates." The coup of 411 B.C.E. was spawned with expectations of support from Persia in the Peloponnesian War, and later included an olive branch extended to the brutish oligarchs of Sparta, their opponent in the war.[28] The takeover in 404 B.C.E. by the "Thirty Tyrants" would have been impossible without the helpful intervention by the oligarchs of Sparta. The final collapse of democratic forces in 322 B.C.E. occurred when Macedonian forces under Antipater sided with a reactionary element among the ruling oligarchs of Athens, who went on to grab land and enrich themselves throughout the Hellenic era.[29]

The threats oligarchs faced from poorer members of the community below them were potentially severe. The rich landlords at the top enjoyed a life of extreme and satisfying comfort compared to the wretched and often brutal conditions endured by the slaves, who generated the surpluses from the mines and on the land. The fine lifestyle of the one was the obverse of the degraded lifestyle of the other. In the middle were the thetes and hoplites, many of whom were armed and at least potentially dangerous. The posture and behavior of these middle strata were crucial both to the wealth defense strategies of the oligarchs and to the successful suppression of the mass of slaves. To understand

[27] The oligarchs of Athens fared far better than their brethren in the area of Arcadia, where, "during a period of *stasis* in 363," Allen (1997, 122) reports, "most of the aristocrats from all the region's cities were thrown into prison in the city of Tegea. The prison was soon full and the public hall had to be used."

[28] Taylor (2002, 91) argues that the assembly was not as resistant to a takeover by the Four Hundred as some readings of Thucydides have claimed. "Although terror, violence, and propaganda have their place in Thucydides' account," she writes, "modern treatments overemphasize them and so ignore or gloss over Thucydides' charge that the Athenian people did not resist oligarchy very strenuously and so bear a large share of responsibility for it." Athenian democracy, she concludes, "was not very hard to end."

[29] Individual oligarchs in Athens could also count on fellow oligarchs in other parts of Greece to provide safe havens when they had to flee into exile after a failed attack on the ruling oligarchy. Whibley (1896, 130) mentions the example of Corcyra in the 430s B.C.E., and the "support given by the rulers to the oligarchic exiles of Epidamnus."

the inner mechanisms of wealth and property defense in Classical Athens, it is important to grasp that the most salient divide was not between oligarchs and non-oligarchs, but rather between the free and unfree. According to Anderson (1974a, 37), "the essential line of demarcation" did not pass through the citizenry, however great its internal stratification. It was always between the slaves and everyone else. "The community of the classical *polis*, no matter how internally class divided," he writes, "was erected above an enslaved workforce which underlay its whole shape and substance."

In most contemporary city-states in the region, there was almost "continuous class war" Jones (1955, 153) writes, and "counterrevolution alternated with revolution." By comparison, Athens was a pond of tranquility. "There was at all times, a small group of wealthy intellectuals who hated the democracy," Jones continues, "but in normal circumstances they found no support among the middle class of hoplites, or even in the upper trierarchic class." The picture that emerges is one of an intensely conservative middle group of citizens who showed little interest in agitating against the oligarchs in general – although they did use their arms to fight when a reactionary segment within the ruling oligarchy attempted to transform Athens from being an arrangement of "oligarchs-plus" to one of "oligarchs-only."

From the perspective of the ruling oligarchs, the thetes and hoplites were strategic allies rather than dangerous democrats. Despite the unusually radical participation afforded to poorer citizens in the assembly, they never used democracy to encroach on the property and wealth of the Three Hundred. "No suggestion was ever put forward for the redistribution of the land or for the cancellation of debts, which more revolutionary democracies conducted," Jones (1955, 153) notes. "This is readily understandable in a society where property, and particularly land, was so widely distributed." Nor did the hoplite and thete majorities push for freeing the slaves, which is understandable given how many hoplites were slave owners themselves. The assembly made exceptions on the slave question only in times of extreme national emergency, when additional bodies were needed in the navy to fill shortages of thete rowers.[30]

Democracy in the *polis* posed no dangers to either the separate or the collective interests of the ruling oligarchs. Indeed, their concentrated fortunes were likely more secure with hoplite and thete participation than without it. Within the assembly, from the highest trierarch to the lowest thete, a "respect for the rights of property prevailed" (Jones 1955, 153). The most astonishing example of this commitment to the status quo distribution of property was evident in 404 B.C.E. after the hoplites helped defeat the Thirty Tyrants in a brief civil war. "Not even now," Jones (1955, 154) admits, "were there reprisals or confiscations." The enjoyment of even modest property amid propertylessness and the taste of freedom amid slavery permanently tamed the lower elements of the citizenry. In the highly unlikely event the hoplites and thetes were tempted

---

[30] "To help man the fleet which won the battle of Arginusae," Jones (1955, 153) writes, "all slaves of military age were called up with the promise (which was honoured) of freedom."

to turn their weapons and overwhelming numbers as voters against the partially disarmed few above them, the oligarchs of Athens could, as a last resort,
threaten to call for assistance from neighboring oligarchies, especially at Sparta.
"This ever-present threat," Lyttkens (1994, 67) writes, "greatly enhanced the
coercive bargaining power of the rich stratum."

With a profound bias in favor of property defense among all citizens, this left
only the dangers posed by slaves. It is in the utter domination and exploitation
of slaves that the merely partial nature of oligarchic disarmament is revealed.
For although Athenian oligarchs suppressed their own individual capacities
for coercion in favor of a lateral-collective force that was quasi-public and
directed outward from the *polis*, they retained and cultivated crucial private
coercive capacities that they deployed constantly to defend their wealth and
property in the form of the slaves they owned, the surplus from their labor, and
the suppression of revolts that could, if large enough, upset the entire social
order. Berent (2000, 266) reports that "internal coercion was not organized
or professional," but was instead carried out by individuals. In the case of
serious offenders in the city, the common practice was for citizens to gang
up and make arrests. They would then hand over the accused to the Eleven –
enforcers who were chosen by lot each year – who would imprison the person
to await trial, and then impose whatever punishments were decided, including
executions.

Oligarchs and Coercion. The absence of regular police meant that being one
of the few martial and armed actors in Athens was a key source of power and
security. As Berent (2000, 261) argues, "the absence of public coercive apparatuses meant that the ability to apply physical threat was evenly distributed
among armed or potentially armed members of the community, that is, the
citizen-body." Thetes and hoplites mainly faced petty crimes of person and
property. It was the oligarchs who had larger fortunes and owned the bulk of
the slaves in society. With almost no involvement or intervention by the official
institutions of the *polis*, oligarchs unleashed a torrent of violence on slaves to
keep them under firm control.

Fisher (1996, 219) notes that "whipping was certainly systemic," while Allen
(1997, 122) mentions that "the Athenians commonly punished their slaves by
binding them with fetters," sometimes for such extended periods that it was
difficult for them to walk upright. Her description of the private imprisonment
of slaves underscores the fact that ruling oligarchs who suppressed the use
of force among themselves nevertheless retained major individual elements
of coercion and enforcement to use against non-oligarchs. Allen (1997, 123)
writes: "In the extant sources, we hear of slaves as punished with imprisonment
in a millhouse, which susceptibility to corporal punishment marked slaves as
such. Only slaves, according to Demosthenes, are responsible in person for their
offences; freemen can protect their persons even in the worst cases, for in most
cases, the law punishes with fines." Public jails existed mainly to hold prisoners
while their cases were in motion, and at most to detain an individual until a
fine was paid. However, Allen demonstrates that in the private realm of the

free and propertied oligarchic estate in the countryside, punitive imprisonment for the unfree was commonplace.[31]

The divide between the free and unfree was also evident in Athenian laws that permitted "judicial torture" – the practice of getting to the bottom of a dispute or crime involving propertied citizens by torturing their slaves into providing pertinent information only they would know. Available sources confirm the law existed but make no mention of its actual use. Yet strangely, even this action was to be carried out privately by the slave-owning citizens themselves rather than by a third party or someone in an official capacity. According to Todd (1995, 90), the torturing of slaves is indicative of "informal domestic punishments and of the general exemption of citizens from such treatment." Regarding the whipping and beating of slaves, Todd makes clear that although they were acts of coercion and enforcement carried out by the rich in a private capacity, it was done in the open so that there was a "public context of such humiliation, as a statement directed not just at the offender but to be read by everybody" – slaves and free-poor Athenians alike.

Berent also highlights the direct and private nature of coercion and enforcement by landowning masters. He emphasizes that in accordance with the majority of slaves being privately rather than publicly owned, the control of slaves was also predominantly private. Oligarchs could count on not only fellow oligarchs, but even hoplites and thetes, to rush to their rescue in situations where matters escalated beyond whipping, binding, and imprisonment in private oligarchic jails. Berent (2000, 264) writes: "In an illuminating passage in the *Republic* Socrates equates the slave-owner with the tyrant. It is the business of the slave-owner to control the slaves. But why is it that 'Such slave-owners . . . don't live in fear of their slaves.'" The answer is that "the entire *polis* would run to help him." Socrates underscores the point with a hypothetical situation:

> But imagine now that some god were to take a single man who owned fifty or more slaves and were to transport him and his wife and children, his goods and chattels and his slaves, to some desert place where there would be no other free man to help him; wouldn't he be in great fear that he and his wife and children would be done away with by the slaves?[32]

---

[31] Allen (1997, 123) draws this conclusion: "The hindrance, then, to the development of a community use of imprisonment was not a lack of a conception of punitive imprisonment, but rather, in addition to the difficulty of transferring the role of imprisoner from individual to community, a need to distinguish between slaves and citizens." On punishment in Athens see Allen (2000).

[32] Berent (2000, 265) amplifies the point: "In Xenophon's phrase in a similar passage, all the slave-owners in the community act together as 'unpaid bodyguard.' The absence of any ready militia to crush slave revolts is complementary to the fact that 'slaves never represented a cohesive group either in their masters' or their own mind so for all their exploited situation they did not engage (for the most part) in social conflict', and that we do not know of any slave revolts in ancient Greece, again with the conspicuous exception of Sparta."

To this arsenal of methods and techniques for subjugation was added a conscious strategy of divide and conquer. The Athenians deliberately mixed slaves
of different races and origins to render them less capable of forming threatening
alliances. Or as Berent (2000, 265) puts it, "disorientation and deracination
were important tools for the control of the slaves."[33]

Wealth defense in the Athenian *polis* was carried out jointly by ruling oligarchs, a stratum of actors at the top of the social formation whose wealth
and power was thousands of times greater than that of the median member
of the community. The partial disarmament of these oligarchs facilitated their
collective rule and enabled them to manage both internal and external threats
to their landed wealth. However, they remained partially armed for the crucial task of defending their wealth individually through the violent subjugation
of slaves who produced the social surplus that was the bedrock of oligarchic
fortunes in ancient Athens.

Rome

Compared to Athens, Rome was massive, more stratified, more violent, possessed more developed institutions, and was less democratic. Particularly during
the Empire phase, Rome controlled much more territory, many more people,
and relied more extensively on slaves for the production of a surplus. As in
Athens, the basis of Roman wealth was property in land. Yet unlike in the
polis, the land of the Roman oligarchs was concentrated into *latifundia* on an
immense scale. By the second century B.C.E., Rome no longer had a middle
stratum comparable to the thetes and hoplites in Athens, nor any self-financed
army of citizen-soldiers. The legions were funded mainly from the treasury of
Rome and from wealthy commanders who were themselves members of the
ruling oligarchy. At the top of the system were the rich and the ultra-rich. From
there the drop-off was steep for the tens of millions of poor and landless below.

The sources of tension and conflict in Rome were greatly amplified by these
extremes, and the ruling oligarchs lived a much more tumultuous existence
with each passing century of the Republic. The sheer power of Rome meant
that collective-lateral threats from neighboring or distant ruling oligarchs were
rarely a significant concern (except in the limited sense of keeping conquered
lands conquered or repelling invaders at the periphery).[34] Rome faced no external dangers comparable to those posed to Athens by Sparta or Persia. Instead,
the greatest threats faced by Rome's ruling oligarchs were internal – from each
other, despite efforts to neutralize lateral dangers, and from below.

---

[33] Berent (2000, 265) goes on to quote this famous passage in *Politics* where Aristotle explains
how best to defeat slaves on oligarchic lands: "The class which farms it should ideally, and if
we can choose at will, be slaves – but slaves not drawn from a single stock, or from stocks of a
spirited temper. This will at once secure the advantage of a good supply of labour and eliminate
any danger of revolutionary designs."

[34] From 367 to 133 B.C.E., the territory of the Roman Republic expanded from 115 to 31,200
square miles (Stephenson 1891, 32).

As in Athens, partial disarmament was a crucial element making a ruling oligarchy a feasible mode of joint domination and property defense. However, the more developed nature of Roman governing institutions, especially the increasingly public provision of legions after the Marian reforms of 104 B.C.E., created a coercive apparatus that could be turned against the ruling oligarchs of Rome if commanded by rich and politically ambitious oligarchs who supplemented out of their own riches the wages of the nonlanded soldiers and promised them free property as veterans. The ruling oligarchs' only hope for defense was a split among the commanders of the legions such that one or two equally powerful generals sided with the status quo rulers in the capital. It was during the late Roman Republic, and especially from 100 B.C.E. forward, that this fatal flaw in the collective defenses of Rome's ruling oligarchy was played out in a dramatic and violent fashion. After a series of famous marches of Roman legions on Rome itself – by Sulla, Pompey, and Julius Caesar – the Republic eventually collapsed under the strain. In the process, the ruling oligarchy was replaced by a more sultanistic form.

Material Power Index. Before analyzing the nature of Rome's ruling oligarchy, it would be useful to estimate the material position and power of the oligarchs, both compared to an average Roman and compared to the pattern evident in Athens. Table 3.2 presents the material stratification of Rome during the era stretching loosely from the first century B.C.E. until the middle of the first century C.E.

Each individual in the first column is assumed to have a family of four.[35] This means that the entire population represented in the table is more than 55 million people,[36] with the city of Rome itself having a population of slightly more than

---

[35] Data for Table 3.2 are drawn from Goldsmith (1984) and Milanovic et al. (2007, hereafter Milanovic). Goldsmith presents information on wealth and income estimates while Milanovic attempts to show all data as income. Income alone presents an incomplete picture of oligarchic power. Particularly when influence over legions became a major arbiter of intra-oligarchic competition, many oligarchic generals used promised distributions of personal fortunes in land to soldiers and veterans as a means of maintaining troop loyalty. Income indicators would only capture allowances these oligarchs could pay to the legions from their own funds.

[36] The upper part of Table 3.2 shows the average property wealth for the various landed strata of senators and equites (knights). By the middle of the first century B.C.E., land ownership outside these roughly 400,000 citizens was minimal. The bottom part of the table refers to landless members of the social formation. Because they lacked property and wealth, their estimated annual incomes are used as a proxy for their average material condition. The assumptions and choices made in estimating these incomes are explained in Milanovic (2007, 54–69). The category "Soldiers and Workers" in Table 3.2 is a weighted average of the following Milanovic categories in their table "Roman Empire 14," p. 64: "Tradesmen and service workers"; "Workers at average wage"; and "Ordinary soldiers." Similarly, the category in Table 3.2 labeled "Officers and Praetorians" is a weighted average of the following Milanovic categories: "Praetorians"; "Centurions"; and "Legion commanders." The basic annual income for slaves and farm labor is rounded for simplicity from Milanovic's 234 to 250 sesterces. The Milanovic table also includes a catch-all category of some 200,000 "other rich people" that is underspecified and is not grounded in estimates available in Goldsmith (1984). This category is not included in Table 3.2.

TABLE 3.2. *Wealth and Material Power in Ancient Rome*

	Number of People	Average Wealth (sesterces)	% Share Citizen Property	% Share Population	Material Power Index
LANDED					
Top Ten	10	100,000,000	1.06	.00007	400,000
Other Senators	590	2,500,000	1.56	.00426	10,000
Equites – Knights	40,000	500,000	21.17	.289	2,000
Municipal Senators	360,000	200,000	76.21	2.60	800
LANDLESS					
Officers and Praetorians	9,300	3,700	0	.07	16
Soldiers and Workers	1,450,000	800	0	10.5	3
Slaves and Farm Labor	12,000,000	250	0	86.6	1

one million. The number of citizens, between five and six million, averaged around 10 percent of the overall population of the empire. The Roman empire at its peak was more than 150 times the scale of the Athenian population at its largest, and the gap between the wealthiest Roman oligarchs and the median member of the society (as reflected in the MPI) was also more than 150 times larger than the same gap in Athens. It is readily apparent that the fortunes concentrated into the hands of the ruling oligarchs at the very top of the Roman empire were many magnitudes larger than those seen in Athens.

Slaves and farm labor made up the bottom of the Roman social formation. There were more than eight million slaves. This is about 15 percent of the population – with the concentration being higher in the Italian provinces than in the other territories (Goldsmith 1984, 271, n39). For purposes of assessing material conditions across the social formation, slaves are not treated separately from the poorest stratum of farm laborers because their juridical status as unfree people did not distinguish them substantially from impoverished free Romans who also had no significant voice in politics. Laws of manumission combined with debt slavery also meant there was a constant shifting of status across the poor-free and poor-slave divide. The late Roman Republic had at its base a vast mass of people living barely above subsistence levels. A small segment was urban while the great majority was in the countryside on the land. With their families, these individuals comprised about 87 percent of the population and collectively owned virtually nothing. Their median annual income was 250 sesterces, or roughly $5,500.[37] For purposes of calculating an MPI, these median inhabitants of the Roman empire have an index of 1.0. They provide the benchmark against which concentrations of wealth and power upward through the remainder of society can be understood.

As in Athens, Rome once had a law requiring soldiers to meet a minimum property threshold and be partly self-financed and self-armed. However, as they were killed in battle or went bankrupt, the soldiers and their families lost their small and medium property to oligarchs who bottom-fed on the soldiers' distress. Thus by the late second and early first century B.C.E., Rome's once independent soldiers joined workers, tradesmen, and praetorians in the ranks of the empire's landless. Some of the officers, including centurions and even legion commanders, were paid generous salaries, but they did not have enough wealth to reach basic land thresholds to join the rich echelons above them and contend for political positions. In all, the landless or near-landless, members of the Roman social formation – both free and enslaved – accounted for fully

---

[37] It is no easier to convert Roman sesterces to modern dollars than drachmae. The admittedly imperfect method used here compares ordinary Roman legion soldiers and enlisted soldiers in the United States. Milanovic (2007, 64) estimates the annual income of an average Roman soldier as 1,010 sesterces. An enlisted E-3 American army soldier with 5 years of experience earned a base pay of $22,300 before taxes in 2009 (U.S. Department of Defense 2009). This yields a rough conversion rate of 1 sestertius = $22, and 1 denarius = $88. Using the purchasing power of bread in 2005 produces a similar conversion of 1 sestertius = $21. For useful comparisons see MacKenzie (1983, 268).

97 percent of the population. Across that broad swath of society, there was a fairly high degree of material compression. The officers and praetorians, admittedly a small group comprising less than a tenth of a percent of the Roman empire, were just sixteen times richer than a common slave or farm laborer. This is roughly comparable to the gap separating the average hoplite from a slave in Athens.

It is in the leap from the propertyless to the propertied in Rome that the indicators of material concentration rise exponentially. Table 3.2 shows that the landed citizens of the Roman empire, although greater in number than the entire Athenian social formation including slaves, constituted a mere 3 percent of the population. The landowning class in Athens was nearly four times broader than in Rome as a proportion of the population. By far the largest element was municipal senators. There were about 120 in each of the 3,000 Roman cities scattered across the empire. The property qualification to be a municipal senator was 100,000 sesterces, or slightly more than $2 million. Most had a net worth of more than twice that amount. They constituted 90 percent of all property owners and owned more than three-quarters of all property. They were significant players in their respective cities, but they were distributed across the territory and lacked the resources as individuals to determine major policies or change the course of the empire. With an MPI of 800, they were, in relative terms, more materially endowed than all but a handful of oligarchs in Athens. However, in Rome, they had above them thousands of actors with far larger resources at their disposal, and who faced greater and more violent threats to their wealth and property.

The real power in Rome was located beginning at the next stratum up – among the equestrian order – the knights. Far fewer in number than the municipal senators, the wealth of the equites was significantly more concentrated. The property threshold for being a knight was 250,000 sesterces (probably more than $5 million), and many had fortunes far larger. On average their net worth in property was 2.5 times that of the urban senators scattered across the empire, although still only a fifth of the average wealth of the 600 senators congregated densely in the Roman capital. Many of the richer equites surpassed some of the more modest senatorial fortunes. A struggle lasting nearly two centuries between senators and equites unfolded early in the Roman Republic as the senators sought to keep the equites from rising in status and gaining access to offices and the incomes flowing from them. By the middle and late Republic, most status distinctions had disappeared, and the term equites "merely denoted all nonsenatorial rich men" (Beesly 1877, 15). It is unlikely that the ruling oligarchy of Rome included all 40,000 equites, but it certainly included the wealthiest among them. Although these knights were less than a third of a percent of the Roman population, they made up 10 percent of those owning land and owned 20 percent of all the property already concentrated in the hands of the few.

The concentration of wealth among the ultra-rich in Rome was extreme. The average net worth of a senator in Athens was perhaps $2.3 million in 2009 terms. In Rome the average was 2,500,000 sesterces, or more than $55 million – a figure substantially higher than the average fortune of even the richest ten senators of the Athenian *polis*. An average Roman senator could count on his property generating an income of 150,000 sesterces per year or $3.3 million (Milanovic 2007, 64). The MPI for a typical Roman senator was 10,000 times that of a common slave, or a hundred times the material gap separating an Athenian senator from the median member of the *polis*. Although only a tiny fraction of the Roman population, all senators combined owned nearly 3 percent of the society's property.

To complete the picture of wealth concentration in the late Republic and early Roman Empire, it is necessary to evaluate the scale of the material power resources owned, controlled, and deployed by the very richest citizens. As in Athens, the leading Roman names and their fortunes should be viewed as indicative of wealth concentration at the apex of the empire rather than as a definitive list of the richest oligarchs. However imprecise the data, it is a certainty based on various writings and archaeological evidence that Rome consistently had a few dozen oligarchs at the top whose fortunes dwarfed even the substantial riches of the average senator. The Younger Pliny, who constantly reminded everyone that his riches were modest for a Roman senator, had 100 slaves and property in land worth around 15 million sesterces, or about $330 million. At the other extreme, the highest recorded fortunes of 400 million sesterces ($8.8 billion) were held by Senator Gnaeus Cornelius Lentulus and Narcissus, a freedman (Alföldy 1988, 107; Davis 1910, 69; MacKenzie 1983, 270).

There are no reliable estimates of the staggering personal wealth of Julius Caesar. After he returned from his victorious campaign in Gaul, the estimated value of the spoils he presented during his triumph at Rome ranged from 600 to 1,750 million sesterces, or $13.2 to $38.5 billion (Jaczynowska 1962, 491; Davis 1910, 70). So great was Caesar's loot that he flooded the gold market and depressed the metal's value by 25 percent. Setting aside the case of Caesar, it is possible to estimate a very conservative average for the top ruling oligarchs of Rome of around 100 million sesterces, or $2.2 billion each.[38] This made them 40 times more materially endowed than the average senator, 200 times more than the typical knight, 500 times the resources of a millionaire municipal

---

[38] In addition to Lentulus, Narcissus, and the Younger Pliny, this estimated average includes the fortunes (in millions of sesterces and billions of dollars) of Seneca (300, $6.6), Pallas (300, $6.6), Augustius (250, $5.5), Marcus Licinius Crassus (200, $4.4), Demetrius (100, $2.2), Tarius Rufus Augustus (100, $2.2), and Gaius Caecilius Isidorus (60, $1.3). The Elder Pliny mentions Isidorus's will as including an estate of 4,000 slaves, 7,200 oxen, over a quarter million head of other cattle. And this was after "he had lost much in the civil wars" (MacKenzie 1983, 271). The average figure of 100 million sesterces also includes a consideration of the fortunes of Marius, Sulla, L. Licinius Lucullus, Augustus, Tiberius, and Pompey. In his triumph after campaigns in the East, Pompey was able to offer the Roman treasury 200 million sesterces, or $4.4 billion (Jaczynowska 1962, 491). Sources for estimates of Rome's wealthiest oligarchs include Alföldy (1988), MacKenzie (1983), Davis (1910), and de Ste. Croix (1989).

senator, and a staggering 400,000 times the material endowment of the median member of the Roman empire at the bottom. These extreme concentrations of material resources conferred immense and quite flexible political power on those in a position to deploy it. However, the riches also attracted threats and attacks to which oligarchs responded with strategies for wealth defense.

Threats to Oligarchs. The net political effect of the propertied and conservative hoplite and thete small farmers in Athens was to dampen conflicts within the social formation. The ever-present threats from slaves were managed with a combination of personal violence and policing by oligarchs, and a system of controls and lateral assistance among landed citizens, both great and small. In Rome there was no moderating stratum and nothing remotely close to the democratic participation they won in the *polis*. The ruling oligarchs in Rome had an "unchallenged authority going far beyond anything we know of in Athens and including a virtually complete monopoly of all forms of political initiative," North (1990, 284) argues. "If there was such a thing as Roman democracy," he continues, "it was nonparticipatory to an extreme degree and therefore in many ways at the opposite pole to the Athenian democracy."[39] Unmediated by a middle class owning modest but secure plots of land, Rome and its ruling oligarchs relied more heavily on collective coercion when major slave revolts occurred and private means of control and enforcement on their landed estates during ordinary times. The best estimates suggest that slavery was particularly intense and brutal in Rome. Even if slaves owned by oligarchs on their country estates are excluded, Rome's 600 senators owned around 250,000 household slaves *in the capital alone* – an average of 400 slaves per household.[40]

Confronting the danger posed by Rome's tens of millions of slaves, farm laborers, and urban underemployed was a major wealth defense problem for the ruling oligarchs. Neither their vast landed estates nor the stream of income the land produced could be defended if direct producers were not suppressed and disciplined. As in Athens, partial disarmament meant that although Rome's ruling oligarchs accepted arrangements that diminished their capacity to exert violence against each other and pooled their resources for the collective coercion manifested in the legions, they nevertheless maintained a direct role in the coercion and enforcement required to secure their personal property, including chattel slaves.

[39] Runciman (1983, 177) concurs, arguing that Rome "was neither politically nor socially democratic under the Republic any more than under the Principate. The Republic, it is true, was governed by elected magistrates, and it was on the overthrow of the monarchy preceding it that its ideology of *libertas* was based. But this liberty extended only to a tiny elite, themselves voted into office by a minority of a minority: of the male citizens eligible, not more than a small fraction could physically appear at elections to cast their ballots and then only under a system heavily weighted and easy to manipulate."

[40] Scheidel (2005, 67) notes that Pedanius had "400 household slaves" and concurs that "the average senator could easily have owned hundreds of slaves, and the average knight, dozens."

Oligarchs and Coercion. A famous Roman proverb warns, "So many slaves, so many foes."[41] However stable and enduring a system of slavery may appear, it always involves the forced labor of socially imprisoned persons. Coercion and violence, or the certain threat of them, lie at its foundations. Harris (1980, 118) estimates that Rome had to capture, purchase, or find almost half a million new slaves each year just to maintain their numbers.[42] Roman slavery represented "the most radical rural degradation of labour imaginable," writes Anderson (1974a, 24–5). It was nothing less than "the conversion of men themselves into inert means of production by their deprivation of every social right and their legal assimilation to beasts of burden: in Roman theory, the agricultural slave was designated an *instrumentum vocale*, the speaking tool, one grade away from the livestock that constituted an *instrumentum semi-vocale*, and two from the implement which was an *instrumentum mutum*."

The exploitation of slaves was relentless. "On principle no freedom of movement whatever was allowed to them – a slave, so runs one of Cato's maxims, must either work or sleep," Mommsen (2006 [1855]) writes. "And no attempt was ever made to attach the slaves to the estate or to their master by any bond of human sympathy." He continues, "the letter of the law in all its naked hideousness regulated the relation, and the Romans indulged no illusions as to the consequences." Slaves, if not psychologically and physically defeated, could pose a serious threat to the persons and property of Rome's ruling oligarchs. Like their Athenian counterparts, they took to heart Aristotle's advice about keeping slaves divided against each other. "It was an economic maxim," Mommsen observes, "that dissensions among the slaves ought rather to be fostered than suppressed."

At the first signs of resistance, oligarchs delivered swift and harsh punishment through the private apparatus of enforcement each maintained. "The violence directed against slaves was never moderated," Runciman (1983, 170) writes.[43] He adds that there is nothing in the sources regarding the brutal treatment of slaves in the mines, Pliny's application of judicial torture to his slaves, or the extreme punishment for captured runaways (impalement if they were masterless) to suggest that violence was anything but ordinary. The application of coercion for the direct defense of one's private property was the domain of the individual oligarch, and this extended to meting out punishment to one's human property. "It was not the ordinary practice to place chains on the slaves," Mommsen (2006 [1855]) explains, "but when any one had incurred punishment or was thought likely to attempt an escape, he was set to work

---

[41] Quoted in Mommsen (2006 [1855]). All Mommsen references are to volume III, chapter XII.

[42] Many were captured in wars or were bought as commodities in massive slave markets supplied from the East. One of the largest sources was from the "exposure of foundlings" due to destitute parents who abandoned children they could not support. "Plutarch says quite simply 'the poor do not bring up their children.' To Strabo it is a remarkable thing about the Egyptians that they rear every child that is born" (Harris 1980, 123).

[43] For a harrowing account of the treatment of Roman slaves, including the mass crucifixion of 20,000 that dared to rebel violently in Sicily, see Beesly (1877, ch. 1).

in chains and was shut up during the night in the slaves' prison." This slave prison was a private creation. Except in instances where large-scale slave revolts occurred,[44] the public and collective instruments of coercion maintained and funded by Rome's ruling oligarchs played no role in the defense of individual oligarchic wealth and property. To meet the everyday challenges of securing wealth and property, the partial disarmament of the ruling oligarchs reserved for each a substantial private capacity to exert coercion and carry out penal enforcement over their slaves.

Rome's increasing reliance on slave labor was intimately linked to two other phenomena: the insatiable conquest of land and the creation of slave *latifundia* – the highest private concentrations of agricultural property ever seen by that point in history. "It was the Roman Republic which first united large agrarian property with gang-slavery in the countryside on a major scale," Anderson (1974a, 60) notes. As small-holding peasants were increasingly fed into the Roman war machine to die or become bankrupt, more slaves were delivered to the empire, and more land was accumulated by ruling oligarchs. Slave labor did not just release common peasant farmers from the land to fight; it permanently displaced them. When the soldiers returned from war, they became either destitute farm laborers living barely above the level of slaves in the countryside, or they joined the masses of barely employed unskilled laborers in Rome and other major cities.[45] When these large and impersonal forces concentrating land upward were not enough, oligarchs added momentum by using their overwhelming power and capacity for violence to grab land from peasants in a process Simkhovitch (1916, 204) describes as the "wiping out of small farms."[46]

The result was slave holdings and land concentration on a scale that reached gigantic proportions. L. Aemilius Paulus had enslaved 150,000 men in Epirus in 167 B.C.E., and a major oligarch like Lucius Domitius Ahenobarbus owned *latifundia* comprised of multiple *villa* estates covering more than 200,000 acres in the first century B.C.E. (Bowman 1994, 55; Anderson 1974a, 61). According to Simkhovitch (1916, 201), Seneca, who was one of the richest landowners of

---

[44] The most notable being the First and Second Sicilian Slave Wars of 136–133 B.C.E. and 104–100, respectively, and the enormous slave revolt of 73–71 B.C.E. led by Spartacus.

[45] Anderson (1974a, 28) summarizes the relationship this way: "The raising of free urban troops for war depended on the maintenance of production at home by slaves; battle-fields provided the manpower for corn-fields, and *vice-versa*, captive labourers permitted the creation of citizen armies."

[46] Simkhovitch (1916, 204) writes: "Thus we are told in the Metamorphoses of Apuleius how the rich man after he despoiled his poor neighbor's flocks 'resolved to dispossess him of his scanty acres and, inventing a fictitious quarrel over the boundaries of their lands, claimed the whole property for himself.' An intimation of similar proceedings is to be found in Sallust's 'Jugurthine War': 'The parents and children of the soldiers, meantime, if they chanced to dwell near a powerful neighbor, were driven from their homes. Thus avarice, leagued with power, disturbed, violated, and wasted everything without moderation or restraint, disregarding alike reason and religion and rushing headlong, as it were, to its own destruction'" (Simkhovitch 1916, 204).

Rome, asks his fellow oligarchs, "How far will you extend the bounds of your possessions? A large tract of land, sufficient heretofore for a whole nation, is scarce wide enough for a single lord."

Confronting Urban Threats. Setting aside for the moment any involvement by oligarchs in agitating the free urban masses, Rome's ruling oligarchs still needed means to maintain order and defend against uprisings from a growing population of urban and rural poor – a significant number of whom had tasted land ownership on a modest scale and had wielded arms in foreign campaigns. Being free and holding Roman citizenship were a source of status and prestige even among the abjectly poor, and they produced an undercurrent of conservatism that helped constrain dangers from below. Free Romans knew firsthand how slaves and noncitizens were treated. However, these restraints provided only a foundation on which a much more direct coercive apparatus of control was established by the ruling oligarchs for their security.

As in the Athenian empire, Roman oligarchs were the undisputed source of violence and enforcement on their lands across the countryside. Runciman (1983, 170) refers to the danger of "being carried off to the private dungeon" of a major landowner. As a condition of their collective rule, and in sharp contrast to the behavior of the warring type, Roman oligarchs refrained from violently attacking each other's estates and *latifundia*, but small peasants enjoyed no such protections. Powerful oligarchs could "arm their slaves or tenants for murder, kidnap, or robbery with virtual impunity, and could encroach on the property of a weaker neighbour simply by pulling up the boundary stones and taking it over" (Runciman 1983, 170).

Matters in the cities, where the terms of collective oligarchic rule were more tightly managed, were a different story. It is well known that Rome, like Athens, lacked anything comparable to a modern, public police force.[47] Some scholars have interpreted this as a penal vacuum and as evidence of insufficient state institutionalization, partly contributing to Rome's eventual collapse. Such conclusions display a decidedly modern bias and misunderstand the more personal and direct nature of social domination and "public" control when oligarchs are fully or partially armed. As Nippel (1984, 20) writes, "It is not the absence but the very existence of such [public police] forces which is exceptional in universal history."[48]

---

[47] For an early assessment of policing in Classical Rome, see Echols (1958).

[48] The emphasis in this book on wealth and property defense, and especially the shifting locus of coercive capacities, is central to understanding this matter. The single most profound transition across oligarchies is not between warring and ruling oligarchies. Making this transition requires, as we have seen, only a partial disarmament of oligarchs. It is the full disarmament of oligarchs that is the truly historic transformation. Nippel (1984, 20) underscores precisely this change: "The delegation of almost all (or at least the most important) functions of law-enforcement to public authorities has had such a decisive impact on the modern perception of law and order that pre-modern societies are often characterized as showing a lack of necessary institutions and provisions." The present study confirms that the "institutions," in the modern sense, were indeed lacking, but the necessary "provisions" most definitely were not.

Fear of mass urban violence on the part of Rome's ruling oligarchs was palpable. Nippel (1984, 24) points out that "the sources reveal the nobility's feeling of vulnerability to alleged conspiracies and the potential danger of autonomous associations in society." All meetings after dark were deemed clandestine by default and the law forbade them. To counter threats from below, domination in Classical Rome involved an ample dose of ideological hegemony, strategic social exclusiveness, and the related effects of status consciousness. However, it also relied on "violence, usurpation, and physical coercion" (Runciman 1983, 169). The structure of the system reflected the mixed nature of oligarchic power and roles in an arrangement of collective rather than separate rule. There existed formal offices empowered to legitimately mete out punishment – from arrests, to beatings, to death sentences. Yet these offices were all occupied directly and without exception by members of the ruling oligarchy. Occupying a transition point from fully private to fully public law and enforcement, Rome had oligarch-officials rather than simple officials.

Every Roman was aware that the wealthy and propertied oligarchs were backed by a formidable military apparatus that they collectively funded and personally staffed. Rome was pervaded by a "military discipline imposed almost permanently on society as a whole" (Nippel 1984, 24). In times of crisis, the wrath of these forces was unleashed on rebellious members of society. "Riots at Rome fill a large place in the pages of Cicero," Brunt (1962, 70) notes, "but their effect on the course of events was limited; the government could in the end always repress urban disorder, if it could command a loyal soldiery." It was exceptional for soldiers to be deployed in the capital – indeed, the ruling oligarchs were terrified of having major coercive forces in the city that could be turned against them by one of their own. Yet the knowledge among the impoverished masses that brutal forces were always at the ready informed their calculations as they submitted to the mundane processes of coercion and enforcement.[49] The result, according to Nippel (1984, 23), was a strong "internalization of respect" for the authority of the magistrates.

All Roman officials enjoying *imperium*, or power, were accompanied by a symbolic retinue of lictors, whose number corresponded to the rank of the official being guarded. A lower official would have only half a dozen, with a maximum contingent of twenty-four accompanying a dictator. When citizens were engaged in a disturbance, a magistrate would arrive to confront them, the lictors having first parted the crowd for this symbol of Roman might to approach. On his authority, the magistrate would settle the matter on the spot

---

[49] Nippel (1984, 25) adds that "the authority of the senate and the stability of the aristocratic regime were not seriously in jeopardy" thanks to the ability of oligarch-officials to "to carry through persecution on an unprecedented scale. Arrests on a very large scale and summary trials of hundreds or thousands of people are only possible with the support of quasi-military forces."

or single out the ringleader and order him arrested by the lictors. This was only possible if the crowd was already thoroughly intimidated by the magistrate because of the immense potential repression he embodied.

The exercise of coercion was highly ritualized. The lictors carried the *fasces* – a bundle of rods tied together with a ribbon and, depending on whether the disturbance was inside or outside the perimeter of the capital, a hatchet was included. The sticks symbolized the collectivity of the regime, the blade of the hatchet signified its potential violence, and the ribbon binding the *fasces* together symbolized restraint in the use of that violence. When a magistrate was losing patience with a crowd that did not heed an order to disperse, or if he felt personally menaced, he would order his lictors to untie the ribbons to release the rods and hatchet. The idea was not that these simple implements would themselves be effective to hold back an angry mob. Rather, it was a sign that the limits of restraint were being tested and a reminder of what would come next if matters escalated. "Maintaining public order derives from the display of magisterial authority," Nippel (1984, 23) writes, "and not vice versa. That is why magistrates are expected to be able to deal with disturbances just by virtue of their presence and eloquence, and why it is assumed that the dismissal of a turbulent public meeting by the presiding magistrate is a sufficient means of restoring order." For this system to work, magistrates also had to avoid situations in which their authority alone would be unlikely to quell a disturbance. Thus, as Nippel notes, "magistrates are also advised not to engage unnecessarily in confrontations which could affect their dignity."

The collective and individual means of coercion deployed to defend against slave, peasant, and urban threats from below were powerfully effective. Although Rome faced disruptions, riots, and revolts across many centuries, they were always successfully suppressed. There were no revolutions from below, and popular uprisings had nothing to do with the fall of Rome. The greatest source of instability was from Rome's ruling oligarchy itself. The arrangements of collective rule solved many of the most debilitating problems plaguing warring oligarchies, but also created new threats on a grander scale. The histories make prominent mention of the "Roman Revolution," but as Runciman (1983, 165) points out, it was a revolution "which wasn't one." "Although the period from 60 to 14 C.E. did, in Syme's words, witness 'a violent transference of power and property,'" Runciman writes, "it was not a transference from one class to another. It was a transference from one set of members of the single dominant class and its hangers-on to another."

Lateral Oligarchic Threats. The ruling oligarchy that was the governing structure of the Roman Republic consisted of an elaborate architecture of arrangements, rules, regulations, and sanctions designed to prevent just such a violent transference of power and property. Evolved from conflicts and solutions spanning generations, the *Mores Maiorum* (Customs of the Fathers) and the *Cursus Honorum* (Course of Honors) summed up the unwritten constitution that made collective oligarchic rule tenable. At the core of these codes was a complex array of checks and balances on power that, if viewed ahistorically, could easily be misinterpreted as democratic limitations on the powers and potential abuses of leaders. The problem with such a perspective is that the "people" never had the power to impose any serious constraints on the oligarchs who ruled them for centuries. Given the consistent top-down domination of Roman society from its inception, these codes must instead be understood as efforts by the powerful to constrain the powerful. They were lateral checks and balances, not vertical. In minute detail, they addressed the pitfalls inherent in collective wealth defense by a ruling oligarchy.

Two challenges were more sensitive than the rest. The first was that collective rule necessarily created "official" positions imbued with powers and prerogatives that all oligarchs had to respect. How could these powers be curtailed so that no single oligarch could threaten the rest? The second concerned coercion. Collective rule by oligarchs created opportunities for pooling coercive capacities into formidable armed forces. This arrangement worked to the advantage of partially disarmed oligarchs in the capital. It lent credibility to their authority over the poor masses below them, and it supplemented them in the countryside when resistance on the land overwhelmed their individual coercive capacities (evident especially in quelling slave rebellions). The collective forces of the ruling oligarchy also guarded against lateral attacks from other ruling oligarchies abroad, and afforded opportunities not just for defending but also enlarging the wealth and property of the oligarchs. However, what could be done to prevent the ultimate oligarchic nightmare: having these forces turned by one oligarch against the collectivity? The unwritten codes of Rome's ruling oligarchy represent the accumulated wisdom and experience of the "ancestors" that facilitated and maintained partial disarmament and collective rule without compromising the core objective of each oligarch to defend his wealth and property.

The Course of Honors sought to control and limit access to offices. On the belief that age and experience in lower offices affected the temperament and predictability of those who reached the most powerful offices, there were rigidly specified age thresholds for each higher office and a set schedule of lower offices to be held before upper ones. To disperse and fragment power, there were minimum intervals between offices that could be held, and there were explicit prohibitions against holding certain offices more than once. In addition to term limits, terms in office themselves were kept short – rarely more than a single year – to keep the power of office constantly in flux and shifting among members of the ruling oligarchy. The same was true initially of oligarchs given commands of legions. No matter how long the war or campaign, the commanders were rotated and changed at the discretion of the ruling oligarchs in the senate to prevent shifts in loyalty by soldiers toward their oligarch-commanders and away from the collective command back in Rome (Jaczynowska 1962, 489).

Certain offices concentrated so much power and created such great potentials for abuse that they had special rules and checks associated with them. Tribunes of the plebeians, powerful officials elected for a year, often locked horns with senators, who held office for life. Tribunes had the authority to veto almost any law or decision, as well as to veto each other. During his year in office, a tribune enjoyed the protection of sacrosanctity – he could not be touched, harmed, coerced, dismissed, or derailed in any way. However, the moment his term was finished, if he had abused his power in the eyes of the senate, he was immediately at risk of trial and punishment, including a sentence of death. The office of consul was also immensely powerful but also heavily curtailed. Two consuls were elected each year, but to be effective, both had to agree as each could veto the other.

Another example is the office of dictator. There were emergency situations when the collective interests of the ruling oligarchs were under such imminent threat that they simply could not be safeguarded through the slow processes of collective deliberation and rule. To meet such emergencies, the ruling oligarchs had a special provision for installing a dictator with unlimited powers, but for a limited duration. In office only for six months, dictators immediately relieved all other magistrates except tribunes of their offices, they had direct power over all civil and military affairs, and could imprison or sentence anyone to death without trial. To make sure a tribune could not get in the way of these desperate measures to safeguard the ruling oligarchy, a decision or action by a dictator was the sole domain over which a tribune had no veto. Unlike all other offices that had multiple holders at each level as lateral checks on each other – tribunes, consuls, and other magistrates – there was only one dictator and he was exempt from any retroactive trials or prosecutions for anything he did during the six-month emergency.

A single office holder abusing his power, violating the time-honored rules of the game, and unsettling the arrangements of collective rule could eventually be managed – including, if matters got out of hand, by simply arranging the death of the renegade oligarch for the good of the group. This was sometimes done through public and legitimate procedures and other times through the private instrument of the assassin.[50] The Romans evolved a special instrument of enforcement within the oligarchy known as *coercitio*. Used by the highest magistrates, *coercitio* could be employed without engaging legal proceedings. According to Nippel (1984, 22), it covers "scourging and execution (by decapitation with an axe), arresting and carrying a disobedient person to prison, imposing a fine up to a *multa maxima* limit or seizing a pledge." In the overwhelming majority of cases, "it was not an instrument to discipline the man

---

[50] Rome's oligarchs also made full use of rewards and other benefits for informants who would squeal on oligarchs plotting treacheries. As Nippel (1984, 24) argues, the system offered "rewards to informers, money for citizens, and liberty (plus money) for slaves. To offer liberty to slave informers implied not only interfering with the property rights of slave-owners; it also meant an instigation of the denunciation by slaves of their masters. The establishment of such an exemption to the rule vital for a slave-owning society that slaves cannot give evidence against their own masters is a significant demonstration of how seriously alleged conspiracies were taken."

in the Roman street, but a weapon to be used as a means of controlling and disciplining members of the ruling class itself."[51] It was also designed not just to punish an oligarch who destabilized the collective order at the top, but to send a strong public message to other oligarchs who might be entertaining similar disruptive ideas. Nippel (1984, 22) writes that applying *coercitio* was "an extremely spectacular procedure, particularly when an example was being made of a member of the aristocracy itself."

These measures are illustrative of the dense array of safeguards put in place to reduce the dangers of lateral threats arising among Rome's ruling oligarchs. By its nature, collective rule generated offices that temporarily conferred potentially disruptive powers on those who held them. The chance that these offices could be turned against the oligarchs by the unpropertied population was blocked by a system of voting designed to guarantee oligarchs a permanent supermajority (de Montesquieu 1748; Anderson 1974a, 5). There was never any doubt that all offices would be populated by the richest Romans. Yet even the system of voting and popular participation contained an element of intra-oligarchic management. North (1990, 287) refers to this as the "arbitrative power" of the assemblies. Most of the vigorous debates about sham democracy center on the Athenian *polis*. Rome, meanwhile, was far more dominated by the ruling oligarchs. North (1990, 285, 287) writes:

> The assemblies were convoked, presided over, addressed, and dismissed by elite members in their roles as magistrates, and they were conducted according to voting systems privileging the well-off and inhibiting the poor from conducting any kind of conflict with the well-off. [...] Rome had no Government, no political parties advocating distinct policies, no representative institutions, no system of allowing mass voting in local areas, and so on.

For the most part, the oligarchs sought to manage most matters without open conflict. The dominant mode of governance was "to fix the business of the Republic through deals and arrangements among themselves, without reference to the views of less important citizens." There was much that was settled cooperatively, and "much lay conventionally within the ambit of the senate or even of negotiations between families or groups, to be settled... by the negotiation of mutual benefits" (North 1990, 285).

However, there were also tense moments when conflicts between entrenched oligarchic factions could not be resolved through negotiation. Aristotle famously wrote that "a [neutral] arbiter always gives the best ground for confidence; and the 'man in the middle' is such an arbitrator" (Aristotle, *Politics* 1296[b]34, quoted in Dietz 2007, 15). North (1990, 284) suggests that the Roman plebeians were allowed to play just such a middle role – but not as

---

[51] Nippel (1984, 22) adds, "It was a matter of a conflict between one magistrate and another, or between a magistrate and a senator: a higher magistrate against a lower one, a magistrate versus a candidate for office who is not properly qualified, the consul summoning the senate against a senator who refuses to appear, the consul being in the chair at a senate meeting against a senator who obstructs proceedings."

an expression of democratic power. Rather, it was yet another safeguard, ironically, to sustain and balance an exclusionary ruling oligarchy. North writes:

> The popular will of the Roman people found expression in the context, and only in the context, of divisions within the oligarchy. So, democratic politics in Rome was a function of the degree and type of competition in progress between oligarchic families, groups, or individuals. It is quite simply a fact that the ruling class accepted the arbitration of popular voting in certain extremely important circumstances, just as they accepted that the power and success of families and individuals should be limited by the rotation of office, regular succession to commands, and so on. These conventions or restraints lie at the heart of the system; as they weaken, so the system collapses.

At the other extreme from this popular component was perhaps the ultimate constraint on ambitious holders of office – the rule that that no king or queen could enter the city of Rome. This meant, by implication, that no Roman oligarch could ever become a sovereign (although this convention did not prevent the title and powers of "emperor," a designation with military rather than royal origins).

Even Roman law, which would later play such an important role in the rise of absolutist states and capitalism, reflects the tensions of intra-oligarchic conflicts and the need to address them if collective rule by semi-armed oligarchs is to be workable. There is very little about Roman law that deals with crime or matters involving the population at large. "The public relationship of the citizen to the State, and the patriarchal relationship of the head of the family to his dependants," Anderson writes (1974a, 65), "were marginal to the central development of legal theory and practice." Rather, the great bulk of Roman law is focused on setting the terms of property ownership – of land and of slaves. This strikes at the heart of oligarchic concerns, particularly if they are partially disarmed and property claims cannot be settled directly by force in a warring fashion. Rome's oligarchs invented the concept of "absolute" property. Anderson (1974a, 66) adds: "no prior legal system had ever known the notion of unqualified private property." This was a crucial innovation that gave some peace of mind to oligarchs obsessed with securing their fortunes.[52]

As important as these many arrangements were for making collective rule possible, they paled in comparison to the rules and conventions surrounding the means of coercion. No single factor posed a greater threat to Rome's oligarchs than the very legions they jointly created, funded, commanded, and deployed across a widening empire. The *Mores Maiorum* specified in great detail where and how coercion could be used. The first regarded the soldiers themselves.

---

[52] Rome's guarantees of private property occupy a middle position between property claims and property rights. The key is in the locus of the coercion that lies behind exclusive property. For property rights to exist, the state must have a monopoly on the means of coercion – which is to say oligarchs must be fully rather than partially disarmed.

To ensure that their interests would align with the oligarchs and their loyalties would be to Rome, soldiers had to be propertied citizens. The manner in which this *mor* broke down would ultimately overwhelm the ruling oligarchy. The partially disarmed oligarchs of Rome were more vulnerable than their fully armed counterparts in warring oligarchies, and therefore strenuous efforts were made to constrain all coercive forces and means within the *pomerium*, the boundary of the city of Rome. Carrying a weapon inside the *pomerium* was forbidden not just as a matter of law, but on religious grounds as well (meaning a violation could be tried as a high crime of blasphemy).

Even when magistrates were accompanied by their lictors carrying the *fasces*, the hatchet blade had to be removed in deference to the conventions on force. When praetorian guards entered the city, they were required to wear civilian attire to cast them as unthreatening. The greatest restrictions were reserved for commanders and their soldiers. First there was the principle of *domi et militiae* demarcating distinct domestic and military realms (Nippel 1984, 20). Rome's legions were not allowed to cross into Italy without first disbanding. The only exception was when they were directed downward for security at rebellious masses of citizens – any other direction being "political." Even greater restrictions applied to the *pomerium* of Rome itself. Neither a provincial magistrate nor a general was allowed to cross the perimeter of Rome without surrendering the authority of their office or command. Indeed, generals and other powerful magistrates were prohibited from returning to Rome without first being officially recalled by the senate. To do so without an invitation was deemed a direct threat to the ruling oligarchy tantamount to a coup.

A triumph was a highly ornate celebration of a general's victory and spoils in war. Slaves and captives would be displayed in long parades, together with the gold and other booty destined for the Roman treasury. However, a general was expected to wait outside Rome with his soldiers until the senate allowed him in, and even then, the general was no longer in active service while in Rome, and could not command his soldiers – who were forbidden from wearing their combat attire while in the city. Again, any deviation from these strict protocols represented a direct threat to the ruling oligarchy. For centuries, the legions guarded Rome against external threats, and the rules and regulations surrounding the legions guarded Rome's oligarchs against a military overthrow from within. It was the gradual violation of the unwritten commandments of collective oligarchic rule that finally ended the Republic and brought first general-dictators and then general-emperors to power. The change marked a transformation of, rather than an end to, oligarchy in Rome.

Breakdown of Ruling Oligarchy. The breakdown of Rome's ruling oligarchy began in 133 B.C.E. with a devastating breach of the norms of joint domination by a tribune named Tiberius Sempronius Gracchus. It took a full century for the architecture of collective oligarchic rule to collapse completely. The end finally came in 27 B.C.E. with the permanent shift in control of Rome's coercive apparatus out of the hands of the senate and into those of Emperor

Augustus. As the first century B.C.E. was coming to a close, Rome had completed its long slide toward sultanistic oligarchy. At the start of the collapse, Rome's ruling oligarchs tried desperately to defend the regime by killing, in the span of four decades, four powerful oligarchs (and exiling another) for blatantly violating the time-honored conventions of collective rule, and for daring to agitate the "large and desperate underclass" (Anderson 1974a, 57) with laws that struck at the heart of the wealth defense interests of the most powerful and conservative oligarchs.[53] Only one oligarch who made similar proposals survived unscathed – by quietly withdrawing his proposal to redistribute land to the poor. This extrajudicial culling of four prominent members of the ruling stratum in just four decades was more than had been murdered collectively (as opposed to executed) in intra-oligarchic battles during the previous four centuries combined. Yet it was a trickle compared to the mutual butchering within the ruling oligarchy that was to follow.

The breaches by these four oligarchs that started in 133 B.C.E., disruptive as they were, only set the stage for a far more debilitating threat to the faltering ruling oligarchy. For the first time in many centuries, the successful shift away from the oligarchic command of private forces "for Rome," toward a more public and collectively regulated deployment of legions "by Rome," experienced a series of major setbacks and finally a complete reversal. Cutting off access for individual oligarchs to regime-threatening coercive power – which was a necessary condition for ruling oligarchy to emerge and flourish as an alternative mode of wealth and property defense – was undone by a succession of martial oligarchs, starting with Marius but becoming truly menacing with Sulla and Julius Caesar, who gained personal and private command over large segments of Rome's legions (Baehr 1997).

However, this re-linking of oligarchs to coercive capacities was different from that existing for warring oligarchs, who separately constitute a multiplicity of relatively competitive coercive forces on a more modest scale. Now individual oligarchs were taking private control of gigantic forces that were built by large collectivities of ruling oligarchs rather than by lone warring individuals. This radically new combination – single oligarchs or small factions being able for the first time to deploy personally the coercive apparatus of a "state" or empire – was what made possible the sultanistic form of oligarchy on a grand scale. The semi-armed ruling oligarchs of Rome had created the raw materials out of which a sultanistic oligarchy could be forged, and, once the means of coercion had been commandeered, against which they could mount neither a separate nor collective defense. The goal in these pages is not to recount the entire history of this more warring period that erupted late in the

---

[53] The immediate reaction of the oligarchs was to defend their wealth and property. "The unanimous attitude of the senate towards the agrarian reforms of Gracchi, its hostility towards even the most moderate bills, shows the desire of all the governing group to maintain a state of property" (Jaczynowska 1962, 486).

life of Rome's ruling oligarchy. It is a terrain well trodden by scholars.[54] The
objective, rather, is to offer a fresh interpretation of this era by focusing on
the architecture of oligarchic power, the nature of threats to wealth and property, and especially the crucial form and shifting locus of coercive capacities in
securing wealth defense.

Tiberius Gracchus (hereafter Tiberius) was a member of a leading oligarchic
family of Rome and had been elected in 133 B.C.E. to the office of tribune of the
plebs. This afforded him a single year to launch an ambitious political gambit
that would reverberate for a century and ultimately bring down the Roman
Republic. Having been a military commander, Tiberius witnessed firsthand
across the empire that the extreme concentration of property in the hands of
a few oligarchs, and the tilling of the soil by slaves rather than small Roman
farmers, was a debilitating trend that could ultimately sap Rome's capacity
to defend itself. He was partly motivated to halt this corrosion. However,
he also had other scores to settle within Rome's oligarchy, and he knew that
championing a radical land reform bill would strike a body blow to his enemies
in the senate. Supported by the Claudian faction, Tiberius called for a new law
that would redistribute public lands to landless laborers in the hope that those
who benefited would become a power base for the tribune. The underclass
gladly welcomed and supported Tiberius's initiatives, however self-serving his
motives.

His initiative was simple but radically threatening to the ruling oligarchy: he
proposed the enforcement of laws already on the books regarding the public
lands of Rome, *ager publicus*. To the horror of the oligarchs in the senate, who
for generations had been illegally grabbing public lands won by military conquest as their own (and bequeathing it to their sons), Tiberius reminded them
that this land could at most be leased and was intended by law to be distributed
to the wider Roman citizenry to maintain small and medium peasants, the better to maintain a fighting force of and for Rome. Appian notes that the law
specified that "nobody should hold more than 500 *jugera* [300 acres] of this
land." Tiberius's proposal was a disaster for oligarchs whose estates formed
latifundia spanning tens of thousands of acres. They were perfectly aware of
the law, but its utter nonenforcement had always been safely in the hands of
the oligarchs doing the grabbing.

Tiberius's bill would cut new teeth for the old law. A commission of *triumvers* would be established to conduct surveys, determine "ownership," and
redistribute the land so that no one exceeded the legal limits. To ensure the commission was not subverted from the start, the first members would be Tiberius
himself, his father-in-law, and his brother Gaius of barely twenty years. Thereafter the members would be elected annually. "This was extremely disturbing
to the rich because, on account of the *triumvirs*," Appian writes, "they could

---

[54] A useful history of the period, especially when read for contrasts with Plutarch, remains that
of Appianus [Appian] of Alexandria (Appian 1912), written in the first century C.E. All quotes
in this chapter are from Appian (1912), Book I.

no longer disregard the law as they had done before; nor could they buy the allotments of others, because Gracchus had provided against this by forbidding sales." As a gesture of conciliation to the ruling oligarchy, Tiberius allowed for an extra 250 *iugera* for each of two oligarchic sons, for a total of 1,000 *iugera*. The extra acreage did not soften the fact that this was the most frontal domestic attack on the oligarchs' wealth and property ever witnessed since the founding of the Republic. The outrage among the wealthiest landed oligarchs was palpable. "All kinds of wailing and expressions of indignation were heard at once."

Tiberius further provoked the oligarchs by taking the legislation directly to the Assembly to be voted on – again breaking with conventions by bypassing the senate, where they could easily block it. With a vote looming, the oligarchs schemed "to prevent its enactment by all means," including bribing another tribune, Marcus Octavius, to use his legal veto in their defense. At this stage, all actors were still fighting the battle through procedural maneuvers and – apart from some worried oligarchs making generous use of their stockpiles of gold to influence Octavius's stance on the matter – playing according to the accepted rules and conventions. Tiberius asked that the clerk read the bill to the assembly. Octavius vetoed the bill by ordering the clerk to remain silent. Tiberius was appalled and reminded Octavius that as a tribune of the plebs, he was (at least in theory) not supposed to side so blatantly with the ultra-rich oligarchs.[55] Having "stationed near himself a sufficient guard, as if to force Octavius against his will," Tiberius reissued the order to read the proposal to the assembly. Despite this unprecedented show of threatening coercion by Tiberius, Octavius exercised his veto a second time and the clerk followed conventions and remained silent. The procedures and protocols that lent stability to Rome's ruling oligarchy were being stretched to the breaking point.

Fearing this tense standoff might escalate into open violence in the assembly, the proceedings were adjourned. In the meantime, Tiberius responded to what he saw as an abusive use of Octavius's veto by abusing his own veto power as well to teach the senate a lesson. The effect of his punishing veto spree was "to suspend public business and public payments" throughout the Roman capital (Beesly 1877, 30). When the assembly reconvened and Tiberius again ordered the bill to be read, Octavius, being watched carefully by his senate allies and still acting fully within his legal authority, used his veto for a third time. Tiberius then shocked the ruling oligarchy by initiating the unprecedented maneuver of having Octavius impeached on the spot on the dubious grounds that he was behaving more like a tribune of the oligarchs than of the plebs.

---

[55] This argument could not have been taken very seriously. From the moment Rome's wealthiest plebeians succeeded in using the poor to gain access to tribune offices equal in stature to those of patrician senators, the rich plebeians tossed the poor aside and allied on material grounds with their fellow oligarchs. When they sided with the underclass, it was always to gain some advantage in intra-oligarchic battles at the top. As Anderson (1974a, 55) argues, "The struggle of the poorer classes had generally been led by wealthy plebeians, who championed the popular cause to further their own parvenu interests."

There are indications Tiberius realized the conflict was veering into dangerous and uncharted political territory. As the impeachment votes mounted against Octavius, Tiberius implored him to withdraw his veto, but the tribune would not yield. "The voting went on," Beesly (1877, 30) writes, "and when Octavius, on his Tribunate being taken from him, would not go away, Plutarch says that Tiberius ordered one of his freedmen to drag him from the Rostra." An impeachment like this having never happened before, no one was sure if it was even legal, but Tiberius pressed on and his agrarian reform law was passed. In the eyes of the ruling oligarchy, not only was this a costly attack on their property, but it represented a reckless disregard for numerous basic conventions that had sustained their joint rule. It was obvious to them that a single oligarch was using the temporary powers of office to greatly increase his own individual position – and, to compound the offense, appeared to be mobilizing Rome's impoverished underclass in the process. Their oligarchic property in land was being threatened individually and their rule was being threatened collectively. The established system of wealth defense was under stress.

The one-year clock was winding down for Tiberius as tribune, and so he and his family-commission of *triumvers* moved quickly. An estimated 75,000 small farmers were created through the land reform. Because a tribune was sacrosanct, the oligarchs, struggling mightily to act within the bounds of their own rules, could not punish Tiberius until his term expired. Yet on his first day out of office, a trial and likely death sentence surely awaited him.[56] Tiberius countered this threat in the only way available: he broke yet another convention of the *Mores Maiorum* and ran for tribune for a second year in a row – "fearing that evil would befall if he should not be reelected." This was too much for the defenders of the status quo, particularly because it appeared Tiberius was going to prevail. The first attempt at the election was adjourned in a flurry of outraged protests by Tiberius's fellow oligarchs. It was clear the procedural means of restraint within the ruling oligarchy were becoming less effective.

The next morning Tiberius assembled his armed allies and prepared a signal to launch a violent response if his opponents used force to block his election. By meeting force with force in a hallowed hall where an election was to take place according to formal procedures, Tiberius likely sealed his fate. He was, according to Appian, "obstructed by the other tribunes and by the rich, who would not allow the votes to be taken on this question." Plutarch wrote that Fulvius Flaccus warned Tiberius "that his foes had resolved to slay him, and . . . were arming their friends and slaves." Tiberius then gave the signal to fight.

> There was a sudden shout from those who knew of it, and violence followed.
> Some of the partisans of Gracchus took position around him like bodyguards.
> Others, having girded up their clothes, seized the *fasces* and staves in the

---

[56] Writes Appian: "The defeated ones . . . talked the matter over, feeling aggrieved, and saying that as soon as Gracchus should become a private citizen he would be sorry for what he had done to the sacred and inviolable office of tribune, and had sown in Italy so many seeds of future strife."

hands of the lictors and broke them in pieces. They drove the rich out of the assembly with such disorder and wounds that the tribunes fled from their places in terror.

The symbolic breaking of the *fasces* was a direct assault on the authority of the ruling oligarchy. Commenting on the response of the senators to this breakdown of order and procedure, Appian writes that "it is astonishing to me that they never thought of appointing a dictator in this emergency." Indeed, their entire response was extrajudicial. Instead of ordering Tiberius's arrest, putting him on trial, and beheading him publicly in the name of Rome, the oligarchs themselves joined in a private slaughter.

The senators, armed with clubs and led by Scipio Nasica – Tiberius's own brother-in-law, who was acting "as a *privatus* and against the will of the responsible magistrate" (Nippel 1984, 26) – attacked the chamber where the renegades were plotting their next move. Tiberius Gracchus and more than three hundred of his associates were bludgeoned to death, and their corpses were dumped that night in the Tiber River. Appian captures well what a turning point this was: "The sword was never carried into the assembly, and there was no civil butchery until Tiberius Gracchus."[57] However, once the precedent of such violence and breaches of protocol was in place, worse followed:

> Sedition did not end with this abominable deed. Repeatedly the parties came into open conflict, often carrying daggers; and from time to time in the temples, or the assemblies, or the forum, some tribune, or praetor, or consul, or candidate for these offices, or some person otherwise distinguished, would be slain. Unseemly violence prevailed almost constantly, together with shameful contempt for law and justice. [...] There arose chiefs of factions quite frequently, aspiring to supreme power, some of them refusing to disband the troops entrusted to them by the people, others even hiring forces against each other on their own account, without public authority.... [R]uthless and indiscriminate massacres of citizens were perpetrated. Some were proscribed, others banished, property was confiscated, and prisoners were even subjected to excruciating tortures.

The grab for power by Tiberius and his murder marked the start of the so-called Roman Revolution. The security of wealth and property deteriorated as Rome's ruling oligarchy began to crumble due to threats from within, not from below. What remained unclear was whether oligarchs would start to fully rearm and the regime would fragment into a warring oligarchy, or consolidate

---

[57] Appian is referring only to the illegal use of the sword, and not to formal decisions to behead fellow oligarchs. Spurius Cassius Vecellinus, a consul of the Republic early in the fifth century B.C.E., may have been the first case of oligarchic retribution against a renegade who threatened the group's land holdings by proposing land reforms. The ruling oligarchs violently opposed him. Although the sources are unclear on what happened, it appears that as soon as Cassius was no longer consul, he was tried and beheaded by order of the senate in 485 B.C.E., supposedly by his own father. The charge was that he had abused his power and agitated Rome's poor in an effort to become a king – a violation of the sacred tradition of no kings in Rome (Encyclopedia Britannica 2009).

TABLE 3.3. *Fate of Oligarchs Who Threatened Rome's Ruling Oligarchy*

Name	B.C.E		Nature of Threat or Reform		
			Agrarian	Citizenship	Comment
Tiberius Gracchus	133	Slain	✓		Bludgeoned by senators
Gaius Gracchus	121	Slain	✓	✓	Gold offered for his head
L. Marcius Philippus	104	Survived	✓		Quietly withdrew reforms
L. Saturninus	100	Slain	✓	✓	Pelted with roof tiles
Sextus Titius	99	Exiled	✓		Had image of Saturninas
M. Livius Drusus	91	Slain	✓	✓	Stabbed by hired assassin

under one powerful individual who would resecure oligarchic property by monopolizing the massive collective means of coercion in a more sultanistic form.

The second defensive killing by Rome's ruling oligarchy against one of its own was that of Gaius Sempronius Gracchus in 121 B.C.E. Like his elder brother Tiberius, Gaius pursued an aggressive agenda as tribune of the plebs that threatened the wealth and property of the senators and upset the stability of the ruling oligarchy. The difference this time was that the senators tried to give the murder a more official status by passing the first-ever *senatus consultum ultimum*, a final decree of the senate (martial law but with no six-month dictatorship), so that unlike the older brother, Gaius and his followers could be killed officially by Rome rather than privately by Rome's alarmed ruling oligarchs.[58]

In addition to the brothers Gracchi, four other prominent oligarchs posed major threats to the ruling group. The six are listed in Table 3.3. Four were murdered extrajudicially (bludgeoned; suicide and beheaded, pelted to death by a mob hurling roof tiles, and stabbed by a hired assassin). Sextus Titius was driven into exile and Marcius Philippus survived because he quickly backtracked when he saw the menacing oligarchic reaction to his legislative proposals.[59]

---

[58] The senate chose Lucius Opimius to execute Gaius. Thousands were killed throughout the day on the Hill and thousands more were later rounded up and strangled. With one of his slaves following, Gaius tried to escape but was cornered in a grove. Rather than die at the hands of his enemies, "he presented his throat to the slave." Gaius's head was severed and his body was dragged through the city and dumped into the Tiber River. His house was torn down, his property was confiscated, and his widow was forbidden to go into mourning (Nippel 1984, 26). It was a savage effort to police the ranks of the ruling oligarchy and prevent ambitious renegades from converting powerful Roman offices into instruments that threaten oligarchic wealth and property and disrupt the terms of collective rule.

[59] Nippel's account (1984, 26) of the slaying of Saturninus and his supporters underscores the fact that Rome's oligarchs, although partially disarmed, could still quickly whip up forces they privately controlled, even if they borrowed public caches of arms. "Senators and knights could arm themselves and were able to supply their followers with weapons. We may assume that in general the majority of the population had no direct access to weapons. In the case of the

All of these oligarchs advanced varying legislative agendas. However, there were two recurring initiatives that were particularly disruptive to the status quo and produced strong and violent reactions from the other ruling oligarchs. The first was the taking of land. Following the lead of the Gracchi, all of the renegade oligarchs proposed some form of agrarian land reform. The formulae sometimes varied. However, in all cases, the nature of the threat to Rome's collective oligarchy was double-edged.

If successful, the reforms would carve lucrative lands directly out of the holdings of the latifundists. This trampled on their shared commitment to defend oligarchic wealth and property, and each oligarch could easily calculate the financial toll this policy would take. Equally ominous, the provision of small parcels of farmland to potentially millions of Rome's poor citizens would instantly mobilize a loyal and enduring power base for the one oligarch among them who championed the reforms. Thus the land proposals would drain the material vitality of the ruling oligarchs while concentrating enough mobilizational power resources in the hands of their foe to make an overthrow of the system conceivable.

The second recurring threat – the offer of Roman citizenship and suffrage to all Italians (who were paying a lot of taxes and supplying tens of thousands of soldiers) – cut two ways. It would create a support base for the reformer on a scale many magnitudes larger than anything the agrarian reform alone could yield. Hardly a hypothetical threat, this was precisely the secret deal struck by Drusus in 91 B.C.E. with allies across Italy, who pledged an oath to be his clients if he won citizenship for them. From a material perspective, the ruling oligarchs could see that a sweeping grant of citizenship would also qualify millions of additional applicants for yet more land parcels. However, therein lay their opening to isolate the renegade oligarch and defeat the measure, as it brought the interests of current and future citizens into direct conflict. The potential power gains for Gaius Gracchus, Saturninus, and Drusus were immense if they succeeded. But the immediate effect instead was to trigger a reactionary alliance that included oligarchs in the senate, the knights, and the plebian underclass of citizens.

Shifting Oligarchic Capacities for Coercion. As Rome was nearing the start of the first century B.C.E., deep fracture lines were already evident in the ruling oligarchy. The challenges being mounted by some oligarchs, including a willingness to use violence and ignore the conservative norms that had maintained collective oligarchic governance without interruption for nearly four centuries, produced deadly responses and procedural violations that only hastened the regime's decline. Nippel (1984, 25) notes that "disintegration within the aristocracy led to the disregard of fundamental constitutional conventions." It was at best foolhardy, and at worst perilous, to try to use the powers and prerogatives of high Roman office to launch assaults on the same ruling oligarchs

proceedings against Saturninus arms were distributed from the public arsenals – a method which still allowed reasonable control."

who constituted the political-economic substratum on which the authority of
those offices stood. This likely explains why renegade oligarchs, who were aristocrats in the fullest sense of the word, turned instinctively to populist appeals
aimed at a large and latent source of alternative power contained in the plebian
underclass.

To harness this latent people power, an oligarch had to do much more than
just dabble at the margins with scattered populist gestures aimed at the poor.
The Gracchus brothers and the others who followed succeeded in activating
Rome's desperate underclass sufficiently to make them scary, but not in a
manner that made them a loyal or coherent social force. "It was the crucial
weakness of the great *populares* of the late second century B.C.," Nippel
(1984, 26) points out, "that they were not successful – in spite of considerable
efforts – in winning lasting and reliable support from the *plebs urbana*." As
wrenching as certain periods were during these four decades of intra-oligarchic
conflict, there is no reason to conclude that the ruling oligarchy could not
have continued for centuries to cut down the individuals who broke ranks
and, for motives selfish or noble, challenged the status quo. "It had ever
been the way of the Roman oligarchy to prune the tallest poppies," observes
Sherwin-White (1956, 6). The difference with the Gracchi and the others was
that the pruners occasionally needed somewhat larger and sharper shears. In
short, the renegade oligarchs shook Rome's ruling oligarchy, but they lacked
independent power resources sufficient to weaken its central pillars.

It was the next wave of challenges that dealt a deathblow to Rome's ruling
oligarchy and to the period referred to as the Republic. This time the threats
did not originate in the contingent powers of office, nor in the potential power
of mass mobilization, but rather in the *recombination* of oligarchic (material)
and coercive (military) power resources in the hands of individual oligarchs
commanding Roman legions. "Hitherto the murders and seditions had been
internal and fragmentary," writes Appian. "Afterward the chiefs of factions
assailed each other with great armies, according to the usage of war, and
their country lay as a prize between them." The events that led to this shift
in the form and locus of coercive power among Rome's oligarchs were not
planned, nor did collective oligarchic rule collapse because the regime failed
to serve the oligarchs' objectives of wealth and property defense. If anything,
Rome's ruling oligarchy was hyperfunctional and succeeded too well. Their
concentrated fortunes were not just secured. They were enlarged to such a
degree and in a manner so exclusive that the collective apparatus for defense,
which needed propertied soldiers to sustain it, began to suffocate.

The turning point came in 104 B.C.E. when General Gaius Marius, facing
a severe shortage of landed Roman recruits for his campaign in Africa, commenced radical reforms of Rome's armed forces. There is an unbroken thread
linking these reforms to the subsequent capacity of key commanders – first
Sulla and finally Julius Caesar – to blend their private oligarchic riches with
a new personal military loyalty that enabled them to march "their" Roman
forces on Rome itself. Rome had been threatened from abroad many times

in the past. It was sacked by Gallic warriors in 387 B.C.E. Yet not for four centuries had Roman oligarchs themselves personally controlled forces mighty enough to threaten Rome and dominate their fellow oligarchs who ruled there. Despite Marius' military reforms, most of Rome's oligarchs remained partially disarmed and respected the norms forbidding bringing coercive forces into the capital. A few became fully rearmed by converting the same coercive apparatus created by, and intended to defend, collective oligarchic rule into their own semi-private forces. No group of diluted ruling oligarchs could long endure with individuals among them who harbored sultanistic ambitions and the offensive capacities to realize them. Rome's collective oligarchic rule yielded to the formidable power of a single oligarch.

It is true that the *latifundia* played an important catalytic role in these events. However, it is the emphasis on oligarchs and particularly changes in their relationship to the means of coercion that distinguishes the argument being made here from all others that cite the role of the *latifundia* in Rome's decline and eventual collapse. It was not extreme enrichment and impoverishment in the sense of class tensions that mattered most. Rather, it was fundamental changes in troop recruitment and loyalty in the Roman legions caused by dispossession of small farmers that enabled the rise of powerfully armed oligarchs to transform the very organization of oligarchy in Rome.

There were many elements to the Marian reforms, but one is particularly relevant to the arguments being advanced here. Frustrated by a lack of property-tied recruits across Italy for the forces he was raising to fight in North Africa, and unwilling to wait for formal action to be taken by the senate in Rome, Marius simply "set aside the property qualification" (Brunt 1962, 74) and began recruiting vigorously across the rural proletariat. Whatever Marius's intentions, the greatest effect of this change was to shift control of Rome's coercive apparatus out of the hands of the ruling oligarchy and into the hands of oligarch-commanders.

Even when they were fighting for "Rome," or at a minimum their own little plot of farmland under the empire, the prospect of spoils from battle always had an allure for recruits. However, from the Marian reforms forward, the prospects for cash and land became paramount. "The greatest need of the poor was subsistence," Brunt (1962, 77) argues, "and the strongest motive for the soldier was the prospect of material gain." Marius not only offered a stipend and a generous part of the spoils, but he promised an allocation of his own private land to "his veterans" after their return to Rome. It was, in effect, turning upside down the property qualification and the initial intent of the *ager publicus* laws that were abused by the oligarchs. Now instead of getting land from Rome, they were getting it from Marius, their commander, and the person to whom they naturally felt the greatest loyalty.[60] Thanks to the constant threat

---

[60] In making orations and appeals to their soldiers, many generals continued to frame their exhortations to battle in terms that referenced higher principles. "Political issues and slogans were thus not a wholly negligible factor in determining the attitude of the soldiers, yet they

of retribution from Marius's veterans, the brilliant but aging commander was elected to an unprecedented seven terms as consul starting in 107 B.C.E., with five terms in a row from 104 to 100 B.C.E.

Marius pioneered the use of legionary threats against Rome's ruling oligarchy. However, it was not until Lucius Cornelius Sulla, Marius's rival, that a commander actually crossed the *pomerium* and marched troops against Rome for personal political ambitions in 88 B.C.E. Brunt (1962, 78–9) writes that "Sulla, the first to turn his army against the government at Rome, probably appealed to their cupidity; his soldiers almost forced him to march on Rome, and according to Appian...they were afraid that if he were replaced in the eastern command, other legions would enjoy the spoils of Asia." When Sulla as dictator in 83 and 82 B.C.E. created new Roman colonies in which his Roman veterans could get some land and retire, it was "his personal policy, not that of the Senate." This behavior did not stop with the Sullan dictatorship, but instead deepened in a way that put a premium among Rome's oligarchs on having enough wealth to be able to raise and deploy thousands of soldiers who would be materially tied and personally loyal to their oligarch-commanders. "Armed men were equally readily available for purchase," Runciman (1983, 160) notes. He adds that it was "the dictum of Crassus that a leading politician should be able to maintain an army from his own resources, and the dictum of Julius Caesar that money and the soldiers they buy are the two things which create, preserve, and augment *dynasteias*."[61]

It was not difficult for soldiers recruited with remuneration on their minds to make the transition to selling themselves as mercenaries to the highest bidder. Runciman (1983, 160) points out that after the murders of the Gracchi, "the heads of rival factions would either refuse to disband the troops under their command or would simply hire private armies for their own account." There was no shortage of former soldiers to draw on. "Discharged veterans were seldom resettled on the land in any large numbers or with any great success, and the inducement to them to sell their experience and services to a patron or commander willing to pay for them must often have been very much more tempting than the alternative of a remote and inadequate small-holding." This changed only after dictatorship in Rome gave way to emperors, whose personal riches could easily outbid other contenders, and who cultivated a high degree

---

were rarely, if ever, decisive," Brunt writes (1962, 76). "Personal loyalty to generals counted for more. It is now usual to say that the armies of the late Republic came to be almost private armies, bound to their generals as clients to patrons."

[61] "It is clear from the conduct of the troops who served under Sulla, the Marian leaders, Pompey, Caesar and the dynasts who struggled for power after Caesar's death," Brunt (1962, 76) observes, "that he was apt to feel more loyalty to his commander than to whatever government could claim legitimate authority at Rome. It is easy to assume that he was entirely indifferent to constitutional and political issues and guided wholly by personal attachments, still more by hopes of material rewards. [...] Appian said in a notable analysis of the conduct of the soldiery in 41 B.C., they were then serving their generals rather than the State, and did not scruple to desert them for rewards, since they knew that the generals needed them only for personal ends."

of personal loyalty. "It is true," Runciman (1983, 160) notes, "that there were no private armies under the Principate and that the attempted rebellion of Avidius Cassius in 175 A.D. collapsed ignominiously. But then the emperors (from Julius Caesar onwards) could outbid anyone else in money as well as prestige."[62]

Far more famous than Sulla's march on Rome was that of Caesar himself, when he decided to cross the Rubicon River into Italy, thus committing to an attack on the capital. Caesar secured the loyalty of his soldiers first with promises of great reward.

> When Caesar crossed the Rubicon, a gesture he made led his soldiers to believe that he was promising to make every man among them an *eques*... Certainly neither he nor his opponents spared promises of great rewards. At his triumph in 46 Caesar gave each veteran 5,000 or 6,000 *denarii* [around $500,000]. After his death rival commanders and the Senate itself vied in undertakings to enrich the soldiers. Ruthless exactions in the East enabled the high-minded Brutus and Cassius, after paying one donative, to promise their men 1,500 *denarii* apiece. (Brunt 1962, 79)[63]

The oligarchic formula that facilitated collective rule for generations worked by subtracting much of each oligarch's private coercive capacities from the mix. From Marius forward, and at a pace that only accelerated as it progressed, private coercive capacities were reconnected with a vengeance to immense personal wealth and formal positions of rule. This potent recombination transformed Rome's oligarchy. Ruling oligarchy would give way to a series of sultanistic oligarchies led by powerful individuals.

Property and Wealth Dimension. Before concluding this section on Rome, it is worth reemphasizing the importance not only of changes in coercive capacities, but also of wealth and property defense itself. For with all of the high drama of armies fighting and powerful Romans jostling and elbowing for tribunates, consulships, and the title of emperor, it is easy to lose sight of the aggressive material motive present and active at every stage. As the first century B.C.E. was grinding to a close, the relationship between material power and coercive power was becoming more mutually reinforcing. Yet seizing wealth

---

[62] Brunt (1962, 80, 77) adds: "After Caesar's death in 44 his veterans feared, not without reason, that if the optimates recovered power, their allotments would be in jeopardy. These fears combined with their affection for Caesar to make them irreconcilable with the 'Liberators.'" "Caesar, by his own account, was so loved in his life that his men would refuse no danger for his safety... and certainly after his death it was his veterans who pressed most strongly for vengeance." Their personal loyalty was not lost on Augustus when he assumed authoritarian control in 27 B.C.E. "Under the Principate, the emperors were large landowners, but they were so as it were in their own right, as private possessors: Augustus in the *Res Gestae* boasts of having used his own personal fortune to buy up land on which to settle his veterans, as Julius Caesar had done before him" (Runciman 1983, 161).

[63] "The lavish monetary gifts made or at least promised to soldiers on whom their generals were dependent might much exceed the sum of 3,000 *denarii* which Augustus thought adequate as a bounty to legionaries who had served for twenty years or more" (Brunt 1962, 79).

for its own sake, and especially if one could take possession of the fortunes of one's mortal enemies within the ruling oligarchy, had great attractions on its own. To understand how this unfolded in the final decades of the Roman Republic, it is necessary first to discuss "proscriptions" – for there was no single phenomenon more materially significant within the ruling oligarchy.

To be proscribed meant you were no longer permitted to exist (Seager 1987). The practice began gradually under the quasi-dictatorship of Marius, but it exploded during the dictatorship of Sulla that arose in 83 B.C.E. The targets of proscription were not the usual suspects – dehumanized slaves or impoverished peasants – but rather oligarchs: knights, nobles, patricians, senators. Sulla announced a list of enemies among Rome's oligarchs that he had prepared in advance. Appian's description captures the horror:

> [Sulla] forthwith proscribed about 40 senators and 1,600 knights. He seems to have been the first to make a formal list of those whom he punished, to offer prizes to assassins and rewards to informers, and to threaten with punishment those who should conceal the proscribed. Shortly afterward he added the names of other senators to the proscription. Some of these, taken unawares, were killed wherever they were caught, in their houses, in the streets, or in the temples. Others were hurled through mid-air and thrown at Sulla's feet. Others were dragged through the city and trampled on, none of the spectators daring to utter a word of remonstrance against these horrors.

Sulla's terror subdued the ruling oligarchy and rendered its procedures and conventions moot.[64] The bloodshed that began so modestly with Scipio Nasica's gang of senators bludgeoning Tiberius Gracchus to death had now matured into the wholesale slaughter of powerful and wealthy oligarchs across the Roman Republic.[65]

One of the obvious fringe benefits of proscribing so many rich enemies was that their great fortunes were now available for the taking. The Sullan dictatorship was a period of massive redistribution of property and wealth within Rome's oligarchy, producing far bigger asymmetries than had existed in previous centuries. This was agrarian reform of the most brutal kind. The grounds for being murdered and having one's land confiscated had nothing to do with laws or abuses of *ager publicus*. The mistake was simply to provide Sulla with a pretense for adding more names to his death lists. The lands grabbed in this manner were likely more than a million acres. "In this period arose new large fortunes of some persons closely connected with Sulla, who

---

[64] "There was no longer any occasion for laws, or elections, or for casting lots," Appian writes, "because everybody was shivering with fear and in hiding, or dumb. Everything that Sulla had done as consul, or as proconsul, was confirmed and ratified, and his gilded equestrian statue was erected in front of the rostra. [...] Thus Sulla became king, or tyrant, de facto, not elected, but holding power by force and violence."

[65] Having enjoyed absolute power for some time, and feeling satisfied with the reforms he introduced, Sulla decided one day simply to retire. After a seemingly casual public mention of his lifelong intimate relationship with a famous male actor (a revelation shocking to Rome and quite possibly also to his wife Metella and their children), Sulla stepped down and moved permanently to one of his country estates.

received estates of the proscribed as gifts or bought them almost for nothing," Jaczynowska (1962, 487) writes. "The proscriptions were the most profitable for the family of the dictator."

Referring rather gingerly to this bloody business of land redistribution within Rome's oligarchy as "economic differentiation," Jaczynowska (1962, 495–6) draws an important contrast with parallel conflicts and responses dating back to the brothers Gracchi:

> The economic differentiation of the senatorial aristocracy has its reflection in the political situation, in the collapse of the solidarity of the governing group. At the end of the second and the beginning of the first century B.C. the *"factiones nobilitatis"* competed with each other, but they were able to show their unanimous attitude when they had to defend the position of the whole group. Such was the attitude of the senate in its struggle against the Gracchi.

As the decades passed, she writes, "the disruption among the *nobiles* and all the senators became more and more marked and it is even difficult to speak of the solidarity of the optimates." Fragmentation and petty narrow interests seemed to predominate as a sense of the interests of collective rule was absent. Ruling oligarchy was gradually being replaced by the sultanistic form.[66] Some of the greatest fortunes in Rome were founded during Sulla's proscriptions and seizures of property. Jaczynowska (1962, 497) notes that Sulla's own wife, Metella, "got numerous possessions as gifts or by what seemed to be a purchase. She also took care of the fortune of her son." Many villas and estates fell into Sulla's own hands. "Sulla's partisans enriched themselves considerably too," Jaczynowska (1962, 497) adds, and "Cicero mentions 'seven tyrants,' who gained large holdings purchasing land during the proscriptions."[67]

The generous provisions of confiscated land Sulla made for his soldiers did not necessarily mean they became firmly established as small-holding farmers. When land grants to the abjectly poor are not combined with seed capital to get them started as farmers, the tendency is for them to quickly sell the acreage. This once again worked to the benefit of the oligarchs allied to Sulla.

---

[66] "At this time the merciless and egoistic struggle for the magistratures, the provinces, and the most valuable booties was more important for the *nobilitas* than the ideological fight. Very considerable changes took place in the political attitude of the nobles in a little less than a century. Under the leadership of Scipio Nasica almost all senators went to crush the 'rebel' tribune of the people. In the camp near Pharsalus the nobles quarrelled about the post of the highest priest . . . on the eve of Caesar's victory" (Jaczynowska 1962, 495).

[67] The fortunes of Q. Hortensius Hortalus, Q. Lutatius Catulus, and L. Domitius Ahenobarbus were all made from the spoils of Rome's crumbling ruling oligarchy. Noteworthy is the "large fortune of M. Licinius Crassus that arose later owing to Sullanian proscriptions," Jaczynowska (1962, 488) writes. "According to the relation of Pliny the Older he had located in land 200 mil. sest.," which is equivalent to roughly $4.4 billion. The oligarchs siding with Sulla were poised like vultures to profit from the slaughter and confiscations. "Another form of income for the powerful nobles were speculations made by the purchase and the sale of possessions or houses in the city," Jaczynowska (1962, 495) observes. "A special field to those profits was opened by the Sullanian proscriptions, when many senators bought estates for next to nothing and after that sold them at lucrative prices."

Thanks to the proscriptions, Sulla was able to "give every soldier of 23 legions his share – nearly 120,000 of veterans received plots of land" (Jaczynowska 1962, 488). Many veterans sold these parcels. "Who could buy them? Great landowners and above all senators," Jaczynowska responds. "In its ultimate effects the agrarian reform of Sulla was profitable for the nobility, whose state of property grew up considerably thanks to direct and indirect 'benefits' of the dictator."[68]

The Roman case reveals the limits of self-regulation among oligarchs attempting to rule collectively despite the temptations for individual or factional domination and lateral material predation. Partial disarmament and the creation of a joint coercive apparatus in the fearsome Roman legions worked well for centuries. Crucial to the formula was the creation of safeguards – manifested as norms, traditions, conventions, and laws – designed to ensure a dispersion of power among the ruling oligarchs and to block (or at least buy time against) rogue individuals. Three things were crucial to the formula: protections against potential abuses of the powers and authority of offices, checks on access to and control over a force of arms Rome's oligarchs knew could overwhelm them, and attempts to construct stronger guarantees of claims to absolute property.

Office alone, although disruptive to the ruling oligarchs, proved to be an insufficient base from which to launch an attack on the propertied collective in charge of the empire. From the Gracchi to Drusus, the pattern was the same. A powerful oligarch would initiate legislation that combined threats to oligarchic wealth and property with thinly veiled hints of a mass base ready to rise up to defend the reforms. The ruling oligarchy would call the bluff, kill the reformer and as many of his followers as they could find, and thus remind everyone who was in charge and just how much focused violence they could unleash at will. The names and legends of the fallen leaders and followers would live on in glory. However, not once did the anger or outrage that followed ever lead to a regime-threatening revolutionary surge or movement from below during the 600 years from Tiberius Gracchus in 133 B.C.E. until the collapse of the Roman Empire in 476 C.E. Rome may have been slowly rotting from within over the centuries, but it was besieged from without by "barbarian" hyenas picking up the unmistakable scent of decay.

It was a different story with the coercive dimension. This was a power resource ripe for redirection after the Marian military reforms forever altered the relationship between oligarchic commanders and armed masses of materially motivated soldiers. Loyalty shifted to oligarchic commanders via a material nexus of cash and land. These were still Roman soldiers. They hailed overwhelmingly from the Italian countryside, not from distant territories speaking languages other than Latin. It still mattered that everyone talked the talk of

---

[68] Jaczynowska (1962, 489) adds: "Not all the senatorial aristocracy, but only its most politically privileged part, took advantage of these reforms. There followed a very considerable enrichment of a little group of the *nobiles* and the impoverishing of some senators (90 among them were proscribed)."

Rome, defending the empire and its glory. Yet in the end they would fight for payment, the promise of spoils, and the prospect of veteran lands and colonies. It was when oligarchic office in the form of military command was combined with enough material resources in the hands of individual oligarchs to buy the loyalty of this apparatus of coercion that ruling oligarchy itself could not endure.

When some oligarchs suddenly have the coercive means to steal each other's fortunes in classic warring fashion, which is the same thing as saying their targets lack sufficient means of wealth and property defense, they do so with a ferocity that belies the genteel rituals of their former cooperation. However, because these warring actors took over an established order rather than destroyed it, the result was a sultanistic oligarchy rather than the warring form. The Sullan proscriptions, and similar policies under different names, continued for decades until the relative peace and amnesties ushered in by the emperor Augustus, who established a dictatorship from 27 B.C.E. forward. Augustus eventually died of natural causes, but as the case of Julius Caesar had shown, when a dictator was safeguarded by a sultanistic monopoly on Rome's means of coercion, the last remaining course of attack for the oligarchs was the individual violence of the conspiracy or assassin. This has occurred repeatedly throughout history and represents the vestigial reverberation of the warring oligarch's individual coercive capacities (whether carried out personally or using wealth to hire the services of an assassin) in the face of daunting new "state" instruments of enforcement.

This chapter closes with a brief comparative consideration of the ruling oligarchies of the medieval Italian city-states, especially the important issue of the form of oligarchic wealth and property (or, how much does property in land matter?).

Italian City-States of Venice and Siena

The locus of coercive capacities is vital for oligarchs engaged in wealth and property defense. It not only shapes the roles oligarchs will assume (rulers, fighters, state managers, or none of these), but also the potential forms and sources of threats they confront. The New Institutional Economics literature is focused on contracts, transactions, and markets. Accordingly, it is mainly concerned with threats and predations "from above" by powerful states with overwhelming coercive capacities. Yet this obsession joins the analysis at a very late stage. The primary and most dangerous threats oligarchs have faced throughout most of history have not been from administrative-bureaucratic states – whose formation oligarchs largely dominated, and over which they retain powerful material and noncoercive means of influence. Rather, they have been from each other, individually or collectively, and from mobilized poor populations from below.[69]

---

[69] For an overview of Old and New Institutional Economics, see Greif (2005). Although still focused on contracts, transactions, and markets, Greif's excellent work stands out among

Ruling oligarchies represent one solution to the problem of wealth and property defense in the face of multi-dimensional threats. However, collective rule by oligarchs assumes a range of forms, depending on whether oligarchs remain fully armed, or forge arrangements of wealth and property defense that permit varying degrees of individual disarmament in exchange for joint control over shared means of protection and coercion. The highly unstable Mafia Commissions occupy the fully armed end of the spectrum while Athens and Rome, with partial disarmament, were in a middle position. The last two ruling oligarchies to be examined, the Italian city-states of Siena and Venice, are at the other extreme from the Mafia Commissions.

Despite their temporal and geographic overlap with medieval warring oligarchies, the Italian city-states of Genoa, Florence, Naples, Milan, Siena, and Venice were important exceptions to the rural-dominated feudalism of the epoch. Within these cases, the ruling oligarchies of Siena during the seven decades under The Nine (*Noveschi*), and of Venice during seven centuries under commercial oligarchs, represent unusually stable regimes marked by a high degree of disarmament among the wealthy actors in power.[70] A key factor shaping the role and locus of coercion in these two oligarchies was the relative dominance of oligarchs whose wealth and property were commercial and urban rather than landed and rural. Before examining what accounts for the exceptional stability and longevity of oligarchy in Venice and Siena, it would be useful to review the highly unstable pattern in the ruling oligarchies of the Italian city-states. As in other cases presented in this chapter, the paramount threat to ruling oligarchies arose from oligarchs themselves. The variations, however, lay in the different solutions pursued in the city-states.

Oligarchic Instability in the Italian City-States. Lorenzo de' Medici captured the creed of ruling oligarchs across medieval Italy when he declared that "in Florence one can ill live in the possession of wealth without control of the government."[71] There is no disputing that government control was firmly and directly in the hands of the wealthy.[72] The central problem for most of the

---

economists for its serious treatment of coercion. Also see Bates, Greif, and Singh (2002). The latter work also represents an important advance in our understanding of the role of coercion, although it views the matter of coercion in a highly stylized manner and theorizes coercion as being in the hands not of powerful actors like oligarchs, but rather "groups" and "citizens."

[70] The ruling oligarchy of Venice was so stable that Thayer (1904, 785) characterizes Florence and Genoa as "political hysteria" by comparison. Tarrow (2004, 454) argues that the Italian oligarchies were "riven with internal conflicts" for most of their histories. This is true for his key case, Florence, and many of the others. However, it was much less true for Siena and Venice. For important contributions to the literature on the Italian city-states, see Bowsky (1962, 1972), Martines (1972), Anderson (1974a), Ferraro (1988), Tilly (1992), Spruyt (1994), Lachmann (2003), and Greif (2005).

[71] Preferring to work through surrogates, bribes, and intimidation, Lorenzo the Magnificent added, "I accepted [formal office] against my will and only for the sake of protecting my friends and our own fortunes."

[72] As Martines (1972, 14) observes, "Whether at Florence or Venice, Padua or Genoa, the affairs and direction of government were bound up with the practical interests of the political families."

city-states, however, was their volatile oligarchic mixture. Collective oligarchic rule was complicated by the fact that a relatively disarmed body of merchant oligarchs was attempting to rule together with a more armed group of landed oligarchs tethered materially to the countryside but residing in the cities. The former were a new stratum of wealthy merchants, bankers, and manufacturers. Their social origins were in the cities and they extended their business activities by land and sea across broad swaths of territory centered on the Mediterranean and Adriatic Seas. The landed oligarchs, drawn from older aristocratic clans and families, were predominantly urban, and yet they shared a basic military orientation with other landed feudal contemporaries across Europe (Molho, Raaflaub, and Emlen 1991).

During the early centuries of the medieval epoch, the commercial side of the ruling oligarchies in the city-states was dominant. The broad pattern, however, was for the more landed oligarchs to prevail by the twelfth and thirteenth centuries. The landed elements, although strong enough to win key victories within the cities, were too weak to convert battles between cities into feudal struggles for territorial conquest. With the exception of Florence's temporary takeover of Pisa, none of the cities consumed the others, nor did any consolidate the entire peninsula during the long period from the fall of Rome through the end of the Renaissance.

With the exception of Genoa and Venice, which were wholly seafaring polities, the Italian cities were independent urban centers extensively linked to, but never dominated by, their surrounding countrysides. Except in the south of Italy, there was no extensive farmer class and no slave economies. The underclasses in the north were urban. As the *Ciompi* revolution in Florence in 1387 demonstrates (Tarrow 2004), the urban poor could sometimes pose major threats to the ruling oligarchies. Overall, the coercive capabilities of the city-republics of Italy were adequate to withstand eruptions from below. Horrific violence was directed against workers to keep them disciplined and intimidated.[73] Oligarchs also used their financial resources to engage segments of the urban populations in factional battles between elements at the top.[74] "The tremendous upheavals in the cities," Herlihy (1972, 150) observes,

Indeed, it is not wholly metaphorical to say that government and the principal families were indivisible; and when they were not, then political violence was profound, men overturned governments and the streets were delivered to lawlessness."

[73] Turner (1948, 97) describes the violence against laborers in Florence: "The workers had no guilds and were denied the right of organization. They were ruled by consuls and watched by police chosen by the employers' guild. Any worker who resisted an employer was subject to flogging or imprisonment. [...] In 1338 all assemblies of any kind by the workers were declared illegal. Harsh punishments for violation of these laws were the rule. Sometimes a hand was cut off. At other times workers were excluded for a year from the list of employable craftsmen. Agitation against the employers, and especially for the establishment of a workers' association, was punished by public hanging."

[74] Anderson (1974a, 158) writes that "the social resentments of the mass of artisans and city poor always remained just below the surface of municipal life, ready to explode again in new crises, whenever the established circle of the powerful became factionally divided."

"were aggravated and sustained through organized factions. . . . The rich had the wealth to grant favors or the power to win them, and inevitably they attracted friends and clients from the lower levels of society, especially the humblest."

Lateral threats between oligarchs were significantly more challenging. Outbreaks of violence among merchant oligarchs were relatively rare because their individual coercive capacities were more modest. The main source of instability was the landed oligarchs resident in the cities. They belonged to powerful clans straddling the city and countryside that retained a capacity to assemble armed forces to settle intra-oligarchic conflicts – most of which were with other landed oligarchs. The ruling oligarchies of the Italian city-states fashioned elaborate arrangements to facilitate collective rule in the face of these threats. They rotated offices frequently, allowed only short tenures in powerful positions, and included the drawing of lots in their selection process to undercut the power of any one oligarch or faction. They swore oaths in grand ceremonies designed to lend gravity to the promises uttered. Still, the ruling oligarchies of the city-states were weak and prone to crises as some oligarchs engaged their own coercive capacities or tried to use the city's powers to defend their wealth and property.

The problem went beyond generic factional fighting. The merchant-landed split within the ruling oligarchy guaranteed that there was a fundamental contradiction in the logic of joint rule and individual wealth defense (Epstein 2000a). The factional use of common resources for private advantage was, as Epstein (2000b, 285) points out, "an intrinsic feature of the city-state regime." The form of government was one of collaboration, but the use of government was divided between common objectives and personal or factional gains in wealth and property. "It thus comes as no surprise that over time the contradiction became increasingly difficult to resolve," Epstein notes. "The threat of a common enemy – a local feudal count, another town, or the Emperor – might generate a temporary sense of unity," Duggan (1984, 42) writes, "but for most of the time (and increasingly in the late twelfth and thirteenth centuries) factional unrest was rife. Pitched battles, with crossbowmen shooting in the streets, buildings being set on fire, and dozens being killed and wounded, became regular occurrences."

Spruyt (1994, 138–9) argues that groupings of powerful factional families "formed armed companies, the *consorterie*, to defend themselves from rival families." The political organization of the factions "paralleled that of the city government. Such factions, too, appointed consuls and had their armed forces." The *consorterie* tended to ally under one particularly wealthy and powerful oligarchic patron. They were, according to Duggan (1984, 42), "primarily sworn associations for self-defence, with the terms of agreement enshrined in contracts."[75] As a key element of wealth defense, oligarchs were compelled

---

[75] Duggan adds: "According to one contract from Lucca in the thirteenth century, members were to meet in times of crisis and decide 'whether to serve the commune or to serve every one of his friends.'"

to make major investments in urban fortifications.[76] Describing these volatile conditions as "permanent revolution," Epstein (2000b, 277) argues that the presence of a landed and bellicose element within the otherwise mercantile urban centers "threatened the city-state's survival as a distinctive mode of organised power." A more stable and enduring ruling oligarchy was impossible as long as the landed oligarchs residing in the cities could not be controlled. To achieve this, they had to be as willing as the merchant oligarchs to disarm and rely on more collective means of coercion and enforcement.

These conflicts were debilitating for commerce and often created opportunities for the poor to fight and struggle from below – a threat even the landed oligarchs were eager to avoid. Thus as a group, the ruling oligarchs sought a method to impose a taming force from above that proved elusive by horizontal means. The instrument of choice was the *podestà*, a policing figure usually drawn from landed martial origins, who was hired through a paid contract. "The *Podestà* was an outsider brought in to fulfill executive powers, particularly police functions," Spruyt (1994, 142) argues. "He was basically an entrepreneurial captain with military skills. He was thus often an aristocrat and accompanied by a small armed retinue."

Although far less threatening than having a Roman oligarch command legions he could turn against the ruling center, allowing a *podestà* to assume a superior coercive position within the cities presented clear dangers. The delicate challenge was to have the *podestà's* concentration of coercive power resources be great enough to overwhelm any single oligarch (or small faction), but not enough to dominate the city's entire ruling oligarchy. To manage these risks, elaborate rules were written and precautions taken to limit the powers of the *podestà*.[77] However, these efforts were not always effective. The job of the *podestà* was to maintain the peace. "Hence he had to control the exercise of violence by the armed noble *consorterie*, and the guilds which likewise possessed armed companies," Spruyt (1994, 143) observes. He also had "a personal incentive to increase his position within the city. The neutralization of other powers left him with a possible monopoly of violence. Hence, the *Podestà* often ended up dominating the very groups that had brought him in."[78]

---

[76] "Each *consorteria* had its fortified tower, a massive stone structure that could rise to a height of 250 feet," Duggan (1984, 42) writes. "This served both for defense and attack in times of unrest: archers and catapults would be stationed on top and fire at neighbouring towers or down into the streets. The skyline of most cities was dominated by a forest of such towers: Florence had at least 150 in the early thirteenth century ... Without any strong executive power, the elite of landowning nobles and wealthy merchants, from whose ranks almost all civic officials were drawn, fought for supremacy."

[77] Greif (2005, 751) provides a summary of the long list of precautions taken to keep a *podestà* from being able to abuse his coercive capacities.

[78] Spruyt (1994, 143) describes the process this way: "A captain might form an alliance with the leading powers in a city. Fellow aristocrats or moneyed men from the upper class might enlist his support against their internal rivals. Other captains enhanced their standing by gaining external support. Foreign powers could prove to be useful allies for aspiring despots. Furthermore, as the conflicts between cities increased, the military capabilities of these professional soldiers became more important."

Lateral threats among oligarchs within the Italian city-states, prompting the *podestà* solution, were compounded by the collective threats oligarchs posed to each other in conflicts between cities. The rise of interurban conflicts created pressures for a shift upward to an even stronger actor – the *signoria*. "Before 1200 relations between city-states were generally amicable," Epstein (2000b, 287) writes, "for their expansion still occurred mainly at the expense of rural lordships rather than of other towns. Soon, however, the cities' boundaries began to touch, and expansion became a zero-sum game in which one city's gains were its neighbour's loss."[79] Oligarchic competition between cities, which had been predominantly commercial, became more violent and territorial. Lacking their own standing armies, the merchant oligarchs in the city-states gravitated toward a commercial solution to the problem: they used their collective wealth to hire forces through contracts, known as *condatta*, with privately owned companies of armed fighters commanded by mercenary contractors, or *condottieri*.[80]

The use of *signorie* was an alternative to battling through unreliable and expensive mercenary instruments. "From roughly 1270 onward," Spruyt (1994, 142) argues, "the temporary *Podestà* transformed into the permanent *signoria*" – rule by a princely petty dictator drawn from the landed oligarchs. This solution to interurban instability was "for the city-state – or rather, for the dominant class, party, or grouping within it – to submit to the lordship or 'tyranny' of one ruler," Epstein (2000b, 287) argues. "Not surprisingly, the first such *signorie* were attempted in Lombardy, where the strength of urban ties and the importance of the major transalpine trade routes made the costs of political instability higher than anywhere else in Italy. Lombard *signori* were frequently successful *podestà* backed by significant landed property, whose families played important roles in local society for several decades."

The overall picture that emerges for the Italian city-states is one of collective oligarchic rule that ultimately foundered because of an incomplete disarming

---

[79] "Conflict and pressures for institutional change arose also between city-states themselves," Epstein (2000b, 283) writes, and "alliances were fickle and short lasting, for each town aimed to monopolise the trade of its hinterland and to divert commerce to the city itself. Agreements between city-states were made and dissolved for opportunistic reasons: long-term cooperation foundered upon commercial and territorial competition. Warfare was just as much a part of everyday life as commercial interaction. No frontier was permanent; boundaries were constantly being pushed to the limits of and beyond the old episcopal districts."

[80] These forces were willing to be hired by any government with enough resources to pay for the troops. Machiavelli was highly critical of mercenary forces in general and believed, following the examples of Athens and Rome, that the Italian city-states should raise their own forces from peasants. Anderson (1974a, 168) points out that Machiavelli failed to understand the important differences in the mercenary forces raised by absolutist kings and those contracted by the Italian ruling oligarchies. "For Machiavelli confused the European mercenary with the Italian *condottieri* system: the difference was precisely that the *condottieri* in Italy owned their troops, auctioning them and switching them from side to side in local wars, while royal rulers beyond the Alps formed or contracted mercenary corps directly under their own control, to constitute the forerunner of permanent, professional armies."

of oligarchs – but not in the sense that all oligarchs retained too much coercive capacity, but rather that the landed segment did. This internal problem was compounded when the city-states extended their reach into their surrounding hinterlands, eventually leading to clashes between ruling oligarchies over property and wealth. Both of these forces pushed power and coercive capacities upward toward single actors, first the *podestà* and then the *signoria*.[81] Torn by wealthy and powerful actors sharing in governance and yet constantly fending off each other's predations, the Italian city-states were a "cauldron of competing interests" (Spruyt 1994, 142). However, there were important and instructive exceptions. Venice for a period of seven centuries, and Siena for a period of seven decades, did not follow the pattern of the other Italian city-states. Their ruling oligarchies were vastly more stable. Attention turns now to these cases for an explanation of why.

Relative Oligarchic Stability in Venice and Siena. The case of Venice will be discussed first and only briefly because the Venetians did not really "solve" the problem of relatively disarmed merchant oligarchs clashing endlessly with more bellicose landed counterparts. It is, rather, a problem they never had. Even more so than Genoa, the other predominantly maritime city-state, Venice was a social formation erected on the water – islands, marshes, and lagoons lying ten miles off the Italian coast in the Adriatic Sea. By the ninth century, the islands had become populated by a landed nobility that had fled Germanic invasions on the mainland. They comported themselves as a landed aristocracy without land. "Deprived of its possessions," writes McClellan (1904, 12) the Venetian aristocracy "brought to Venice nothing but a sentiment and a tradition – the sentiment of loyalty felt by the people for their masters and the tradition of holding in its grasp the reins of government."

Laying an early foundation in the royal mode, Venice had a doge (*dux* or duke) whose succession was supposed to be dynastic. However, it turned out that "sentiment and tradition were of themselves insufficient props to sustain a permanent aristocracy." The landless nobility lacked a solid foundation and was quickly overwhelmed by a rising stratum of merchant oligarchs whose wealth formed the backbone of the city-state. "With no lands to inherit, a landed aristocracy was an impossibility," McClellan (1904, 10) notes. "Being of necessity a commercial state, the only aristocracy she could develop was that of wealth. And it is this fact which in great measure explains the peculiar form of her evolution."[82]

---

[81] What these forces did not produce anywhere in Italy was an absolutist state that could unite the peninsula. Contending explanations for why Italy failed include Anderson (1974a), Tilly (1992), Spruyt (1994), Lachmann (2003), and Tarrow (2004).

[82] McClellan (1904, 15) adds: "There were no feudal seigneurs in the Venetian aristocracy, no landowners, no rulers of castles or of towns, no soldiers. All were merchants engaged in the pursuit of wealth, through commerce. For them the acquisition of wealth was the sole and necessary path to eminence and power. For them wealth and power and wealth and success became synonymous. They appreciated the fact that the prosperity of the individual merchant depended upon the welfare of the commercial class as a whole; and that for the benefit of the

Over a period of centuries, the commercial oligarchy stripped the doge and the old landed families of all their powers – first blocking dynastic succession to the dogeship in 1033, then making the doge an office elected by a Great Council of oligarchs instead of by the people in 1172; and finally, in 1297, by excluding from the Great Council itself anyone whose ancestors had not been Council members. This created a closed aristocracy based not on birth, but on having been from families that were rich for decades or even centuries – effectively obstructing not only the old nobility but also the new rich. The merchant oligarchs of Venice built maritime forces to defend their trading enterprises, they had a relatively easy time maintaining peace on the islands (angry mobs could not readily assemble and attack because boats were needed to move between islands), and what remained of the landed nobility had lost its violent and coercive edge. Being a "doge of Venice" became synonymous with having all pomp and no power.

Despite being in frequent conflict with the much larger Byzantine Empire, Venice enjoyed a level of prosperity and a degree of internal stability throughout the Medieval period and Renaissance that no other city-state in Italy could boast. During these centuries, Venice did acquire territories on the mainland, but these were absorbed and exploited by merchant oligarchs rather than spawning landed oligarchic challengers. The ruling oligarchy seated at Venice was firmly established, and all subsequent acquisitions were on its terms. If anything, the acquisition of mainland territories sapped Venice's strength in a different way – by drawing the island state into the land battles and conflicts of the Italian peninsula and Europe generally. To meet these challenges, Venice, always stronger at sea, was forced to hire expensive mercenary *condottieri* to fight its battles. The regime ruling Venice ranks as perhaps the single most stable, continuous ruling oligarchy in history. The key to that record was that oligarchs within the regime were decidedly more disarmed than was the norm in ruling oligarchies dating back to antiquity. Also important was that the ruling oligarchy was able to fend off lateral attacks from other oligarchs in the region by mobilizing their wealth to jointly hire coercive force sufficient to defend and even expand their territory. Attention now turns to the even more unusual case of Siena.

If it were not for the emergence of the Oligarchy of the Nine (also known as "the IX" or the *Noveschi*) in 1287, Siena would be indistinguishable from the general pattern of oligarchic instability across the Italian city-states.[83] A satellite and main rival of Florence in Tuscany, Siena charted a different path

class everything else must be subordinated. As wealth increased, class feeling became stronger; influenced not only by the wish to retain what had already been acquired, but by the desire to exploit the unlimited field of possibility throughout the world."

[83] Their full name was the "Nine Governors and Defenders of the Commune and People of Siena." This section relies on the extensive historical excavations of the *Noveschi* by Bowsky (1962, 1972).

by establishing a ruling oligarchy specifically designed to manage the debilitating problem of violence and coercion originating from landed oligarchs living in the city. For nearly seven decades of remarkable stability and prosperity, until the regime of The Nine was finally overthrown in 1355 in the aftermath of the Black Death, Siena was ruled by a closed group of merchant oligarchs that explicitly excluded all landed oligarchs – the *casati* (referring to castles) or *magnati* – from participation. Their stated objective was to establish and maintain "the pacific state of the city of Siena" (Bowsky 1972, 237). Only the merchant oligarchy of Venice lasted longer.

The Nine were not an entrenched group of the same oligarchs ruling like dictators for years or even decades, but rather were a governing council whose members served for two months. Outgoing members of The Nine (and their close relatives) had to wait twenty months to serve again. In a dizzying turnover of leadership spanning nearly seventy years, at least a thousand different individuals held office as "the *Noveschi*."[84] The law establishing The Nine dealt frontally with the chronic problem of the merchant-landed split within the oligarchy. It stated that members of The Nine "are and must be of the merchants," and "among them there may not be any members of the *casati*." Bowsky (1962, 370) describes the *casati* as a set of "specifically named Sienese noble houses – families whose frequent acts of violence often made them a public menace."[85] The Nine appointed all the highest officials of Siena and made all the major decisions of policy.

The distinction between the merchant oligarchs entitled to sit on The Nine and the landed oligarchs that were excluded was not based on scale of wealth, but rather whether the primary basis of that wealth was agricultural or commercial. Many of the landed oligarchs were engaged in commercial ventures, and most merchant oligarchs owned plots of land in the *contado*. "Many were no less noble than the families legally excluded from the IX." Bowsky writes, "and were Sienese citizens as early as they can be traced." Both sides of the divide had oligarchic members whose wealth varied significantly. The problem between the two groups was not that they remained socially and economically separated, but rather that the landed oligarchs, still heavily armed and dangerous, had a far greater capacity for dealing with conflicts and competition through violence – and frequently did so.

---

[84] With the composition of The Nine changing six times a year over seven decades, the posts were filled more than 3,700 times. However, Bowsky (1962, 372) points out that some individuals served eight times while many served at least three times. He shows that fewer than a hundred families, and probably as few as sixty, dominated the membership of the *Noveschi* during its existence.

[85] The *casati* had, according to Bowsky (1972, 268), "a special proclivity for violence" that was "directed against fellow magnates at least as often as against burger merchant, *contado* [countryside] peasant, or villager." "They possessed numerous city palaces, towers, squares, and shops as well as vast *contado* holdings. Often they included directors of imposing international banking and mercantile enterprises" (Bowsky 1962, 372).

The integration between the merchant and landed oligarchs was extensive. Bowsky (1962, 379) notes that members of The Nine, "worked closely with members of the legally excluded nobility, as their partners, bankers, customers, and agents." These linkages extended into the realm of the family and marriage. "Members of the IX and their relatives from at least twenty-eight different families wed no less than forty-seven excluded nobles from more than ten houses," he adds. Although many of The Nine were as rich as the richest *casati* oligarchs, overall they were second-tier merchant oligarchs. That is, it appears that for the most powerful *casati* houses to accept rule by The Nine, it was a necessary compromise that they not be drawn exclusively from merchant oligarch counterparts at the very top, but rather from a less materially threatening stratum below. "The government of the IX," Bowsky (1962, 381) observes, "appears to have been a combination of more numerous but individually less powerful men against those more powerful but less numerous." He adds that "Siena's most successful and long-lived government... was made possible in part by mutual jealousies among the *casati*."

The functioning of Siena's ruling oligarchy can perhaps best be understood by briefly considering one of its most shaky moments – the *casati* rebellion of 1318. The first signs came in 1311 that the ruling oligarchy needed to be more vigilant against landed nobles seeking to topple The Nine. Addressing the Siena City Council, Friar Bernard reported that "some persons of the city of Siena, in a not moderate number, both nobles and magnates and *popolani*... had made and composed a sect, sworn plot, and conspiracy or company... by reason of which the state of the city of Siena and of the people could be disturbed." Not wanting to foment an even stronger reaction, the Friar added that "The Nine, meeting with many secret councils of wise men, agreed that the *Podestà* should proceed no further with this matter" (Bowsky 1972, 241).

Instead, The Nine stepped up their protections and defenses against such plots by powerful oligarchs. Bowsky (1972, 266) describes the measures enacted after 1311. To undermine the opportunities of some landed oligarchs to forge alliances with exploited classes in Siena, the ruling oligarchs instituted a deliberate policy of providing "abundant and inexpensive food for the great masses of the urban populace, even when this meant curtailing profits that they and the magnates would have gained from the sale of grain at whatever inflated prices the market would bear." They also made the punishments against rogue oligarchs and those who helped them much harsher.

> Conspirators' property was to be confiscated and they themselves executed, or, at the government's pleasure, exiled. Normal legal restraints and safeguards did not apply in the investigation of such plots: the *Podestà* could not only use torture, but could also generally proceed in those ways that seemed best to him. Any official, including a member of the Nine, who impeded justice was subject to an enormous £1,000 fine for each violation. Informers were promised anonymity and sizable rewards if they themselves were not implicated, and immunity if they were. Any judge or notary who revealed the name

of a witness [informer] was to be treated as a forger and burned alive. (Bowsky 1972, 243)

These arrangements augmented the coercive capacities the *Noveschi* already had in place to safeguard the ruling oligarchs against attacks by menacing landed nobles. Twenty-four armed companies had been established in Siena under the control of The Nine. "The total picture to emerge is that the companies were headed by persons most trusted by and loyal to the ruling oligarchy," Bowsky (1972, 237) writes, "and that the Nine maintained absolute control over these organizations." This system of defense was refined even further by creating a subset of special forces within it. "Stricter still was the regime's hold over a special elite corps composed of eight men from each company," he adds, "who at times of disturbance were to hasten to the palace of the Nine (the communal palace) and not leave without the Nine's express permission."[86]

During the summer and fall of 1318, the ruling oligarchs had assembled and then quickly dismantled a group of fighters to attack the neighboring town of Massa Marittima. Feeling cheated out of spoils from the conflict, the fighters protested angrily. Capitalizing on the tumult, Deo Tolomei, a powerful landed oligarch, entered the conflict on the side of the angry soldiers. The Tolomei were, according to Bowsky (1972, 264), "holders of numerous *contado* castles and lands, members of prominent banking and commercial firms, possessors of valuable urban real estate – and men well supplied with armed followers in Siena, and with noble connections in Florence and elsewhere." Deo Tolomei was plotting to be made *podestà*, the first native Sienese to hold the post in more than a century. "Success would have given the Tolomei a marked advantage over their fellow magnates," Bowsky points out, "and a base from which to attempt to establish a personal or family signorial regime similar to those of the Visconti in Milan or the Scaligers at Verona."

Backed by the Tolomei and other landed oligarchs, the rebels struck. "Several hundred well armed men burst into the Campo [main square]. With shouts of 'Death to the Nine!' they tried desperately to storm the communal palace, the residence of the Nine and the *Podestà*." The defenses of the merchant ruling oligarchs proved more than adequate. The armed companies and especially the elite corps responded quickly and brutally, and were supplemented by mercenary forces hired as backup defenses. "Bells rang out to summon support," Bowsky (1972, 249) reports. "The commune's defenders were well served by huge catapults and by a contingent of the military companies specially skilled in the use of the crossbow. The hundred mercenary infantry or police (*birri*) of the Nine fought bravely."

The defeat of the rebellion was not only because of strong defenses. The movement itself was deeply divided in ways that gave The Nine important advantages. The first was a lack of unity between the rebels carrying out the

---

[86] "So crucial was their role that each member of this group had to leave behind in his own company at least one close relative, and the special corps was renewed annually by two men from each company personally chosen by the Nine" (Bowsky 1972, 237).

attack and the landed oligarchs plotting and assisting from behind the scenes. At the crucial moment when the attack was launched, the leaders of the Tolomei adopted a cautious posture. As Bowsky (1972, 249) writes, they "withheld the bulk of their forces in the courtyard of the chief Tolomei palace, in Piazza San Cristofano, only about a block from the raging battle, probably waiting to see how the tide would turn." This prevarication suggests that these actors were coming together with a minimum of linkages to each other and with quite different agendas and calculations of risk.

These splits extended into the upper reaches of the landed oligarchy as well. Although a very powerful family, the ambitious Tolomei clan was neither the richest nor the most influential of the landed oligarchs residing in Siena. More important than the involvement of the Tolomei and other *consorterie* controlled by other landed oligarchs was the unwillingness of the other major *casati* to participate in the Sienese rebellions. "The overwhelming majority of magnate families did not participate in the revolutionary movements," Bowsky (1972, 265) points out. Their reaction, rather, was to "fear the establishment of a Tolomei *signory*, and of a regime in which their own ambitions might be less favored than under the Nine" (Bowsky 1972, 268). The battles were never over representation. The objectives were to "replace one oligarchy with another, to control the commune completely, and allow free reign to their own ambitions, economic or signorial" (Bowsky 1972, 265).

In the aftermath of the armed rebellion of 1318, the *Noveschi* took a series of important steps to safeguard the continuity of the ruling oligarchy. First, they hired extra crossbowmen and mercenaries to guard the seat of power in Siena for the remainder of 1318. Personal protections were also provided for members of The Nine who were in office at the time of the attack: "They received permission to have two bodyguards each, paid at communal expense, and to carry both offensive and defensive weapons in the city." The treatment of members of the lower classes who took part in the rebellion was ferocious. Those captured immediately were tortured, tried, and beheaded. Dragnets were established to find the conspirators, and enormous rewards were offered for "merely pointing out the location of a sentenced rebel" (Bowsky 1972, 252).

The treatment of the landed oligarchs at the center of the rebellion was far more cautious and accommodative. Immediately following the attack, all of the urban properties of the Tolomei were torched. However, Deo Tolomei himself and his fellow landed nobles escaped and took refuge outside Siena. The Nine in Siena wrote a formal letter to The Twelve in Volterra asking them to watch for the presence of key rebels and to arrest them on behalf of Siena if they were discovered. The letter mentioned several middle-class members of the conspiracy, but did not mention Deo Tolomei or any of the other landed oligarchs who conspired with him. Bowsky (1972, 255) argues that The Nine did this "so as to leave room for accommodation with the rebellious nobles." Their access to wealth and coercive means was simply too great to risk further antagonism.

Deo Tolomei was given a death sentence for his part in the rebellion. During his years as a fugitive, he accumulated four additional death sentences, "including those for his capture and temporary seizure of the *contado* castle Menzano in 1320 and his leadership of a large mixed company of mercenaries that had ravaged the Sienese Valdichiana [the vast alluvial valley of Chiana in central Italy] and Valdorcia [a region of Tuscany, central Italy, which extends from the hills south of Siena to Monte Amiata] in 1322 and 1323" (Bowsky 1972, 251, n60). In 1339, The Nine accepted a princely fine of 1,000 gold florins from Tolomei to have all of these charges dropped. He returned to the commune soon after and became a respected citizen in good standing.

Conclusions

The ruling oligarchies discussed in this chapter range from the volatile Mafia Commissions to the stable oligarchies of Venice and Siena. All reflected the pursuit of wealth defense through collective arrangements. Whatever threats these ruling oligarchies may have faced from below (and the dangers were constant), the greatest dangers arose not from mobilized mass movements, but instead from fellow oligarchs at home or abroad, who everywhere exploited and dominated the direct producers below them.

All the oligarchs ruling jointly remained partially armed. However, the extent of their coercive capacities varied widely, as did the scale and independence of coercive capacities raised and commanded collectively. No single factor was more important in shaping the character and longevity of these ruling oligarchies. The American and Sicilian Mafiosi barely disarmed at all. When joint coercion was deployed through Commission hit squads against a threatening don, members temporarily loaned their separate coercive forces. At the other extreme, the oligarchs making up the ever-shifting membership of The Nine in Siena were exclusively merchants because they were the actors least capable of using force to disrupt or take over the ruling oligarchy. The armed and dangerous oligarchs drawing their wealth from the land were explicitly excluded, giving the Sienese ruling oligarchy its decades of longevity. Venice alone sustained a ruling oligarchy for centuries because it lacked a dangerous landed element, and individual merchant oligarchs and small cabals were no match for the collective coercive capacities the Venetian ruling oligarchy could muster.

The ruling oligarchies of Greece and Rome suggest that degrees of wealth stratification are important, but also that the destabilizing effects of official position alone are unlikely to be enough to overwhelm collective rule – especially when rules and norms on rotation and other safeguards are in place. However, official positions, combined with extreme concentrations of wealth that allow individual oligarchs to take over the funding of state armies, as occurred in Rome, create power positions that can overwhelm a ruling oligarchy. The role of coercive capacities is vitally important. Yet it is the potent fusion of material power, official positions, and instruments of coercion in the hands of ambitious oligarchs that spells ruin for ruling oligarchies. In a warring oligarchy, wealth defense, rule, and personal self-defense amount to the same thing. In a ruling oligarchy, the collective arrangements of oligarchic domination and each oligarch's other efforts to achieve wealth defense are related, but they follow different and sometimes clashing logics.

4

Sultanistic Oligarchies

In a warring oligarchy, wealth defense is accomplished directly by armed oligarchs who separately rule their own domains. In a ruling oligarchy, the arrangement is collective and requires at least partial disarmament for the system to be stable. A sultanistic oligarchy is a third mode of wealth and property defense. Oligarchs are either fully disarmed or coercively overwhelmed, tend not to rule directly, and yet enjoy protection from a single powerful oligarch against potentially devastating lateral and vertical threats. The primary locus of coercion to defend wealth rests "above" all oligarchs, but not in the law-bound institutions of an impersonal bureaucratic state. The defense role remains in oligarchic hands – but those of one oligarch whose overarching rule is direct and personalistic. As in the other oligarchies already considered, there are no absolute property rights under a sultanistic oligarch. There are only property claims, which sultanistic regimes enforce systemically but also with the vicissitudes that accompany personalistic rule. The stability of a sultanistic oligarchy depends vitally on how well the lead oligarch manages wealth defense for oligarchs in general, although, ironically, this usually involves sultanistic predations on individual oligarchs to be effective.

The concept of sultanism originates in the writings of Max Weber, who theorized it as an extreme form of patrimonialism. It was later reintroduced by Linz (1975), and then developed more fully by Thompson (1995) and Chehabi and Linz (1998). Despite its Orientalist and even religious-sounding name, sultanistic regimes refer neither narrowly to rulers in the Middle East nor to caliphates. Sultanism is secular in its origins and operation. Three elements are particularly prominent in defining sultanistic regimes. First, sultanistic rulers govern personalistically and exercise extreme discretion over all political-economic matters of significance. They enhance their power and discretion by blocking rather than building independent institutions. Such laws and institutions that exist are subordinated to the prerogatives of the ruler.

Second, sultanistic rulers maintain strategic control over access to wealth and deploy material resources as a key part of their power base. The relationship within the oligarchy between the one and the rest is symbiotic, but also fraught with tensions. Third, sultanistic rulers strive to establish and maintain discretionary control over coercive power within the state or regime. This includes controlling the armed forces, intelligence, police, the judicial apparatus, and sometimes engaging paid bands of paramilitaries, enforcers, and thugs. Even if a sultanistic ruler cannot fully disarm other oligarchs in the system, he or she commands enough firepower to intimidate and overwhelm most of them. In sum, a sultanistic regime is a personalistic rulership in which institutions and laws are enfeebled and the leader governs through the use of coercive and material power to control fear and rewards.

Sultanistic oligarchies as an ideal type share certain common features, and they also exhibit some similarities and differences with warring and ruling oligarchies. Wealth and property defense as an oligarchic imperative does not disappear just because the task of securing the material position of oligarchs shifts out of their individual or collective hands. The historical record is rich in examples demonstrating that oligarchs can adapt to changing arrangements for securing their wealth against threats. However, for existential reasons, what they cannot accept is a generalized failure to defend.

Being disarmed does not alter the fact that oligarchs can usually use their material power resources to guard their fortunes against frontal threats. In extreme situations, this means rearming – a pattern that is particularly likely in cases involving oligarchs who hold a substantial proportion of their wealth in land or in extraction and mining. For urban oligarchs whose wealth and property are primarily commercial, it typically means deploying material resources in a manner that destabilizes a sultanistic ruler – including wrenching transfers of wealth out of the economy, covertly funding mass rallies, hiring agitating vigilante militias, or financing alliances with commanders in the armed forces willing to restore a secure property regime. Oligarchs can also hasten a ruler's exit by signaling their lack of support in a crisis. Concentrating a huge amount of wealth and coercive power in the hands of a single sultanistic actor gives that individual a great deal of discretion. However, in the presence of a stratum of independent and matured oligarchs, that discretion is complicated by broader oligarchic demands for wealth and property defense.

The fact that all oligarchs except one are disarmed, or at a minimum one holds overwhelming coercive capacities (most often those of the police and armed forces), means that oligarchs as a group are unlikely to rule directly. Although some oligarchs gain access to high offices – which, in turn, helps spawn new oligarchs through corruption or allocating business opportunities – the proportion of all offices held by oligarchs is greatly reduced compared to patterns seen in ruling oligarchies. In addition, unlike in a ruling oligarchy, where elaborate methods are devised by oligarchs themselves to rotate offices, spread access, and impose term limits on key positions to avoid destabilizing power concentrations, in a sultanistic oligarchy the lead oligarch pursues strategies first to concentrate his or her power of office, and then to use access to key posts to reward supporters and subvert competitors. Individuals who hold important and potentially powerful offices, whether oligarchs or elites, are heavily dependent on the sultanistic oligarch. All oligarchs holding political positions do so because of their association with the lead oligarch and serve at his or her discretion. Thus, no matter how many oligarchs are in office at any given time, the regime never constitutes collective oligarchic rule of the kind seen in Athens, Rome, Venice, or Siena.

Despite these characteristics evident across most sultanistic oligarchies, there are also important differences and sources of variation. The Indonesian and Philippine cases presented in this chapter illuminate a range of factors that affect the politics of oligarchy under a sultanistic figure. A focus on wealth defense, and especially the property defense component, means that the locus of coercion is always a key variable. Suharto in Indonesia and Marcos in the Philippines were both sultanistic oligarchs. However, the extent of their power, the stability of their rule, and their capacity to dominate their national oligarchies differed significantly because of differences in the coercive capacities of oligarchs in the two cases – particularly, how and when the oligarchs arose in the first place. The comparisons between Venice and Siena showed that the nature of ruling oligarchies varies depending on the extent to which oligarchs are disarmed. Although sultanistic oligarchies involve a much higher concentration of coercive power in the hands of a single dominant actor, the presence of oligarchs who are only partially disarmed continues to be an important factor.

The general pattern is that oligarchs who are exclusively urban are more likely to be fully disarmed – the exception being when their riches are linked to mafia-style operations, smuggling, or trafficking in illegal substances. For oligarchs with large land holdings in the provinces and countryside (whether agricultural, mining, or forest concessions), disarmament is usually incomplete or always a latent threat that can be quickly revived. Oligarchs in Suharto's Indonesia, for instance, were completely urban-based and thoroughly disarmed. Even when the sources of their wealth later included plantations, mines, and concessions in the regions, their base of operation remained the cities and the security forces engaged in the provinces were either subcontracted as freelancers from a state security apparatus Suharto commanded from the center, or his state security forces could always be counted on to be overwhelming were a clash to occur.

The pattern in the Philippines was inverted for most of the twentieth century. Some Filipino oligarchs were exclusively urban and based in Manila. However, until the closing decades of the century, when the distribution became more balanced, most oligarchs had major sources of wealth and entrenched political bases in the provinces, where their families or clans maintained a significant footprint even if the head oligarch had operations in Manila and resided there permanently.

This urban-provincial dimension and the matter of coercive capacities have direct consequences for the relationship between oligarchs and a single sultanistic oligarch, and between oligarchs and the formation and function of institutions. The first is a question of timing and origin. It matters whether the stratum of oligarchs in a social formation exists prior to the emergence of a sultanistic ruler, who, in turn, originates from their ranks. This was the pattern seen in Rome at the end of the Republic when Caesar and subsequent emperors assumed a dominant position and displaced a preexisting ruling oligarchy. Such oligarchies are generally much harder for sultanistic rulers to control because oligarchs tend to be well established, more independent, often retain coercive capacities, and possess multiple layers of power that augment their bedrock material power resources.

Oligarchs in the Philippines arose long before Marcos emerged and tried to dominate them. Moreover, the formal institutions of representative government implanted during the American phase of colonial rule were populated by these oligarchs and functioned for decades at the provincial and national level as the seat of the country's ruling oligarchy. Until the Marcos disruption, these institutions also served as the main apparatus through which oligarchic behavior was channeled, cooperation was managed, and conflicts were resolved. With their system of collective rule damaged by Marcos's abuses, Filipino oligarchs have been unable to return to the *status quo ante* despite the dictator's overthrow.

Indonesia is at the other extreme. Suharto arose as a sultanistic leader not from the ranks of an existing oligarchy (which, depending on the case, could be absent for a variety of reasons), but instead played a central role in creating a stratum of oligarchs over which he assumed the position of progenitor and *primus inter pares*. Cases following this pattern tend to be populated by oligarchs who lack independent coercive capacities, arise at or near the center of the regime, and are dependent on their oligarchic incubator sometimes for decades until they develop the means to pose challenges.

When institutionalization occurs under sultanistic oligarchs, it is of a kind that departs fundamentally from the legal-rational ideal. Institutions arise neither as entities on a path to becoming independent and impersonal bureaucracies, nor as bodies oligarchs themselves occupy and use to rule, but rather as instruments of sultanistic control over oligarchs and to manage their proliferation. This is the case even when the institutions in question are (or give the appearance of being) formal and otherwise ordinary bodies for governance. One consequence of these differences is that Suharto was better positioned to tame Indonesia's oligarchs over a longer period of time than Marcos could in the Philippines. These same factors also help account for the very different patterns of violence in the two social formations – particularly the violence oligarchs could generate and the nature of the threats they faced from all directions.

Power relations between a sultanistic oligarch and the remainder of an oligarchy are also influenced by the composition of the oligarchs themselves. The capacity of the lead oligarch to dominate the others depends on whether factors such as race, religion, or ethnic-regional origin prevent members of the oligarchy from converting their tremendous material resources into regime-challenging political power – via parties they found or fund, movements they facilitate with their resources, or "rent-a-crowd" mass mobilizations in the streets they sometimes hire. In Indonesia, for instance, the fact that a significant segment of the oligarchy is ethnic Chinese and Christian in a country dominated by Malay Muslims severely limited the intra-oligarchic challenges Suharto faced, and also segmented the kind of electoral ruling oligarchy that emerged after he fell. Few such obstacles exist in the Philippines.

The cases examined here demonstrate that these variables are crucial in shaping the form and politics of sultanistic oligarchies. But there is also an important dynamic element woven into the discussion. In both cases, the sultanistic oligarchs were overthrown and replaced by electoral ruling oligarchies. For Indonesia, the transition in 1998 represents the country's first experience with ruling oligarchy in the modern era. For the Philippines, the sultanistic period under Marcos both interrupted the country's ruling oligarchy and transformed it into a far more unstable arrangement once it was restored after 1986. In addition to the central focus on sultanistic oligarchies in this chapter, attention is also paid to how and why they collapsed, and the nature of the electoral ruling oligarchies that emerged in their wake. Several basic themes evident in the historical cases of ruling oligarchy explored in Chapter 3 also appear in these modern cases.

Indonesia

Scholars of Indonesia's modern political economy agree that a significant stratum of wealthy actors did not appear until after Suharto took over in the late 1960s. There has been much less consensus, however, over how to interpret these actors – including even what to call them. They have been viewed as "the rich," "budding entrepreneurs," "emerging capitalists," "conglomerates," "crony capitalists," and "politico-business families." Although approaches have varied, a major preoccupation of scholars has been to interpret these actors and Indonesia's political system within a capitalist-developmental framework.

The result has been a sometimes skewed reading of the nation's political economy, identifying classically capitalist actors that were not really present, and perceiving political processes and developments associated with capitalist transformations that were not really underway. In an important study, Richard Robison (2008 [1986]) focuses, for instance, on what he terms the "rise of capital" – an exploration of an emergent domestic capitalist bourgeoisie that he theorized would eventually shape Indonesia *qua* capitalists. The actors he points to were certainly getting very rich, and the entities they ran looked a lot like generic capitalist businesses. However, they were not ordinary entrepreneurial capitalists or even proto-capitalists – a view Robison himself advanced in his earlier work (Winters 1988) and later reembraced.[1]

---

[1] Departing from the rise of capital view, Robison and Hadiz (2004, 43) argue that the Suharto regime had not been producing "a class of capitalists that would outgrow and challenge it."

The *oeuvres* of Donald Emmerson and William Liddle differ markedly from the critical work of Robison, but share a common thread of interpreting modern Indonesia within a developmental-capitalist paradigm. They portray Indonesia under the Suharto regime as a nation on a definite, if somewhat meandering, path of modern political "institutionalization." According to Emmerson (1983, 1239), the spread of capitalism, markets, and the emergence of an increasingly "complex" economy was creating a regime that was "stable" and "institutionalizing." Contrary to critics, Suharto's dictatorship was exhibiting what Emmerson argues were signs of "bureaucratic pluralism" – a comforting choice of words for the regime's Western partners. Emmerson (1983, 1223) chides those who describe the regime as "militaristic, sultanistic, or clientelistic" for their failure to notice that it was actually "more legitimate, and thus more likely to become institutionalized" than observers had acknowledged.

Liddle goes well beyond Emmerson's version of the Suharto regime as a legitimate-institutionalizer. Long before the regime had even reached its full authoritarian potential, Liddle (1985, 70, 87–8) argued that there was "clear evidence of the institutionalization of the New Order," and – although nothing of the sort was occurring – that institutionalization had "begun to replace personal rule." Contrary to Emmerson, Liddle does not think this orderly developmental process was caused by anonymous forces of increasing complexity driven inexorably by Indonesia's engagement with global capitalism. Rather, it was a direct bonus of "the skillful political management of President Suharto." Calling for a more respectful "appreciation of Suharto the politician," Liddle complains that "foreign specialists and other observers of Indonesian politics have not been inclined to give the president much credit for his achievements." The brilliance of the Suharto dictatorship, according to Liddle, is that this Indonesian *capo di tutti capi* was one of those rare autocrats in history who actively built strong institutions even if it undercut his own personal rule in the process. Neither of these interpretations provides an accurate account of the Suharto regime and its inner dynamics.[2]

The perspective presented in this chapter finds neither the building of bureaucratic-pluralist institutions at the heart of Indonesia's modern political economy nor the achievements of a great developmental leader. On the contrary, Suharto's successful creation and management of a sultanistic oligarchy depended crucially on his ability to thwart institutional development in the ordinary sense and bend the process to suit his objectives of personalistic rule. Moreover, the arguments presented here focus not on the "rise of capital," but on a somewhat different "rise of oligarchs." The former refers

[2] This optimism continued until the regime collapsed. At the March 1998 national meeting of the Association for Asian Studies in Washington, DC, Liddle argued from the floor that the most likely course of events for Suharto, who was beset by the Asian Financial Crisis and a surge in student demonstrations, was an "actuarial scenario" – meaning Suharto would remain in office until he died of natural causes. Emmerson, a panelist on the dais, concurred with this assessment. Suharto was pushed from the presidency two months later and died a virtual recluse in 2008. (Personal notes from the 1998 AAS session.)

to specific economic actors and activities characteristic of the capitalist mode of production. The latter refers simply to the extreme concentration of wealth into private hands, by whatever means, and the associated politics of wealth defense. Depending on the place and historical period, this concentration has sometimes been done by capitalist entrepreneurs. However, as the other examples already presented in this study clearly show, it has also been done in other ways by actors whose wealth accumulation had little to do with capitalism, markets, institutionalization, or the rule of law.

The argument in brief is that a spectacular process of personal enrichment of a small stratum of society took place in Indonesia; that at the time of this enrichment Indonesia was intricately embedded within, and extensively linked to, a system of global capitalism; and that fortunes were amassed and oligarchs were created by a muscular process of taking, skimming, and outright stealing of the country's natural resource wealth and its public treasure. In the Indonesian case, this process has been a much more vigorous pursuit of wealth extraction than of wealth creation. As Suharto consolidated his power, he dismantled what remained of Indonesia's independent legal and political institutions to remove all obstacles to his system of personalized power. It was a "system" in the paradoxical sense that institutions arose to lend order and effectiveness to sultanistic oligarchy – but in a manner ensuring that the power of persons would be paramount. The implications of this for Indonesia's political economy have been deep and lasting.

This perspective differs in important respects from the pioneering interpretation of oligarchs and oligarchy presented in Robison and Hadiz (2004). First, their work is a deep exploration of a particular oligarchy rather than a general theorization of the phenomenon. Although no longer viewing Indonesia's enriched stratum as an emerging capitalist bourgeoisie, Robison and Hadiz remain focused on the question of global and domestic forces of market capitalism eventually "disciplining" what are termed "politico-business oligarchs." Their main theoretical attention is trained on the evolving structure of Indonesia's political economy in a changing global context – "how an oligarchy fractured and weakened by crisis has reorganised its power by holding out against the 'disciplines' of those global markets so instrumental to its rise, and by hijacking new institutions of governance and forging new social alliances" (2004, xiv).

In their final chapter, they ask if "oligarchy can survive" against liberal democracy and markets – a question that never arises in the present study because the theory advanced here posits no inherent opposition between oligarchy and democracy, nor between oligarchy and any particular mode of production. For the same reasons, it is not a major puzzle that Indonesia could be ranked in 2009 as both the most democratic and the most corrupt country in Southeast Asia (Freedom House 2009; Agence France-Presse 2009).[3] Indonesia

---

[3] In 2005, Freedom House coded Thailand and the Philippines as "free" and Indonesia as "partly free." Since 2006, Indonesia has been the only "free" country in Southeast Asia. For several years,

is best described as a criminal democracy in which oligarchs regularly participate in elections as the instrument for sharing political power, while using the intimidating and cajoling power of their wealth to overwhelm the legal system.[4]

Indonesia's Sultanistic Oligarchy. The spectacular concentration of wealth into the hands of oligarchs is one of the most profound transformations Indonesia has undergone since independence. At the end of World War II, it was a society that had a far more flat pattern of material distribution. Within three decades Indonesia was already sharply stratified with an extremely wealthy group of oligarchs at the top. During the decades that this was occurring, Indonesia was not simultaneously laying the economic foundations to burst onto the international stage as a powerhouse of capitalist production like South Korea, Taiwan, or China.

Despite achieving an average growth rate of 7 percent per annum during the long Suharto regime, and despite having one of the largest domestic markets in the world as a potential consumer base, Indonesia in 2010 still had no domestic car industry, no aviation or ship-building industry, no domestic electronics industry, and was not a significant producer of steel or chemicals. There is no sector in which Indonesia is a world-class producer of goods or services from firms Indonesians own or have founded. Because of the way Indonesia's oligarchy was formed and has evolved, the country developed as (and largely remains) an economy of extraction and a supplier of primary or input goods.

Yet, the record is appalling even in the realm of simple extraction. The most revealing case is the state oil company Pertamina. Despite Indonesia having significant oil and gas deposits for decades and being a member of the Organization of the Petroleum Exporting Countries (OPEC), its state oil company atrophied rather than grew as an explorer, driller, producer, and refiner. Instead of being a regional or world player like Petronas (Malaysia),

---

Transparency International (2009) has listed Indonesia, Vietnam, and the Philippines as strong contenders for the title of most corrupt in Southeast Asia. However, the Political and Economic Risk Consultancy (PERC 2010) based in Hong Kong, which polls mid-level and senior Asian and expatriate executives working in the region, has much more consistently ranked Indonesia at the very bottom.

[4] O'Donnell (2004) tries to resolve the thorny problem of thriving electoral democracies coexisting with the weak rule of law by making it a matter of the "quality of democracy." On this view, choosing government representatives through genuinely competitive elections is a lower quality of democracy than doing so while also taming oligarchs via the legal system. On normative grounds this approach is attractive. It paves the way for restoring important elements of the "classical doctrine of democracy" attacked by Schumpeter (1975 [1942], 250–68). However, analytically the argument obscures more than it reveals. There is far more at stake than the "quality" of democracy in the differences between places that make transitions from authoritarian rule to electoral democracy, and yet cannot tame their oligarchs through the law, and those where oligarchs submit to a genuine rule of law (not an authoritarian leader) but in the absence of democracy. Wood (1989) analyzes "oligarchic democracy." See also O'Donnell, Cullell, and Iazzetta (2004). The relationship among oligarchs, democracy, and the rule of law is explored in greater detail in Chapter 5.

PetroBras (Brazil), or even CNOOC (China), Pertamina positioned itself as one of the world's leading oligarchic skim operations, while the actual hard work of oil and gas production was contracted to foreign firms.

Indonesia's thorough integration into global capitalism and markets has been of far greater importance to foreign actors and firms than to Indonesia's rising oligarchs. If one were to subtract the nation's virgin forests full of timber, its mines laden with gold, silver, coal, and various minerals, and its oil and gas both onshore and off; and if one were also to take away the colonial Dutch firms that became state-owned companies functioning since the late 1960s as oligarch-enriching theft machines, one would also erase Indonesia's oligarchs. Their story is one of coercively taking, grabbing, and seizing the nation's wealth. Under carefully constructed conditions of control and intimidation, this national wealth was readily available to be appropriated into private hands. Put simply, Indonesia has been politically and materially plundered by its own insatiable elites, some of whom were transformed into oligarchs because of a largely criminal process of wealth stripping that retarded rather than fueled wealth creation. Indonesia required neither market forces nor functioning legal institutions nor competitive entrepreneurs to achieve this outcome – only a well-ordered oligarchy.

Before Indonesia's wealth could be grabbed efficiently, it was important that certain developments fell into place first that facilitated the seizure of the nation's riches. The nature of Indonesia's oligarchy and the country's developmental path would have been very different had oligarchs emerged during the Dutch colonial period or even the early years after independence when the country had reasonably professional and effective institutions of law and an open political system. Instead, oligarchs were a creation of the Suharto dictatorship that came to power nearly two decades after independence. The imprint of this delay and the changes in the political-legal context during the first three decades of independence would profoundly shape Indonesia's oligarchy and economy well into the twenty-first century. Suharto's New Order regime refined to a high art the elementary principles of wealth accumulation by theft and stripping embedded within a context of forced sharing among oligarchs. An important social myth in Indonesia is *gotong royong*, a folk notion glorifying cooperation to get things done. One key to Suharto's longevity in power is that he imbued Indonesia's oligarchy from its birth with a sometimes voluntary, sometimes forced version of this sentiment.

As nascent oligarchs set about grabbing and squeezing the nation's wealth for themselves, they adopted a creed of *bagi-bagi* – which commonly means "share" or "distribute," but in the context of Indonesia's oligarchy translates more accurately as "the obligatory sharing of oligarchic spoils."[5] Violating the *bagi-bagi* ethic is one of the few acts that risks having high-end theft by Indonesian oligarchs treated as a punishable crime. In the rare instances

---

[5] I am grateful to Jonathan Pincus for several discussions in the 1990s in which he advanced perceptive interpretations of Indonesia's system of *bagi-bagi* (pronounced "bog-ee bog-ee").

when this occurs, the laws on the books are selectively invoked, creating the appearance of a functioning legal system with regard to oligarchs. However, the actual result is that laws in Indonesia operate not to tame oligarchs in general, but to enforce an intra-oligarchic code of wealth sharing through *bagi-bagi*. The consistent losers in this system are the great majority of Indonesians positioned too far from the heart of the action to capture anything but a tiny fragment of the largesse.

Although Suharto is long gone, oligarchy in Indonesia continues to be strongly influenced by the legacies of these origins. The story of Indonesia's oligarchy contains several basic elements that merit mention at the outset. First, because of the devastating effects of Dutch colonialism and war, there were virtually no Indonesian oligarchs at independence after World War II.[6] The two decades that followed under Sukarno's leadership were far too chaotic politically and economically to spawn a stable stratum of oligarchs. However, key developments during these years nevertheless played a major role in the form Indonesia's oligarchy would assume when it did emerge.

Second, with the rise of Suharto's military dictatorship after 1965, Indonesia had a sultanistic regime before it had a sultanistic oligarchy. Although Suharto veered the country decisively into the Western-capitalist fold internationally, he was uninterested in (and probably incapable of) creating a system of competitive capitalist production. He was intensely hostile to independent institutions of governance, particularly those associated with law and enforcement. The oligarchs created early in the Suharto period began as wholly dependent tentacles for wealth extraction and transfer for the regime, with the crucial function of wealth defense being supplied personalistically by Suharto.

Finally, the chronic pathologies in Indonesia's political economy that persist, despite the establishment of a robust electoral democracy after 1998, represent the long-term costs the nation now bears for the specific manner in which Indonesia's oligarchs were incubated and matured under Suharto. They evolved into a powerful domestic force that skillfully managed the old general's overthrow and went on to thoroughly dominate and debilitate the country's politics and economy ever since.

The starting point for analyzing oligarchs and oligarchy in modern Indonesia centers, as in all cases, on the concentration of extreme wealth in the hands of a few private individuals. This was not achieved in Indonesia until the 1970s. Prior to this transformation, Indonesia was dominated by all manner of elites – political, military, religious, and intellectual – but never by oligarchs. As for the presence of oligarchs and oligarchy in earlier epochs, the history of the mostly Malay people of today's Indonesia began before the nation existed as a bounded or unified entity. Over the millennia the islands were dominated by warring and sultanistic oligarchies organized into kingdoms of varying size

---

[6] Vandenbosch (1930, 1002) cites evidence of one exception to the pattern in the pre-war period. At his death in the late 1920s, an ethnic-Chinese entrepreneur in the Dutch colony left an estate worth $160 million, a fortune that in 2008 would be valued at slightly more than $2 billion.

and reach that competed for control over the population and the agricultural surpluses they produced.

This was followed by a period of gradual European colonization that began with the arrival of the Portuguese and the Dutch in the early 1600s. Although Dutch control of the archipelago was not complete until the middle of the nineteenth century, foreigners had by then thoroughly destroyed all indigenous bases of concentrated wealth, coercive power, and independent political organization. Local oligarchs of Malay ancestry were displaced by Europeans whose advantages in technology and organized coercion permitted them to dominate the islands materially and administratively. As a consequence, the development of indigenous oligarchs was interrupted by Dutch colonial occupation and actively suppressed for centuries. The Europeans were well positioned to ensure that all concentrations of material power accrued to themselves or to a handful of ethnic-Chinese traders. However, they were less successful, especially by the early 1900s, in preventing the emergence of Indonesian elites able to organize impressive mobilizational power resources. Accelerated by the crippling disruption of World War II, Dutch hegemony over the archipelago would ultimately be ended through a mobilized resistance led by these elites, chief among them Sukarno.

A useful demarcation for the start of the contemporary era is the defeat of the Japanese, who had seized control of Southeast Asia early in World War II. It was during the period following the Japanese surrender in 1945 that Indonesian oligarchs had an opportunity for the first time in centuries to establish themselves materially and, eventually, to dominate the nation's political economy. To trace how Indonesia's sultanistic oligarchy arose and evolved, the years since 1945 can be usefully divided into three major periods: the two decades dominated by President Sukarno from 1945 to 1965, the roughly three decades from 1966 until 1998 of authoritarian rule under General Suharto, and the democratic period since Suharto was eased out of power in 1998.

Attention now turns to the three major periods through which Indonesia has passed since declaring independence, and an explanation of how the material and property foundations were laid during the Sukarno years for the emergence of Indonesia's oligarchs under Suharto. The discussion begins with an examination of battles over the property regime, followed by an account of how the devastation of key governing institutions facilitated the rise of sultanistic oligarchy in Indonesia. The first of these periods is noteworthy for how the foundational struggles over Indonesia's property regime and control over the archipelago's vast riches set the stage for the explosive rise of Indonesia's modern oligarchs in the late 1960s and early 1970s. It is also noteworthy for the destruction of the fragile institutions of law and government staffed by trained professionals in the Indonesian bureaucracy and judiciary at the end of the Dutch and Japanese regimes.

Laying Foundations of Property and Wealth. The twenty years between 1945 and 1965 were tumultuous for Indonesia. Although conflicts of ideology, religion, regionalism, and even personalities were in the foreground during these decades, gritty struggles over who would take possession of and benefit from the country's abundant resources were always just below the surface. The formation of Indonesia's oligarchs, enriched through a process of stripping and taking overseen by Suharto, was preceded by twenty years of pitched battles among the nation's elites that shaped who would get the prime pickings and who would receive the leftover and crumbs.

Although the nation was overrun with elites of every kind, virtually all were of modest means.[7] This meant that materially the country was up for grabs, and the grabbing would prove to be frantic and brutal. What eventually unfolded was a process of accumulation through a logic of shared theft. However, before this could happen, struggles arose over the terms of enrichment – particularly the status of and control over property and riches in Indonesia. The battles that were fought, and the particular manner in which they were resolved, would determine not only if a layer of local oligarchs would emerge, but who and where they would be, the political-economic role they would eventually play, and the form oligarchy would assume. The material foundations laid in these first two decades have continued to shape Indonesia's political economy into the twenty-first century.

From the end of World War II until 1965, the fundamental material struggles in Indonesia were manifested in three key conflicts. One was over the immense wealth and resources of the so-called Outer Islands. At issue was whether the dominant elites on Java would successfully implant a domestic version of colonial extraction ensuring the rise of oligarchs at the center, or, whether the riches of islands like Sumatra, Borneo, New Guinea, and Sulawesi would create a group of regionally based oligarchs distributed across the archipelago. The second conflict was over Dutch business assets left over from the colonial period. The Dutch vigorously negotiated their right to keep their enterprises on granting independence, but these fragile claims were erected on illegitimate foundations. If Dutch firms were seized, it was of enormous importance into whose hands they would come to rest.

The last conflict was the most important for laying the material foundations of an independent Indonesia and the oligarchy that would arise. At stake was whether Indonesia would remain integrated into the international capitalist system and uphold basic tenets of private property on which unarmed oligarchs rely to defend their massive fortunes. Would Indonesia's formidable Communist Party (PKI) succeed in moving the country into the property-threatening domain occupied by the Soviet Union and China (neither of which had oligarchs), or would this impediment to the rise of Indonesian oligarchs be eliminated? By the beginning of 1966, all three of these questions had been settled decisively by the same actor, Indonesia's armed forces, and in a manner that would have major implications for oligarchs and oligarchy in the country.

---

[7] "They were an intelligentsia with backgrounds in political activism and government service," Ricklefs (2008, 294) writes of these elites. "Few had business interests or landed wealth. Politics was what they knew and their only significant source of status and reward."

Although occupied by the Germans and devastated by the war, the Dutch were determined in 1945 to re-take the Indonesian archipelago. Assisted initially by the British and Americans, the Dutch fought for five years to suppress the movement headed by Indonesia's mobilizing nationalist elites. By the end of 1949, the Europeans finally gave up and negotiated a formal transfer of sovereignty. The nationalist elites spearheading the resistance were certainly materially more prosperous than the vast majority of Indonesia's illiterate peasant farmers. Some had attended local Dutch schools and even traveled to Europe earlier in the twentieth century. However, no Indonesian individuals or families possessed sufficient concentrations of wealth for material resources to be the primary basis of their power.

The tremendous material battles of the 1950s and 1960s erupted soon after the Dutch peace was signed. The first clash involved the balance of power between Java and the Outer Islands, and had both religious and regional dimensions overlaid on its decidedly material-property foundations. Although Indonesia lacked a set of oligarchs to organize and spearhead the fights over wealth and property, there existed a stratum of small-scale traders and entrepreneurs whose origins dated back to the arrival of Islam at the end of the thirteenth century. Organized mainly under the banner of the Masyumi party, they were overrepresented on the islands outside Java, particularly Sumatra and Sulawesi. Java was densely populated but lacked natural resources. The situation was reversed for the Outer Islands, which were less populated, but endowed with oil, gas, mines, timber, and matured plantations. Until the first national elections of 1955, leaders of the Masyumi party mistakenly believed that they were the largest political force in Indonesia and that they were positioned to win the elections by an outright majority. They were wrong on both counts.

With the 1955 vote finally tallied, it became painfully apparent to Masyumi that the Java-based parties and interests were going to dominate parliament and the cabinets. This meant that unless elites in the Outer Islands asserted greater regional autonomy, Java and especially Jakarta would seize control over the trade and natural resources based outside Java. Masyumi elites and small-scale traders had performed far better among voters on the Outer Islands, where they had also forged alliances with local military commanders to set up lucrative smuggling operations – which Anderson (2008, 51) terms "Outer Island warlordism" – to capture a much larger share of the export trade and withhold it from Java and Jakarta.[8]

If not interrupted, oligarchic fortunes could easily have been amassed for the regional elites involved. Overdetermining the conflict was the fact that Masyumi was much more committed to an Islamic state for Indonesia than were the Java parties, and the PKI was openly hostile to the prospect. In

---

[8] "Some provincial military commanders," Anderson (2008, 50) writes, "headed towards warlord status, began to create their own hidden budgets by protecting smugglers, controlling local export revenues and practising extortion, especially of Chinese entrepreneurs who nonetheless found these commanders useful at the price."

1957 and 1958, the *Pemerintah Revolusioner Republik Indonesia* (PRRI) and *Permesta* rebellions broke out on Sumatra and Sulawesi. The rebel leaders, all of whom were party and military elites, argued that they were defending the interests of the populations of the Outer Islands, whose wealth was being sapped by Java. They were also defending their disproportionate access to that same wealth as the key power holders in the regions. Had their rebellions succeeded, it is a virtual certainty that regional oligarchs would have arisen extremely rapidly in the territories outside Java.

The effect of the rebellions was to unite forces on Java that had been squabbling for years. Jakarta elites and the army's central command – deeply committed to a unitary Indonesian state and jealous of the riches the rebels were attempting to seize – agreed that the rebels should be crushed. For its part, the PKI was pleased to see its main Islamic and petty bourgeois antagonist, Masyumi, dealt a serious setback. The armed forces attacked the civilian and military renegades. When the regional rebellions were finally suppressed, both the dominance of Java over the Outer Islands and the strength of the armed forces were enhanced. The oligarchic potential for actors in the regions was thoroughly eclipsed. For decades to come, oligarchs on Java, working in intimate association with officers in the armed forces and foreign partners, would extract and take for themselves the great riches of the major islands off Java.

The second wrenching material clash also erupted at the end of the 1950s. The Dutch had negotiated onerous terms for Indonesia's independence. The Indonesians were forced to assume colonial debts, significant parts of which were costs the Dutch incurred waging a bitter war against the independence movement. The Dutch refused to cede control of certain territories, particularly the western half of the large and mineral-rich island of New Guinea. They also retained ownership of companies that had served as the main instruments of economic extraction and wealth transfer to Dutch oligarchs and the royal treasury. When Amsterdam's intransigence over West New Guinea intensified in 1957, worker and farmer unions linked to the Indonesian Communist Party started taking over Dutch firms – the most valuable business assets in the country.[9] It was the army that again acted decisively. General Abdul Haris Nasution immediately took charge of the Dutch firms and placed them under military control. They would eventually become state-owned enterprises – entities that from the late 1950s until the present have served as a crucial channel for massive wealth transfers from public to private hands, creating legions of Indonesian oligarchs.

These first two clashes restructured Indonesia's material wealth in a manner that set the stage for the emergence under Suharto of Java-based oligarchs

---

[9] The Dutch firms comprised nearly 250 factories and mining companies, as well as banks, shipping lines, and a range of other service industries. The Dutch companies accounted for 60 percent of all foreign trade and fully 90 percent of plantation production. The major Dutch trading companies were restructured in 1958 and controlled 70 percent of imports and were given monopolies in the import of thirteen basic commodities ranging from rice to textiles (Robinson 2008 [1986], 72).

linked to the state and the military. The victory over the Outer Island rebellions ensured that the elites based in Jakarta would be able to commandeer the archipelago's natural resources for their own elevation to wealthy oligarchic status.[10] Seizing the Dutch firms provided an important set of institutional structures within which political and military actors could be incubated into oligarchs as well.

The third and final clash, which pitted the Indonesian armed forces against the Indonesian Communist Party, was the most critical and traumatic of all because it dealt preemptively with the property-defense aspect of oligarchic wealth defense. If the PKI had prevailed, amassing private property and private wealth on an oligarchic scale would have been an impossibility. The resources in the regions and the former Dutch firms certainly would have fattened a *nomenklatura* party elite in Indonesia, with local equivalents of *dachas* and other perks. However, in the absence of private fortunes controlled personally rather than through membership in a PKI politburo, there would have been party elites but no Indonesian oligarchs (just as there were no Soviet, Chinese, or Vietnamese oligarchs during the Communist regimes).

The only party with a serious grassroots organization, the PKI had performed far better in the 1955 national elections than anyone had expected, and their showing in the regional elections of 1957 was even better. National elections were scheduled for 1959, but all the major parties except the PKI demanded at the end of 1958 that they be postponed indefinitely (Ricklefs 2008, 320). The threat was that the PKI would win at least a plurality and possibly a majority of the votes, making it the first peaceful Communist takeover of any country through legitimate democratic elections. With the electoral door slammed shut, the PKI maneuvered for position throughout the early and mid-1960s as the only party able consistently to deliver a solid mass base for President Sukarno. Closer ties were also forged with China, which offered to facilitate the creation of a "fifth force" – the direct arming of workers and farmers under the PKI.

By 1964 and 1965, PKI tensions with propertied Islamic strata on and off Java and with the armed forces had risen dramatically. PKI farmers took matters into their own hands on a land reform bill that had been stalled for years and started seizing property from small and medium landlords, especially on Java. Meanwhile, the military despised the Communists on nationalist grounds, believing the PKI's ideology and behavior displayed a stronger commitment to European-inspired global Communism than to Indonesia itself.[11] The officers

---

[10] The number of Indonesians who could profit handsomely from the business and trading opportunities during the Sukarno years was limited. Robison (2008 [1986]) provides a comprehensive list of these budding oligarchs in a chapter entitled, appropriately enough, "The Failure of Domestic Private Capital: 1949–1957."

[11] Out of personal curiosity, Major General (ret.) Prabowo Subianto had reviewed the internal army files on D. N. Aidit, the head of the PKI. Aidit was captured in Central Java and executed by firing squad without a trial late in 1965. Emphasizing the deep commitment of the Communists to the international movement, Prabowo noted that "Aidit's last request was to

were alarmed by the prospect of an armed PKI mass base and they were aware that the party was actively infiltrating branches of the armed forces.

With President Sukarno's role as balancer between Indonesia's opposing elements finally strained to the limit, and presented with the opportunity to blame a failed *putsch* in Jakarta in the fall of 1965 entirely on the PKI, the military joined with conservative Islamic forces to unleash a ferocious attack on the party and its followers (Roosa 2006). The party's leaders were assassinated upon capture, executed after show trials, or detained indefinitely in gulags. The PKI was outlawed and peasants and workers associated with the party were rounded up by the hundreds of thousands in a barbaric slaughter. Any potential threat oligarchs might have faced from below had been dealt with preemptively years before Indonesia's oligarchs had even emerged as a significant stratum. Indeed, all mass threats to Indonesia's property regime were erased practically overnight. Under conservative military domination, the country moved decisively into the welcoming embrace of the anti-Communist nations led by the United States.

Institutional Devastation. For a sultanistic oligarchy to arise under Suharto, these key changes in the property and material realm were not enough on their own. Another obstacle was the reasonably effective and independent government institutions that were in place and functioning at the time of the transfer of sovereignty at the end of 1949, especially in the legal realm. These institutions were staffed by confident and trained Indonesian professionals, and destroying them was an important precondition for the kind of political economy Suharto later implanted – key characteristics of which survived after the collapse of his regime in 1998. The work of systematic institutional devastation was carried out in the 1950s and 1960s by Indonesia's ambitious political and military elites who attacked and undermined the fragile but promising institutional base inherited from the Dutch and Japanese occupiers.[12]

Pompe (2005, 35) writes that at the end of the colonial era in Indonesia "the place and role of courts was respected and secure." Contemporary Indonesians are incredulous when told that their nation began with remarkably strong institutions of law and a reasonably professional bureaucracy. They often express the view that the country is trapped in a "culture of corruption," as if rampant theft at all levels were a genetic defect of society since its inception. Having witnessed an endless series of failed attempts to control corruption, one exasperated young Indonesian professional opined that the only solution was to "outsource the entire government." On a flight home from their studies in the

sing *The Internationale*. Tan Malaka had done the same," referring to another major Indonesian communist who was the Comintern's Southeast Asia designate, had spent long periods in Moscow, and had published in Russian. In fact, unlike with Aidit, no record was kept of Tan Malaka's 1949 execution by the Indonesian army. Prabowo likely heard this version from his military network, and it clearly fit his sense of what an insufficiently nationalist Tan Malaka would have done. Interview in Jakarta with Prabowo Subianto, September 18, 2009.

[12] Daniel Lev's (1965, 1985, 2000, 2007) scholarship on the early years of the Republic provides the most sophisticated interpretation of the late colonial and parliamentary periods, and this section relies heavily on this work.

United States, despairing Indonesian students argued that the only way to fix the country's broken institutions and stop the debilitating effects of organized theft by officials and rising oligarchs was to "bring back Dutch colonial rule for fifty years."[13] These sentiments of hopelessness are compounded by the fact that they were expressed by a new generation of educated and informed Indonesians whose views were shaped mostly after Suharto had fallen and a procedural democracy was in place.[14]

The first setback for the rule of law in Indonesia occurred during the Japanese occupation when crucial decisions were made about unifying the divided legal system left over from the colonial period. To facilitate the economic plunder of the archipelago and to administer it in a manner that made full use of local hierarchies of domination, the Dutch controlled the colony through a dualistic legal and bureaucratic system based on race and ethnicity.[15] Europeans had one set of courts, laws, and procedures based on strong European codes and protections, while the vast majority of Indonesians were controlled through traditional (*adat*) laws and courts, which provided much weaker individual protections and deferred to secular and religious elites who operated a patrimonial, authoritarian, and discretionary system of rule down to the local level. Both tracks had trained legal professionals, complete with lawyers, clerks, and judges.[16] Indonesians sat in judgment of Indonesians on the basis of *adat* traditional law and used relatively authoritarian legal procedures; meanwhile, the Dutch sat on one set of panels that adjudicated Europeans in one jurisdiction and a second set that adjudicated Asians in another.

[13] The comment by the young professional was during a private conversation in Jakarta in October 2009. The students argued their point aboard a United Airlines flight from Los Angeles to Hong Kong in June 2001.

[14] Lev (2007, 252) argues that the new reform generation "was denied historical knowledge necessary to understand just how the New Order came to be and what exactly it did. High school and university offerings have long suppressed information on, not to mention debates over, the parliamentary, Guided Democracy, and New Order periods. [...] The quality of judicial institutions then, and how they were subverted, is unknown. Few are aware of the 1950 Constitution and fewer have read it." In an interview conducted on the eve of Suharto's removal from power, the late Y. B. Mangunwijaya (1998), a progressive Jesuit priest famous for his novels set in the colonial period, takes the argument one step further. A staunch critic of the repressive Dutch regime, Romo Mangun (as he was called) reminds his readers that especially in the areas of education and law, the Dutch system was superior to the conditions in place by the end of Suharto's New Order. "If we take the performance of the Dutch East Indies as the metric, we have declined in everything. Don't think the Dutch East Indies didn't perform. It's that the Indonesian Republic was supposed to outperform. Take for instance the realm of education during the colonial period – it was completely fine. There were no lawyers and judges who could be bought. In those days the professors and lecturers from the Dutch law schools in the colony sent a petition to the government in Holland criticizing the way Sukarno had been arrested. They viewed Holland's actions as a violation of the law. Do we see anything like that now? Not at all, which is a setback."

[15] On how the Indonesian civil service (first the *pangreh praja* and later the *pamong praja*) was structured to maximize the delivery of agricultural goods from Indonesian peasants to the colonial masters, see Anderson (1972).

[16] The Dutch had created schools of higher education for legal and bureaucratic professionals, and in 1924 the first law school for Indonesians was established in Batavia.

Despite this sharp separation, there was also an overlapping grey area in the middle. For instance, Japanese nationals resident in the colony were treated as Europeans, ethnic-Chinese Christians had special status, and a small number of elite Indonesians received quasi-European treatment as well. It is also noteworthy that in the case of the *Landgerecht* courts established in 1914, which adjudicated petty crimes and misdemeanors, Indonesian judges actually sat together on panels with Dutch judges and jointly heard cases involving defendants of both local and European origin (Lev 1985, 60). Indonesian and Dutch jurists had argued throughout the first half of the twentieth century that the system should be unified, and that the basis of the single legal structure should be the Dutch laws and especially the European legal procedures, which had stronger standards of evidence, gave the judiciary much greater autonomy from officials in the executive and administrative branches, and was significantly less prone to authoritarian abuses and intimidation.

A choice had to be made about this bifurcated legal structure. In the committees set up under the Japanese to prepare Indonesia for independence, the nationalist lawyer Muhammad Yamin argued in favor of establishing the new nation on a foundation emphasizing the more democratic and independent European track of the system. He did not succeed in blocking what Lev terms the colonial "Indonesian side" of the legal and bureaucratic infrastructure. Yamin's proposals were rejected, Lev (1985, 70) writes, "largely on the basis of arguments by the famous *adat* law scholar, Supomo, whose very conservative views were rooted deeply in the colonial Indonesian-side establishment. That Supomo won, with support from Soekarno, among others, can only be attributed to a predilection, particularly among Javanese political leaders in the revolutionary heartland, for the assumptions that governed the Indonesian side." Those assumptions were that a traditional and patriarchal system was a better fit for Indonesian society.[17] The revolutionary Republic had adopted

---

[17] Lev (1985, 70–1) adds that the Dutch procedural codes were "attractively 'modern' but symbolically 'European,' and might still work to the advantage of European and ethnic Chinese commerce. *Adat*, which had been used to keep Indonesians in their place, could by a slight turn of imagination become a nationalist symbol of their distinctiveness, but it was generally regarded as too primitive for the law of a modern state. The dilemma favored the legal status quo until there was time to resolve the issues." The 1945 Indonesian Constitution was hastily drafted with the notion that Indonesians would get back to it and fill in the gaping holes once the commotion of the independence struggle had passed. Lev writes, "Most public and private lawyers and legal scholars took it for granted that Indonesia, as a modern state, would eventually create a new legal system based on 'modern' codes." This did not happen. Instead, as Lev continues, Dutch domination through the use of a racially constructed "Indonesian side" for law and administration would instead be adapted to class domination by local elites. "*Adat* continued to invoke, symbolically, the racial criterion of the colony over and against ethnic Chinese, whose law is written in the civil and commercial codes and special provisions. But the succession of ethnic Indonesian political leadership necessarily implied the disappearance of racial and caste overtones in the relationship between state and ethnic Indonesian society. Racial domination easily mutated into class domination, however, for the legal system was ideologically suitable for either."

"the most repressive side of the plural colonial legal establishment" (Lev 2007, 236).

Favoring the *adat* side of the system and failing to adopt the stronger European procedural codes made it much easier for Indonesia's military and political elites to gut the legal system of its autonomy and subordinate it to executive power. This decision set the stage for the complete absence of legal restraints that would later facilitate Suharto's creation of a sultanistic oligarchy. Nevertheless, Indonesia's legal infrastructure, even with this latent vulnerability at its core, was vastly more professional and independent in the 1950s than anything seen from 1960 onward. This characterization runs counter to the view widely implanted in Indonesia through armed forces propaganda that the parliamentary period from 1950 to 1957 was chaotic, fragmented, ineffective, overly "political," and likely structured to be this way on purpose by the Dutch, who insisted on the federal 1950 Constitution adopted during the negotiations for sovereignty.

Lev (2007, 238) offers a strikingly different assessment of the early years of the Republic.

> Judicial decisions from those years provide ample evidence that judges from the first instance up through the *Mahkamah Agung* (Supreme Court, Indonesia's highest court) not only managed litigation but, as best they could in difficult circumstances, began to adapt old substantive law to new conditions. Moreover, their decisions were implemented as a matter of course, in distinct contrast with judicial practice under the New Order. Similarly, the prosecution and police, equipped with capable leadership, were, by and large, oriented to law, not particularly to political authority, which did not always hesitate to make use of them but as often as not failed. It was, in short, a fairly effective legal system, one that evidently had the respect of those who came in contact with it.

Some government officials tried to use their office for self-enrichment, as did political parties starved for operating funds. "Compared with Guided Democracy and the New Order years, however, 1950s corruption seems amazingly picayune and even subject to some controls, not least by way of legal process."[18] Lev (2007, 238) concludes that "the legal system inherited from the colony worked impressively well under the parliamentary government" despite needs for funding, facilities, and equipment, and that "legal institutions by and large were respected and trusted."[19]

---

[18] In sharp contrast to the weakness of the judicial system from the 1960s onward, Lev (2007, 239) points out that during the parliamentary years "legal process was given its due by most cabinets; and the top ranks of the judiciary, prosecution, and police had no compunction about enforcing the law, even against prominent political figures. Political leaders tested boundaries often enough, and sometimes crossed them, but for the most part the lines held."

[19] Lev (2007, 237) notes that that this version of the parliamentary period runs counter to the "constructed mythology about how bad it was." He admits there were challenges. And yet, "parliamentary governments produced strong education and health policies; debated and promulgated substantial legislation; unified the judicial system and extended it throughout the country; planned and held the first national elections."

The attack against this legal system was fierce, with Sukarno playing a complicit role, but with the greatest damage being inflicted by the armed forces under the leadership of General Nasution. Under a constant threat of an army coup from October 1952 forward, General Nasution pushed Sukarno to declare martial law in 1957 and advanced the concept of the military's "dual function" so that officers could play a direct role in politics. Nasution also scrapped the work of the Constituent Assembly, which was busy between 1955 and 1959 writing a better and stronger constitution, by forcing Sukarno's hand in reinstating the authoritarian 1945 Constitution by presidential (and arguably unconstitutional) decree. "The changes that followed were dramatic," Lev (2007, 240) writes, "and for some – including judges, private lawyers, some prosecutors, and assorted other legal functionaries – paralyzing."[20] The result was that a legal system that had functioned remarkably effectively despite its liabilities had "quickly lost its ideological and political moorings."

> It was during this period, from 1959–60 on, that the legal system began rapidly to collapse. Such institutionally oriented officials as Prosecutor-General Soeprapto and police commandant Soekanto were dismissed and replaced with leaders less independent and more sensitive to political purposes. A few judges, prosecutors, and police officials objected or quietly retired, while many of those who remained turned from law to political compliance and its rewards. The same was true of the administrative bureaucracy. As highly placed civil servants were incorporated into a state edifice tied directly to regime leadership and freed from both institutional and nonregime controls, a tacit understanding took shape by which, in exchange for political loyalty to the President or to the army leadership or to both, officials were tacitly allowed to extract compensatory rewards wherever they could find them (Lev 2007, 241).

Although Indonesia's legal system and institutions of governance showed signs of strength and independence when the new nation was founded, they were far too new to endure the relentless attacks on their foundations by the armed forces and key figures like Sukarno. By the early 1960s, with a second generation of legal specialists moving into the system, there was little will to hold on and defend their profession or autonomy. Lev (2000, 8) writes:

> Unlike their predecessors, with memories of judicial standards, integrity, and prestige in the colony, and a sense of pride in the judicial independence of the 1950s, younger judges settled into a lesser station. Pressured to do the Government's bidding, suffering from declining real income and loss of status, judges were easily enticed into corruption, not least by rising star prosecutors. Guided Democracy's bureaucracy became pervasively corrupt, though it

---

[20] "Authority and power were increasingly concentrated in Jakarta," Lev (2007, 240) adds. "Political parties were pushed to the margins of legitimacy and their number was reduced. Nongovernmental organizations (NGOs) of various sorts, denied the useful access they once had to parliament and elsewhere in the government, went rapidly into decline.... In short time, military officers were in the cabinet; active in regional administration; and in charge of Dutch commercial enterprises nationalized in 1958."

proved capable of becoming even more so later, but no part of it was scarred more deeply and lastingly than the judiciary.[21]

In a speech before the legislature in 1960, Sukarno severely weakened the judiciary by announcing Indonesia's government would have no separation of powers. Laws were adopted in 1964 and 1965 that "allowed for direct government interference in the course of justice and, as part of the general abolition of the separation of powers, explicitly ended judicial autonomy" (Pompe 2005, 52). The last independent institutional obstacles to Suharto's lawless sultanistic regime had been removed, and the stage was now set for the emergence of a stratum of oligarchs that could be nurtured in a context of controlled theft.

Suharto and Indonesia's Sultanistic Oligarchy. Major General Suharto seized command of the armed forces at the end of 1965, wrestled power from President Sukarno, and placed him under house arrest until his death in 1970. He also personally oversaw the violent execution of hundreds of thousands of Indonesians whose only mistake was to be associated with a legal leftist party. With reverberations of that trauma still haunting all progressive politics more than a half century later, it is not an exaggeration to assert that this massacre was probably the single most transformative event affecting the prospects for Indonesia's oligarchy in the country's entire pre- and postcolonial history. It not only settled, in a manner that was absolute, the last major material-property battle for this new nation, but also left the country in the hands of an inward-looking military autocrat who had not graduated from high school, had minimal exposure to the international world, and displayed the mentality and ambitions of a retro-Javanese potentate.

Suharto frontloaded the violence of his regime in an act of mass murder so terrifying that it was possible for the New Order to remain in power largely unchallenged from below despite exerting a relatively low level of brutality against the population over the next three decades (the same cannot be said for neighboring populations in Timor Leste). The regime had nipped most resistance in the bud early while adopting a punitive strategy to control the press, education, and ideas. The result was that even the most fabulously wealthy oligarchs that arose under Suharto's rule never experienced even a fraction of the fear and nervousness felt by the much more modest upper classes threatened by the PKI in the 1950s and 1960s. As the gap between ultra-rich Indonesians and everyone else widened under the watchful protection of Suharto, oligarchs

---

[21] "In the judicial system," Lev (2007, 241) states, "prosecutors put their control over preliminary investigation to use by arresting well-off entrepreneurs, often ethnic Chinese, and holding them for ransom. In a short time, prosecutors began to recruit judges, needy and disappointed in their own institutions, who shared the take in exchange for favourable decisions when necessary. Soon after, judges went on to accepting bribes directly from litigants in both criminal and civil cases. Judges and prosecutors who objected at all either retired or were set aside to do routine or meaningless work. Finally, to complete the circle, advocates who understood that winning cases had a price attached joined what came to be known later as the 'judicial mafia.' By 1965 much of the judicial system was infected."

felt no urgent need to invest in the coercive aspects of wealth defense. Lacking the threats and anxieties present in other theft-driven authoritarian regimes, oligarchs in Indonesia also had no safety concerns pushing them to move their gains abroad. Rampant resource grabbing combined with keeping the capital at home helped fuel growth, but not necessarily development, during Suharto's sultanistic rule.

No effort is made here to recount the political economy of Suharto's New Order regime. There are numerous sources that cover the period capably and from a range of perspectives.[22] Instead, the more modest objective is to explore the contours of Indonesian oligarchy, first in its sultanistic form under Suharto, followed by the changes in oligarchy that took place once Suharto was removed from the picture. At the heart of the discussion is how Indonesia's oligarchs came into existence, the nature of the threats they faced once constituted, how wealth and property defense were achieved, and the tensions that arose within Suharto's sultanistic oligarchy finally culminating in its collapse. Wealth and property defense in the post-Suharto period are also discussed, together with the transition from a tamed to a wild oligarchy.

It would not be easy to find another country where so much fabulous wealth could be held by oligarchs who are surrounded by so many millions of people living in so much poverty and frustration, and yet those oligarchs face no imminent threats from below and somehow operate economically without the protections of property rights based on the rule of law. An arrangement like this might seem plausible if it were the repressive Suharto regime that was being described, but instead, this is a description of post-Suharto Indonesia. Even more remarkable is that the material extremes existing in contemporary Indonesia remain utterly undisturbed despite an electoral-democratic transformation during the brief "reformasi" period after Suharto's fall that introduced a rambunctious freedom of the press, full rights of assembly and dissent, and an end to torture, kidnappings, and disappearances (except in resistance zones still dominated by the military).

Although Indonesia's oligarchs face a range of constant and often annoying complications in defending their property and wealth, they are never because of serious threats from their impoverished brethren. In fact, the threats oligarchs have faced since the collapse of Suharto's sultanistic regime have been entirely from each other and from figures within the state (not from "the state"). Among countries where property rights are weak or even nonexistent, and where wide swaths of the population (in Indonesia's case many tens of millions) scratch out wretched lives earning less than $1 a day, Indonesia ranks as one of the happiest and most secure places in the world to be an ultra-wealthy oligarch. Even more extraordinary is that this absence of threats from below has existed without interruption since the PKI massacres in the mid-1960s.

Indonesia is a nation spilling over with a lively politics complete with surprising twists and turns, outcomes unknown in advance, and a healthy dose of

---

[22] Robison (2008 [1986]), Winters (1996), Robison and Hadiz (2004), Friend (2003).

intrigue and scandal. Indonesians have also duly gone to the polls and elected a string of mostly incompetent and ineffective presidents since 1998, only one of whom had managed to get elected to a second term as of 2011. Indonesia's politics is profoundly distributive, but only in the lateral sense at the top, never vertically to the poor. That is, Indonesia's democratic contests are exclusively a game of shifting groupings of oligarchs (and elites who want desperately to become oligarchs) struggling to take power for purposes of wealth defense and personal (or group) enrichment. The urban and rural poor, workers, farmers, and trampled segments of the population in general are usually sideshows to this process.

This situation is inexplicable without an understanding of the specific conditions under which Indonesia's sultanistic oligarchy was formed, and how it later evolved. If a massacre set the tone for the Suharto regime, what made the bloodshed especially chilling was that it was led not by a raving demagogue, but rather by a soft-spoken and unassuming general of simple tastes, who had never stood out in the turbulent politics of the Sukarno era. "Suharto terrified people," Anderson (2008, 45) writes, "not only on the basis of his blood-stained record, but by his demeanour – chilly, silent, masked."[23] Although General Suharto's grip on the instruments of coercion in Indonesia was firm from the start of his rule, he took immediate steps to establish total control by co-opting and sidelining all potential challengers from within the armed forces (Crouch 1988), a task finally completed by 1974. Thereafter, he repeatedly elevated favored officers to positions of tremendous power – mainly so that they could execute ruthless policies of suppression – only to clip their wings and push them into positions of stunned and frustrated marginality.

There was an endless supply of equally ruthless military men to replace the discarded and discredited generals who came before. Lev (2007, 242) notes that with the Outer Islands subjugated, the legal system and institutions of governance thoroughly undermined, and the PKI exterminated, Suharto enjoyed the "advantage of a cleared field" as he worked to consolidate his power. The key component was his control over core elements of the army, which was the institution most responsible for the destructive political work done since 1950. Suharto's preferred method of power consolidation was patronage and *bagi-bagi*, which was always backed by the "widely understood premise that brute force, exemplified by the slaughter of late 1965, was always available in reserve" (Lev 2007, 242). "For him, he wasn't interested in money for luxuries," notes Prabowo. "Money was a tool. For him it was power."[24]

Suharto created and nourished Indonesia's oligarchs and organized them under a sultanistic oligarchy that he ruled personally. However, it does not necessarily follow that he intended to create this oligarchy, and indeed he

---

[23] Asked if he had ever heard his father-in-law so much as raise his voice, retired general Prabowo replied, "Never. He knew he was too powerful ever to have to yell. It was just not his way." Conversation at Hambalang Ranch with Prabowo Subianto, November 14, 2009.

[24] Interview in Jakarta with Prabowo Subianto, January 31, 2009.

probably did not. His motives from the outset were to shore up his power and stabilize his rule under conditions that were chaotic and sometimes violent. Indonesia's economy in 1966 was in shambles. Unemployment was in the double digits and inflation was in the triple digits. Indonesia's production and commerce had ground to a halt or gone underground into smuggling and black markets. Suharto needed fast money and staple goods, not only to get through the economic crisis, but to buy support and buy off opponents. However, to tap Indonesia's wealth and use it to stabilize his rule he would need a lot of help and partners. The United States led the effort to supply Suharto with a rapidly dispersing flow of emergency resources and generous credit. Although convincing private investors that Indonesia was a safe place to invest would take longer, the United States assisted with that project as well (Winters 1996; Simpson 2009). The problem with these external resources is that they came with constraints attached that conflicted directly with Suharto's power needs for material accumulation and disbursement on the domestic side.

After the destruction of the PKI, Indonesia's sultanistic oligarchy arose and evolved in three stages. The first, the military-Chinese phase, spanned the years from 1965 when Suharto took command of the armed forces until early 1974 when he defeated his last major military competitors. During this phase he signaled Indonesia's return to the Western capitalist fold and made gestures on the economic side to stabilize the economy by tapping Western credit, aid, and investment through an enclave of technocrats that were given just enough influence to achieve these objectives. Guided by a pragmatic logic of regime consolidation and security, and embracing the ethos of *bagi-bagi*, Suharto's core activity centered on aggressively mobilizing and privatizing the nation's wealth – in the readily exploitable agricultural and natural resource sectors – into the hands of a strategic group at the top. The two sets of actors to benefit from this wealth concentration were generals, who posed the most immediate coercive threat to Suharto, and ethnic-Chinese merchants, who were in the best position to help Suharto yield cash quickly.

The transition to the second stage of oligarchic expansion, the indigenous phase, followed a convergence of several major developments: a quadrupling of oil prices starting at the end of 1973, regime-threatening demonstrations and riots in January 1974, and the successful sidelining of intra-military elements encouraging the disruptions. Although Suharto's momentum was briefly stalled in 1975–6 by a domestic financial crisis of epic proportions – caused by oligarchic stealing gone wild through Pertamina – he entered the late 1970s stronger than ever. The second and larger surge in oil prices in 1978 provided the resources Suharto needed to enlarge the rising oligarchy beyond the ethnic Chinese and the generals to include indigenous Malay "*pribumi*" elements as well.

The third stage, the family phase, commenced in the mid- to late-1980s not because of any major shocks or profound changes in Indonesia's political economy, but instead because Suharto held on long enough for his brood of six children to grow up and start grabbing a major share of the oligarchic action.

This development, combined with clear indications that Suharto was laying the groundwork for a dynastic succession, became a source of friction and instability within a now more matured and diversified Indonesian oligarchy. Suharto's children, sheltered by the extreme security of their father's rule and having no direct experience with the pitfalls and dangers of a mismanaged Indonesian game of spoils, behaved in a predatory manner that violated the oligarchic creed of *bagi-bagi* and exposed Suharto's sultanistic rule to conflicts and threats it had not faced in nearly two decades. These three stages are examined in turn.

Military-Chinese Phase. Given that the Suharto regime lasted more than thirty years, it is easy to imagine that he established his rule with little effort. The reality is that Indonesian politics has long been dominated by an array of ambitious elites who jostled tirelessly with each other for power and advantage. Immediately on taking over the army and crushing the 1965 *putsch*, Suharto had to contend with a decade-long process of consolidating his power and constraining potential opponents, especially those with access to coercive power resources. During this first phase of the New Order regime, Suharto desperately needed to mobilize resources for his consolidation. This logic of consolidation explains how and why he ended up founding the nation's oligarchy and dominating it in a sultanistic fashion. The unintended consequence was that Suharto created a powerful stratum of oligarchs that ultimately become independent from him, that would step aside leaving him exposed when his regime came under attack in the late 1990s, and would go on without him to dominate the country's politics with neither the constraints nor the order his sultanistic regime once imposed.

President Sukarno was weakened by the events of 1965 and his political relationship to the PKI. However, despite the murders of the generals in the October 1 attack, he held on to the presidency and retained a great deal of popular support. Complicating matters for General Suharto was that a number of officers who had recently risen to high positions across the armed forces were unenthusiastic about him suddenly taking over. As Crouch (1988, 159) notes, many generals worried that if Suharto was allowed to consolidate his power and depose Sukarno, "they too would be replaced because Suharto would want to appoint his own men to key posts." It was one thing to accept Suharto within the boundaries of his position as commander of the army, but they were "not willing to cooperate in moves designed to enhance his power at the expense of the president." There was also the matter of the other branches of the armed forces. The air force, the navy, and the police were determined to maintain the independence from the army that Sukarno had helped them gain. Suharto had to contend with these other armed branches in addition to obstacles within the army itself.

Crippled by his wavering behavior on the night of the failed *putsch*, General Nasution, the armed forces chief of staff, held the highest military rank but was in a largely administrative post. Suharto undermined him with relative ease. A more formidable opponent within the army was General Soemitro, commander of the Brawijaya army division in East Java. In October 1966, as Suharto's maneuvers against President Sukarno were intensifying, Soemitro helped form the "Great Brawijaya Family," consisting of current and former officers. In February 1967, as Suharto was engineering a parliamentary dismissal of the president, Soemitro led a delegation of military top brass from the Great Brawijaya Family that met with Sukarno to express their support.[25] Decades later in his memoir, Soemitro (1994, 148) recounts a conversation with General Nasution in the months after the failed 1965 *putsch* in which he told "Pak Nas" [Nasution] that "especially among the senior officers . . . no one, including me at the time, wanted Pak Harto [Suharto] to replace Bung Karno [Sukarno]. We wanted Pak Nas."

The differences were not ideological. Soemitro and other problematic officers in the armed forces were as reactionary, authoritarian, and ambitious as Suharto. What they sought were guarantees that they would gain key positions and bountiful resources from the political upheaval underway. These urgent pressures from within the armed forces constituted the first stimulus for Suharto to create an apparatus that would – in the shortest time possible and despite the economic devastation Sukarno had left behind – generate patronage resources he could command and disburse. By granting ethnic-Chinese businessmen exclusive segments of the Indonesian market, and then pairing them with military commanders so that funds could flow to the generals for personal enrichment (and sometimes for basic provisions for troops and subordinates), Suharto was able to establish leverage over all key military commands in the army by 1969.[26]

However, major contenders like General Soemitro continued to pose a significant threat and were harder to neutralize. Patronage in the form of positions and money usually buys compliance, but the same resources can also enable determined and ambitious figures to launch challenges against the patron. Suharto's successes in positioning himself as the nexus between officers and flows of largesse enhanced his coercive capacities and laid the groundwork for

---

[25] Crouch (1988, 215) writes that *El Bahar*, a newspaper sponsored by the navy, published an article saying the Brawijaya officers "had assured the president that their division stood firmly behind him" – causing the paper briefly to be banned. Decades later in his memoir, Soemitro (1994, 142, my translation) denied the meeting was to support Sukarno. "The point of the discussion," he explains, "was to advise Bung Karno to adjust to the new reality and not stubbornly resist. We emphasized this by way of illustration. But we didn't say it in so many words. . . . " The shocking *El Bahar* article appeared on February 14, 1967, and Soemitro took a full week to assess the damage and finally issue a "clarification" in *Kompas*, Indonesia's largest newspaper.

[26] "Military men had become deeply involved in business activities," Crouch (1988, 304) notes, "and after taking power in 1966, the chief concern of many senior officers was to create conditions conducive to expanding commercial opportunity which they hoped to exploit in association with their business partners." Suharto used the ethnic Chinese because their operations were generally larger and more extensive than entrepreneurs of Malay descent, and because the deals being cut were corrupt. As Christian, Buddhist, and racial minorities, they were far more vulnerable to attack and thus less likely to divulge the details of these partnerships.

the rise of a sultanistic oligarchy he would dominate. However, these same moves generated frictions because the conservative societal groups who helped Suharto destroy the PKI and bring down Sukarno believed he was going to end corruption, not refine and enlarge it to a scale never seen before. Students, intellectuals, and religious figures felt betrayed when they realized that Suharto was erecting a bewildering apparatus of skimming, theft, and patronage – and cutting deals with foreign corporations and monetizing the nation's natural resources to do it. As this anger grew throughout the late 1960s and early 1970s, General Soemitro attempted to harness it to destabilize Suharto and the inner circle around him that had kept Soemitro marginalized.

The abstract technocratic logic behind establishing Indonesia's National Logistics Agency (BULOG) in 1967 was to manage and stabilize the supply of basic commodities like wheat, sugar, soybeans, and rice. The concrete sultanistic logic behind BULOG's implementation was initially to dampen potential social disruptions from wild price swings, but in a manner that facilitated oligarchic enrichment and yielded regime-supporting largesse. Both goals were different parts of a linked strategy of regime stabilization and entrenchment. BULOG operated through an array of Suharto-linked companies, six of which belonged to Liem Sioe Liong, a rising ethnic Chinese oligarch. Liem's Bogasari flour mills were given a partial and then a full monopoly on the import, milling, and distribution of wheat and flour. Liem and other similarly positioned businessmen profited handsomely, but it was always understood from the beginning that in exchange for these lucrative deals, Suharto could direct key military officers or elite political figures to Liem and others to be taken care of in generous *bagi-bagi* fashion. Sometimes this only meant envelopes stuffed with $100 bills, sometimes it meant meeting operational needs for troops or building barracks, and sometimes it meant setting up important players in juicy subsidiaries – seeding the rise of second-tier oligarchs.

Skimming from the country's farmers or profiting from imported commodities whose marked-up prices were passed on to consumers was just the beginning. The most lucrative areas for stealing were not in agriculture, but rather in natural resources – especially oil and gas, which was funneled through Pertamina. Suharto had placed General Ibnu Sutowo in charge of this state-run company. Although the president would later remove Sutowo for forgetting who was in charge and trying to build his own mini-empire,[27] the pace at which military and government elites were attaching like leeches to Pertamina

---

[27] As Dhakidae (1991, 174) observes, "The majority of the top management of Pertamina lay in the hands of relatives of the president director," General Sutowo. Dhakidae shows that Sutowo's general assistant was a brother-in-law, as was Pertamina's technical director for exploration; the director of administration and finance was a nephew; the head of the transportation division and the head of the personnel screening team was a lieutenant colonel and a close associate from Sutowo's hometown of Palembang; the head of the division for coordinating oil contracts with foreign companies was a major general and a relative of Sutowo by marriage; and the junior director of domestic supply had been the chief of staff in the army division in which Sutowo served.

and skimming public funds was not only rapidly creating a new layer of oligarchs, but also attracting considerable attention and criticism.

Mochtar Lubis, the editor of the daily *Indonesia Raya*, launched a series of articles in 1969 that would be one of the last examples of investigative and critical journalism in Indonesia for a generation. The series began with the provocative headline: "Pertamina, Does It Want Diversification-Conglomeration or to Establish a Personal 'Economic Empire?'"[28] Lubis and his reporters uncovered evidence showing that instead of pooling resources and expertise for national development, major entities like Pertamina were distributing patronage that was spawning a network of private oligarchs. In an editorial justifying the publication of their damaging exposé, *Indonesia Raya* declared:

> ... the aim of this series of reports is to attract the attention of the government and the people of Indonesia to Pertamina that commands one of Indonesia's richest natural resources, which due to its management policies, lie beyond control and outside the national budget. This report is written as objectively as possible, without any bad feeling towards individuals within Pertamina, including Ibnu Sutowo. For the sake of salvaging the nation's wealth, however, which is acquired by Pertamina, and for the safety of the greater Indonesia, we understand that it is our patriotic responsibility to give our contribution to salvage Pertamina, so that it could be managed as a motor and source of development to achieve our people's just and equal welfare.[29]

Lubis, who had the honor of being jailed by both Sukarno and Suharto, presented devastating evidence of grand theft not only through Pertamina, but also through BULOG, which managed rice production and distribution for the whole country, and a range of foundations established by the military and members of Suharto's inner circle.

Although General Soemitro was excluded from these lucrative money flows, his stature and the support he enjoyed from officers closely allied to him compelled Suharto to accommodate him with a powerful post in the regime. Just six months after being made commander of the notorious security arm, Kopkamtib (the Operational Command for the Restoration of Security and Order), Soemitro began to make his move. He visited university campuses around the country promising a "new pattern of leadership" for Indonesia (Crouch 1988, 313). Soemitro was supposed to be repressing dissent and criticism, but his visits to campuses encouraged and emboldened student leaders who were outraged at Suharto's corruption and theft of the nation's riches.

Student demonstrations erupted during the January 1974 state visit of Japanese Prime Minister Tanaka. Unfortunately for General Soemitro, what began as disciplined protests exploded into two days of urban rioting that left 11 dead, 300 injured, 775 arrested, and extensive property damage. Suharto

---

[28] *Indonesia Raya*, November 22, 1969, my translation. The words *economic empire* were in English in the headline. See Dhakidae (1991, 172, n105).

[29] *Indonesia Raya*, December 9, 1969, cited in Dhakidae (1991, 171–2, his translation).

dismissed Soemitro after a shocked armed forces closed ranks behind the president. This was the first and last direct challenge to Suharto's power by a fellow general. The president seized the moment to attack the press, student leaders, universities, and all dissenting organizations across society. What little remained of independent institutions of law, police, or justice was extinguished. With the defeat of Soemitro and the process of wealth concentration advancing rapidly, Suharto's transformation from authoritarian general to sultanistic oligarch was complete.

Indigenous Phase. The first cohort of military-Chinese oligarchs had been formed by 1974 and Suharto's grip on them was solid. The oil booms of 1974 and 1978 fundamentally changed the dynamics of oligarchic creation and control. Whereas the first group played a critical role in Suharto's regime consolidation, the windfall resources pouring into the state's coffers permitted Suharto to broaden the oligarchy to include *pribumi*-Malay elements whose exclusion was possible initially but politically untenable over the medium and long term. The ethnic Chinese were entrepreneurs in their own right. They would have never grown into the bloated conglomerates they became by the 1980s without becoming an adjunct of Suharto's extraction apparatus, but they would have survived as medium-scale entrepreneurs and traders. Suharto's control over them, in the last instance, was because of a dangerous cocktail of economic, racial, and religious jealousy and hatred always barely below the surface of Indonesian society. The richer the Chinese oligarchs became, and the more they fulfilled their resented function as Suharto's conduit for spoils, the more dependent they became on the protection-racket aspect of the Suharto regime. An official policy of discrimination against the Chinese combined with periodic pogroms by angry mobs of *pribumi*s kept the ethnic Chinese not just on a short leash, but a choker chain.

Suharto's leverage over indigenous Malay oligarchs was primarily material, but also perversely institutional. His personal control over access to the state's petro-dollars, cheap bank credit, and the granting (or blocking) of permits for businesses across all sectors meant that indigenous oligarchs were under his sway from the deposit of their first royalty checks until the opening of their offshore accounts in Singapore, or, for the largest players, in Switzerland and Austria. As with the use of BULOG and Pertamina, the enlargement of Indonesia's oligarchy was given greater organizational coherence through the use of state banks, the ministries of forestry, agriculture, public works, and semi-public foundations established by Suharto and others. However, these were never bureaucratic institutions that could function independently or stand impersonally over oligarchs. They were institutions administered to lend order and regularity to oligarchy itself under Suharto. This contrasts sharply with the collective institutions of a ruling oligarchy, through which fully empowered oligarchs manage their joint affairs and mutual defense. Indonesia's institutions, whatever their outward appearances, were instruments for creating and controlling oligarchs according to the strategic and tactical signals given by the sultanistic oligarch standing above the institutions. In short, these were institutions operating for oligarchs rather than institutions run directly by them or empowered independently over them.

Nothing was more emblematic of this phenomenon than the creation of "Team 10."[30] The abstract technocratic logic for establishing Team 10 in January 1980 by presidential decree was to address short-term problems of inefficiency, waste, and ministries working at cross-purposes in the course of government procurement. Meanwhile, the concrete sultanistic and oligarchic logic pursued through this institution was to manage the injection of windfall oil and gas receipts into the hands of budding indigenous oligarchs – almost always on a no-bid basis. When Team 10 was set up, the government was sitting on an unspent surplus of $1.4 billion that Suharto could distribute immediately. Team 10 was headed by two notoriously corrupt Suharto protégés in the State Secretariat, and during the next three years the president would issue five decrees widening the reach of the Team's control over government procurement while taking over ever-smaller expenditures. The first decree made Team 10 a permanent body. The effect of the next decrees included ordering all purchases by state companies, especially Pertamina and state banks, to go through Team 10; extending the Team's reach to provincial government procurements; lowering the threshold of no-bid contracts from $800,000 to $320,000; spawning mini-Team 10s in each government ministry to link to the main Team in the State Secretariat; requiring all procurements using foreign credits to get Team approval; and finally in 1985, giving Team 10 control over military and security procurements.

The scale of wealth funneled through Team 10 was staggering, and much of it was a monetized form of the nation's oil, gas, timber, and mining resources. During its eight years of operation, the Team awarded Rupiah 52 trillion in government procurements to indigenous clients of the regime. This was roughly equal to $60 billion and was almost four times the total realized domestic private investment during the same period. A portion of this money purchased actual goods and services. As much as $25 to $30 billion in free funds was skimmed by a few hundred rising oligarchs launching their fortunes.[31] On top of these riches, Suharto doled out monopolies, opportunities to become "sole agents" to import thousands of products, forestry concessions (especially to figures in the armed forces) to fell trees across millions of hectares with no costs for replanting, and mining concessions in coal, copper, silver, and gold.

As the figure in charge of this sultanistic oligarchy, a key role Suharto discharged was to provide wealth defense for oligarchs who had never been armed. They were wholly urban, mostly on Java, and heavily concentrated in Jakarta. Their reliance on the coercive capacities of Suharto was complete. Minor disputes among oligarchs were settled by prominent figures known

[30] A full analysis of Team 10 is presented in Winters (1996, 123–60).
[31] The best broad-brush estimates are that a third of Indonesia's ordinary project expenditures are stolen – and that is when tenders, bidding, and audits temper the larceny. None of these safeguards was in place on the funds flowing through Team 10.

to have direct access to Suharto. The president intervened directly in major conflicts involving the strongest oligarchs, especially if the matter involved damaging ripple effects that could engulf the banking sector or the broader economy.

If Suharto is to be saluted for anything, it would be for his ability to blend a capacity for cold cunning with a keen awareness that a well-played game of *bagi-bagi* would extend the life of his sultanistic rule. Indonesia's elites and soon-to-be oligarchs had repeatedly demonstrated a penchant for infighting, social agitation, and regional destabilization. Strong impersonal institutions of law would be one way of taming them, but Suharto's technique was an unusual institutionalization of personal rule. He built and ran Indonesia's oligarchy in a manner that was remarkably orderly, predictable, and with barely a hint of autocratic whim or snit. Commenting nostalgically on making money with and under Suharto, one Indonesian oligarch emphasized the premium the president placed on personal integrity despite all he had done to undermine any recourse to law or justice. "With Suharto a deal was a deal," the oligarch observed. Lucrative arrangements and monopolies forged through Suharto involved a "reasonable" payment up front in exchange for the president's blessing and protection.[32]

Crass dollar or rupiah amounts were discussed with the president's closest associates, themselves major oligarchs, whereas actual meetings with Suharto usually consisted of little more than tea and pleasantries in his living room. This audience and a friendly handshake on the way out sent signals to everyone who mattered that a budding or established oligarch had "access" and, more importantly, protection. Implicit in the arrangement was the understanding that a relationship of mutual assistance was being forged – the oligarch might be asked to contribute off the books to the coffers of Suharto's party machine, Golkar, at election time or provide funds or a share of the market to help launch a minor client of the regime. Investing material resources in this corrupt and semi-corrupt way was itself a vital method of oligarchic wealth defense. Failing to be generous would violate the spirit of *bagi-bagi* and expose an oligarch to predatory encroachments by other oligarchs as Suharto stood aside, or, more ominously, attract the president's direct retribution. The system was thoroughly corrupt, there was no rule of law, and yet it had calculable rules, norms, channels for recourse, and was legitimized and softened by a creed of sharing and taking turns that was inclusive across a widening layer of oligarchs extending first from Jakarta and eventually outward to the Outer Islands.

Compared to governments with impersonally functioning institutions, regimes based on personal rule are prone to chronic instabilities. However, Suharto developed a remarkably effective formula for regime longevity. To contain threats from below, he pursued a relentless attack on civil society and punished pockets of resistance according to a sliding scale of responses. Depending on the nature of the threat and the social position of the individual

[32] Confidential interview in Jakarta with Oligarch "A," February 2, 2009.

or group behind it, the responses ranged from petty bureaucratic harassment and obstacles to promotion, up to beatings, jail, torture, disappearance, or group slaughter. The methods for control used at the elite and oligarchic level were as gentle as those directed at the lower classes were brutal. The hallmark of Suharto's sultanistic oligarchy was a system of material extraction and enrichment managed through an elaborate pyramidal structure.

Access to opportunities for becoming (or remaining) an oligarch extended outward from Suharto as a share of the spoils flowed inward and upward to enrich the lead oligarch personally, but also to lubricate and provision a regime apparatus that was badly starved for taxes and other legitimate resources. This system elevated proximity to Suharto to the most prized and profitable asset an Indonesian oligarch could hope to acquire. Proximity played a major role in who could become rich, remain rich, and enjoy the most reliable protections so crucial to wealth defense in a sultanistic oligarchy. It also raised the political significance of access management and oligarchic protection by Suharto for the resilience of his sultanistic oligarchy.

Family Phase. The maturation into young adulthood of Suharto's children commenced not only a third stage in the evolution of Indonesia's sultanistic oligarchy, but also triggered its most radical and destabilizing transformation. For two decades Suharto had pursued a carefully calibrated politics of proximity. A critical element in this mode of access was its unitary character focused on the person of Suharto himself. This allowed the dictator to shape and dominate Indonesia's oligarchy as he provided a high degree of predictability and a general defense of property that he could also selectively withdraw. "The system worked for a time," observed Prabowo Subianto, Suharto's son-in-law.[33] However, this proven formula began to falter badly when Suharto was confronted with the proximity dilemmas that arose when his own offspring began aggressively demanding a share of the oligarchic takings in a manner that did not comport with the established norms of *bagi-bagi*.[34]

No existing or potential oligarch could match the access and protections afforded to Suharto's own family members, but it was not merely a matter of family favoritism and related jealousies. The addition of Suharto's children into the operation of the sultanistic oligarchy actually disrupted Suharto's capacity to deliver reliable wealth defense. The result was a loss of equilibrium as the frictions from a new and seemingly unstoppable pattern of predation and threats increased to levels never before reached during the New Order. It was also a loss of legitimacy and support among the oligarchs as the spirit and practice of *bagi-bagi* was violated in ways that were alarming and appeared likely to worsen. By the mid-1990s, Suharto was grooming three of his progeny for succession and dynasty, which meant that the turbulence they were creating threatened to become a permanent element of the evolving oligarchy.

---

[33] Interview in Jakarta with Prabowo Subianto, January 31, 2009.

[34] Schwarz (2000, 146) quotes a 1992 interview with a long-serving Suharto cabinet minister: "As long as his children are not involved, the president makes very rational economic decisions. But when the kids get involved, rationality loses. Then it's the father that speaks, not the president."

Continued support for Suharto became synonymous with entrenching the kids possibly for decades to come.

Suharto's children invaded Indonesia's oligarchy with remarkable force and speed, becoming dominant oligarchs in their own right practically overnight. The crucial difference was that unlike any other oligarchs that had been built up since 1965, their proximity and relationship to the sultanistic oligarch afforded them protection on terms that were not transactional. Moreover, as members of the family, they were empowered to be protectors themselves in ways that went far beyond the contingent protection a close Suharto client-oligarch might offer. Table 4.1 provides a snapshot of the children and some of the differences among them.

A first observation is that two of the six children – Titiek and Mamiek – never concentrated enough personal wealth to become major oligarchic figures on the Indonesian stage. This did not, however, prevent them from becoming irritating second-tier access brokers.

With $100,000 of seed capital, Tommy Suharto got his start in 1984 at age 22. Within ten weeks his Humpuss Group already had twenty subsidiaries, which soon ballooned to sixty. A year later he acquired Perta Oil Marketing, a subsidiary of the state oil company Pertamina, instantly making him a major crude-oil broker and transporter. Perta generated profits of $1 million per month. Most of Indonesia's toll roads were built and operated by the state-owned firm Jasa Marga, with untold markups and opportunities for skimming and theft for oligarchs as the projects were completed. In 1989, Suharto issued a decree granting his daughter Tutut 75 percent of profits from all toll roads her group operated jointly with Jasa Marga, driving costs up still further. Bambang positioned his group as a partner of major foreign power companies and forced the state-run power company, PLN, to buy electricity at inflated rates (Guerin 2003).

Initially focusing their theft and skimming on natural resources and the state sector, effectively robbing the nation and the treasury, their business groups soon mushroomed and diversified. Their conglomerates survived by forming partnerships with actual competitive companies, often Chinese or foreign, and providing access and protection as their main contribution to the venture. Until they started stepping on each other's toes, the children ensured that competition was minimal and profits were eye-popping. In addition to the sixty firms in Tommy's group, Tutut's group consisted of more than ninety companies ranging from telecommunications to infrastructure. Bambang's conglomerate expanded to more than one hundred subsidiaries before consolidating down to fifty and then twenty-seven.

In the years before the 1997 Asian financial crisis and the collapse of the Suharto regime, these methods of enrichment produced a sprawling family of major oligarchs. In 1997, *Forbes* magazine listed Suharto as the fourth richest person in the world with an individual net worth of $16 billion, despite drawing an annual salary in his last peak year of only $21,000. The Suharto family owned or controlled 3.6 million hectares of prime Indonesian land, an area comparable to all of Belgium. They also owned 100,000 square meters of

TABLE 4.1. *Profile of Suharto's Children*

Suharto's Children	Born	Group (founded)	Revenue 1992 (million)	Net Worth 1999 (million)	Comments
Siti Hardiyanti Rukmana ("Tutut")	1949	Citra Lamtoro Gung Group (1983)	$400	$700	At age 25 given 14% (later 16%) share of Liem's BCA. More than 90 subsidiaries and $1 billion in net worth before 1998 crisis.
Sigit Harjoyudanto	1951	Humpuss Group (1984)		$800	Given 16% share of Liem's BCA plus 40% holding in Humpuss Group. Formed Arseto Group in 1978.
Bambang Trihatmodjo	1953	Bimantara Citra (1981)	$500	$3,000	100 subsidiaries by 1993.
Siti Hediati Hariyadi ("Titiek")	1959	Maharani Paramita (1992)		$75	Fortune reached only $150 million. Partnership with Tirtamas Group owned by brother-in-law Hashim Djojohadikusumo.
Hutomo Mandala Putra ("Tommy")	1962	Humpuss Group (1984)	$500	$800	Only 22 when his group was founded with brother Sigit. 60 subsidiaries.
Siti Utami Endang Adiningsih ("Mamiek")	1964	Manggala Krida Yudha (n.d.)		$30	Entered business too late to profit like siblings.

TABLE 4.2. *Suharto Family Cash and Assets Acquired over 30 Years in Power (billions)*

Oil & Gas	$17.0
Forestry and Plantations	$10.0
Interest on Deposits	$9.0
Petrochemicals	$6.5
Mining	$5.8
Banking & Financial Services	$5.0
Indonesian Property	$4.0
Food Imports	$3.6
TV, Radio, Publishing	$2.8
Telecommunications	$2.5
Hotel & Tourism	$2.2
Toll Roads	$1.5
Airlines & Aviation Services	$1.0
Cloves monopolies	$1.0
Automobiles	$0.46
Power Generation	$0.45
Manufacturing	$0.35
Foreign Property	$0.08
TOTAL	$73.24

Source: Table 4.2 and other figures in this paragraph, unless otherwise noted, are from the May 24, 1999, cover story in the international issue of *Time* magazine on Suharto and his family by John Colmey and David Leibhold. Research for the issue, in which I participated and that included an article by me, spanned four months and included investigations in eleven countries.

exclusive office space in the Jakarta market alone. The family directly owned or had controlling equity in at least 564 companies, and no sector was left untouched. According to one estimate, the total wealth amassed by the family over three decades in power was more than $73 billion. Table 4.2 presents the estimates by sector.

Setting aside $9 billion earned from interest on deposits, three-fourths of this wealth was derived from grabbing the country's oil, gas, and mining resources, or muscling in on state corporations and major government contracts. The entrepreneurial value added from this politically powerful but otherwise undistinguished group of children was, by all accounts, almost zero, while the inflated costs borne by the nation were staggering.

In the late 1960s and throughout the 1970s, the complaints about the country's rising oligarchs came from outside the oligarchy. Students and activists protested loudly about the rampant corruption, while the indigenous *pribumi* elites were upset that they were being ignored as oligarchic enrichment was accelerating. Suharto silenced the activists with an iron fist while accommodating his *pribumi* elite critics by using Team 10 to launch them as oligarchs. When a new round of criticism erupted around 1990, it was different from what had come before. Focused on the Suharto clan, and especially the children, this attack originated for the first time from within Indonesia's oligarchy. An investigative report appearing in the *New York Times* (Erlanger 1990) placed in the public record withering criticisms of the Suharto family that could already be heard as whispers among oligarchs in Jakarta in the late 1980s, but rarely expressed so openly and bluntly.[35] The article wondered aloud if Suharto might step down in 1993, or whether the growing need "to protect the large and burgeoning business interests of his children" had locked Suharto inside a presidential cage. The article noted that the children had "emerged in the last five years as privileged corporate players and objects of increasingly pointed criticism."

The shock value of the piece lay in the sources quoted and the direct mention of the Suharto clan. An unnamed minister in Suharto's cabinet shared with the *Times* reporter a joke circulating in Jakarta: "'India has the Taj Mahal,' he said. 'We have the Toll Mahal.'" The reference was to Tutut's toll roads – although the reporter robbed the joke of half its fun by neglecting to mention that *mahal* means "exorbitant" in Indonesian. The enrichment of Suharto's children had "expanded so quickly, and their involvement in most major government projects has become so egregious, that some well-connected Indonesians, including the hierarchy of the armed forces, fear that such excess is undermining . . . the renowned stability of the country."[36]

A prominent media editor added, "People have stopped covering it all up. Cabinet ministers tell jokes and want to hear them." A senior member of Golkar, the party vehicle through which oligarchs could be launched, stated that "the family is an acrimonious issue, and worse, it's self-destructive." Another top member of the ruling party added, "It started out O.K., but now there is a sense of excess and moral rot. First it was his wife and half-brothers, now his children, and soon his grandchildren. It has become a real issue for the future." An unnamed Indonesian scholar estimated that "at least 80 percent of major government projects go in some form to the President's children or friends." Another observer noted that it was unlikely anyone, including in the army, would move against Suharto. Yet there were "only disgruntled loyalists now."

Confidential interviews with Indonesian oligarchs, both indigenous and ethnic Chinese, reveal that the agitation within the once quiescent sultanistic

[35] One of the exceptions was when General Benny Moerdani dared to tell Suharto to his face that the new pattern of nepotism and corruption involving the children constituted a potential threat to national stability. For this warning from one of Suharto's most loyal generals, Moerdani was removed in 1988 from his threatening position as the commander of the Indonesian armed forces.

[36] In a speech quoted in the article, now former commander of the armed forces, General Moerdani, jabbed at the family by saying that with rapid growth "in 20 years we can afford to pay the tolls."

oligarchy was caused by a complex mixture of factors associated with this third family phase – the most fundamental being a surge in lateral threats to oligarchic wealth and a faltering system of wealth defense from Suharto himself. Oligarch "D" explained how the children began in certain lucrative areas, but how the patterns changed.

> At the beginning they had their own special areas. We all knew don't touch certain businesses. For instance, we all knew don't get involved in LPG [liquefied petroleum gas] carriers or oil tankers, which was what Sigit or Bambang were doing. We all knew that. Don't even think about oil trading because all of that was the business of the kids. And the ones who ran the show for them were the Bakrie boys under the name of Permindo.[37]

The family's method of enrichment expanded in two key ways. They started to take larger shares of deals and contracts, often contributing no capital, and they spread into far more lines of business already populated by established oligarchs. Referring to changes in how Suharto's children were behaving, Oligarch "F" noted:

> They were a lot more greedy. Now it was a fifty-fifty split. Before, the take was 10 percent, sometimes 20. When it went to 50 percent, that's what irritated everyone. But then when they started getting involved in everything, it ate up people's business. A lot of us had monopolies, but a few were in tough markets, and when you have to give away 50 percent, what's left?

Asked if Suharto himself ever took this kind of cut before the children arrived on the scene, Oligarch "F" replied, "Never, never, never, never."[38]

Another source of disruption was that the children started to engage in intra-family battles over opportunities for further enrichment. When oligarchs outside the family made damaging lateral grabs, Suharto did not hesitate to intervene to maintain an orderly sultanistic oligarchy. Asked if oligarchs feared retribution from Suharto, Oligarch "A" replied: "Oh yeah, definitely. No one dared to cross him."[39] His children did not share this hesitation. According to Oligarch D, who had extensive contacts with the family, the task of placing limits on the offspring fell to Mrs. Suharto: "The one who controlled the kids was the mother. She tried to keep the kids from being too greedy. The father was busy running the state."

Conflicts between the children would drag other oligarchs into the fray, sharpening horizontal frictions. "The first thing that brought the end of the era was kids fighting with kids. It made us very uncomfortable. One kid was supported by one player and the other kid was supported by another, then they both become enemies, fighting with each other, and sometimes it got quite ugly," explained Oligarch "F." "Of course it depends on the Old Man

---

[37] Confidential interview in Jakarta with Oligarch "D," March 18, 2009.
[38] Confidential interview in Jakarta with Oligarch "F," June 17, 2009.
[39] Confidential interview in Jakarta with Oligarch "A," February 2, 2009.

[Suharto], who he wants to give it to at the end of the day. And then the competition starts all over who can give the Old Man more."[40]

The actions of Suharto's children had a direct and negative effect on the coherence and stability of the nation's oligarchy. However, the greatest damage they inflicted on their father's sultanistic rule was indirect. The presence of the children, and the fact that Suharto enforced few limitations on them, dramatically undercut his capacity to provide Indonesia's oligarchs with reliable wealth defense. The reason was less because of the individual or collective predations of the children themselves, although these caused considerable agitation among Indonesia's oligarchs. It was rather because the absence of limits on Suharto's children created opportunities for actors around the children to join the game of grabbing the nation's resources and wealth. This unleashed a torrent of predations by scores of ambitious and aggressive people acting in the name of the kids and their extended families. Almost overnight there spread a pandemic of lateral threats against oligarchic wealth. And given that the core of the problem was the children (even if they were not directly responsible for everything done in their names), direct appeals to the sultanistic ruler himself for relief were foreclosed.

Referring to this proliferation of threats, especially the ones caused indirectly by the children, Oligarch "B" reported: "The more they spread into every sector and the more petty they got, the more irritated the ones [oligarchs] already there became." And, he added, "it was also getting so cheap."[41] This was a reference to the unseemly characters that had infiltrated the inner circle of the kids. Oligarch "B" described his disgust:

> Around Suharto it was always big players. But his children moved the game down market. So now it was not just the big boys at the table, but small boys showed up too. Around the kids were a lot of undesirable characters, some of whom were known to be bandits and thugs. It was like tentacles that were multiplying and growing. Can you imagine what this is like for a major player?

Oligarch "B" provided an example.

> I had a big piece of prime land, and this guy said he wants an appointment and uses the name of [a Suharto offspring]'s mother-in-law. And so of course I let him in because I thought it was a message from the mother-in-law. And he shows up with these guys who look like a bunch of thugs and he says, "Oh, by the way I own this land." I asked him what he was talking about and he says my land belongs to [a Suharto offspring]'s mother-in-law, and so I have to pay her, through him, so much. Extortion, you see? And that would drive us crazy. Imagine some disgusting thug shows up out of the blue and says your land belongs to the mother-in-law of one of the kids. Of course you get pissed off. Turns out he owned a very small bakery shop.[42]

[40] Confidential interview in Jakarta with Oligarch "F," June 17, 2009.
[41] Confidential interview in Jakarta with Oligarch "B," March 11, 2009.
[42] Confidential interview in Chicago (by telephone to Jakarta) with Oligarch "B," February 9, 2010.

Still referring to the extortionist, the oligarch continued, "What he didn't know was that I knew the mother-in-law quite well." She was aware the man was doing the land-grab operation and she expected to receive a cut of the extortion money. "But she never bothered with the details of it," said Oligarch "B." "And when I talked to her I said, 'Listen auntie, this happened to me, and are you really involved?' And she said, 'Oh it's you, I'm sorry I didn't know.'" As an in-law of one of Suharto's children, the woman felt confident she could dispatch various shady characters to extort members of the oligarchy. However, there was too much of this going on for her to be bothered with the details of who was being squeezed. It was inevitable that she and others attached to the kids would occasionally be involved in extorting millions from personal acquaintances.

"It's the breadth and the crudeness of the arrangements that's so harmful," the Indonesian media editor told the *New York Times* (Erlanger 1990). "Since 1966, under Mr. Suharto's New Order, Indonesia has been a collaborative system of cooptation," he added, "where people have happily lived and profited by the five D's: *datang, duduk, dengar, diam, duit.* Come, sit, listen, silence, money." When the system of oligarchic grabbing and skimming radiated from Suharto alone, it was more orderly, safer, and less offensive to members of the upper classes. The oligarch facing the land grab was lucky that he had a personal relationship with the mother-in-law and could shame her into stopping the theft. If he did not have this arbitrary fall-back defense, he would likely have forfeited the land or paid a high fee to keep it. Going to Suharto was out of the question because the oligarch would have been forced to criticize the president's children and their family. The risks of offending or embarrassing Suharto were potentially far more costly than the cash value of the prime piece of land or the extortion payment demanded to keep it. Going to the courts was utterly out of the question. Oligarch "B" saw the problem as a loss of protection and recourse.

> It's like a "me too" game. Everyone connected to the kids starts to play the game. They [the children] were so involved in everything, and they start to accommodate all their friends and family and cronies, and it begins to get to be too much. It was nonstop trouble. And Suharto was nowhere to be seen, and no one even dared to bring it up to him. Everyone saw what happened to Benny [Moerdani] when he mentioned that the kids were becoming a serious liability. It was this group connected to the kids who ruined everything, actually. They added flame to the fire, on top of the kids themselves increasing the greed level, fighting with each other, adding in the grandkids, and even the grandchildren's circles. By the time the in-laws and other hangers-on of every stripe got involved, the system Suharto had built was ruined.[43]

The family phase of Indonesia's oligarchic evolution fundamentally disrupted what had been a reliable and stable system of wealth defense. "Under

---

[43] Confidential interview in Chicago (by telephone to Jakarta) with Oligarch "B," February 9, 2010.

Suharto there was a feeling of security," said Oligarch "A." "We felt protected and his word meant something – and when the kids grew up it fell apart."[44] A new and virulent form of lateral danger had arisen, and oligarchs had nowhere to turn for protection.

Indonesia's oligarchs were eternally grateful to Suharto for their very existence and for the decades of order and stability he provided during their aggressive and often illegal enrichment. However, the arrival of the children, the grandchildren, and especially the entourage of threatening characters they brought with them, introduced a deep and unsettling transformation within the oligarchy. As the evidence mounted that Suharto was preparing some of his children for political roles, a nightmare scenario was emerging. If Suharto was engineering a dynastic transition that promised to transform a simmering problem into a permanent one, then from the perspective of Indonesia's oligarchs, the president had become a net liability and had overstayed his welcome. This view, already widespread by 1990, grew more acute during the next eight years.

Suharto Sidelined. The broad outlines of Suharto's fall from power are well known.[45] The proximate cause occurred in the summer of 1997, just as the regime was completing its latest round of rigged parliamentary elections. A thousand miles to the north in Thailand, the *baht* was slowly imploding, causing a financial ripple effect across Asia. The damage to regional economies varied, but no country was harder hit than Indonesia (Winters 1999, 2000). By the late 1990s, Indonesia's economy was deeply integrated into potentially high-velocity capital flows, and almost two-thirds of all loans in the domestic banking sector were technically in default, but were being hidden and sustained by external short-term borrowing.[46] As the regional financial crisis widened, capital outflows reached a record pace and funds for short-term loans dried up, triggering defaults on the mountain of bankrupt loans that were suddenly revealed across a liberalized Indonesian banking system that operated in practice as a public theft machine.

By the fall of 1997, with the value of the rupiah sinking, Indonesia turned to the International Monetary Fund (IMF) for a bailout. As part of its austerity demands, the IMF forced Suharto to cancel a host of major government projects and close sixteen ailing banks. These measures caused a cascading collapse of contracts for large firms (especially in construction) and a loss of confidence in

---

[44] Confidential interview in Jakarta with Oligarch "A," February 2, 2009.

[45] For a range of interpretations, see Sidel (1998), Aspinall (2005), Lane (2008), and Pepinsky (2009).

[46] Indonesia's technocrats and their allies in the World Bank and IMF had recklessly pushed for banking and financial liberalizations, figuring the dangers of doing this in an environment devoid of any safeguards would generate enough fear to finally get safeguards on the agenda. This never happened. Instead, Indonesia's oligarchs responded to financial liberalization by opening hundreds of new private banks, taking the deposits of average Indonesians, and then lending it to themselves without collateral for schemes no regulated or arms-length banking system would have funded. This was a new method of taking the public's resources, it was widespread, it was technically "illegal," but no apparatus existed for regulation and enforcement.

the rest of the banking system beyond the few that had been shut down. The rupiah came under enormous pressure, losing 35 percent of its value in one trading day, before finally settling at just one-quarter of its pre-crisis value.

By early 1998, with the economy in wild fibrillation, the Suharto regime was forced by the IMF to remove subsidies on food and fuels, prices for the latter rising 70 percent overnight. Students exploded in a flurry of protests and demonstrations, with pockets of urban poor erupting in several cities as well. Initially contained within their campuses, students continued their protests from February 1998 through the end of April. In the middle of this agitation, and behaving as if nothing was happening, members of parliament chosen in the rigged 1997 election joined with representatives appointed by Suharto to vote unanimously in March 1998 to give the dictator a seventh five-year term. Just before dusk on May 12, while an overconfident Suharto was in Egypt attending an international gathering, a deployment of snipers on a Jakarta overpass fired on students milling around their university after a demonstration. Six died, some shot in the back of the head, and sixteen others were wounded.

For three days in the middle of May, Jakarta and other major cities were rocked by riots that left more than one thousand people dead and unleashed a pogrom against the ethnic Chinese that included the rape of nearly two hundred women and young girls, and destroyed four thousand shops and homes in Jakarta alone. Apart from the Chinese, the mobs seemed to be targeting businesses and buildings linked to the Suharto family. Suharto rushed back to Indonesia just as students, swelling to 60,000, occupied the parliament building – guarded by marines. As Harmoko – a Suharto confidant, head of Golkar, and speaker of the parliament – called for his patron to step down, the president stalled for time by announcing reforms and promising new elections.

Fourteen members of Suharto's cabinet informed him they would not serve in an interim government. Abandoned and actively supported only by his family, Suharto hastily arranged a ceremony for the morning of May 21 to announce the transfer of the presidency to Vice President B. J. Habibie. The head of the armed forces, General Wiranto, stated that the Suharto family would be protected, and the president returned to his private home defended by a cordon of soldiers holding back demonstrators calling for the president and his cronies to be jailed. Suharto was in no danger and made no arrangements to flee abroad.

There is no serious disagreement about these basic facts, but there is considerable debate over explanations of the regime's collapse. Everyone concurs that the 1997–8 financial crisis played a necessary role: no external shock, no regime change in the spring of 1998. However, the crisis was not sufficient. As destabilizing as the economic turmoil was across Asia (and through contagion, well beyond), no other government collapsed in the middle of the financial devastation. Moreover, the Suharto regime had survived major crises and bailouts in the 1970s and 1980s. Why should the shocks of the late 1990s bring down Asia's strongest sultanistic oligarch? Lane (2008) argues that the regime collapsed as a consequence of a people-power movement. This contends with the argument that deep and prior disruptions at the oligarchic and elite levels weakened the regime first, robbing Suharto of the support and unity he needed to do the same thing in 1998 he had done without hesitation in the past – crush threats from below with the swift and fierce use of violence and repression.

It is beyond dispute that student protesters showed great courage and made enormous sacrifices, several paying with their lives in the struggle. Yet it would be inaccurate to label the demonstrations, protests, and days of rioting as a "movement." There was no mature or coherent movement underway in 1997 and 1998, much less afterwards. A more apt characterization of this uprising would be a "mobilization of the last minute" triggered by a sudden external shock. The protesters helped finish off what was, by the early months of 1998, a mortally wounded regime. They managed this despite what Aspinall (2005, 264) describes as an "absence of a strongly organized threat from below." The weakly organized and largely inchoate mobilization was certainly not a sufficient condition for the regime's collapse, although it was likely a necessary one.

If, counterfactually, the prior financial convulsions unleashed in the second half of 1997 were removed, there is every indication that Suharto would have faced no serious mobilizations, much less the challenge of a people-power movement. The president was on track for a seventh term in office that, barring poor health, he would likely have completed. Likewise, if one were to remove the deep resentments among elites linked to the increasingly vulgar behavior of the Suharto clan and the growing alarm among oligarchs over a faltering system of wealth defense, the result would have been a far more solid core of powerful actors at the top supporting Suharto and his generals. Such backing would have emboldened a set of actors who were hardly squeamish about the use of coercion, and it would have greatly increased the likelihood of a Tiananmen-like attack on demonstrators.

The timing and character of Suharto's fall must be traced to deeper pathologies that were already present by 1997 and that overwhelmed the status quo when the financial crisis disrupted politics and business as usual. To understand the regime's stability and possible sources of vulnerability, a key starting point is the fact that Indonesia faced no external security threats of any kind. The survival of Suharto's New Order was a wholly internal affair predicated on managing wholly internal threats. Domestically, the potential threats could come from below or from powerful actors at the top – specifically, elites deploying various kinds of power resources (military might, positions and office, capacities to mobilize religious, ethnic, or regional threats) or, once established and materially empowered, oligarchs capable of using their growing material power resources to challenge the godfather at the head of what had evolved into an extended Indonesian mafia economy.

Suharto's formula of rule was remarkably simple – use horrific violence and ongoing intimidation of the most petty kind to check threats from the lower classes. As needed, this intimidation was extended to elements of a middle class that gradually took shape from the 1970s forward. As a crucial complement to these means of control directed downward, Suharto pursued a deliberate strategy of maintaining unity and cohesion at the top, first by defending elites and oligarchs against any and all threats from below, and second by an accommodating, secure, and predictable system of *bagi-bagi* as the nation's wealth was siphoned and shared.

As long as Suharto weaved foreign investors into the mix (and he did so without much fuss because few rising local oligarchs had the skills or inclination to do the actual work of resource extraction, building infrastructure, or producing goods), Western powers contributed generous grants and loans on easy terms to support this domestic formula. The lion's share of the wealth from this system went to those strategically positioned to become Indonesian oligarchs. Another portion was distributed liberally across a satisfied layer of national and local elites – who did their luxury shopping at malls in Singapore until gaudy and opulent shopping complexes were erected on the land of displaced urban slums (and operated securely despite yet more slums kept at a perimeter just far enough not to offend the beauty of the megaplexes). What remained trickled down to the rest of society, who got pieces of the spoils as jobs were created and as basic tasks inevitably got done – in spite of the waste and theft at the heart of Indonesia's political economy.

In accounting for the regime's implosion, the key analytical question turns on the elements in the formula that changed the most in the period leading up to Suharto's fall. This can be answered initially by noting what changed the least. First, until the onset of the Asian crisis itself and an unusually tough posture from Robert Rubin's Treasury Department in the United States, there had been no wavering in foreign support, loans, assistance, and investment. Second, anger and resentment from below was a constant across the entire New Order. However, there are no indications that capacities and opportunities to organize civil society had improved significantly since the massacre of the PKI in 1965 and the shutting down of independent student organizations in the 1970s. There are no indications, moreover, that the regime had softened its approach in the 1990s to dissent, activism, organizing, and resistance from below. Suharto's reputation for using violence was well deserved, and the brutal death in 1993 of Marsinah, a labor activist, provided a chilling reminder of the consequences one could expect for daring to fight back. In July 1996, concussion bombs and extreme violence were used against regime critics at the Jakarta headquarters of Megawati Sukarnoputri's Democratic Party, killing dozens of activists.

On the other side of the ledger, what did change dramatically was the degree of unity and coherence at the level of elites and oligarchs. From an oligarchic perspective, Suharto as sultanistic head of the system had grown more isolated in the 1990s. By the onset of the 1997 financial crisis, he had been abandoned. It is not that he faced an uprising from oligarchs or from elites in the armed forces. They did not overthrow him. It is rather that deep fissures had replaced unity and coherence at the top, particularly between Suharto and Indonesia's most powerful actors. Only a few oligarchs provided covert support to the demonstrations in the opening months of 1998 and during the dramatic occupation of the parliament. At most this amounted to minor expenditures for food, water, and sometimes for banners and transport.

What was far more significant was their willingness, apparent to everyone at home and abroad, to allow Suharto and his family to face the brunt of the crisis alone and exposed. They withdrew their support from Suharto and engaged in pathological behaviors that undercut his frantic efforts to stabilize the system and hold on to power. They did so without the fear of retribution from Suharto they had displayed across a period of decades. At a time when saving Suharto demanded that they rally their resources to the regime, they moved nearly $200 billion of their fortunes offshore. As the IMF injected tens of billions of dollars in cash into the crumbling banking sector, the oligarchs brazenly stole the funds and used it to speculate against their own national currency. Although the conditions imposed by a series of IMF "letters of intent" spread pain across the oligarchy, the onerous terms set forth in the agreements seemed to be tailored to hit Suharto's kids the hardest – something oligarchs across the system privately relished.

This breach among powerful actors at the top – which involved not just oligarchs, but also elements in the armed forces, party elites, leaders of Islamic mass organizations, and even members of Suharto's cabinet – created a vital political space for a mobilization of the last minute that could be reasonably secure against frontal retribution and thus gain enough momentum to overwhelm the regime. "Everyone is piling on now and kicking him because they know he's down," commented Rizal Ramli in February 1998.[47] General Wiranto (2003, 60), who became commander of the armed forces that same February, writes that in the days leading up to Suharto's fall, he drafted a position paper for the president arguing that "demand for change had not only come from university campuses but also from all walks of life including... retired ABRI officers."

During the second half of 1997 and especially during the first months of 1998, it was Suharto's own children who emerged as spokespeople making pronouncements and defending the president. This began months before the explosion of student protests. The fact that no one among the elite or oligarchs was willing to defend Suharto was an open invitation for demonstrations and shockingly frontal criticism. When ambitious actors in the military deliberately shot unarmed student protesters on May 12, 1998 – likely without orders from Suharto – they raised what had been a simmering resistance to a furious boil. Once Suharto returned to Jakarta from Egypt, any inclination he may have had to use wholesale slaughter to stop the demonstrators was tempered by a keen awareness that he lacked broad support across the stratum of actors at the top – an awareness the protesters shared.[48] When Suharto finally authorized

---

[47] Conversation in Chicago (by telephone to Jakarta) with Dr. Rizal Ramli, February 24, 1998, former Coordinating Minister of the Economy under President Wahid.

[48] Interview in Jakarta with (Ret.) General Wiranto, March 28, 2003.

a harsh response in the closing days, the instruction was uncharacteristically ambiguous and, even more unusual, not followed by the commander of the armed forces.[49]

Democratic and Oligarchic Transitions. The fall of Suharto in May 1998 marked the beginning of Indonesia's transition to an electoral democracy. It became a political system with free competition among parties and candidates to win votes that are freely cast (Schumpeter 1942, 271).[50] This transition was real and even radical. Indonesians held their first post-Suharto national elections in 1999, and five-yearly elections occurred on schedule in 2004 and 2009. Citizens participate and vote in a political environment marked by open and critical debate at open forums, on campuses, on the streets, and in the press; the competition among dozens of political parties for seats in the national and regional parliaments; and, since 2004, the direct election of presidential tickets. Violence during election campaigns is minimal, candidates are not harassed or assassinated, and voters, although highly manipulated, are not seriously intimidated. The outcomes of elections are not known in advance and transfers of power have been orderly and constitutional.[51]

---

[49] On May 18, 1998, Suharto handed Armed Forces Commander Wiranto a presidential instruction placing indefinite and almost unlimited martial law powers into the general's hands and authorizing him to take "any means necessary" to restore stability. Wiranto (2003, 60–2) writes that "what surprised me a great deal as the President put the document in my hands was his statement: 'Whether or not you make use of this letter is up to you.' I was startled by the remark. It was something very unusual, as normally in such a situation a head of state would think very thoroughly about the risks involved before issuing such an instruction: when he gives it to the person he chose, there would be no more bargaining." When Wiranto returned with the presidential instruction to armed forces headquarters, his fellow officers were fearful their commander, who had been Suharto's adjutant and was close to him personally, might opt for saving the regime through the repressive means the document called for. If he were to "take total repressive actions," Wiranto reasoned, "the New Order government would survive the ordeal for some time." However, he was convinced that the support did not exist at any level to sustain the regime for the medium or long term. He told the officers he would not attack. "Spontaneously, all officers at the headquarters shook my hands. Then and there I realized that the burden pressuring them for some time [being ordered to massacre ordinary Indonesians by the thousands for a lost cause] had been removed by my statement and attitude."

[50] In ordinary usage, democracy connotes vesting the power of deciding issues in the electorate, significantly expressing the will of the people (setting aside whether there is such a thing), or somehow reflecting the most important interests of the majority of citizens. Procedural or electoral democracy is a narrower and more technical concept. It refers to a political system that fulfills minimum, although certainly important, criteria of free contestation in the selection of the government in power. No deeper democratic notions are relevant. A procedural democracy presents voters with choices that may represent wide or narrow societal interests. There is no inherent contradiction between a system scoring high marks as an electoral democracy and yet being dominated by a tiny minority of actors in setting the agenda and policies pursued by the democratically elected government.

[51] Allegations of fraud having to do with computer manipulations of counting and results as well as of voter lists, especially in 2009, have been adjudicated by the courts – resulting in some re-voting at the provincial level, but no outright cancellations of elections at the national level.

However, this was only the most visible transformation. The democratic transition was accompanied by an equally deep transition whose effects are profound and yet unintelligible without a theory of oligarchs and oligarchy. Suharto was not merely the sultanistic guarantor of secure wealth for Indonesia's oligarchs. He also supplied the taming factor that regulated and constrained oligarchic behaviors toward the state, society, and each other. Suharto did this through a personalistic system in which all taming capacities were monopolized by the president through a process of deliberately undercutting the legal institutions that could, if empowered and functioning impersonally, tame Indonesia's oligarchs and ruler as well.

Suharto's removal had a dual effect with divergent consequences. It resulted in a transition to democracy, but it also caused a quite distinct transition to an untamed ruling oligarchy. Suharto was sidelined and the armed forces were weakened by decades of having their top officers selected based on their lack of courage and inability to lead. This cleared the way for an invigoration of the institutional forms and procedures of democracy. Instead of being carried out by civil society, which in Indonesia was much too disorganized and debilitated to play such a role, democracy was easily captured and dominated by oligarchs. Electoral democracy presents no inherent limitations on oligarchs. On the contrary, in Indonesia it provided a new means of pursuing individual and collective oligarchic interests. Democratic institutions have enabled rather than constrained Indonesia's oligarchs since 1998. They have provided an arena in which oligarchic cooperation and competition has flourished.

The institutions of law must be treated separately. Invigorating them has no necessary connection to electoral democracy and involves radically different power dynamics. Effective institutions of governance and enforcement, particularly if empowered in a way that is impersonal, are by definition stronger than even the strongest individuals in the system. They do not do away with oligarchy – that is a strictly material matter. However, they constrain and limit the behaviors of oligarchs, and are therefore by definition unavailable to be captured or dominated. The dual transitions of 1998 – democratic and oligarchic – presented new opportunities and challenges to Indonesia's oligarchs. They altered the context for wealth defense and shifted the nature of threats oligarchs faced. Indonesia's devastated institutions of law have proven to be no match for the materially empowered stratum of oligarchs Suharto created, controlled, and then unleashed by his departure.

The failures of law and enforcement explain why the institutional successes accompanying the democratic transition did not catapult the country in the direction of a civil oligarchy. Indonesia lurched instead in the direction of a poorly functioning ruling oligarchy, organized as an electoral democracy, in which the only actors who can dominate the political stage are oligarchs with massive personal wealth, and elites with a capacity to attract or extract sizeable resources from the state. The result is a criminal democracy in which untamed oligarchs compete politically through elections. Attention now turns to a brief examination of the electoral ruling oligarchy that emerged once Suharto's sultanistic oligarchy had collapsed.

Untamed Ruling Oligarchy in Indonesia. The previous chapter on ruling oligarchies emphasized the importance of the extent to which oligarchs were armed or disarmed. The direct and sometimes personal involvement of oligarchs in the coercive aspects of wealth defense has major implications for intra-oligarchic relations and the form and stability of ruling oligarchy itself. The central challenge is for oligarchs to achieve at least a partial disarmament while creating collective capacities for coercion, and then to prevent those formidable collective capacities (organized armed forces on a major scale) from being commandeered by rogue members of the ruling oligarchy. Forging a stable solution was complicated in Athens, Rome, and the medieval cases by situations in which oligarchs were partially disarmed at the ruling center but retained vital coercive roles in the countryside. The Roman case was further complicated by oligarchs who transformed temporary commissions as Roman generals into permanent positions of domination over the ruling oligarchy.

The specific circumstances of Indonesia's new ruling oligarchy solve this chronic problem of oligarchic coercion in advance. The country's oligarchs appeared late in the modern period with a postcolonial state already formed. They were the product of a sultanistic oligarch rather than an established cohort over which one among them seized control. In addition, Indonesia's oligarchs were fully disarmed from the beginning. No single factor is more important than this last one in accounting for the remarkable stability of Indonesia's electoral ruling oligarchy after 1998, despite an array of profound class, religious, ethnic, and regional tensions churning across the archipelago. The contrasts with the Philippines on all of these points are significant.

The reduced risk of intra-oligarchic violence does not mean oligarchs operate in an unthreatening environment. The question is the source of the threats and the means employed to achieve wealth defense. The transition to a vibrant electoral democracy has not translated into significant threats from below. Indonesia's civil society, particularly anyone associated with the Left (which in Indonesia still has crippling PKI associations), remains too fragmented and unorganized to mount any coherent challenges to oligarchs. Instead, oligarchs confront a proliferation of lateral threats and predations from above. These dangers do not emanate from "the state" in the impersonal sense of taxation or the taking of property, but rather from a dizzying array of freelancing elites using government offices and administrative posts in Jakarta, the provinces, and districts (*kabupaten*) to squeeze wealth from oligarchs in an updated and less genteel game of *bagi-bagi*. In confronting all of these threats, oligarchs are forced to deploy substantial material resources to pursue their core objectives of wealth defense.

The most vital power resource in Indonesia since Suharto's removal from office is money.[52] This is as true in the realm of Indonesia's new democracy as it is in the new game of competition and defense among Indonesia's untamed

---

[52] This is not to say that the ability of oligarchs to hire and deploy coercive forces is entirely absent. In fact, the use of *"preman"* and goons, once the preserve of military elites under Suharto, is one of the factors that is evolving rapidly among oligarchs in Indonesia. See Ryter (2009).

ruling oligarchs. For the first time in Indonesia's modern history, its politics are more dominated by oligarchs than by fractious elites. This includes military elites, who lack any independent institutional professionalism and are as easily swayed by money as all the other elements of the political system.

Capgemini (2008) calculates that in 2008 Indonesia had about 25,000 millionaires. The Merrill Lynch firm further estimates that an additional 20,000 Indonesian millionaires with combined assets of more than $90 billion (much of it tainted by illegality) lived in Singapore to safeguard their wealth and ensure their personal safety. The wealth management division of PT Bank Mandiri, Indonesia's largest bank, identified three hundred Indonesians with a net worth of at least $20 million. *Forbes* (2010) reports that Indonesia's richest forty citizens had roughly $42 billion in net worth. The top twelve on the list were all billionaires and held combined assets of $28 billion. The largest oligarch on the list had a personal fortune of $7 billion, while the oligarch ranked fortieth had a net worth of $240 million. The average for the forty was $1.05 billion (Nam 2009; CapGemini 2010; Ellis 2010; Koh 2010). Representing a tiny fraction of the population at the top, Indonesia's oligarchs control enormous stockpiles of concentrated wealth, but also exhibit a typical pattern of extreme stratification among oligarchs themselves.

Material power resources are used by oligarchs in different ways in post-1998 Indonesia, with the biggest variation being that the political exclusion of ethnic Chinese oligarchs from high state and party offices presents indigenous *pribumi* oligarchs with a far wider range of uses of their funds. Although there are spectacular exceptions, *pribumi* oligarchs on average control smaller fortunes than their ethnic Chinese counterparts, but *pribumi* oligarchs have a monopoly on opportunities to supplement their material power with funds stolen directly from state institutions. These resources play a crucial part in the *pribumi* battles over the highest offices in the nation, whereas the multifaceted battles themselves constitute a unique drain on the oligarchic resources of the *pribumi* contenders. Efforts are made to defray these costs by squeezing vulnerable ethnic Chinese oligarchs. However, this only works when the *pribumi* oligarchs demanding funds can credibly threaten to trigger costly problems for political "donors" No single case better illustrates the myriad uses of oligarchic material power since Suharto's fall than that of Akbar Tanjung.

Hazards of the Oligarchic Middle. Akbar Tanjung is a *pribumi* oligarch who is big enough to play in the perilous game of post-1998 oligarchic competition, but not big enough to win when in direct competition with far wealthier contenders.[53] This makes his trajectory especially useful for illuminating the threats oligarchs face and the methods of defense they deploy against each other

[53] Tanjung is personally wealthy, but the scale of his wealth is hard to estimate because most of it was accumulated via government and party positions he has held for decades. One element in the definition of an oligarch includes being able to deploy nonpersonal resources *as if* they were personally owned. This channel has been especially important for a figure like Akbar Tanjung whose elite positions have been a key bridge to his oligarchic status.

in the context of Indonesia's electoral democracy. Although the country's oligarchy underwent a profound transformation since 1998 from tamed to wild (and from sultanistic to ruling), the transition was nevertheless one of almost perfect oligarchic continuity. The feeble institutions of law not only posed no serious threats to Suharto and his family, but virtually no one from the New Order regime was prosecuted and jailed, no matter what the offense.[54] Twenty-two members of Suharto's 1998 cabinet continued in Habibie's cabinet, and sixteen of these were in identical posts.[55] Akbar Tanjung, who first became a minister in the late 1980s and served in Suharto's last three cabinets, was one of the survivors who shifted cabinet posts in May 1998 to become President Habibie's Minister of the State Secretariat.

Tanjung's power resources were multi-layered in that he could deploy his own wealth as material power, as well as flex his muscle through elite political offices. Reflecting Tanjung's extensive institutional base within Golkar, which would only grow stronger and wider in subsequent years, he was elected party chairman in July 1998, a post he held until December 2004. He managed to add to this impressive portfolio the office of speaker of the parliament from 1999 until 2004, despite Golkar taking second place in the 1999 elections. As Golkar chairman, Tanjung made a bid to become the party's presidential candidate in April 2004, and later that year tried to hold on to his chairmanship. Despite his impressive institutional power within the party, he was defeated in both instances by the sheer material firepower exercised by the competing oligarchs he confronted.

The Akbar Tanjung saga began with a garden-variety embezzlement of public funds. As Minister at the State Secretariat under President Habibie, and as chairman of Golkar, Tanjung stole the rupiah equivalent of almost $5 million from BULOG, the state's agricultural logistics agency, and used the funds to shore up his position in the party and strengthen its chances in the 1999 elections. Tanjung claimed it was technically not embezzlement because the president had instructed him to divert BULOG funds to help the poor. No record exists of this order. Indonesian elites and oligarchs often display some of their most brilliant creativity when constructing covers for their larceny – less because they fear the law than because they fear how *pribumi* oligarchs in office or strategically placed elites in government might selectively invoke laws for intra-oligarchic advantage or forced *bagi-bagi* if an easy trail is left behind. However, this theft from BULOG was so small by Indonesian standards

---

[54] Bob Hasan, an ethnic-Chinese crony of Suharto, was thrown to the wolves and jailed. Suharto's youngest son, Tommy, served four years of a fifteen-year sentence for ordering the 2001 murder of a supreme court justice who refused a bribe and upheld a lower court ruling against him. This was a rare act of violence at the top of the system. The irony is that Tommy probably could have avoided jail time on the original charge had he not killed a high court official over the matter. Since his release from jail, he circulates freely among Jakarta's elites and regularly enjoys fawning press coverage.

[55] Every strategic ministerial post except the minister of finance made the transition from Suharto to Habibie without change.

that Tanjung and his associates appear to have been careless in concealing their tracks.

Nothing happened until 2001, when Rizal Ramli, who had been jailed decades earlier as a student activist opposing Suharto, became the head of BULOG and audited the accounts. Tanjung, then the Golkar chairman and speaker of parliament, scrambled to account for the funds. Instead of dispersing the assistance to the poor through an established government channel, he claimed he had transferred the money to a private foundation, but could not recall its name. Once identified, the shady foundation could show no proof it had given assistance to the poor. The evidence was overwhelming that the money had become part of a slush fund Tanjung was free to deploy as he wished. The money became his. As the case unfolded, it became clear that following the money was not what mattered to the authorities, and they never investigated the actual flow of funds into Golkar. The target was Akbar Tanjung, an oligarch with presidential ambitions.

Excluding ethnic Chinese oligarchs from office during the New Order never conferred any significant advantages to *pribumi* oligarchs because proximity to Suharto provided better security than anything else during his sultanistic rule. However, the balance of power within Indonesia's oligarchy shifted dramatically after 1998 when Suharto's removal enhanced the power of *pribumi* oligarchs and elites, who could capture the power of office to make threats and offer protection, and who were now dispersed across hundreds of key posts at the national and provincial levels. Since independence, high government positions had been used for extortion and protection rackets. During the New Order, these same offices were relatively useless against the oligarchs radiating out from Suharto. Squeezing had to be focused on actors below the oligarchic circles fanning out from the president. Suharto's fall suddenly exposed oligarchs at every level. This created new incentives for *pribumi* oligarchs to invest their material power resources to control the augmented powers of office.

Contending for high political office also had advantages for oligarchic defense. *Pribumi* oligarchs began to invest major resources in party politics and the pursuit of high positions in an effort to shield themselves against threats to their ill-gotten fortunes and various other crimes they had committed before and after Suharto's fall. One of the biggest transformations since the democratic transition is that the major media, owned by oligarchs and used extensively in intra-oligarchic battles, constantly blare headlines about often mind-boggling levels of corruption. Party affiliation and being a contender for high office allows the accused to dismiss accusations as being purely political.[56]

---

[56] This has been a key element in the response of Laksamana Sukardi, who is alleged to have appropriated tens of millions of dollars while serving as a minister in President Megawati Sukarnoputri's cabinet, and who founded and chairs a new political party. (Interview in Bandung with Laksamana Sukardi, December 10, 2006.) Sukardi was no longer a minister once President Megawati lost the 2004 election. He was immediately flooded with phone calls from

Numerous oligarchs have been attracted to engaging directly in politics to enable them to deploy this important deflecting mechanism – expending significant personal resources to move up within existing parties or to found entirely new ones. It is also the case that a respectable showing by a party (which in Indonesia means winning as little as 5 percent of the popular vote), can secure lucrative cabinet posts or major cash payments in the frenzy to form coalitions to support presidential tickets.

The other side of the equation is that being a major contender, especially for the presidency, can attract fire and complications from other oligarchs and influential elites. When the "BULOG-gate" scandal erupted in 2001, Akbar Tanjung's powerful positions as Golkar chairman and speaker of the parliament made him a serious prospect for the presidency. His sway within the parliament, an institution in which almost nothing moves forward or is stopped without money changing hands, allowed him to block the formation of a "special investigation committee." However, Tanjung was enough of a threat that his major political rivals, even inside Golkar (which houses the largest number of big oligarchs), saw utility in weakening him by pushing his corruption case along in the lower courts.

When he was officially indicted, the media carried demands that he step down as speaker. He refused, saying he was innocent until proven guilty. When he was found guilty and sentenced to three years in prison in September 2002, he argued he deserved to continue as speaker until his case was heard on appeal. Despite his conviction being upheld in January 2003, he clung to his posts in Golkar and parliament claiming the decision was unjust. Tanjung's last hope was the supreme court, Indonesia's highest court of appeals. Its verdict of not guilty came in February 2004.[57]

Three things were crucial to Tanjung's vindication, none having anything to do with logic or legal principles. Tanjung's defense was that he was merely carrying out a direct presidential instruction. Prosecutors anticipated this, arguing that Tanjung should have disobeyed an order to engage in embezzlement.[58] However, if the supreme court upheld Tanjung's conviction, there was a danger former president Habibie, an oligarch whose family virtually ran the Batam Island special zone as a personal fiefdom, could become embroiled in the matter.

---

people attempting to extort funds. "We're getting all these calls asking for money, even though we don't have any," explained Sukardi's wife. "So, he changes his number every few days." (Personal conversation with Rethy Sukardi in Jakarta at the Gran Melia Hotel, October 25, 2004.) Sukardi was officially named a suspect in a massive corruption case involving Pertamina tankers on November 3, 2007, but has never been jailed or convicted of any crimes.

[57] Far more shocking than Tanjung's vindication was that he had actually been found guilty by two lower courts. A well-placed political source for Indonesia's *Tempo* (2004) magazine commented on the eve of the final verdict: "If Akbar [Tanjung] is found not guilty, the country's political scene will remain 'normal,' without any significant turbulence or surprise."

[58] The indictment stated that the law obliged Tanjung to challenge his superior: "Akbar Tanjung should not have agreed or should have suggested to the president that . . . the Bulog nonbudgetary fund should not be used" (*Tempo* 2004).

According to a source quoted in the media before the decision, the thinking among the justices was: "If you want to convict Akbar Tanjung, then you must also convict [former president] Habibie" (*Tempo* 2004).

The second reason is that with Tanjung's reputation now ruined, it was beneficial for the other players in the system to keep him in place as party chairman and parliament speaker in an effort to debilitate Golkar. By the time of the actual supreme court decision, calculations within President Megawati's camp, itself enduring an almost constant barrage of corruption allegations, had shifted away from weakening Tanjung (mission accomplished) and toward forcing Golkar's numerous oligarchs to expend massive resources to unseat a figure widely understood to have one of the most formidable institutional party bases and networks of any Indonesian politician. Retired Armed Forces Commander Wiranto, whose influence in Golkar was limited, gained momentum for a presidential run in tandem with each public humiliation Tanjung endured during the months leading up to the 2004 party convention to choose a presidential candidate. Media reports made it clear that President Megawati feared a Wiranto bid for the presidency, and "some of her political colleagues had made no secret of their hope that the official clearing of Mr. Akbar's name could cripple the general's campaign" (Perlez 2004).[59]

The third factor was Tanjung's oligarchic material resources. As will be evident presently, he was far from the richest oligarch on the Indonesian political stage. However, as the BULOG corruption case demonstrates, Tanjung was able to augment his personal resources for political advantage and wealth defense by deploying party and public resources as if he owned them. In the weeks following the supreme court decision ending Tanjung's ordeal, evidence surfaced that money played a crucial role in producing a verdict of not guilty. A self-described "case broker," known in Indonesian as a *makelar kasus* (or "*markus*" for short), brought a civil suit against Tanjung for breach of contract for failing to pay all the fees for fixing his court cases.

Kito Irkhamni, a former assistant to the attorney general, admitted cashing checks from Tanjung for nearly $35,000 in "operational fees." He further stated in his suit that the parliament speaker had agreed to pay him about $115,000 as a "commitment fee for his services in providing information on the development of Akbar's corruption case from the district court to the Supreme Court," and to "convince judges" of Tanjung's innocence. Irkhamni claimed he had honored his side of the case-fixing bargain and was seeking full payment plus almost half a million dollars in damages. Not only did this civil suit fail to trigger a criminal investigation, but, incredibly, a judge was appointed to assist the sides in mediating the dispute (Sri Saraswati 2004; *Jakarta Post* 2004).

---

[59] "A *Tempo* source at the Indonesian Democratic Party of Struggle (PDI-P) said that many of Golkar's rival parties were indeed interested to see Akbar exonerated. They believe that his exoneration will trigger a conflict among convention participants in Golkar." Bagir Manan, the chief justice of the supreme court, felt compelled to state that "there has been no attempt to influence the justices" (*Tempo* 2004).

Prior to 1998, Tanjung could have avoided such defensive expenditures. At the height of Suharto's sultanistic rule, falling within the personal orbit of the intimidating president provided oligarchs with maximum protection. No one in the government, and especially not in the legal system, dared to pursue legal matters against individuals known to be linked favorably to Suharto. During the New Order, the case broker business was more significant at the oligarchic margins for those whose distance from the center left them vulnerable to predations. This arrangement changed dramatically when Suharto fell. Case brokers moved up the oligarchic pyramid and the *markus* business has flourished under conditions of wild oligarchy since the taming role of Suharto disappeared. The reengagement of Indonesia's legal system since the democratic transition has not produced rule of law, but instead a booming industry of brutish *bagi-bagi*. Wealth defense and security for oligarchs is achieved through cash payments that settle legal matters in the oligarchs' favor, or prevent them from arising in the first place.

Oligarchs vastly richer than Tanjung have their own in-house operators whose full-time job is running a wealth defense machine. For a middle oligarch like Tanjung, whose various posts and offices also afforded him a modicum of protection, a case broker was indispensable. One *markus* admitted that fees for their services could reach Rp 20 billion (more than $2 million) per case (Tempo 2010). "It all depends," observes Neta Pane, an Indonesian specialist on corruption in the legal system. "If it's a high-profile case... it costs more. If another broker is involved, it becomes even more expensive" (Rayda 2009).

Akbar Tanjung's oligarchic mettle was tested again at the Golkar Convention less than a week after his *markus* lawsuit made national headlines. Held on April 20, 2004, the convention was originally intended as a device to leverage Tanjung's powerful institutional base within the party. Some factions in Golkar had been calling for the embattled chairman to step down over the BULOG scandal and demanded Tanjung pledge not to represent the party in the presidential contest in July. Rully Chairul Azwar, the Golkar secretary in charge of the 2004 parliamentary campaign and a Tanjung protégé, devised a ploy to deflect these demands by announcing, in the new spirit of democracy, that Golkar would hold its first-ever convention to allow party delegates, the bulk of whom were Tanjung loyalists, to elect Golkar's presidential nominee.[60] Holding a convention would put the matter to a vote – a contest Tanjung's faction was confident he would win.[61]

Hundreds of party officials from across the archipelago owed major political debts to Tanjung for his favors and assistance to them over the years. Many could not have moved up in the party without Tanjung's help. Ordinarily, a

---

[60] Interview in Jakarta with Rully Chairul Azwar, April 19, 2004.
[61] Ikrar Nusa Bakti, independent analyst at the Indonesian Institute of Sciences (LIPI), argued that Tanjung was most likely to prevail in the convention because of "the clout his position lent him and his powerful influence over party officials nationwide." "It is useless for them [the other contenders] to campaign," Bakti stated, "because Akbar [Tanjung] will eventually win the race" (Khalik 2004).

phalanx of party loyalists like this would have been enough to guarantee a victory for Tanjung. However, his experience in 1999, when President Habibie used overwhelming oligarchic financial resources to win Golkar's nomination for president, should have given Tanjung pause about his chances at the 2004 convention.[62] Although none of the eight candidates at the convention won a majority of delegates in the first round, the predictions that Tanjung's institutional base would give him an advantage seemed validated: he led the pack of eight, followed by Wiranto.

One of the other contenders, an oligarch who had apparently underestimated how much had to be spent to hold delegates to their promises, was shocked when he did not win in the first round. "Yesterday, I had a majority," he said in disbelief. "They all swore with their hands on the Koran!"[63] The decisive moment came during the short recess before the runoff vote. An oligarch who had participated in the convention referred to this interlude as "the minuet," during which a classic display of pure oligarchic material power was used to ensure a bewildered Tanjung was defeated by his own party loyalists in the next round. "They came in with suitcases at the last minute. A big push," the oligarch recalled, referring to how the cash was brought to the convention. "It was a real learning experience for me," he added.[64] Wiranto won the presidential nomination by a decisive margin.

The final showdown for Tanjung came in December 2004 at the party's National Congress in Bali. Wiranto had fared poorly in the July presidential election and Tanjung, still chairman, had reasserted his control over Golkar in the final months of 2004. When he gave his accountability speech recounting his stewardship of the party through the difficult years after the collapse of Suharto's New Order, he received two thunderous standing ovations from a hall filled with regional representatives. Tanjung's reelection to the post of party chairman looked secure until Jusuf Kalla and Aburizal Bakrie, two major oligarchs within Golkar, pooled their financial resources to reverse Tanjung's momentum. Oligarch "E" recounted the turning point:

> At the Denpasar [Bali] National Congress, money was brought out in the toilets! People were wavering in the vote. And you know what they did? They took hand phones into the voting booth to prove that they voted for "A" or for "B." So you were given half [the promised cash], and then after that when you showed that you had voted for Jusuf Kalla, they will give you the rest.

[62] Robison and Hadiz (2006, 235) write that supporters of President Habibie "gained the clear upper hand when they were able to assure his nomination in a National Leadership Meeting in May 1999 – primarily over Akbar Tanjung – during which money politics was allegedly pervasive." The media reported "the occurrence of large-scale bribery of party regional delegates taking place on Habibie's behalf."
[63] Conversation at the Golkar Convention in Jakarta with one of the candidates immediately following the first vote count, April 20, 2004.
[64] Confidential interview in Jakarta with Oligarch "E," April 24, 2009. This oligarch claimed that Wiranto's team paid part of the money before the vote and promised to pay the rest after their candidate won. "And he didn't pay the remainder," he added.

No other political figure in Indonesia had a stronger reputation for being an effective party player, a tireless party networker, and a master of party politics and maneuvers than Akbar Tanjung. And no other Indonesian party was as thoroughly institutionalized and "modernized" as Golkar. Yet Tanjung, a minor oligarch, was repeatedly outdone by much more formidable oligarchs – all of whom had major legal vulnerabilities in their past. These oligarchs could sway major votes, reverse key political moments, and purchase specific political and legal outcomes by exercising material power on a scale that trumped all other power resources that could be brought to the contest. Reflecting in frustration on his struggles within the party, Tanjung observed: "The most important thing in Golkar is not power, it's money."[65]

Ethnic Chinese Oligarchs. Racial and ethnic splits among oligarchs can have a major influence on an oligarchy. Ethnic Chinese oligarchs in Indonesia have been more constrained than their *pribumi* counterparts in how they can deploy their material power resources since 1998. Winning high offices, holding top party positions, and having strategic party affiliations have played an important role in the wealth defense strategies of ethnic Malay oligarchs like Akbar Tanjung, Wiranto, Prabowo Subianto, Aburizal Bakrie, Jusuf Kalla, Arifin Panigoro, Hashim Djojohadikusumo, and Laksamana Sukardi. Some have even invested their personal fortunes in founding entirely new parties.[66] Except in countries where public funds are a major source of finance for political campaigns, finding the money needed to be a political contender is always a challenge.

In Indonesia, where no public funds are available and where small-donor funding for parties or candidates is almost nonexistent, there are only three options. Incumbents, who are almost always oligarchs, can try to squeeze the state apparatus, including state-owned corporations, for "support" – all of which is illegal but difficult to trace. Other political contenders can be oligarchs rich enough to dominate entire parties and sustain their own campaigns. Or

---

[65] Interview in Jakarta with Akbar Tanjung, July 15, 2009. Tanjung understands that money is a form of power – but one he views as distorting and illegitimate. Golkar performed poorly in the 2009 parliamentary election and its presidential candidate did even worse. Debate over turning to a younger generation erupted on the eve of the party's national congress to choose a new chairman. Yuddy Chrisnandi, a rising legislator and candidate for the post, pointed out that only money determined who would lead the party. "There are a lot of young men just like myself in Golkar who are ready to step up," he said. "However, the reality is that integrity and idealism mean nothing in the party. The only thing that really matters is financial power." The chairmanship was won in 2009 by Aburizal Bakrie, one of Indonesia's richest oligarchs (*Jakarta Post* 2009).

[66] Laksamana Sukardi created the Democratic Renewal Party, Susilo Bambang Yudhoyono created the Democrat Party (with borrowed funds), Wiranto founded The People's Conscience Party (Hanura), Prabowo and his brother Hashim created the Great Indonesian Movement Party (Gerindra), and Surya Paloh used his massive resources to found the National Democrats social movement (designed to be convertible into a party before the 2014 elections). All of these players except Sukardi splintered off from Golkar, a party that is especially hard to dominate because so many oligarchs can bring huge financial resources to the battle. "That's why in the end I just decided to leave Golkar," stated one of these oligarchs. "It's cheaper." Confidential interview in Jakarta with Oligarch "I," February 14, 2009.

finally, they must have such a high prospect of winning that they can attract the financing from a limited pool of oligarchs. *Pribumi* oligarchs populate the first two modes and ethnic-Chinese oligarchs provide most of the outside financing via the third method.[67] The higher the political office and the more expensive the campaign (either within a party, as the Tanjung example showed, or against candidates from other parties), the higher the concentration of oligarchs contending for and winning the positions. The net result is that high political offices in government and in parties are disproportionately held by oligarchs or by actors who can capture significant oligarchic resources. It is tantamount to having a system in which a wholly self-funded figure like U.S. presidential candidate Ross Perot is the norm rather than the exception.

Ethnic Chinese oligarchs are constantly squeezed for enormous sums across the entire spectrum of political players. Wealth defense and security is the overwhelming motivating factor shaping to whom these oligarchs surrender funds and at what levels. The first consideration is whether the individual gathering funds is operating on behalf of an incumbent, such as a sitting president, or for a challenger. Incumbents enjoy many advantages in Indonesian elections, and the fact that they could be in office for years to come is a major risk to an ethnic Chinese oligarch.[68] However, they can also inflict punishment immediately by signaling to the police or the attorney general that languishing legal problems, even ones that have been suspended in writing (and at great cost) for "lack of evidence," must be revisited.

This risks a flurry of damaging headlines and a cascading torrent of predations that are costly to contain. A member of one of Indonesia's richest oligarchic families was asked, in a private conversation with another oligarch, how much he had "donated" to the campaign of a sitting president seeking reelection. He replied that he had paid more than $10 million for the presidential election alone, and far more if donations to the party for the parliamentary elections were included. None of it was part of any official campaign finance report by the candidate. Asked why he gave so much, the oligarch answered: "I have all kinds of dirt they can dig up." The inquiring oligarch then asked: "Does paying give you any certain security?" "No," replied the big oligarch, "but not paying will guarantee me having trouble."[69]

---

[67] This is true at all levels of the political system. Parties actively recruit the wealthiest actors they can find in the regions to run for regional and national parliamentary seats because party funds tend to be scarce, and even when the party headquarters try to distribute resources to the regions, campaign operations are notoriously porous.

[68] As President Megawati Sukarnoputri's loss in the 2004 election demonstrates, all the perks and money flows accruing to incumbents do not guarantee a victory. In Indonesia's electoral democracy, access to massive financial resources is crucial for winning a top party post or getting on a presidential ticket. However, the resources cannot secure victory because Indonesia's population is simply too large to be reliably bought at the polls. The political role of money in Indonesia ensures oligarchs are dominant, but does not determine which oligarchs will win in any given contest.

[69] Confidential interview in Jakarta with Oligarch "G," November 13, 2009. This conversation was recounted to me in 2009, but which post-1998 election this discussion is referring to has

A slightly different oligarchic calculation applies in deciding how much to surrender to nonincumbents. The key variable is the likelihood that the politician, fellow oligarch, or party pressuring for payments will win or perhaps sit in the coalition cabinet. Funds are distributed across almost all of the major parties and contenders. As polling numbers go up or as momentum is lost, subsequent tranches are increased or withheld. The calculations are never for policies, movements, or political principles. The motivating factor is the threat of an asset-destroying attack coming at any time, and the deployment of material power in advance is defensive. "Most of the big guys do it because they are afraid and the law is so screwed up that you're in trouble if they turn on you," said one oligarch. "They are buying security so that they don't get disturbed by the people who come to power," he explained. "The game is to make everybody happy." The goal is to avoid catastrophe rather than pursue further enrichment. "It's like buying insurance," the oligarch added. "If you also get business, it's a bonus."[70] An especially well-networked oligarch estimated that the lion's share of all donated funds for all the parties and all the major candidates in the 2009 parliamentary and presidential elections came from fifty to one hundred oligarchs, with the biggest funders numbering no more than ten to fifteen.[71]

The legacy of manifold illegalities dating back to the Suharto period and its collapse has generated an unlimited supply of legal cases that can, under conditions of intra-oligarchic friction and elite jealousy, expose oligarchs to endless rounds of attack. The experience of one Indonesian oligarch is instructive. When the name of his business conglomerate appeared in a very negative light on the front page of a leading newspaper, the oligarch began receiving threatening phone calls that same morning from an individual claiming to be a prosecutor in the attorney general's office. The oligarch was told that if he did not immediately transfer $10 million into a numbered foreign account, the prosecutor would pursue the allegations contained in the news item, possibly leading to charges being filed. The oligarch then spent the next forty-eight hours trying to buy time as he contacted his own connections at the attorney general's office to find out if the extortion was originating from an actual prosecutor.[72]

Even this was dangerous because merely inquiring about an attempted extortion could trigger a real and costly one. To guard against this, since 1998

---

been deliberately obscured to protect the source. In a restaurant of a luxury Indonesian hotel, I overheard a brief exchange between two ethnic Chinese oligarchs who were comparing notes on how much they had been squeezed to pay to the incumbent's campaign war chest (how funds are used is never made clear). "How much?" asked one. "One M," the other replied. "Me too," said the first. Depending on the context, "one M" can refer to a billion rupiah (one *milyard* or about $100,000) or a million dollars. I later discovered that in this case "M" stood for a million dollars.

[70] Confidential interview in Jakarta with Oligarch "H," April 30, 2009.

[71] Confidential interview in Jakarta with Oligarch "G," November 13, 2009.

[72] The system offered no institutional recourse. "Suharto would have stepped in to stop this endless bleeding, or it never would have even been done this way in the first place," the oligarch commented. Confidential interview in Jakarta with Oligarch "C," May 18, 2009.

oligarchs have been forced to maintain a small army of officials in the attorney general's office, the tax office, and the police on retainers so that these actors would feel obligated to assist when problems like this arose. If the threat was from a real prosecutor, the oligarch in this instance intended to wire the money as instructed. If not, it could be ignored. Over time, the same extortion game came to include corrupt figures in the media. Aware that a negative news item could trigger a costly extortion process for an oligarch, some editors or even ambitious reporters would alert oligarchs that they or their firms were about to be mentioned very unfavorably in a story, but that the damaging reference could be deleted from the article for a fee.

The Indonesian case has been highly dynamic over the period covered in this chapter. There were insufficient concentrations of wealth in the early decades after independence to produce a significant stratum of oligarchs. Under Suharto, Indonesia evolved into a sultanistic oligarchy whose members were thoroughly disarmed and who arose in a staged fashion that eventually disrupted the regime's wealth defense arrangements, contributing to its collapse. The transition to an electoral democracy unfolded in a context of weak legal institutions that could not replace the controls Suharto had imposed. Indonesia experienced a second and simultaneous transition to an untamed oligarchy. The system became more volatile politically and economically – an effect commonly attributed to the untested character of the new democracy, but, seen from an oligarchic perspective, is equally traceable to the disruptive effects caused by wild oligarchs.

As Suharto's authoritarian regime ended and the sultanistic form of oligarchy with it, what kind of oligarchy has democratic Indonesia become? The Indonesian state and its coercive capabilities remained intact during the transition, preventing a move toward the warring form. The rise of democracy without the strong institutions needed for impersonal guarantees of property and enforcement also prevented Indonesia from becoming a civil oligarchy. Still in a mixed middle zone, Indonesia has moved decisively in the direction of a ruling oligarchy as *pribumi* oligarchs have increasingly captured and dominated the open democratic process.

Indonesians are now freer and oligarchs are more freelancing. They use their material power resources for wealth and property defense in a political economy overflowing with threats and uncertainties. Transforming Indonesia into a system that is both a procedural democracy and a civil oligarchy requires a political process that is much harder than overthrowing an aging sultanistic ruler. The nation's oligarchs and its elites must be overpowered and tamed by impersonal institutions of law and governance that are stronger than the most empowered individuals in the system. This process is made easier by the fact that Indonesia's oligarchs are fully disarmed, but could still take decades.

This chapter turns now to a brief comparative examination of the Philippines. The intention is not to present a case with the depth and detail offered on sultanistic oligarchy and its aftermath in Indonesia. Rather, the goal is to focus on key areas of comparison that highlight important aspects of oligarchic theory and practice. The Philippines under Marcos is an example of a sultanistic oligarchy, but one that contrasts sharply with Indonesia. The section opens with an overview of the key factors accounting for variations between the cases – particularly the much more volatile sultanistic oligarchy in the Philippines.

The Philippines

Like Suharto, President Ferdinand Marcos of the Philippines ruled a sultanistic oligarchy. However, the duration of his rule (from 1972 to 1986) was less than half that of his Indonesian counterpart, and his dominance over Philippine oligarchs was far more contested. The differences between the two sultanistic oligarchies provide important insights into the kinds of threats oligarchs face – especially the menace they can pose to each other – and the range of power resources at their disposal to manage the threats. There are four significant sources of variation between the cases. First, not only were Filipino oligarchs a fully matured element of society prior to the sultanistic period, but they had thoroughly dominated the archipelago's politics as a stable ruling oligarchy for more than a century before Marcos seized power.

Second, from the start, Filipino oligarchs were armed and played a direct role in the coercive aspects of wealth defense. At no point from the Spanish period in the nineteenth century, through the American period in the twentieth, to the contemporary period in the twenty-first century have oligarchs in the Philippines ever been fully disarmed. A significant segment has retained formidable coercive capacities – ranging from standing private militias in the countryside, to bands of soldiers that can be hired as needed from the Philippine armed forces, to motley goon squads that can be raised and unleashed in the provinces and sometimes in Manila. This has meant that the threat of lateral violence and predation has been a constant element of wealth defense for all Filipino oligarchs, including those in the capital and major cities, who tend to have far more limited means of coercion.

A third difference is that splits among Filipino oligarchs do not cut along racial-ethnic lines. For reasons dating back to Spanish and American colonial influences, the geographic distribution and networking of Filipino oligarchs has been more evenly balanced between the capital and the countryside than was the case in Indonesia, and religion has presented no major obstacles in the Philippines to integration for the Chinese diaspora community. Finally, because neither Filipino oligarchs nor the state ever dealt peasants and workers the sort of deathblow Suharto delivered in the 1965 massacre, oligarchs have faced constant challenges and threats from below. They have consistently employed private means of violence, backed up by government troops and paramilitary units, as part of their strategy of wealth defense against these threats. Despite all this coercion, electoral democracy has played a perversely stable and central role in the organization and politics of oligarchy in the Philippines. The case is especially important for the lessons it teaches about the relationships among oligarchs, their capture of procedural democracy, and the fundamental disconnect between electoral politics and the "high" rule of law needed to constrain the behavior of a society's most powerful actors.

Armed and Dangerous Oligarchs. A civics textbook used widely in high schools across the Philippines in the late 1930s casually presents the following scenario for class discussion: "During a political meeting one of the candidates pulled his revolver and killed his opponent, who had made an insulting remark. The man was tried and found guilty of murder." Students are then encouraged to debate "why" – that is, why the man should be viewed as a murderer, not why one candidate would shoot another. This somewhat jarring exercise is part of a chapter devoted to the "protection of life, liberty, and property."[73] The book appeared early in the Commonwealth phase of American colonial control, and Filipinos, whose democracy dates back to the turn of the century, had recently elected Manuel Quezon as their first president in 1935.

Given the frequency with which political murder was followed by impunity for Filipino oligarchs and elites in the 1930s, students of the day could be excused for struggling mightily with the civics exercise. The same year Quezon was elected, the man who would become the nation's tenth president, Ferdinand Marcos, killed the newly elected congressman from his district with a single shot. Conspiring with his father Mariano Marcos among others, Ferdinand was outraged that the candidate who had just defeated his father paraded arrogantly past the Marcos home. A co-conspirator testified at trial against Marcos and a raft of damning circumstantial evidence was presented. Yet, on appeal the supreme court found the young Marcos not guilty in a logic-bending decision penned by Justice José Laurel, himself an oligarch, who had received his doctorate in law at Yale University and went on to become president after Quezon.

It would not get any easier over the next eight decades for students to explain why political killing among oligarchs should necessarily lead to imprisonment. In the late 1950s, the notoriously violent Justiniano S. Montano, Sr. made headlines for "whipping out his .45 revolver before fellow congressmen on the floor of the House of Representatives" (Sidel 2009, 112). Yet, he enjoyed a long career with impunity. No one was brought to justice after oligarch and former senator Benigno Aquino was assassinated in 1983 by a single shot to the head at the Manila airport as he returned from exile to challenge the nation's sultanistic oligarch, Ferdinand Marcos, for the presidency. In November 2009, the private militia of the sitting governor of Maguindanao province staged an attack on the entourage of his opponent *en route* to file election papers. All fifty-eight people in the entourage were butchered in the ambush, thirty of them journalists tagging along to document the event. The governor was

---

[73] See Benitez et al. (1937, 244). In another chapter, students were invited to grapple with the foundations of oligarchic wealth in the Philippines: "Is it best that the land and other natural resources of a country be owned and controlled by a few people or by as many as possible? Why?" (Benitez et al. 1937, 3).

a close political ally of then President Gloria Macapagal Arroyo, and many Filipinos speculated openly that it was unlikely he would be held accountable for the atrocity.[74]

Oligarchs gained an early foothold in the Philippines. Dutch colonialism impeded the emergence of local oligarchs in Indonesia, delaying their appearance in the modern era until well after World War II. However, Spain's approach in the Philippines was less invasive, treating the islands as a colonial afterthought until early in the nineteenth century when the galleon trade ended in the Americas. By the time the Spaniards decided to strengthen their grip on the colony's economy and politics, a stratum of local oligarchs had already taken root and was growing immensely wealthy and powerful. The turning point in the nation's oligarchic history came in 1836, the year sugar from enormous plantations owned by Filipinos became the colony's chief export.

Haciendas in Pampanga and Western Negros provided the agricultural vehicle for the unusually early founding of the archipelago's landed oligarchs (Larkin 1993, 24).[75] The formation of this wealthy element in the Philippines was a gradual and structured process. The Spanish administration and its army of 7,000 Filipino conscripts provided a basic framework of order just strong enough to prevent a slide into warring oligarchy. It also hindered local oligarchs from collectively taking over the islands as a ruling oligarchy. The Spanish, and later the Americans, ruled the colony as a whole

---

[74] The International Crisis Group (2009, 1) reports that "the immediate trigger for the killings was the decision of one man, Esmail 'Toto' Mangudadatu, to run for governor of Maguindanao province, which for the last decade has been the fiefdom of the Ampatuan family. Political patronage by successive governments in Manila, most notably by the Arroyo administration, allowed the Ampatuans to amass great wealth and unchecked power, including the possession of a private arsenal with mortars, rocket launchers and state-of-the-art assault rifles. They controlled the police, the judiciary, and the local election commission." The report continued: "The Ampatuans' exercise of absolute authority was made possible not only by political patronage from Manila, but also by laws and regulations permitting the arming and private funding of civilian auxiliaries to the army and police ... the ease with which weapons can be imported, purchased, and circulated; and a thoroughly dysfunctional legal system."

[75] Sugar had created a core of indigenous oligarchs who, "despite their disparate provincial origins, acted together with the collusion of foreigners to shape the course of Philippine modernization" (Larkin 1993, 8). No other country in Southeast Asia experienced such an early and enduring formation of local oligarchs. Anderson (1988, 6) argues that the Philippines never had a "substantial *criollo* hacendado class." Although it is true that friar estates were the dominant form of land holding until the American conquest, this did not exclude the emergence of secular landed oligarchs. "Land grabbing was by no means the exclusive preserve of the religious orders," Riedinger (1995, 44) points out. "As restrictions on Spanish settlement in the provinces were terminated in the nineteenth century, private haciendas were established through royal grants." Riedinger admits that the friar estates were larger and more numerous. He adds that royal grants to private locals were "often substantially augmented through usurpation of adjacent lands previously cleared and occupied by natives who lacked formal titles." Filipinos were able to "usurp vast tracts of theretofore untitled communal or individual farmlands."

while emerging oligarchs were left to play a direct and personal role locally in defending their rising fortunes as they ruled over expanding agricultural estates.

The earliest and most successful landed oligarchs blended the mutually re-inforcing aspects of coercive and material power. The 1800s were a time of frontier expansion across the Philippines, with millions of hectares of land opened up, privatized, and rapidly concentrated into haciendas. Oligarchs used a range of techniques to consolidate land into modern *latifundia*. Larkin (1982, 617) writes that "the more powerful landlords and entrepreneurs utilized land laws and brute force to coerce the independents off the land or into tenant bondage." The scale of landholdings by oligarchs varied. "In all settled por-tions of the archipelago," Larkin (1982, 619) notes, "powerful local families increasingly fed off particular territories. Some families owned whole villages and some, major portions of provinces; once in command, moreover, these families retained their grip, and some still possess it today."

Because these oligarchs were armed and personally engaged in the violence needed to secure their wealth and property, the line between landowner and local ruler became blurred. "There developed in the Philippines a kind of culture of control," Larkin (1982, 620) explains. It was based on the idea that in each area or region, "all of the land and other resources as well as almost all of the labor belonged to a single *amo*, a quasi-patriarchal landlord who dispensed justice and favors in return for the complete subservience and total loyalty of his labor force."

There are elements of both continuity and change across the long arc of oligarchic domination in the Philippines (Hutchcroft 1991, 1998). "As revolu-tions, empires, and regimes have come and gone over the past two centuries," McCoy (2009, xi) writes, "the Filipino oligarchy has survived from generation to generation, amassing ever greater wealth and power with every twist in this tangled national history." They have also evolved in important ways. Oligarchs in the Philippines arose as a social force based on concentrated wealth in rural land, and to a degree land in the provinces remains a key base for many in the twenty-first century. They eventually derived their wealth from a much broader range of sources, including some based exclusively in Manila.

Sidel (2004, 55) differentiates, for instance, between dynastic and single-generational oligarchs by how dependent their fortunes were on wealth linked to the state. Dynastic oligarchs who have held power since the nineteenth century are comprised of families whose material resources were not derived from the state. Single-generational oligarchs have not only fed more directly on state resources, but their fates have also been far more determined by power brokers at the provincial or national level who could supply or restrict access to state largesse. What is striking for most scholars, however, are the deep political effects of continuous oligarchic domination. "Although its economic base and social composition are in constant flux," McCoy (2009, xi) argues, "the country's oligarchy has persisted for over a century as a cluster of families, knitted together by ties of blood and marriage, that combines political power and economic assets to direct the nation's destiny."[76]

The early and unbroken domination of the nation by oligarchs has shaped the Philippine state. Hutchcroft (2000, 278) focuses specifically on the formative interaction between local oligarchs and foreign administrators during the decades of American colonial rule. Filipino oligarchs came to dominate a state that was "quite distinctive in the annals of colonialism." Decentralized landed oligarchs in the provinces became woven into the colonial institutions of administration and control at all levels of government – "from local bodies up to the executive agencies in Manila," producing a system that operated "at the expense of central authority."[77]

Oligarchic networks not only straddled the divide between Manila and the provinces according to the kinds of oligarchs prevalent in each sphere, but also through an urban-rural division of roles within major oligarchic families (Larkin 1982, 619). The patriarch of the family might be involved in finance, trade, and hold a senate seat, while powerful relatives in the countryside might own a sugar or coconut plantation and be governor of the province or representatives in the lower house. The oligarchic balance of power that evolved over the twentieth century was one in which tremendous political power was exercised simultaneously and somewhat incoherently from both the regions and the center. The result was what Hutchcroft (2000, 278) describes as "a complex web of central-local ties in which Manila can seem to be at once overlord and lorded over." Although power brokers in Manila intervene in allocations to the regions, national politicians "must commonly rely heavily on local power (and the brokering of arrangements with local bosses and their private armies) in order to succeed in electoral contests."

Hutchcroft's reference to private armies highlights the fact that the single most consistent factor across all periods of oligarchic domination in the Philippines is that at no time have all oligarchs been fully disarmed. Even Sidel (1999, 18), who downplays the influence at the national level of armed oligarchs in the provinces in the decades after World War II, admits that an important legacy of oligarchic influence on state formation in the Philippines is that it "permitted the survival of private, personal control over the instruments of coercion and taxation." The Philippines never experienced, he writes, a phase in which "the means of coercion and extraction [were] expropriated from autonomous

---

[76] McCoy's edited volume, *An Anarchy of Families*, is one of the best collections of essays available on oligarchic domination a single country, but it is also strangely titled. McCoy and his contributors show that the country has been solidly ruled by a minority of wealthy actors who are "so strong, so persistent, and so pervasive that the term *oligarchy* seems merited" (McCoy 2009, xiii). Their rule has thwarted the emergence of a strong and independent legal regime, but it has not been anarchy.

[77] Sidel (1999, 18) writes that "it was the American imposition of 'colonial democracy' from 1901 onward that determined the nature and extent of local strongman rule in the archipelago."

and private powerholders through their subordination or incorporation into central state bureaucracies."

The land-consolidating oligarchs that arose in the 1800s had to be armed to survive the myriad dangers they faced. Known as the *principalia*, oligarchs and their powerful families were largely on their own in defending against the vertical and lateral threats that menaced their rising wealth (Simbulan 2006). Larkin (1993, 30) reports that in 1848 in the sugar province of Pampanga, there were only nineteen Iberians among a population of 140,000 Filipinos. With Spanish officials too sparse to provide reliable protection, local oligarchs built and administered private systems of coercion and enforcement – establishing a capacity for violence that would prove crucial when they fomented revolution against the Spanish colonial regime in the closing decades of the nineteenth century. Bankoff (1996, 137) notes that there existed "unofficial police forces based on large estates," and that from 1850 until the collapse of the Spanish regime it was not uncommon for the colonial state to call on the armed "guards that some hacienda or estate owners have."[78]

The odd combination of political violence and democratic longevity evident in the Philippines is explained by the fact that oligarchs retained significant coercive capacities for wealth and property defense while also channeling their power struggles through democratic institutions that oligarchs themselves had captured from their inception. Comprised of semi-armed Filipinos straddling the center and the countryside, an electoral ruling oligarchy was installed under American tutelage. However, from the outset the system was plagued by two sources of instability. The first was the classic problem explored in Chapter 3 on ruling oligarchies: how to manage lateral threats among partially or fully armed oligarchs attempting to rule collectively? The second was a more modern problem: how to dampen the latent threat of a sultanistic ruler overwhelming an electoral ruling oligarchy that, by institutional design, also empowers a single oligarch in executive office commanding an armed state? This is something Athens did not have to confront, and is tantamount to imposing a dangerous Caesar on the senates and councils of Rome from the beginning, rather than have his appearance on the scene become a key factor in the collapse of the Republic.

It is challenging enough to manage intra-oligarchic competition, avoid major episodes of violence, keep the powers of office rotating among members of the ruling oligarchy, and defend the norms and codes that make all this possible. The task is complicated by the menace of an oligarch-president who could abuse the formidable material and coercive resources of a modern state. It is

---

[78] The Guardia Civil, "the first truly interprovincial police force in the colony," was not established until 1868. With just three regiments of a thousand guardsmen each, it was a weak instrument of enforcement. The Guardia Civil was chronically underfunded and lacked horses. Common bandits, or rustlers working for rival oligarchs, would steal the finest steeds from rich landlords, with guardsmen giving chase on foot. To supplement their incomes, guardsmen were hired by oligarchs as enforcers in their private militia and armies. Sometimes guardsmen became notorious bandits themselves. Bankoff (1996, 136).

unlikely electoral democracy would have been implanted and endured until 1972 without the moderating influence of an external power to tame the more pathological behaviors of local oligarchs. The United States deliberately engineered the wholesale oligarchic capture of democracy in the Philippines, but also enforced a set of constraints that prevented the electoral ruling oligarchy this produced from tipping in either a warring or sultanistic direction (McCoy 2009, xiv).

A crucial component in this formula was civilian control over the police and armed forces, which was also imposed by the Americans. The flaw in the arrangement was that oligarchs were neither fully disarmed nor were they consistently compelled to submit to impersonal institutions of law and governance. Electoral democratic momentum, combined with a certain minimum of fair play and deference to succession rules at all levels of government, gave the appearance for decades that the rule of law existed and that the nation might be on a path toward a civil oligarchy. In fact, however, the Philippines has only managed to experience the warring, ruling, and sultanistic forms throughout its history. Even a decade into the twenty-first century, civil oligarchy remains elusive.

Although electoral democracy in the Philippines always lacked "democratic substance" (Hutchcroft 2000, 294), it lasted for decades. Before martial law in 1972, it was facilitated by a fluid system of rotation in office and an absence of ideological divisions across parties and factions. The dangers that state power posed to ruling oligarchy in the Philippines were greatly reduced once those tempted to abuse their temporary offices realized they would soon be replaced and vulnerable to similar abuses or retribution. Any oligarch who resorted to extreme measures to gain office signaled to the rest that the safeguards of rotation were in peril. Thompson (1995, 6), whose work is important for this section, writes that prior to the Marcos dictatorship, Philippine politics was a vigorous electoral contest between "two oligarchical parties that competed for power according to democratic rules." They behaved like two factions of the same party, and oligarchic rotation was robust as they "alternated in office with almost mechanical regularity" (1995, 15). Not only did the parties alternate, but the oligarchs running for office further dampened threats and stabilized the system by moving freely between parties.

> The parties were not ideologically distinguishable and were weakened by constant turncoatism to achieve maximum factional advantage. The factions' goal was winning at the polls in order to reap the economic rewards of running the state. [...] This system of elite party alternation could work only if elections were reasonably fair. Although pre-martial law polls were characterized by vote buying, violence, and fraud, balloting remained competitive as long as these violations of democratic norms stayed within certain limits (Thompson 1995, 10).

The weak American colonial apparatus gave wide latitude to Filipino oligarchs, especially in the provinces (Hutchcroft 2000). However, before and after World War II, the United States played a direct role in the system of rewards and punishments undergirding the smooth rotation of offices. Although violence was prominent in all elections before 1972, stability was maintained by "repeated U.S. government intervention" (Thompson 1995, 16). Even after independence, the Americans stepped in either to favor a candidate or to moderate the excesses of particularly dangerous and stubborn oligarchs. American intervention was important in 1953, 1959, 1961, 1986, and American jets even roared into the fray to defend President Corazon Aquino from a coup attempt.

Oligarchic rotation was particularly sensitive for the office of president. A Philippine president was not just commander in chief, but also oligarch in chief. He was the single most threatening actor in the system as long as he was in office – always manifesting, as Anderson (1988, 18) writes, "The potentiality of dislocating cacique democracy." The "stability of the system, and the solidarity of the oligarchy," he continues, "depended on the Congress, which offered roughly equal room at the top for all the competing provincial dynasties. The one-man office of president was not, however, divisible, and came to seem, in the era of independence, as a unique prize." Regular and rapid presidential succession also operated as an important restraint on predatory behaviors and limited the time any one oligarch had to accumulate enemies across the entire stratum of oligarchs. Leaving office had to be a safe prospect for a Filipino president.

From the election of Quezon in 1935 until that of Marcos in 1965, the norm of rotation worked so well that no incumbent president won election to a second term.[79] "A crucial but fragile rule of the political game was presidential succession," Thompson (1995, 23–4) writes. "With a stranglehold on public patronage, the Philippine president exercised an extraordinary amount of influence. It is therefore not surprising that several defeated incumbents considered retaining power. Yet every sitting president who lost his bid for reelection yielded office." Yielding office was linked to calculations of risk and safety for a president who was about to lose significant defenses and resources. Shorter terms in power inherently reduced the risks of retaliation and facilitated peaceful rotation. Avoiding a lurch into sultanistic oligarchy required vigilance, particularly because the threats many oligarchs faced from below in the countryside provided a ready pretext for an emergency grab for power by a president at the center. Thompson (1995, 6) argues that there was an "almost continuous procession of unsuccessful peasant-based revolutionary movements in the twentieth century, as well as intermittent rebellion by Filipino Muslims."

Marcos finally fulfilled the latent danger of sultanism in 1972, but the limits had already been severely tested in the 1949 presidential election. The rupture in the system arose when the incumbent president Elpidio Quirino, who had

---

[79] The victory of incumbent President Elpidio Quirino in 1949 was not a reelection. He was defeated after his first full term, and turned the presidency over peacefully to President Magsaysay in 1953.

been in office only a year following the death of President Roxas, used the presidency to wage a campaign that violated all oligarchic norms for the use of coercion and wealth to secure victory. "Terror employed by pro-Quirino goons was widespread," Thompson (1995, 24) notes. According to one contemporary report, "hired killers and hoodlums of the Quirino group have broken up political meetings in the provinces, beat up oppositionist candidates and supporters and prevented certain [José P.] Laurel . . . followers from registering new voters."[80] The United States intervened in an attempt to prevent the violence from reaching levels that could damage the institutions of electoral democracy that were being tested for the first time since the end of the Commonwealth period. Fellow oligarchs made it clear on the eve of the 1953 election that a repeat of the 1949 breach would be met with violence. They backed up their threats with privately raised "armed muscle." "Laurel publicly warned Quirino that another fraudulent poll would lead the opposition to 'turn off the lights and start shooting'" (Thompson 1995, 25).[81] Quirino backed down and lost his bid for reelection.

Sultanistic Oligarchy under Marcos. The election of Ferdinand Marcos to the presidency in 1965 was unremarkable. Had he followed the established pattern of being rotated out of office after a single term, his name, and that of his wife Imelda, would be as unfamiliar to people around the world as those of fellow presidents Roxas, Garcia, or Macapagal. However, Marcos won a second consecutive term in 1969, and his victory disrupted the delicate balancing act at the heart of the nation's electoral oligarchy. The path to martial law in 1972 was laid by the means Marcos deployed to engineer his 1969 victory. He redirected so much of the state's resources to securing his advantage at the polls that he triggered a fiscal crisis on a level not seen since Quirino used similar maneuvers two decades earlier. Equally alarming to fellow oligarchs was how he transformed the armed forces into a personal tool of coercion, first for reelection, then for sultanistic rule. "Marcos undertook the largest reorganization of the armed forces in Philippine history, promoting his relatives and loyalist to top positions," Thompson (1995, 35) observes. "During his first term in office several special forces were established; these paramilitary groups were . . . linked to pro-Marcos politicians and turned their guns on traditional oppositionists."

Using money and violence was common in Philippine elections. Anderson (1988, 18) argues that especially from the 1940s forward, armed groups were

---

[80] Quoted in Thompson (1995, 24). "Instead of curbing excessive violence," Thompson adds, "the military gave warlords who were friendly with the administration free reign. In the worst case, Negros Occidental Governor Rafael Lacson fielded a private army of one to two thousand men, which was charged with assaulting or otherwise intimidating dozens of oppositionists to assure that Quirino won in Lacson's province by more than two hundred thousand votes."

[81] "Coercion, however, was always a means to an electoral end for traditional oppositionists," Thompson (1995, 11) points out. "After 'punishing' a rule-breaking administration, the opposition would return to the electoral arena to make another attempt at winning power through the ballot."

deployed "mainly in intra-oligarchy competition." It was the degree to which Marcos escalated the use of these instruments of direct oligarchic rule that was unprecedented. Quimpo (2005, 235) points out that one result was a record level of violence in the 1971 legislative elections, with 905 deaths and an additional 534 violent incidents. The sheer act of fighting in this extreme manner to remain in office, combined with the additional damage Marcos inflicted on broad swaths of the ruling oligarchy during his second term, raised the dangers of leaving office after eight years to unacceptable levels. Clinging to power reinforced the need to cling to power. It also extended the period during which resources from the treasury could be stolen and the fortunes or lands of rival oligarchs could be threatened, plundered, or redistributed to family and allies. By defying oligarchic norms of rotation, Marcos multiplied his enemies with each passing year and increased his risks of severe retribution were he to lose the offensive and defensive resources of the presidency.

Marcos' reelection in 1969 posed a greater threat to the nation's ruling oligarchy than had any previous democratic outcome. The president's predicament had only grown worse as the 1973 elections approached. Term limits prevented him from running again. Every president before Marcos had surrendered office in an orderly ritual of succession. However, no previous president had ever stayed in power long enough to so thoroughly antagonize and infuriate the nation's powerful oligarchs. They were certain to crush Marcos the moment his formidable coercive and material power resources evaporated following the 1973 inaugural transfer.[82] He had surpassed Quirino in violating oligarchic norms of rotation and trampled the boundaries of ordinary abuses of executive office. It was not unreasonable for Marcos to expect that many oligarchs would strongly support seizing his family's fortune and jailing him for a long list of crimes. As early as 1970, he began mentioning his plan to remain in power by suspending democracy and imposing martial law. When Marcos established his sultanistic oligarchy in 1972, it was as much an act of desperation by an ambitious oligarch who had left no viable exit options as it was a grab for yet more power.

Wealth Defense under Marcos. Like Suharto, Marcos ruled through a combination of fear and rewards. In addition to converting the Philippine armed forces into his personal instrument of coercion – an act of military politicization subsequent presidents proved unable to reverse – he also seized control over the granting of permits, licenses, and opportunities to do business on a major scale. This made Marcos the single most important variable in the wealth and property defense calculations of all Filipino oligarchs. He had concentrated enough coercive and material resources to make or break even the

---

[82] This matter only got worse the longer Marcos remained in power. Explaining why he had no choice but to cling to the presidency indefinitely and could only be removed by overthrow in 1986, Thompson (1995, 5) states that Marcos's "'politics of plunder' and arbitrary repression alienated so many segments of Philippine society that he could hardly expect to find a place in it if he stepped down."

most powerful opponents in the oligarchy. Prior to 1972 – a "rule of law" era Anderson (1988, 27) places in quotation marks because oligarchs imposed the constraints on themselves – there were no strong property rights in the sense of being externally or impersonally guaranteed for oligarchs rather than by them. Instead, there existed property claims among the ruling oligarchs that were mutually recognized and enforced through a combination of collective and individual means of coercion. As in other ruling oligarchies, laws were oligarchic rather than impersonal and independent.

It was the regime governing how property claims were enforced that shifted radically when Marcos seized sultanistic control. "From the very earliest days," Anderson (1988, 22) writes, "Marcos used his plenary Martial Law powers to advise all oligarchs who dreamt of opposing or supplanting him that property was not power, since at a stroke of the martial pen it ceased to be property." The president's goal was not to eliminate Filipino oligarchs. It was to dominate, control, and tame them. "Marcos had no interest in upsetting the established social order," Anderson points out. "Those oligarchs who bent with the wind and eschewed politics for the pursuit of gain were mostly left undisturbed."

Among the many oligarchs Marcos targeted was the Lopez family of Iloilo. Few oligarchic clans better illustrate the intersection of wealth and rule than the brothers, Fernando and Eugenio Lopez. Fernando served as vice president during the Quirino administration in the early 1950s, and during both Marcos terms spanning 1965 to 1972. His brother Eugenio had climbed to the apex of wealth in the Filipino oligarchy. McCoy (2009, 429) writes:

> For over thirty years, Lopez had used his presidential patronage to secure subsidized government financing and dominate state-regulated industries, thereby amassing the largest private fortune in the Philippines. After declaring martial law in 1972, Marcos used the same state power to demolish the Lopez conglomerates and transfer their assets to a new economic elite composed of his kin and courtiers.

Anderson also cites the example of the 500-hectare Hacienda Osmeña, which was selectively targeted for "land reform." With these maneuvers, Marcos demonstrated to the entire oligarchy that he could attack and devastate even the most powerful among them. The evidence is clear that oligarchs had anticipated this threat and several had expended massive resources both before and after the 1969 election in an effort to drive Marcos from power.[83]

---

[83] Thompson (1995, 38) notes that major parts of the anti-Marcos media, including the *Manila Chronicle* owned by tycoon Eugenio Lopez, "were owned by oligarchs who either were allied with opposition politicians or had been alienated by the administration." This included such prominent oligarchic clans as the Roceses, who owned a media conglomerate that included the *Manila Times*, J. Antonio Araneta, publisher of *Graphic* magazine, Teodoro Locsin, owner of the *Philippines Free Press*, and the Jacinto family who published the *Asia-Philippines Leader*. Thompson adds that Fernando and Eugenio Lopez had turned against Marcos "when he would not let them build a lubricating oil factory and a petrochemical complex, or purchase Caltex Philippines and the reclaimed areas of Laguna Bay for an industrial complex."

204   *Oligarchy*

These spectacular acts of intimidation against selected members of the oligarchy were surgically chosen by Marcos to consolidate his power. To position himself as the sole arbiter of whose wealth would be defended and whose would be taken, he sought to divide and disorient the nation's oligarchs through a shifting pattern of material attacks and rewards. However, the fact that Philippine oligarchs were entrenched long before Marcos arrived on the scene, and that the bases of their power included private armies, made them a force the president could, at most, hold at bay but never fully control as Suharto had done in Indonesia. The indicators of this difference were manifold. Marcos was openly opposed by Filipino oligarchs before, during, and after his authoritarian turn commencing in 1969 and culminating in his scramble into exile in Hawaii in 1986.

Suharto was never openly challenged by the oligarchs he helped spawn. After stepping down in 1998, he calmly went home to his private residence in the Menteng neighborhood of Jakarta and remained there unperturbed until his natural death a decade later. Marcos was compelled to lift martial law long before he was overthrown. Although elections during his sultanistic rule were always tainted by massive fraud and violence, he faced significant and repeated electoral challenges from oligarchs using political parties as a vehicle of opposition. New parties were actually founded and old parties forged new alliances while Marcos was in power. Under Suharto, dozens of parties that could potentially oppose his Golkar machine were squeezed against their will into just two parties, one for the "secular nationalists" and one for the Islamists. Despite half a dozen rounds of national elections under Suharto, the resulting three-party system was never effectively challenged until the two incoherent amalgams were unbundled to contest Indonesia's first democratic elections in 1999.

The single most important indicator of the degree of unrelenting oligarchic resistance Marcos faced was the person of Benigno S. Aquino. In his heyday, Aquino had risen to the senate after winning the governorship in his home province of Tarlac, where, like most oligarchs of his stature, he maintained a large private army. He had also married into the wealthy Cojuangco family, owners of Hacienda Luisita, a sprawling sugar plantation in Tarlac province. For Marcos, Aquino posed a direct challenge as a contender for the presidency. Prior to Aquino's arrest in the sweeps after martial law was declared, he was the favorite to win the 1973 presidential elections. Held in solitary confinement and sentenced to death, Aquino was the highest-ranking political figure to be treated so harshly by a fellow oligarch since Emilio Aguinaldo engineered the arrest and execution of his opponent Andrés Bonifacio in 1897.

Political murder was hardly a shocking event in Philippine politics. Table 4.3 shows that even in the twenty-first century, it is not uncommon for dozens of candidates to be wounded or killed in the course of democratic campaigns.

However, the vast majority of these assassinations was linked to contests in the provinces and, at most, involved candidates for governor or congressional seats. No Philippine president has ever been assassinated (indeed, even attempts

TABLE 4.3. *Election Violence in the Philippines*

Year	Killed	(candidates)	Wounded	(candidates)
2001	111	(21)	293	(9)
2004	148	(40)	261	(18)
2007	121	(37)	176	(24)

Source: UNDP. 2007. *Democracy, Electoral Systems, and Violence in the Philippines.* IPER Country Report.
Note: 2004 included a presidential contest.

on the president are remarkably rare for a political milieu marked by so much violence), and until the presidency of Corazon Aquino in the late 1980s, no military coup had ever been attempted, and none has been successful. Although intra-oligarchic competition has always contained an element of violence, it had never been used by oligarchs against each other at the apex of the system. Partly because of the danger of triggering a slide into warring oligarchy, this is a characteristic common to many ruling and sultanistic oligarchies. However, it was also the line crossed by Marcos with the murder of Senator Benigno Aquino in 1983. It was a step too far, and it briefly united an otherwise fractious stratum of oligarchs around the common objective of forcing the offending president from power.

When Suharto's regime sank into crisis in 1997, the sentiment was widespread among oligarchs that the same sultanistic ruler who had helped most of them build their fortunes had faltered in providing reliable wealth defense. It was plainly evident to everyone holding concentrated wealth that the threats from Suharto's progeny had become chronic and were only going to get worse if the dictator held on long enough to found a dynasty entrenching his kids and their unsavory associates. Indonesia's oligarchs did not engage in open revolt against the "Old Man," but they stepped aside and offered no support as waves of mounting challenges to the regime eroded even Suharto's confidence. Suharto had been abandoned, his exposure was palpable, and the signal of encouragement this sent to opponents of the regime was as empowering to them as it was dispiriting to the dictator.

The oligarchs in the Philippines, whose power base was far more independent, behaved quite differently. Their challenges to Marcos were open and frontal, and the instruments of attack they employed included engaging their private material power resources to fund resistance, using their armed paramilitaries in the provinces to render Marcos' control of certain regions highly contingent, organizing and backing political parties to contest elections, and supporting international lobbying efforts focused especially on the United States to undermine the economic, diplomatic, and military assistance Marcos relied on to sustain his sultanistic dominance of the oligarchy.

In the 1987 legislative elections, the first to be held after Marcos was deposed, the oligarchs that had formed a phalanx of active resistance before 1986 constituted the single largest group of winners in the new democratic era. Citing data from the Institute of Popular Democracy in the Philippines, Anderson (1988, 28) notes that 102 congressional seats were won by powerful families "identified with the pre-1986 anti-Marcos forces," compared to 67 who were pro-Marcos. It happens that all 169 of these House members and twenty-two of twenty-four senators elected could also be traced to powerful oligarchic clans dating back to the pre-martial law period. Anderson interprets this as a return to "cacique democracy," and Hutchcroft (2008, 144) concurs, arguing that President Corazon Aquino was "an *elite restorationist*, since her major achievement was to rebuild the elite-dominated structures undermined by her authoritarian predecessor."

It is true that the oligarchic families were back and an electoral ruling oligarchy had replaced Marcos' sultanistic regime. However, what arose after 1986 was nothing like the pre-1972 electoral ruling oligarchy, which had been damaged beyond restoration. The arrangements and norms of power-sharing, of oligarchic rotation, and of moderating oligarchic violence by keeping it mainly in the provinces, restricting it to middle and lower rungs of the oligarchy, and directing the lion's share of it at peasants and workers were gone. No one has been able to figure out how to depoliticize the Philippine armed forces and security apparatus – which contains ambitious elite figures and would-be oligarchs – and return them to a pre-1972 state in which civilians were in control and presidential coups were unheard of. Most important of all, not only did the transition to democracy not include a parallel strengthening of the rule of law, but even a return to a self-imposed oligarchic "rule of law" has proved elusive.

Conclusions

At the start of the twenty-first century, Indonesia and the Philippines, despite the important differences in their oligarchic histories and the nature of their sultanistic regimes, are in some ways more similar polities than they have ever been before. Both have emerged from sultanistic oligarchies. Both have achieved democratic transitions with lively freedoms of press, assembly, and participation. Both have became electoral systems thoroughly captured by their respective ruling oligarchs. Wealth as one of the most important bases of political power is central to both systems in general, and to property and wealth defense for oligarchs in particular. Finally, neither ruling oligarchy has been able to forge an internally derived "rule of law" that constrains the oligarchs collectively, and neither country has developed legal institutions that are strong enough to tame the most powerful actors in the system.

However, there the similarities end. The single greatest difference between the electoral ruling oligarchies in the Philippines and Indonesia is that oligarchs in the former constitute a far more violent force than in the latter. Not all Filipino oligarchs are armed, but many continue to field private armies and others can readily purchase coercive forces when needed. Indonesia has violent mafia figures who are very rich and dominate certain territories or rackets. In addition, every major political party, and a number of Islamist groups, have "*satgas*," defenders, enforcers, and motley bands of *lumpen* youths. Yet none of these is a parallel to the paramilitary forces commanded by oligarchic clans and individuals in the Philippines, who are armed with assault rifles and machine guns instead of bamboo rods and swords (Onishi 2010). The Indonesian military and police are also politicized – but much more so as institutional wholes, with shifting power centers within them, than as fragmented elements headed, as in the Philippines, by charismatic officers launching coups and other coercive (and extractive) operations at the center and in the regions.

The fact that Indonesian oligarchs are not (yet) armed and thus rely almost exclusively on expending substantial sums of money from their ill-gotten fortunes to defeat the rule of law bodes well for the country's prospects for eventually making a transition to a civil oligarchy (possibly even a democratic one). The central obstacle in Indonesia is an overwhelming oligarchic capacity to engage in wealth defense by paying bribes and fees (a degraded version of *bagi-bagi*) to police, prosecutors, judges, press editors, and legislators. Despite its much longer history of elections, and the fact that so much of it was civilian-dominated and reasonably orderly among oligarchs themselves, the Philippines is further away from achieving a strong and impersonal legal regime – a civil oligarchy (democratic or otherwise) – than Indonesia. The provision of wealth defense by a Philippine state holding a monopoly on the means of coercion is blocked by hundreds of armed oligarchs scattered across the country. Disarmed oligarchs are far easier to tame externally and from above than armed or semi-armed ones. The divergent experiences of Suharto and Marcos suggest that this is as true for a sultanistic ruler seeking to dominate an oligarchy as for a bureaucratic state attempting to establish a civil oligarchy based on laws individual oligarchs violate at their peril.

5

Civil Oligarchies

Civil oligarchies differ from the other forms examined in this study in four fundamental ways. In a civil oligarchy, all oligarchs are fully disarmed, the coercion that defends oligarchic fortunes is provided exclusively by an armed state,[1] a civil oligarchy is the only type in which no oligarchs rule (if they hold office, it is never *as* or *for* oligarchs), and the coercive state defending property for oligarchs is governed impersonally through bureaucratic institutions. This combination of factors has several important implications. One is that in civil oligarchies, strong and impersonal systems of law dominate oligarchs rather than oligarchs dominating (or being) the law. This, in turn, changes the character of property ownership from being claims enforced by oligarchs to being rights enforced by the state.

These two shifts – oligarchs submitting to laws in exchange for states guaranteeing property rights – occurred in tandem over centuries and, together, constitute the single most important transformation in the history of oligarchy. Finally, although oligarchs are relieved of the violence and political burdens of defending property themselves, the emergence of a state apparatus that takes on these roles raises novel threats to oligarchs in the form of taxation and possibly redistribution focused on incomes. In civil oligarchies where existing property and fortunes are secure – no matter the scale of wealth or the degree of stratification within a given society – oligarchs for the first time devote virtually all of their material power resources to the political challenges of income defense.[2]

---

[1] Although this is easier if everyone in society is disarmed, the availability of weapons across a population for hunting or personal defense is not the relevant consideration. A modern state's monopoly on the means of coercion is historically meaningful only with regard to how property is defended, and specifically whether oligarchs are armed and play a direct role in the defense. Except in the case of kidnappings and ransom, which are rare in civil oligarchies, having bodyguards or riding in an armored limousine is the defense of person not property.

[2] Property rights in modern states provide strong protections for what is owned, but much weaker safeguards for what is gained as income. The classical definition of income as "the amount that

A civil oligarchy cannot exist without a strong system of laws. However, the key question is not whether laws work or are enforced in a general way across a society. The salient political issues of law arise more narrowly with regard to oligarchs and elites. This is evident in a host of countries like Indonesia and the Philippines. They are recognized as having serious rule-of-law problems, and yet daily civic life for the vast majority of ordinary citizens is reasonably orderly. This is because most people submit routinely to the same legal systems that oligarchs distort and intimidate just as routinely. The great bulk of rule-of-law problems originate in the defeat of laws by the powerful. The "low" rule of law at the mass level is relatively easier to achieve because average citizens lack the power resources individually to bend legal outcomes or block prosecutions altogether.[3] A legal system might be riddled with imperfections of organization, inefficiency, poorly trained personnel, or laws on the books that are simply "bad" for a variety of reasons. Such a legal infrastructure would produce many injustices and inconsistencies. However, the cause would not be the power of ordinary defendants to sway the system of law and enforcement. The ultimate test of a legal system is not its routine or systemic performance, but whether it is stronger than the most powerful actors in society – signifying the achievement of "high" rule of law. If the law tames oligarchs and elites, it will consistently tame everyone else. The reverse relationship does not always hold.

The trade-off is that oligarchic fortunes are defended generally in exchange for oligarchs themselves being as vulnerable to the law – for the first time in history – as are others in the community whose individual power resources are less intimidating.[4] These strong guarantees mean that property cannot be

can be spent without depleting net worth" (Aaron, Burman, and Steuerle 2007, xvii) underscores the distinction between income and existing property and reflects important differences in how they are treated. It also helps account for the widespread occurrence of income taxes on new gains versus the much rarer policy of wealth taxes on the fortunes of living persons. A dead person can no longer own anything. Thus, an estate tax is not a wealth tax on someone's property, but rather on the *transfer* of property, which is a gain to another person's net worth. Policies intended to prevent transgenerational aristocracy do not undercut the material power of oligarchs during their lifetimes, although they do stimulate many oligarchs to engage services to help them defend their material positions for those who survive them in death. A minority of citizens refuses to recognize these distinctions, viewing annual gains to net worth as property like any other. Taxes on income at any rate, by this definition, are a violation of property rights. Most citizens accept that neither the state nor its services or public goods could exist without taxation, and thus are willing to treat property and income as distinct categories – one inviolable, the other contested.

[3] For instance, the mundane turning of the Indonesian wheels of justice resulted in 89,000 prisoners in 396 jails, according to a 2006 government report. Most were people of simple means and many were serving sentences for narcotics crimes. See MacDougall (2008). For comparisons with Russia, see Hendley (2009).

[4] Part of the exchange includes being vulnerable to threats to income in the form of taxes. Theodore Roosevelt, justifying a more progressive system of taxation in 1906, referred to this trade-off. "The man of great wealth," he argued, "owes a peculiar obligation to the State, because he derives special advantages from the mere existence of government" (Avi-Yonah 2002, 1405).

attacked and taken by the state without just cause or compensation, nor can it be threatened laterally by other oligarchs or by the masses of nonpropertied citizens – whether or not they enjoy universal suffrage. As long as property is secured in this manner, there is a ground shift for oligarchs in the politics of wealth defense away from engaging in the coercion and rule linked to property and toward a focus on defending income. However, the shift to electoral democracy is less universal. Civil oligarchies are indifferent to democracy. They neither require it to function nor are they seriously threatened by its existence. This suggests that there are many possible combinations of property defense regimes, the rule of law, forms of oligarchy, and democracy.

For instance, Indonesia after Suharto and the Philippines after Marcos became robust electoral democracies coexisting with weak legal systems that have been relentlessly trampled by oligarchs.[5] Both were described in Chapter 4 as criminal democracies. Meanwhile, in places where the rule of law is undeniably strong, there is wide variation in the degree of democracy and authoritarianism among cases. Impersonal legal regimes that are stronger than oligarchs exist in all civil oligarchies. However, their politics can range from being participatory and democratic like the United States to exclusionary and authoritarian like Singapore. Indeed, the broad variations in civil oligarchies are brought into relief precisely by juxtaposing such otherwise divergent cases.

The United States is presented as an example of how disarmed oligarchs who do not engage in direct rule pursue their objectives of income defense by using their enormous power and resources to shape political outcomes in their favor. Singapore offers insights into how one civil oligarchy arose through a deliberate process of taming oligarchs by strengthening legal institutions. The case is significant because Singapore's civil oligarchy was founded and strengthened by a single dominant figure, Lee Kuan Yew, who could have opted instead to found a sultanistic oligarchy. It is also noteworthy that taming oligarchs through strong laws in Singapore has not been accompanied by advances toward democracy. Indeed, the Singaporean case is analytically challenging because the same legal infrastructure that so reliably defends property and adjudicates oligarchs on the merits also produces distorted outcomes against dissenting political elites, whose power resources tend to be mobilizational rather than material.

The next section advances several arguments about oligarchs and oligarchy in the United States. It presents evidence that a small fraction of American society owns highly concentrated wealth, and that these actors are oligarchs who are no less determined than any others to defend their material position from threats. To argue that the United States is a thriving civil oligarchy does not imply that American democracy is a sham. Winters and Page (2009, 731) write that "oligarchy and democracy are not mutually exclusive but rather

---

[5] Many oligarchs lament this situation because of the increased risks it causes. They yearn for a return to a time when they were well tamed – whether under Suharto or before Marcos. This nostalgia notwithstanding, the fact remains that ruling oligarchs have captured and dominated the electoral systems in both countries, and yet they are restrained by the law in neither.

can coexist comfortably – indeed, can be fused integrally."[6] There are many policies about which oligarchs have no shared interests. Their influence in these realms is either small or mutually canceling. "Oligarchy can exist with respect to certain limited but crucial policy issues," Winters and Page continue, "at the same time that many other important issues are governed through pluralistic competition or even populistic democracy." Oligarchy is focused specifically on the political struggles related to wealth defense. "In the U.S. context, as elsewhere," Winters and Page conclude, "the central question is whether and how the wealthiest citizens deploy unique and concentrated power resources to defend their unique minority interests."[7]

The United States

The definitions of oligarchs and oligarchy do not change when applied to the United States. Regardless of political context or historical period, oligarchs are defined consistently as actors who claim or own concentrated personal wealth and are uniquely empowered by it. They are a social and political by-product of extreme material stratification in societies, and such stratification is inherently conflictual: oligarchs desire to keep their fortunes, while others threaten to take it. Oligarchy refers to the politics of defending wealth – a challenge for oligarchs that varies widely according to a range of factors that have been explored in this book. Although oligarchs have participated directly in rule for much of history, this has always been linked to the manner in which wealth was defended. Active engagement in rule has never defined oligarchs. In many of the cases already discussed, some oligarchs have ruled while others have been on the sidelines. During the New Order, Suharto himself was the only oligarch ruling directly. This did not make the rest of the members of Indonesia's oligarchic stratum disappear, a point that became obvious when *pribumi* oligarchs began dominating the country's electoral ruling oligarchy after 1998. As in other civil oligarchies, oligarchs in the United States do not

---

[6] A full discussion of the broader issues of oligarchy in the United States, as well as a review of the relevant literatures, is available in Winters and Page (2009) and is not reproduced here.

[7] A key ideological battle waged on the Right is to deny that extreme material inequality is related to extreme political inequality, especially in electoral democracies. Karl Zinsmeister, George W. Bush's chief domestic policy advisor and a former magazine editor at the American Enterprise Institute, knows that a few Americans are very wealthy and the rest are not. Yet he argues that "the idea that the United States has separate classes is dubious." The free market "is democracy," according to Zinsmeister, "with pluralities of economic actors exerting votes" (Frank 2006). This statement contains a kernel of truth, but it conceals the fact that concentrated wealth allows some to "vote" for certain things others cannot. For instance, pluralities of ordinary citizens intending to brush their teeth may "vote" with their money for Colgate over Crest, while pluralities of oligarchs seeking to evade and avoid paying taxes may "vote" for offshore tax havens using LLCs versus onshore tax shelters using S-corporations. The existence of class in the material-power sense lies in the chasm separating these two universes. Oligarchs also buy toothpaste, but ordinary citizens never buy tax products – although all contribute to a common tax bill.

rule directly. This does not diminish their determination to defend their wealth against threats, although it does modify how they go about it.

In 2005, Citigroup (Kapur et al., 2005, 22) offered its high net-worth clients in the United States a concise statement of the threats oligarchs confront. "Organized societies have two ways of expropriating wealth," according to analysts in the Investment Research division: "through the revocation of property rights or through the tax system." The good news for oligarchs is that "in developed capital markets, governments have learnt the lessons of level playing fields, regulatory certainty, and the sanctity of property rights." States are still capable of "revoking property rights." However, such moves are "exceptional and generally counterproductive," and, according to Citigroup's economists, highly unlikely under present conditions in advanced capitalist countries. "The more likely means of expropriation is through the tax system," they warn.

According to the authors, a "plutonomy" is an economy with a stratum of ultra-rich citizens at the top who drive spending. "At the heart of plutonomy is income inequality," which is made possible by "capitalist-friendly governments and tax regimes." A danger to this arrangement is that "personal taxation rates could rise – dividend, capital gains, and inheritance tax rises would hurt the plutonomy."[8] Thus, the bad news for oligarchs in the United States is that the same government that so reliably defends property rights also poses grave and constant threats to oligarchic incomes. Annual gains for oligarchs from compensation and capital income are typically thousands of times the entire net worth (even including home equity) of the average American. Since ancient times, taxation has always been a central and conflictual matter in political economy. Tax rates and burdens are a direct reflection of power. Although discussions of taxation can be mind-numbing, who pays taxes and how much they pay is linked to important notions of justice, fairness, morality, legitimacy, and citizenship.

At the center of civil oligarchy in the United States is the expression of material power by oligarchs to defend their incomes against taxation. The politics of income defense unfolds on many levels. Oligarchs seek to drive down their "nominal" or "marginal" tax rates, which are the highly visible published percentages everyone pays in their tax brackets. They also benefit from pushing down the bottom threshold of the highest bracket. This shifts the

---

[8] Citigroup's analysts add that in addition to taking property or increasing taxes, states can also threaten the material position of oligarchs by changing the rules so that labor gets a larger share of the economy's surplus. "There is a third way to change things though not necessarily by expropriation, and that is to slow down the rate of wealth creation or accumulation by the rich – generally through a reduction in the profit share of GDP. This could occur through a change in rules that affect the balance of power between labor and capital. Classic examples of this tend to fall under one of two buckets – the regulation of the domestic labor markets through minimum wages, regulating the number of hours worked, deciding who can and cannot work, etc., or by dictating where goods and services can be imported from (protectionism)" (Kapur et al., 2005, 22). This "Industry Note" from Citigroup Global Markets Inc was distributed to wealthy clients in dozens of countries.

tax burden downward to a far more numerous stratum of citizens who are well off – known in the wealth management business as the "mass affluent" – but who lack the material power resources oligarchs can deploy for income defense. As important as these policy objectives may be, by far the most intensive use of these power resources is to widen the spread between the published tax rates for oligarchs and what they actually pay. In the jargon of tax specialists, this is the difference between the nominal tax rate and the effective tax burden. This Income Defense Spread is a key measure of income defense success for oligarchs.[9]

Before offering a more detailed analysis of these claims, it would be useful to present the argument in brief. First, data are presented documenting the concentration of wealth in a few hands to establish a pattern of extreme material stratification in the United States that is characteristic of all oligarchies. Second, it is argued that these oligarchs are keenly aware of the threats posed to their material interests, and that they engage a portion of their wealth to defend against these threats. They must do this individually to reap the benefits of income defense, and the great majority of oligarchs participate in the process according to a common logic of threat management.[10] Third, pursuing income defense in a civil oligarchy consists of two components. One is hiring the services of armies of professionals – lawyers, accountants, lobbyists, wealth management agencies – who have highly specialized knowledge and can navigate a complex system of taxation and regulations, generating a range of tax "products," "instruments," and "advice" that enable oligarchs to keep scores of billions in income annually that would otherwise have to be surrendered to the Treasury.[11] Collectively these professionals comprise an extensive and entrenched Income Defense Industry.

The other component is the nitty-gritty political battles and legwork of making and keeping the tax system sufficiently porous so that there is complexity

[9] Even gaining access to anonymous IRS data that would enable analysts to measure the spread has involved overcoming major political hurdles shielding oligarchs and the extent of their income defense efforts from scrutiny. Johnston (2010a) points out that data on the 400 highest-income taxpayers are available "only from 1992 to 2006," and these were available only because the Obama administration "overturned the George W. Bush policy of treating the data as a state secret." Figures presented later in this section also include estimates for 1961 that were never intended to be revealed, but which Johnston admits were only possible to discover "because of a quirk in the Statistics of Income report for that year."

[10] This is in addition to the victories oligarchs win collectively through the political efforts of bodies that lobby vigorously on behalf of the ultra-wealthy.

[11] The hiring of income defenses by oligarchs is qualitatively different from average citizens hiring tax preparers or buying cheap software (what might be called "TurboTax payers") to find deductions that are commonly missed, or just to make sure confusing returns are filled out correctly. Professionals defending the incomes of living oligarchs (and frequently helping them avoid estate taxes at death) fashion new means and unique methods of tax avoidance that are often tailor-made for the individuals buying them. TurboTax payers cannot afford the services of income defense providers, and there is virtually no advantageous porosity or uncertainty structured into the tax system for those with incomes below the 99.5 percentile.

and uncertainty. Some "speed dial" oligarchs influence officials in the legislative and executive branches directly, phoning senators and congressional representatives to complain about laws and rules or to ask for policy assistance. However, most do not. Actors within the Income Defense Industry, whose fees siphon off a share of annual oligarchic gains, constitute a highly coherent, well-financed, and aggressive network for political pressure to ensure that oligarchs are able to defend their material interests. Income defense providers are motivated intermediaries who give concrete political expression to core oligarchic demands. However, oligarchs and their interests are always the primary driving force. The crucial theoretical linchpin in this argument is that oligarchic interests and the active deployment of oligarchic power resources explain the entire enterprise and propel it. Both as service providers and as political agents, the Income Defense Industry exists only because of the substantial material threats oligarchs face and the material power they exercise to counter them. This argument specifies the interests oligarchs have and traces the mechanisms through which power is used – and political outcomes are achieved – to address those interests.

Oligarchs and Material Power in the United States. An appreciation of the asymmetries in power between oligarchs and other members of society begins with an estimate of differences in the material positions of actors across the social formation (Fraser and Gerstle 2005). The notion is that regardless of the other ways in which political power might be equal – such as one-person-one-vote or an equal right to speak or participate – yawning differences in material power create enormous inequalities in political influence and account for key political outcomes won by oligarchs. Winters and Page (2009) present data based on income and wealth in the United States that offer a glimpse of the extent of material power concentration. Their estimates are updated in Table 5.1 based on the most recent Internal Revenue Service (IRS) data from 2007.

The last column, the Material Power Index (MPI), reflects each successive income level as a multiple of the average income among the bottom 90 percent of America taxpayers. Crossing the threshold to the top 10 percent of incomes is four times the average at the bottom, but still a modest average income level of slightly more than $128,000 a year. The MPI then starts a trend of roughly doubling at each successive threshold to seven, fifteen, then thirty-two. Even at more than thirty times the average income of the bottom 90 percent of Americans, an average annual income of $1 million for those in the top one-half of 1 percent is still too modest to qualify as oligarchic. These citizens are certainly rich. However, their material power resources are still insufficient to engage anything beyond the cheap foot-soldier services of the Income Defense Industry.

The pattern changes dramatically at the next threshold – the top 1/10th of 1 percent of incomes. Instead of doubling, the MPI suddenly quadruples from 32 to 124, and then leaps another sixfold to 819 for those with incomes in the top 1/100th of 1 percent. There were about 150,000 Americans whose average annual incomes were $4 million and above in 2007. For reasons that

TABLE 5.1. *Material Power in the United States (based on 2007 incomes)*

Threshold of Taxpayers	Number of Taxpayers	Average Income	% of All Income	% Income Cumulative	Material Power Index
Top 400	400	$344,800,000	1.6	1.6	10,327
Top 1/100th of 1%	14,588	$26,548,000	4.5	6.1	819
Top 1/10th of 1%	134,888	$4,024,583	6.2	12.3	124
Top half of 1%	599,500	$1,021,643	7.0	19.3	32
Top 1%	749,375	$486,395	4.2	23.5	15
Top 5%	5,995,000	$220,105	15.1	38.6	7
Top 10%	7,493,750	$128,560	11.1	49.7	4
Bottom 90%	134,887,500	$32,421	50.3	100.0	1

Notes: Based on IRS tabulations of individual income tax returns for 2007, CPS-estimated number of potential tax units and National Income Accounts total income figures. Income includes realized capital gains. Each income level is exclusive of the category above it. Average income of the top 400 taxpayers is from the Internal Revenue Service (2009). The total number of taxpayers filing returns in 2007 is 149,875,300, and the total reported gross personal income is $8,701 billion.

Sources: http://elsa.berkeley.edu/~saez/TabFig2007.xls, Table 0, "Thresholds and Average Incomes in Top Income Groups in 2007," revised August 2009, updating Piketty and Saez (2003); computations by the author.

will be explained presently, this is the threshold at which oligarchs dominate the landscape. The final category at the top, the 400 highest taxpayers in the United States, had an average income of $345 million. Their MPI was more than *twelve* times the group immediate below them, and more than *ten thousand* times that of the average American income in the bottom 90 percent.[12]

The MPI for the 400 highest American taxpayers is many magnitudes greater than the indices even for the top of the Athenian trierarchy, and is nearly identical to the concentrated wealth of Roman senators. The degree of material concentration in the United States is vastly greater if estimates are based on wealth rather than income. Depending on whether home equity is included, the MPI of the wealthiest oligarchs in the United States shown in Table 5.2 ranges from 21,000 times to 108,000 times that of the average household in the bottom 90 percent of the society.[13] Based on income, the asymmetries in material power resources in the United States are enormous. Based on wealth, they are simply too staggering to fathom. Moreover, it is impossible to operationalize precisely how much more political influence oligarchs have if they command 1,000, 10,000, or 100,000 times the material power resources of an average citizen. What can be said with confidence is that this does not look like garden-variety pluralism (Winters and Page 2009, 737).[14]

The wealth gradient in American society is important for assessing the distribution of material power across the population. However, how much wealth and material power is needed to make someone an oligarch in the United States? Designating any particular income or wealth level as a line of demarcation is necessarily arbitrary. The significance of being designated as an oligarch lies in the power capacities certain individuals derive from their personal wealth.

---

[12] Johnston (2003, 41) points out that in 2000 the top 1/100th of 1 percent of Americans (about 15,000 people) earned as much income as the bottom 96 million citizens combined – with each segment accounting for roughly 5 percent of total earnings. Attempting to "visualize the enormity of this chasm," Johnston writes that the ultra-rich "would occupy just one-third of the seats at Yankee stadium," while those at the bottom would include everyone from Kansas west, plus Iowa. By 2007, the same fraction at the top had increased their share of all American incomes to 6.1 percent while the proportion earned by the bottom 96 million had contracted.

[13] Home equity is a major component of net worth for average citizens but only a small portion for the rich. Because homes are rarely a source of financing for political engagement or for income defense, excluding them provides a more realistic estimate of the relative material power available to actors at each level of wealth.

[14] Concentrations of wealth and income have changed over the course of the nation's history. The expectation until the middle of the twentieth century was that as less income came from capital and more from work and salaries, income equality would improve. Spengler (1953, 249) notes that in the United States from 1800 forward, the proportion of income coming from property and capital was decreasing. This was supposed to produce a virtuous cycle. "Accordingly, a decrease in the fraction of the national income going to property, coupled with an increase in the wage-salary fraction, tends to be accompanied by a decrease in income inequality," Spengler theorized. "A decrease in income inequality tends to be consequential also upon a decrease in property-ownership inequality, because of the increase in the relative number of property owners." Piketty and Saez (2003 and updates) show that income inequality not only increased dramatically during the twentieth century, but accelerated especially after 1970.

TABLE 5.2. *Material Power in the United States (based on 2004 household wealth)*

	Including Home Equity		Excluding Home Equity	
	Net Worth ($ million)	Material Power Index	Net Worth ($ million)	Material Power Index
Top 100	8,110.0	59,197	7,396.0	108,765
Top 400	2,970.0	21,679	2,709.0	39,838
Top 1%	14.8	108	13.5	199
Top 10%	3.1	23	2.2	32
Bottom 90%	0.137	1	0.068	1

Notes: Data for net worth "including home equity" are from Table 2 (with minor adjustments from *n* = 100 and *n* = 400). The calculations for net worth "excluding home equity" are based on Wolff's (2007) survey of consumer finances data. On average, when homes are excluded, net worth declined by 8.8% for the top 1% of households and by 50.8% for the bottom 90% of households. Applying an 8.8% decline in net worth is very conservative for the top 100 and top 400 brackets. A midpoint decline of 29.8% was estimated for the top 10% bracket.
Source: Adapted from Winters and Page (2009, 736), Table 2; computations by author.

What matters politically is the threshold of wealth above which actors are able to afford the costly services and interventions of the Income Defense Industry. Focusing on who is able to hire the armies of professionals in the Income Defense Industry provides a clear indication of the level at which wealth takes on oligarchic characteristics. Such a method also adjusts to the costs of these political services across countries as well as within them over time. Thus, in a civil oligarchy, not just any rich person is an oligarch. Oligarchs are those rich enough to convert their money into the professional firepower needed to defend their wealth and incomes. Johnston states that "this can sometimes be an outlay of $10 million to avoid $30 million in taxes, and other times spending only $1 million to save the same amount."[15] The KPMG "mass market" tax shelter scandal, examined in greater detail later, suggests that discount tax products cost about $350,000. However, the same case shows that income defense on the cheap exposes borderline oligarchs to extreme legal risks and costly penalties – a danger rarely faced by oligarchs able to pay retail.

Income Defense Industry. Although mobilizational power can be transformative for a group or society, one of its weaknesses is that both the actors who mobilize and the social forces that become mobilized must invest enormous personal time and effort in building this power resource. Because they are so demanding, mobilizations are difficult to sustain. Oligarchs using material power resources do not face this problem because they can set in motion armies of actors – whether thugs, militias, demonstrators, or income-defense professionals – based on remuneration rather than ideological commitments. It is unnecessary for them to lead or inspire, nor must they convince anyone of the goals to be pursued or interests to be served. Oligarchs issue directives to be

[15] Telephonic interview with David Cay Johnston, April 12, 2010.

Oligarchy

followed as commands, and the actors being paid to carrying out those orders do so even if their own political interests are not served. Moreover, oligarchs as principals can disengage personally from the political influence they seek to exert once agents have been hired to do the actual work. The scale, intensity, and duration of this kind of political activity and influence are limited only by the level of material power resources oligarchs have.

In a civil oligarchy, the burdens of political engagement for income defense are rarely borne by oligarchs themselves, but fall instead to others they set in motion. Collectively these actors constitute a lucrative Income Defense Industry whose participants are motivated by the profit-making opportunities generated by the threats oligarchs face and desire to overcome. Johnston (2003, 7) reports that in 2003 there were 16,000 lawyers specializing in trusts and estates, which is only one component of the industry. The Income Defense Industry skims a share of the tens of billions of dollars in income defended annually. Oligarchs get to keep the rest. A report by the U.S. Senate (2003, 2) on the tax shelter industry states that "respected professional firms are spending substantial resources, forming alliances, and developing the internal and external infrastructure necessary to design, market, and implement hundreds of complex tax shelters, some of which are illegal and improperly deny the U.S. Treasury of billions of dollars in tax revenues."

At the heart of this industry are "professional organizations such as accounting firms, banks, investment advisors, and law firms." The report defines an abusive tax shelter as "a device used to reduce or eliminate the tax liability of the tax shelter user," which is accomplished through "complex transactions" that permit the taxpayer to "obtain significant tax benefits in a manner never intended by the tax code."[16] More than complex, they are transactions that would never occur if wealthy taxpayers were not engaging in income defense. Graetz (2002, 278) describes an abusive tax shelter as "a deal done by very smart people that, absent tax considerations, would be very stupid." For decades, these devices had been "custom-designed for a single user." However, an alarmed Senate discovered that some income-defense providers were creating shelters that were "prepared as a generic 'tax product' available for sale to multiple clients" (U.S. Senate 2003, 1). It was the widening of the industry's clientele to the lower reaches of the American oligarchy that triggered congressional hearings.[17]

---

[16] In testimony before the Senate Finance Committee, former IRS Commissioner Mark Everson stated that "abusive transactions that are used by corporations and individuals present formidable administrative challenges. The transactions themselves can be creative, complex, and difficult to detect. Their creators are often extremely sophisticated, as are many of their users, who are often financially prepared and motivated to contest the Service's challenges" (U.S. Senate 2003, 21).

[17] Refined dealings between oligarchs and their high-priced attorneys and wealth advisors had somehow become unseemly. "During the past ten years, professional firms active in the tax shelter industry have expanded their role, moving from selling individualized tax shelters to specific clients, to developing generic tax products and mass marketing them to existing and

Because trust and confidentiality are vital in the services oligarchs receive from income-defense providers, relationships are often initiated by referral. The industry serves what are called High Net-Worth Individuals (HNWIs), defined on the low end as clients with at least $2 million in investable financial assets, and Ultra High Net-Worth Individuals (UHNWIs), defined as those with $30 million in assets and above.[18] The industry is multifaceted and global in its spread and integration.[19] Nearly every major U.S. law firm has a division of specialists devoted exclusively to "wealth preservation," "wealth management," "estates and trusts," and "tax planning." The very top tier of global players is known in the trade as "magic circle" firms. These include prominent law firms like Clifford Chance, Linklaters, and White & Case.[20]

Perhaps the most exclusive firm in the magic circle for wealthy clients is Withers. Founded in 1896 in Britain, its practice grew to include "a number of the most aristocratic families in Britain," especially the royal family. The firm merged in 2002 with a major U.S. firm focusing on taxes and income defense, "creating the first international law firm dedicated to serving the needs of successful people and their families."[21] Withers notes that some of its clients "are worth more than major public companies." With an emphasis on defending income by navigating through a globally complex tax regime, Withers specializes in "wealth structuring" to help their clients "preserve their wealth now and for future generations."[22] Some of Withers' clients "are international families with family members who have UK and/or U.S. connections and want

potential clients. No longer content with responding to client inquiries, these firms are employing the same tactics employed by disreputable, tax shelter hucksters: churning out a continuing supply of new and abusive tax products, marketing them with hard-sell techniques and cold calls; and taking deliberate measures to hide their activities from the IRS" (U.S. Senate 2003, 22).

[18] By comparison, profits "are quite rare" for income defense firms trying to serve the larger but less wealthy market segment known as "mass affluent clients," whose net financial assets are in the modest range of $100,000 to $1 million. Although this group far outnumbers oligarchs, the return on resources invested to provide the mass affluent with wealth management and income defense services is minimal. "The emergence of the mass affluent customer as a new market segment in the 1990s was greeted with enthusiasm by the financial services industry," write analysts for Capco, a global provider of services to the financial services industry. "Numerous institutions spent time and money trying to generate a successful formula for profitably servicing these customers. To date, most have met with limited success" (Del Col, Hogan, and Roughan 2004, 106). Capgemini (2008) uses $1 million as the threshold for HNWIs.

[19] The Wealth Resource Center markets a profile entitled "The Global Wealth Management Industry" that identifies more than 2,500 institutions "from the largest multinational wealth management corporations through to small private banks in offshore tax havens, and from the wealth management divisions of large retail banks through to discreetly run private investment offices serving ultra high net worth families." Available at: www.wealthbriefing.com/webshop/the-global-private-bank-and-family-office-database-64.html.

[20] Other key firms cited by Johnston (2003, *passim*) include Milbank, Tweed, Hadley, and McCloy; Weil, Gotshal, and Manges; Freeman, Freeman, and Smiley.

[21] See www.withersworldwide.com/about-us/history.aspx.

[22] See www.withersworldwide.com/practice-areas/personal/wealth-structuring.aspx.

to mitigate their exposure to tax."[23] Toward this end, Withers advises its oligarchic clientele on "all aspects of wealth structuring, using domestic and international trusts and foundations, private trust companies in local as well as offshore jurisdictions."[24]

Serving oligarchs does not end with devising strategies for maximum wealth defense. It includes advocating their cases aggressively against tax prosecutors when those strategies and instruments are challenged as illegal. "As part of our U.S. practice," Withers states, "we represent clients whose financial affairs are being audited by the taxing authorities and regulators, and appear before the courts in tax matters." The firm is especially proud of its track record in achieving favorable settlements out of court and shielding its wealthy clients from embarrassing public exposure.[25] Services designed to defend income and wealth are expensive in part because the techniques employed are complex and sometimes risky. Whereas the discount end of the wealth services industry is populated by "product pushers," HNWIs and UHNWIs "do not tolerate such treatment" (Research and Markets 2010). Instead, they expect highly person-alized "relationship managers" to devise customized strategies and instruments for income defense.[26]

Political Mechanisms. It is a significant analytical advance to identify a set of actors in the United States that satisfy the definition of oligarchs, show that they are strongly motivated to defend their income, prove they possess power resources unavailable to ordinary citizens to mount their defense, and point to concrete political outcomes showing wealth is successfully defended. However, a strong theory of civil oligarchy must also specify how this is done by

[23] "We have acted for successful people and their families for over 100 years," Withers states on its Web site. "We have built up an in-depth understanding of the personal tax needs of our high net worth clients, and we can help them mitigate their exposure to tax both during their own lives and for future generations." See www.withersworldwide.com/practice-areas/personal/tax.aspx.

[24] An ability to navigate transnationally to avoid taxes in any one location is one of Withers' areas of greatest expertise. "We help international clients to achieve significant tax benefits through our understanding of the cross-border regime regarding residence and domicile." See www.withersworldwide.com/practice-areas/personal/tax.aspx.

[25] One of the more unusual areas of expertise for Withers is the creation of "family offices" for oligarchic families. A family office is "an entity set up to run a family's affairs which has separate legal personality from the family." Withers estimates that "there are 11,000 family offices in existence – with 2,500 to 3,000 in the U.S., a further 2,500 in Europe, and 200 in Australia. This number is expected to grow in time, as the needs of wealthy families become more complex. Having looked after successful people, their families, and advisers for over 100 years, we have real insight into the concerns of wealthy families. This insight helps us when we assist our clients to set up and operate their family offices." See www.withersworldwide.com/practice-areas/personal/family-office-family-business.aspx.

[26] The New York law firm of Curtis, Mallet-Prevost, Colt & Mosle LLP, for instance, provides each oligarch or family with a "relationship partner" who coordinates the professional services of "client teams" drawn from across the firm's many offices. Specialized "Curtis Alerts" serve as an early warning system that informs wealthy customers about impending threats and the implications of proposed legislation, especially on taxes and wealth. See www.curtis.com.

connecting the dots among interests, power, and outcomes. By what political mechanism is oligarchic power expressed? A preliminary point is that civil oligarchy has very little in common with elite theory as it evolved in the U.S. context. Central to the debates in elite theory are arguments about elite "rule," which necessarily implies that democracy in the United States is a façade for minority control and constitutes mass deception.[27] By contrast, the claim in this study is that oligarchs do not rule in a civil oligarchy. This shifts the analytical focus away from how oligarchy and democracy displace each other and toward how the two are durably fused.

The most direct and personal form of oligarchic engagement in income defense lies in their dealings with the Income Defense Industry, which supplies the concrete means of tax evasion and avoidance. Oligarchs participate barely at all in fighting the political battles at the heart of income defense. A minority of oligarchs takes an active role leading highly public battles, but most do not. The political trench warfare that makes income defense possible, that maintains the system's basic architecture, and that constantly adapts it to changing conditions is fought by the same Income Defense Industry that survives by managing (but never entirely removing) the threats oligarchs face. This indirect mechanism of political influence demands a high degree of coherence, organization, planning, and coordination. However, none of these burdens falls to oligarchs themselves beyond the provision of the financial resources that set the political apparatus in motion. Even that role is accomplished as atomized principals propelling a phalanx of organized and integrated agents moving in a common direction against minimal resistance.

The existing structure for income defense in the United States relies on uncertainty. No Income Defense Industry could thrive if oligarchs faced the same tax certainty that applies to the vast majority of Americans – for whom no parallel industry has emerged. The differences between tax certainty at the bottom and uncertainty at the top are commonly attributed to forms of income. "Low- and

---

[27] Mosca (1939, 333), whose work set the tone for the ruling-elite debates in the United States, implied that electoral democracies were a ruse. "All those who, by wealth, education, intelligence, or guile, have an aptitude for leading a community of men, and a chance of doing so – in other words, all the cliques in the ruling class – have to bow to universal suffrage once it is instituted, and also, if occasion requires, cajole and fool it." In a trenchant critique of elite theory, Dahl (1958, 463) chides the approach for resorting to "an infinite regress of explanations" for locating who was truly in power behind the democratic façade. "If the overt leaders of a community do not appear to constitute a ruling elite," Dahl writes, "then the theory can be saved by arguing that behind the overt leaders there is a set of covert leaders who do. If subsequent evidence shows that this covert group does not make a ruling elite, then the theory can be saved by arguing that behind the first covert group there is another, and so on." Writing decades later on "democracy and the economic order," Dahl (1985, *passim*) takes the problem of concentrated material power much more seriously. However, instead of viewing the matter oligarchically, which means to focus on materially empowered individuals, he examines the matter at the level of the firm. His solution is "democracy within firms." Other important critiques of elite theory include Hughes (1954), Meisel (1958), and Rustow (1966).

middle-income taxpayers who have income only from wages, interest, and dividends," Graetz (2002, 279, n91) writes, "have virtually no opportunity to underreport income taxes." Capital income earned by the ultra-rich is much harder to track. It is typically described as "nonmatchable," as if this were some immutable financial law of nature. What this interpretation misses is that the difficulty in taxing the rich is itself a political outcome reflecting prior exercises of oligarchic power. That power shapes the way the rules have been written.

What is "matchable" by the IRS depends on decisions made and enforced about information collected. It would be impossible to tax the incomes of 200 million Americans without first designing and building a tax infrastructure that provides detailed and reliable information on masses of people who move and have shifting or multiple sources of income. It is no surprise that a tax architecture designed to track compensation income for the many is poorly suited to track capital income for the few. Presumably, an infrastructure designed primarily to track and tax the changing material fortunes of oligarchs would be ill equipped to tax hundreds of millions of workers making small wages – who would then constitute the "nonmatchable" category.[28] Nonmatchable taxpayers are twelve times more likely to misreport their incomes to the IRS (Bloomquist 2003, 3). This first aspect of uncertainty is not only a long-term and cumulative expression of oligarchic power (especially given that the federal income tax began in 1913 solely on the wealthy), but ensuring that the system remains capital-income disabled requires constant political effort.

Actors in the Income Defense Industry play a key role managing a second and more important dimension of uncertainty: that of maintaining a delicate balance between tax threats against oligarchs and the complexity and porosity in the system needed to deflect the threats. Absolute tax certainty at any tax rate for oligarchs would kill the Income Defense Industry. Oligarchs provide resources to the industry to lobby for lower tax rates and even the elimination of some taxes. However, the complete removal of all tax threats would devastate the industry. The real political action in income defense, and the area of most intense oligarchic power expression, is in the struggle over the gap between the published tax rates and what oligarchs actually pay. This is the Income Defense Spread, and achieving a high spread requires that players in the Income Defense Industry maintain a healthy mixture of uncertainty, complexity, and porosity in the tax regime. Legislators do part of the task on their own when they avoid direct policy decisions by using tax incentives to support or oppose something. However, what the legislators start, the Income Defense Industry finishes by deploying legions of professionals and lobbyists to insert material into the tax

---

[28] There is nothing insurmountable about the problems posed in taxing the ultra-rich. If the power that accompanied their wealth was less potent, and the matter was more purely technical, it would be fairly straightforward to devise proxies for assessing the annual tax bill for oligarchs. The fact that peasants in France and Russia were hard to track because they did not engage in cash transactions was overcome through the proxy of the head tax. Matters of taxation are always political before they are technical.

code that is favorable to oligarchs, cut sections that cause problems, and block threats on the horizon (Herber 1988, 392).[29]

The Income Defense Industry lobbies for myriad incremental changes to the body of tax codes and regulations on a case-by-case basis. However, it also has a vested interest in the overall complexities and uncertainties of the tax system. The Internal Revenue Code is, according to a tax judge trying to sort through the morass, "a sprawling tapestry of almost infinite complexity" (Moldenhauer 2007, 1, n2). The resulting confusion of the regulations permits those defending oligarchic incomes to transform matters of questionable legality into murky disputes of interpretation. The instrument for doing this is the "tax opinion letter" (or "tax letter") – perhaps the most important weapon in the income defense arsenal and something most taxpaying mortals have never heard of.[30] A single tax opinion letter from a leading firm can range in price from hundreds of thousands of dollars to millions, depending on the complexity of the tax contortions being attempted. When everyone from the mass affluent down to the actual masses engage in tax evasion or "abusive avoidance," there is little porosity for interpretation (or what the IRS calls "doubt about liability"). They face charges in criminal courts and prison sentences if they go too far.[31]

---

[29] Also see Herber 1981. Nearly all firms in the Income Defense Industry participate in lobbying on behalf of their oligarchic clientele. However, those based in Washington, DC do so with a special intensity. Patton Boggs is a prominent and particularly aggressive provider of "wealth preservation" services and a leader among hundreds of similar firms. They count the Mars candy family and the Gallo wine family among their richest oligarchic clients. Like Curtis, they also issue alerts informing their clients about legislation that could affect their wealth and income. "As a firm with deep public policy roots," writes Patton Boggs of their advocacy-lobbying services, "we are proud of our ability to help clients exercise a right enshrined in the U.S. Constitution by petitioning their government. We have been at it since 1965, when Jim Patton encouraged a young White House aide named Tom Boggs to help him build a different kind of law firm, one that understood that all three branches of government could provide solutions to challenging problems. By combining political know-how, legislative experience, and substantive knowledge of the law, they had a vision for helping clients achieve success." This text is on pages 8–9 in the following Patton Boggs document: www.pattonboggs.com/files/News/4de2a317-b30b-4213-a0a5-03294f27841d/Presentation/NewsAttachment/9628c17d-46f9-402d-8348-0abe65ca06ee/PB_100Days_2009Assessment.pdf. The firm describes other services for wealthy clients at the following link: www.pattonboggs.com/estateplanning/.

[30] "A tax opinion letter, sometimes called a legal opinion letter when issued by a law firm, is intended to provide written advice to a client on whether a particular tax product is permissible under the law and, if challenged by the IRS, how likely it would be that the challenged product would survive court scrutiny" (U.S. Senate 2003, 11).

[31] This is true even when tax evasion by ordinary taxpayers is unintentional. Complexity and confusion work in the opposite direction for these citizens. The instructions for filing Form 1040 ballooned from four pages in the 1950s to more than 120 pages by 2010. However, the difference is that confusion on the part of the taxpayer is never a defense. It is confusion on the part of the IRS, judges, and juries over what the law says and requires that matters. By design, tax problems involving the incomes of average citizens are far more straightforward even if the taxpayer is befuddled into errors of underreporting that get treated as criminal evasion.

By contrast, oligarchs, who are armed with enough resources to fight cases for years, routinely negotiate compromises and settlements through income defense professionals. Going to court, much less to jail, is the exception rather than the rule. The IRS states that it takes into consideration the "necessary expense" it might incur in pursuing taxpayers, and adds that in certain cases "compromise is a viable collection tool." Doubt about the tax code and the ability of an individual to litigate are prime considerations in the IRS's willingness to settle. "The determination of the amount accepted to resolve a doubt as to liability case," the IRS advises, "should be made by reference to the expected hazards in litigating the case" (Internal Revenue Manual 2010). The key factor in raising this hazard is the wealth of the taxpayer. "If you've got the resources," states a senior international tax attorney, "the IRS faces a big risk of litigation. That means that you're going to be able to cut a better deal."[32]

The complete body of regulations used by a firm to produce tax opinions, shelters, or other complex instruments is published as Commerce Clearing House's (CCH) "Standard Federal Tax Reporter." In 2010, it spanned twenty volumes filling 71,684 pages.[33] Table 5.3 shows the changing size in pages of this complete representation of the tax code.

The system is so complex, Kotlikoff and Rapson (2006, 6) observe, that "no one can claim to fully comprehend its provisions." The frustrated tax judge agrees. "To thread one's way through this maze," he writes, "the business or wealthy taxpayer needs the mind of a Talmudist and the patience of Job" (Moldenhauer 2007, 1, n2). In fact, oligarchs need neither. They deploy an armada of income defense providers to thread through a maze the industry helped create and on which it thrives. President Barack Obama (2009) emphasized the vital political role the Income Defense Industry plays for oligarchs when he described the labyrinth as "a broken tax system, written by well-connected lobbyists on behalf of well-heeled interests and individuals."

A central tenet of interest-group pluralism arguments is that for every set of actors lobbying for one agenda there are others lobbying in other directions. The sum total of this activity leaves no one with a permanent advantage. This competitive mechanism is virtually nonexistent for the Income Defense Industry. Because there is no industry countervailing the one serving oligarchs, the droning network of firms tirelessly dispatching thousands of lobbyists and professionals faces very little resistance, and the lion's share of the industry's

[32] Confidential interview with a U.S. tax lawyer working for a "magic circle" firm, June 2, 2010.
[33] The "Tax Code," formally known as "Title 26 of the United States Code," is the part written by Congress and consists of 3,387 pages. Added to this are 13,458 pages known as "Title 26 of the United States Code of Federal Regulations," which are churned out by the IRS. The remaining 54,839 pages are filled with "amendment notes, related statutes, proposed regulations, excerpts of committee reports, as well as annotations of cases and rulings beginning in 1913" (CCH 2010).

TABLE 5.3. *Pages in the CCH
Standard Federal Tax Reporter*

Year	Pages
1913	400
1939	504
1945	8,200
1954	14,000
1969	16,500
1974	19,500
1984	26,300
1995	40,500
2004	60,044
2010	71,684

Source: www.cch.com/wbot2010/
WBOT_TaxLawPileUp_%2829%
29_f.pdf

micro-interventions occur off the political radar screen and with no debate.[34] The few public interest organizations arguing for "tax justice" on behalf of average citizens are outstaffed and outfunded by ratios that parallel the MPIs for oligarchs reviewed earlier. In addition, most of their focus is on battling over the published tax rates and brackets. The Income Defense Industry, assisted ideologically by think tanks and movements funded by oligarchs who remain mostly unseen (Phillips-Fein 2009), vigorously fights this much more visible part of the battle.

These efforts have achieved major reductions in marginal tax rates on the rich while the burdens on average households have mounted since World War II. However, the industry has only managed to erode progressivity in the tax brackets, never fully eliminate it. Eliminating progressivity is reserved for a very different and far less visible kind of political effort – the one aimed at increasing the Income Defense Spread for oligarchs. Operating virtually unopposed, these efforts have not just eliminated progressivity, they have successfully inverted the entire system so that effective tax rates are strongly regressive. The further up the oligarchic scale one climbs, the lower the effective tax rate becomes. It is not just that oligarchs have lower tax rates than the merely rich or the

---

[34] The Center for Responsive Politics (2010c) tracks the "major issues before Congress and who's trying to influence the decisions," emphasizing what the "special interests [are] looking to get." Of the thirty-two issues tracked across thirteen sectors ranging from agriculture to terrorism for the 107th to the 109th Congresses, none focused on how the ultra-rich were trying to influence decisions to shift tax burdens to the strata below them, nor on tax shelters and offshore havens used exclusively by the wealthiest citizens to defend their incomes. Under the "Finance" sector, the issue of Social Security reform was listed. However, the focus was entirely on proposals to set up "personal" savings accounts and how much benefits were being cut, rather than questions of how the richest Americans could be made to shoulder more of the burden.

upper-middle class. They often have lower rates on their incomes than secretaries, teachers, and electricians.

The most contentious part of winning such political outcomes comes not from having to defeat activists defending the interests of average citizens. Although the implications for the majority are huge, neither they nor anyone working on their behalf is significantly involved in this realm of politics. The real fight unfolds in the stratospheric border-zone separating oligarchs from the merely wealthy strata directly below them. That is, what little political resistance oligarchs confront arises entirely *within the top 1 percent of incomes*, with the highest 1/10th of 1 percent fighting against the lower 9/10ths of 1 percent. Democratic theory provides a persuasive account of why tens of millions of Americans who are uneducated and poor are underserved by a political system that responds far better to citizens who are highly educated, paid well, and can form networks to advance their agendas. What democratic theory cannot explain is why a mere 150,000 oligarchs comprising roughly 1/10th of the highest 1 percent of U.S. incomes consistently delivers political defeats to the 1.35 million citizens making up the remainder of the top 1 percent. The merely rich have financial resources, they are highly educated, and they outnumber oligarchs by a ratio of nine to one. The former should be no match for the latter. Yet tax burdens have shifted downward from the ultra-rich to the mass affluent.

What is missing from the analysis is the intensity of material power. Table 5.1 showed that the merely rich enjoy MPIs ranging from 15 to 32, whereas the MPIs for oligarchs range from 124 to more than 10,000. The Income Defense Industry exists and wins victories for oligarchs because they have the concentrated material resources – individually not collectively – to fund it. The collective income of the bottom 9/10ths of 1 percent is roughly equal to that of the top 1/10th of the same percent, but individual incomes for the bottom 9/10ths are far more modest. Not only is the drop-off in incomes steep beyond the top 1/10th of 1 percent, but whenever the Income Defense Industry has attempted to move down-market and respond to the income defense demands of the merely rich by offering cheaper generic tax shelters to those who cannot afford custom services, legislators and tax enforcers have reacted harshly. Nearly every episode of "cracking down" on tax evasion by the rich has targeted those at or below the oligarchic cusp.[35] The case material presented in the remainder of this section provides supporting evidence of these theoretical claims about the political contours and mechanisms of civil oligarchy in the United States, beginning with the origins of the income tax.

---

[35] Graetz (2002, 279) argues, for instance, that the Tax Reform Act of 1986 "halted the widespread use of tax shelters by individuals." This is true only if the emphasis is on "widespread," since the 1986 reform focused only on shelters used by the mass affluent. They had begun using real estate tax shelters to accrue losses they could apply against their compensation income. This was commonly used by professionals like doctors and lawyers. Section 469 on "passive loss" rules closed this loophole. This method of tax avoidance was never significant for oligarchs.

Income Defense. The federal income tax was deliberately imposed on the wealthiest Americans in 1913 because of a highly effective but short-lived episode of mobilizational power. Its impact on oligarchs, substantial at first, was undone because of an even more effective and long-term campaign of material power set in motion by oligarchs. The fate of the income tax across the twentieth century offers a microcosm of the battlefront in the sometimes uneasy fusion of oligarchic and democratic power in the United States.[36]

The struggle began in 1894 during the populist movement and immediately followed a severe economic crisis (oligarchic power in civil oligarchies is far more effective during ordinary times and vulnerable during crises). Under the leadership of William Jennings Bryan in the Democratic Party, and supported by the Populist Party, poor citizens burdened by heavy consumption taxes mobilized behind a movement to impose an income tax on the wealthiest Americans.[37] The first such tax had been imposed in the 1860s, but only as an emergency measure to fund the Civil War. The tax's significance declined by 1868 and was repealed in 1872. The 1894 initiative was different because the rich were being specifically targeted for a tax during peace time. The ultra-rich viewed the federal income tax as proof of the kind of dangers latent in extending suffrage to the unpropertied masses. The material threats to oligarchs were enormous, direct, and unprecedented.[38]

Members of Congress (including at least two millionaires) defending the interests of the rich on the floor of the House attacked the bill as "class legislation" – an apt description.[39] The tax would only affect 85,000 out of 65 million Americans, roughly the richest 1/10th of 1 percent. Opposition to the bill was fierce. One representative attacking the law argued that "the men who would be reached by the income tax were only such men as those who controlled the manufacturing and transportation industries of the country," the same men who were "making the country worth living in." Another opponent said that the bill would "impose a tax on a man because he was rich," adding that this "was not Democracy, it was Communism." Yet another opponent decried the legislation as a predatory move by the many poor against the rich few. "Those who demand its enactment," he argued, "are they who by its provisions are exempted from paying it." "It is a shame," he concluded, "that the successful should be made the legal prey of the unsuccessful."

---

[36] The United States was paying a high price in trade for its increasing reliance on tariffs. Farmers in the south and west, fearing taxes on their land would be increased if the rich were not taxed instead, allied with workers in the north and east against the wealthy. Useful histories of the federal income tax are available in Whitte (1986) and Herber (1988).

[37] The Populist Party advocated a graduated income tax on the rich in its 1892 platform. Under Bryan's leadership, the Democratic Party backed the 1894 income tax and proposed it again in its 1908 platform.

[38] The threat was enormous only in the sense of opening the door to further taxes on the rich. The Wilson-Gorman Tariff Act of 1894, to which the income tax bill was attached, imposed a modest 2 percent tax for a period of five years on any gains, profits, and incomes more than $4,000. In 2007 dollars, this was the equivalent of exempting the first $95,000 of income.

[39] All quotes from this debate appear in *New York Times* (1894).

Although the bill passed, oligarchs mounted an immediate defense through legal teams that aggressively carried the fight up to the Supreme Court, which struck down the tax in a 5–4 decision in 1895.[40] It would take an additional eighteen years of struggle for popular forces to pass the Sixteenth Amendment to the Constitution in 1913. It prevented oligarchs from fighting the federal income tax through the courts and marked one of the most extraordinary and direct democratic challenges to oligarchs in U.S. history. However, the victory was short-lived. In the years and decades that followed, oligarchs mounted a sustained campaign of income defense to counter the new threats to their material position. The battle had two consequences. As tax rates on the wealthy were increased – prompted by the onset of World War I – oligarchs used their formidable capacities for resistance and evasion to force the government to lower rates and shift the burdens increasingly onto the wealthy strata immediately below them, who were far more numerous but less able materially to mount an effective defense. Confronted with the costs of the New Deal and World War II, and facing a wall of powerful resistance from oligarchs who quickly refined their techniques for income defense, Congress turned the federal income tax against the much poorer majority who supported it initially precisely because it exempted everyone but the rich. The oligarchic prey had turned the tables on the democratic predator. Figure 5.1 captures the transformation vividly.

The income tax was strictly oligarchic in its impact only during its first four years. The rise in the percentage of households filing tax returns during World War I reflects the shift of part of the burden from the ultra-rich to the merely wealthy. It was among these strata at the top that the tax wars were initially waged. At no time before 1940 had more than 17.3 percent of American households met the exemption threshold for filing a tax return, and during most of this period the level was far lower.

Once the need for war financing had subsided, changes in exemptions allowed the lowest strata of wealthy Americans to avoid having to file returns, and the filing rate dropped again to less than 10 percent between 1925 and 1936. However, the burden never returned to oligarchs alone. A significant portion of the tax bill had been effectively shifted downward to the mass affluent and the moderately wealthy. On the eve of World War II in 1939, the filing rate inched up to slightly less than 14 percent of households. By 1942, what had begun in 1894 and 1913 as a wealth tax became a mass tax, with more than 63 percent of households compelled to file returns and pay income taxes (following the Great Depression, all workers had to begin paying a 2 percent Social Security tax). According to Herber (1988, 393), "The original impetus behind the Sixteenth Amendment, its provision for 'fairer' tax burdens for low- and middle-income persons, was being violated without challenge." The filing rate for households never again dropped below the 80 percent level after 1945

---

[40] *Pollock v. Farmers' Loan and Trust Company.* The majority opinion referred to the income tax on the wealthy as a "communistic threat."

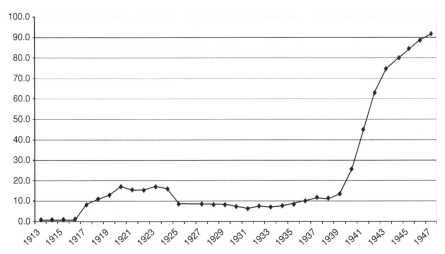

FIGURE 5.1. Percentage of Americans Filing Income Tax Returns, 1913–1947.
Source: Piketty and Saez (2003, Table A0, column 3).

and the 90 percent level after 1965. The explanation for the dramatic change
shown in Figure 5.1 is not just that World War II was expensive. It is that the
income defense capacities of oligarchs had improved significantly after 1913
while investments in the tax infrastructure and design emphasized extracting
resources from many people with modest incomes rather than a few with massive ones. Indeed, the government's response to mounting oligarchic resistance
to a tax intended exclusively for them was not to design better systems to
track and tax oligarchic incomes, but rather to lower rates on the wealthiest
while lowering the threshold of the highest bracket to force the merely rich to
pay more. The state retreated from the richest actors with strong defenses and
pursued those less wealthy with weaker capacities.

An explanation of how and why this happened begins with the dramatic
tax cuts enacted in the 1920s. The cuts reflect an immediate and overwhelming
assertion of oligarchic power. Smiley and Keehn (1995, 285) argue that the
"primary motive for the tax cuts of the 1920s was the desire to reduce the tax
avoidance by wealthier individuals that occurred as a result of the previous tax
rate increases and that the tax cuts enacted did reduce tax avoidance." Pushed
by the war, published income tax rates on oligarchs had risen from 7 percent
in 1915 to 67 percent in 1917 and peaked at 77 percent in 1918. Oligarchs
responded by pursuing immediate avenues for wealth defense. Congressman
Ogden Mills cited "strong evidence that wealthier individuals had successfully
avoided the income surtaxes." Although total dividends for the ultra-rich had
increased between 1916 and 1921, taxes paid by oligarchs dropped sharply.
"On incomes over $300,000," Mills complained, "we collected as much at
10 percent in 1916 as we did at 65 percent in 1921" (Smiley and Keehn 1995,
288).

As tax rates increased, oligarchs fought not only to push them back down, but also to make sure they did not face higher rates than the merely wealthy. Oligarchs had far broader capacities for defending their incomes than the strata extending down to the mass affluent. The challenge was to eliminate progressivity among the rich by making sure those earning $1 million in the early 1920s did not have to pay a higher tax rate than those earning $100,000. Equivalent incomes in 2007 dollars would be $11 million and $1.1 million, respectively. In 1917, oligarchs making $1 million were assessed a published tax rate of 65 percent, which was almost 35 percentage points higher than that assessed on the average affluent American. However, by 1925 the gap had been closed to zero. That year the same top tax rate of 25 percent applied to everyone making $100,000 and above. Thus, although the federal income tax was still societally progressive in the 1920s, it was a major victory for oligarchs to eliminate all progressivity within the wealthy strata.

Income defense for oligarchs was achieved in several ways between 1916 and the tax cuts enacted in 1921, 1924, and 1926. Assisted by tax lawyers and specialized accountants, oligarchs moved some of their wealth into tax-exempt securities at the state and municipal level. They also formed specially structured companies and partnerships to avoid the higher taxes. They started receiving dividends in the form of stock instead of cash, and then lobbied Congress and fought in the courts to frustrate efforts to tax the stock dividends. They also withdrew their compliance. Figure 5.2 shows that there was a sharp drop in the number of tax returns filed by oligarchs after 1916 when tax rates began to rise.

Smiley and Keehn (1995, 294) note that "the number of returns in the upper tax brackets indeed fell (rose) as tax rates rose (fell) and the effect was more dramatic the higher the net-income tax class." Figure 5.2 separates wealthy taxpayers into two groups divided at the $250,000 annual income level (about $2.85 million in 2007 dollars). Using the number of returns filed in 1916 as a baseline, the data reveal that oligarchic compliance plunged and remained below 1916 levels until 1925. During the intervening eight years, the average filing rate for oligarchs was 50 percent of the returns filed in 1916, and in 1921 compliance fell to only 19 percent. The resistance that year was most spectacular for oligarchs whose incomes were more than $1 million, sinking to only 10 percent of 1916 filing levels.[41]

By contrast, the mass affluent strata filed a larger number of tax returns every year after 1916, outpacing 1916 filing levels by an average of 32 percent during the eight years from 1917 to 1924. The average decline in filing levels for those with incomes greater than $250,000 was 48 percent during the same period, despite a rising number of Americans in this tax bracket. In response to these myriad income defense maneuvers by oligarchs, legislators could have enacted

---

[41] "The evidence indicates that there was a significant tax-avoidance response by taxpayers to changes in marginal tax rates during this period," Smiley and Keehn (1995, 301) conclude, "and that this responsiveness was larger the higher the net-income class."

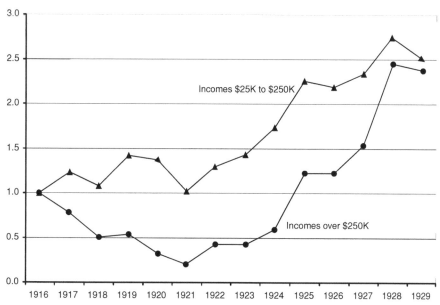

FIGURE 5.2. Annual U.S. Income Tax Returns Filed Relative to 1916 Base Year.
Source: From Smiley and Keehn (1995), Table 2; computations by the author.

changes in the tax infrastructure that blocked and punished questionable methods of avoidance, noncompliance, and outright criminal evasion. Instead they
retreated. "In the end," write Smiley and Keehn (1995, 292), "Congress found
the difficulties of dealing with tax avoidance that was taking place through
the use of corporations and tax-exempt securities too formidable," and in the
early 1920s passed "a substantial reduction in personal income tax rates as the
primary device to reduce tax avoidance." The changes were especially dramatic
on capital gains taxes. Until the 1921 tax cuts, capital gains were taxed at the
same rate as all other income, a rate that stood that year at 73 percent. Starting
in 1922, the highest tax rate on incomes dropped to 58 percent. However, far
more dramatic was the reduction of the rate on capital gains to 12.5 percent,
where it remained until 1934. The tax rate on other income continued to be
reduced until it reached 25 percent in 1925. These reversals in tax rates reflect
a major display of material power and income defense on the part of American
oligarchs.

In addition to data on filing rates, another indicator of the battle oligarchs
were winning against the rich strata below them is evident in the data on the
share of taxes paid by each group. Figure 5.3 tracks the income tax burdens
borne by the merely wealthy and oligarchs, and it illustrates that the overall tax
bill for those earning a 2007 equivalent of between $285,000 and $2.85 million
paid a consistently higher share of total taxes between 1917 and 1927 than
Americans with incomes over $2.85 million. Oligarchs paid a sharply declining
share of the tax bill during their years of greatest resistance, with their share

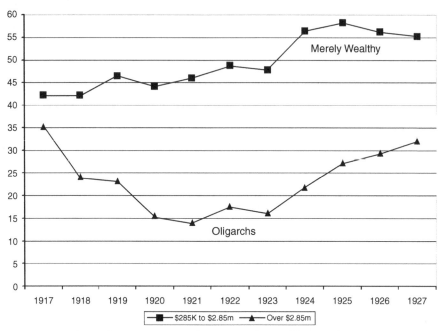

FIGURE 5.3. Share of Income Tax Burden on Merely Wealthy vs. Oligarchs, 1917–1927 (percent, adjusted $2007).
Source: From Smiley and Keehn (1995), Table 3; computations by the author.

rising in response to tax cuts. This pattern is typically misinterpreted as a "supply-side" response.

From the 1890s through 1913, oligarchs had been on the defensive. They fended off the first attempt at taxing the ultra-rich via the courts, only to lose the fight over the Sixteenth Amendment to well-organized popular forces. Oligarchs responded to the new and rising tax on the rich by engaging in aggressive methods of income defense. The achievements were highly successful. Overall rates were cut and progressivity among the wealthy was eliminated, thereby shifting a greater share of the tax burden to the less wealthy strata possessing weaker means of resistance (despite their far greater numbers).

Following the Great Depression, new but modest national taxes were imposed on lower- and middle-income Americans. However, by the outbreak of World War II, the stage had been set for the income tax to be deflected away from oligarchs and applied even to those in the bottom half of all income earners in the nation. The remainder of the twentieth century saw rates fall for those in the highest bracket and rise for those further down. What began in 1913 as the most progressive material victory average Americans had ever won against the ultra-rich had been reduced in a matter of decades to a system that was dramatically less progressive. The most significant part of the story is that what little remained of societal progressivity applied only to the mass affluent, who were now lumped into the same tax bracket as oligarchs far richer than they were, but without the income defense capacities oligarchs possessed to evade paying the bracket tax rate. By the 1950s and 1960s, the system had become absolutely regressive for oligarchs because they alone among the wealthy could engage the services of an Income Defense Industry that could reduce their effective income taxes even below those paid by average citizens (an achievement beyond the reach of the merely wealthy). The focus turns to how this was done.

Offshore Havens. The second half of the twentieth century witnessed an explosion of new instruments and techniques for widening the Income Defense Spread for oligarchs. One of the most significant developments especially after 1970 was the proliferation and use of offshore tax havens (Robinson 1995; Doggart 1997; Palan 2002). Of the $40.7 trillion in financial assets held in 2008 by the world's 10.1 million high net-worth individuals (HNWIs), roughly one-third, or $13.6 trillion, is estimated to be held offshore.[42] An International Monetary Fund study at the end of 2009 suggests a far higher level of $18 trillion of HNWI assets held offshore – a number the IMF believes is conservative.[43] At this rate, the existence of the offshore world permits oligarchs to avoid and evade about $400 billion in taxes globally each year.[44]

Working through an array of specialists, American oligarchs hiding wealth and income offshore engage in deliberate acts of income defense that yield tens of billions of dollars in tax savings. Senator Carl Levin (2010) describes how the services hired by oligarchs operate.

> A sophisticated offshore industry, composed of a cadre of international professionals including tax attorneys, accountants, bankers, brokers, corporate service providers, and trust administrators, aggressively promotes offshore jurisdictions to U.S. citizens as a means to avoid taxes and creditors in their home jurisdictions. These professionals, many of whom are located or do business in the United States, advise and assist U.S. citizens on opening offshore accounts, establishing sham trusts and shell corporations, hiding assets offshore, and making secret use of their offshore assets here at home.

[42] See Capgemini (2008) and Palan, Murphy, and Chavagneaux (2009). Capgemini's annual *World Wealth Report* underestimates wealth because it only tracks investable financial assets. Real estate held offshore would add an additional $2–3 trillion. Capgemini defines HNWIs as those persons with at least $1 million in financial assets. Ultra high net worth individuals (UHNWI), estimated to number 103,300 people in 2008, have financial assets of at least $30 million. Palan's (2002) analysis of tax havens emphasizes their historical roots.

[43] This $18 trillion figure would be significantly larger if it included Switzerland. "What is even more striking," writes Gian Maria Milesi-Ferretti, an economist for the IMF in Washington, "is that this number is likely to be an underestimation given the data problems with offshore financial centres" (Bain 2010).

[44] This level of tax losses follows calculations done by the Tax Justice Network (2005). A 2009 study by Global Financial Integrity showed that developing countries alone forfeit almost a trillion dollars a year in taxes because of oligarchs and corporations hiding assets in offshore havens (Kar and Cartwright-Smith 2006). The Tax Justice Network estimates that 60 percent of all global trade is routed through tax havens (www.taxjustice.net).

Citing committee investigations and hearings, Senator Levin estimates that wealthy individuals using offshore tax havens cause annual losses to the Treasury of nearly $70 billion – a level equal to about seven cents on every dollar of taxes paid honestly.[45] Johnston (2006) reports that "so many superrich Americans evade taxes using offshore accounts that law enforcement cannot control the growing misconduct." Senator Levin admits that "the universe of offshore tax cheating has become so large that no one, not even the United States government, could go after all of it" (Johnston 2006).

The rates at which oligarchs defend their assets by placing them offshore vary geographically with the perceived threats to income and property.[46] A 2003 report by the Boston Consulting Group (cited in Tax Justice Network 2010) estimates that North American oligarchs, enjoying secure property and moderate income tax predations, move roughly 10 percent of their assets offshore. European oligarchs, facing higher tax rates, make more aggressive use of offshore havens – relocating between 20 to 30 percent of their assets.[47] In Latin America, where a larger number of fortunes are from corruption and the threats the rich face are as much to property as to income, oligarchs move assets offshore at a rate of 50 percent.

The term *offshore* creates an impression of pesky enclaves around the world against which major countries are helpless as they pursue tax-evading oligarchs and corporations. The image is that they are a regrettable consequence of international sovereignty. However, Christensen (2006) points out that major powers are far more complicit in the existence of the offshore world than is commonly understood.

> Despite the evocative images conjured up by the term "offshore," it would be wrong to think of offshore as disconnected and remote from mainstream nation-states. Geographically, many of the offshore tax havens are located on small island economies dispersed across the spectrum of time zones, but politically and economically the majority of tax havens are inextricably linked to major OECD states, and the term "offshore" is strictly a political statement about the relationship between the state and parts of its related territories.

[45] The Senate also relies on Guttentag and Avi-Yonah (2006).
[46] There are also clumping effects in the placement of offshore wealth that result from word-of-mouth among oligarchs and the habits and expertise of local income defense industries. Russian oligarchs, for instance, flock to Cyprus whereas Indonesian oligarchs use nearby Singapore.
[47] The published national income tax rate on oligarchs in the United Kingdom in 2009 was 50 percent, substantially higher than the 35 percent upper bracket in the United States. Tax losses for the UK from oligarchs moving their assets offshore were about $20 billion in 2008, according to a study published by Britain's Trades Union Congress (Tax Justice Network 2010). Adjusted for GDP, British oligarchs were using offshore havens for income defense at roughly twice the rate of their American counterparts. Levels are even higher for Continental Europe, including in the Scandinavian countries. Avi-Yonah (2002, 1398) argues that German oligarchs use offshore havens aggressively and that "tax evasion by capital owners is estimated to be rampant (about 50 percent of interest income by German residents is estimated not to be reported)." See also Avi-Yonah (2000).

Focusing on the European cases, he continues:

> In the British economy, for example, the bulk of offshore transactions are con-
> trolled by the City of London, albeit that many City financial intermediaries
> operate out of centres located on UK Overseas Territories and Crown Depen-
> dencies. These centres have a tangible form, with functional banks, trust com-
> panies and law offices, but in practice they do not function autonomously from
> the mainstream economies. They are primarily of use to the City because they
> offer zero or minimal tax rates combined with secrecy arrangements (including
> nondisclosure of beneficial ownership of companies and trusts) and regulatory
> regimes which are more permissive than those prevailing in onshore economies.

Given this close political connection, it is puzzling that countries such as the
United States and the UK do not take stronger actions to control the offshore
problem.

Responding aggressively to offshore havens that help rob the U.S. Treasury
of tens of billions of dollars in unpaid taxes annually, political leaders could
recast oligarchs as unpatriotic or a threat to national financial security. Instead,
tracking assets offshore is portrayed as an invasion of corporate or personal
privacy. As Johnston (2009) points out, this change in framing would open the
door to a different sort of invasion.

> The Obama administration could tell the Caymans – now fifth in the world in
> bank deposits – to repeal its bank secrecy laws or be invaded; since the island
> nation's total armed forces consists of about 300 police officers, it shouldn't
> be hard for technicians and auditors, accompanied by a few Marines, to fly
> in and seize all the records. Bermuda, which relies on the Royal Navy for
> its military, could be next, and so on. Long before we get to Switzerland
> and Luxembourg, their governments should have gotten the message. Barring
> gunboat diplomacy (tempting as it is), there is no reason we cannot pass laws
> to block financial transactions with tax havens or even, Cuba-style, make
> it a crime for Americans to visit or do business with them without special
> permission. Congress could declare the hiding of funds a threat to national
> security and require that anyone with offshore assets disclose them to the IRS
> within 30 days and pay taxes, interest, and penalties within 180 days. For the
> holdouts, temporary special teams in the IRS and Justice Department could
> speedily pursue civil or criminal charges.

The reality is that countries like the United States and the UK do not act aggressively against the offshore world. Christensen (2006) argues that, if anything,
the opposite is true – the major powers have worked to block the cooperation
needed to curtail offshore operations.

> Most reasonable observers might expect that governments of onshore states
> would act collectively to prevent tax and regulatory degradation, but in prac-
> tice key actors, notably Switzerland, the UK and the USA, act to restrain
> efforts at achieving global cooperation. The UK, for example, allows its Crown
> Dependencies to persist with facilitating tax evasion, despite the fact that it
> is ultimately responsible for ensuring the good governance of those islands.

Notwithstanding the "smoke and mirrors" appearance of quasi-independence, all domestic laws enacted by the governments of the Bailiwicks of Guernsey and Jersey need prior approval from the Privy Council. It is therefore safe to conclude that the UK Department for Constitutional Affairs, which is responsible for government relations with the Crown Dependencies, would resist any laws it considered contrary to UK interests.[48]

In the middle of massive public bailouts to the financial system and large bonuses on Wall Street, President Obama (2009) proposed stronger measures to counter "tax cheats" using offshore havens. A White House press release entitled "Cracking Down on the Abuse of Tax Havens by Individuals" admitted that "wealthy Americans can evade paying taxes by hiding their money in offshore accounts with little fear that either the financial institution or the country that houses their money will report them to the IRS." Speaking in the Grand Foyer, Obama said, "For years, we've talked about shutting down overseas tax havens" and about "stopping Americans from illegally hiding their money overseas, and getting tough with the financial institutions that let them get away with it."

Obama's rhetoric was aggressive but his proposals were not. The president urged Congress to support efforts being discussed in the G-20 to sanction nations that maintained secrecy on bank accounts and corporate entities, and he sought funding to hire 800 additional IRS agents "to detect and pursue American tax evaders abroad." However, there were a number of immediate problems. One was that the United States is listed as one of the largest and most opaque offshore locations in the world because of secrecy laws on forming corporations in Delaware and Nevada (Tax Justice Network 2009). Actors around the globe take advantage of this gaping hole in the U.S. system. Another is that although the Senate believes upwards of $70 billion is lost per year (a finding of one key committee on which the president sat as a senator), Obama's proposals were projected to save a total of $8.7 billion over ten years – barely 1 percent of the losses. Finally, the proposal received a lukewarm response from Democrats and outright hostility from Republicans, who argued that denying corporations access to offshore havens would cripple their ability to compete globally.[49]

Jeff Poor (2009), a senior fellow at the Cato Institute, a think tank heavily subsidized by wealthy Americans, responded to Obama's proposals by defending tax havens as "outposts of freedom" and applauding the role they serve in helping oligarchs evade and thus weaken income tax rates that the ultra-rich reject as excessive. If Americans are concerned that "individuals are moving their money to countries with better tax law, that should be a lesson to us that we should fix our tax law," he argued. "That's the right way to get the rich

[48] Finn (2009, 20) points out that the head of state for the offshore micro-nation of Jersey is Queen Elizabeth II – "though she exercises authority on Jersey as the Duke of Normandy." He adds that "the local currency is the Jersey pound, convertible on a one-to-one basis with its mainland namesake."

[49] McArthur et al. (2010) analyze this latest effort by Congress to address tax abuse and evasion.

people to pay more." Unmentioned is that only oligarchs and corporations can avail themselves of such instruments of political persuasion and change.

In testimony before Congress, Leonard Burman (2003, 3) of the Urban Institute argued that "these people who face the highest marginal tax rates have the most to gain from tax evasion, and the most opportunities to engage in it." A crucial bridge for individual oligarchs between their onshore operations and offshore tax evasion is provided by "pass throughs." According to Charles Rossotti, former commissioner of the IRS, "enormous amounts of money...flow through 'pass-through entities' – such as partnerships, trusts, and S-corporations." Burman (2003) notes that these entities are "ideally suited to hiding income." The irony is that Congress created tax benefits for S-corporations and limited liability companies (LLC) to help small businesses thrive against much larger corporations.[50] The abuse of these entities would be easier to detect if it were illegal to own corporations in secret in the United States. Owners of pass-through entities would be more "matchable" if they had to declare who they were and perhaps supply a social security number in the states of Delaware and Nevada. In Senate testimony, Jack Blum (2009) argues that stemming tax evasion is impossible if the most basic information about beneficial ownership of corporations is allowed to remain secret.

> The single most important tool in the toolkit of people trying to hide money from law enforcement and tax collection is the anonymous shell corporation. These shell corporations have no physical place of business, use nominee officers and directors, and as a rule do no business in the place of incorporation. Their sole purpose is hiding where money is, who controls it, and where it is moving, from law enforcement and tax collectors. These shell companies should not be allowed to remain anonymous. States that offer corporations to individuals without insisting on information on beneficial ownership are undermining the efforts of law enforcement to prevent crime, recover stolen assets, and collect tax. [...] From our perspective gathering basic information about ownership for government use is essential to protect national security and to limit financial crime and tax evasion.

Pass-through entities are even more opaque when cross-border transactions and tax havens are involved.

The KPMG Case. Assembling data on the income defense activities of the average American oligarch is difficult by design. The IRS rarely pursues these taxpayers and information is not published. In the rare instances when the courts are involved, the cases are almost always civil negotiations rather than criminal pleas or verdicts, and such cases are typically sealed. If an oligarch works through a tax lawyer, then attorney–client privileges are invoked. In 2003, there was a small breach of this fortress of secrecy when the Senate held

---

[50] Pass-through entities must have fewer than one hundred shareholders and the entities themselves are not taxed. Instead, both their profits and losses "pass through" to the personal income tax returns of owners. The Income Defense Industry uses S-corporations and LLCs (which are even less restricted) for oligarchs as instruments that can pile up losses and reduced personal taxes.

public hearings and later published detailed reports about tax shelters created by KPMG.

The case provides a rare glimpse into how the industry works and how the players involved, especially oligarchs, are treated by the executive branch through the Department of Justice and the IRS, as well as the legislative and judicial branches. The evidence suggests that KPMG's biggest error was to allow greed and fierce intra-industry competition to tempt the firm into applying an aggressive marketing logic to a realm that is embarrassing politically and has survived mostly untouched by government because income defense services had been provided to oligarchs individually and in secret. Trying to reach a broad range of oligarchs to sell them tax shelters while keeping a low profile proved to be contradictory agendas.

The Senate repeatedly raised the generic nature of the KPMG tax shelters in reports and documents related to its investigations (U.S. Senate 2003, 2005, 2006). "None of the transactions examined by the Subcommittee [in the KPMG case] derived from a request by a specific corporation or individual," the Senate writes. Rather, "all of the transactions examined by the Subcommittee involved generic tax products that had been affirmatively developed by a firm and then vigorously marketed to numerous, in some cases thousands, of potential buyers" (U.S. Senate 2003, 2). A key participant in creating these generic shelters was Sidley Austin LLP, a firm with 1,700 attorneys and "over a century of experience" proudly representing and advising "high net-worth individuals and families," including those with "significant inherited wealth" (www.sidley.com).

The Senate's complaint about generic tax products implies that if 600 oligarchs had shown up separately at the doors of Sidley Austin LLP and each requested an expensive, custom-written tax opinion letter supporting abusive tax shelters, the Senate would have been less alarmed. However, for Sidley Austin to serve the same number of oligarchs through a single marketing channel (in this case a wealth management firm called Presidio) and sell them all one generic tax opinion was unacceptable to the Senate.[51]

Tax shelters may be odious in a general way, but marketing them like hamburgers instead of caviar is a step too far. "There is a bright line difference between responding to a single client's tax inquiry and aggressively developing and marketing a generic tax shelter product," the U.S. Senate (2003, 2) argues. "While the tax shelter industry of today may have sprung from the former, it

---

[51] Sidley Austin, formerly Brown & Wood, was investigated by the IRS for the 600 tax letters it wrote in support of illegal tax shelters and was sued by clients who, when exposed, had to pay back taxes and penalties. A single partner, Raymond Ruble, was convicted in 2008 for his role in drafting the letters. Despite its involvement in a massive conspiracy to defraud the U.S. Treasury of billions in income taxes on oligarchs, Sidley Austin remains open for business. Without a hint of irony, the firm's Web site boasts that Sidley's "Federal and State Tax Controversy practice provides thoughtful and experienced advocacy on behalf of clients in federal and state tax disputes nationwide." Their tax controversy lawyers "have an in-depth understanding of tax matters arising in controversies." See www.sidley.com/taxcontroversy.

is now clearly driven by the latter." Elite professionals had suddenly become disreputable hucksters who gave their tax shelters names like BLIPS, FLIP, OPIS, and SC2.[52]

> During the past 10 years, professional firms active in the tax shelter industry have expanded their role, moving from selling individualized tax shelters to specific clients, to developing generic tax products and mass marketing them to existing and potential clients. No longer content with responding to client inquiries, these firms are employing the same tactics employed by disreputable, tax shelter hucksters: churning out a continuing supply of new and abusive tax products, marketing them with hard sell techniques and cold calls; and taking deliberate measures to hide their activities from the IRS (U.S. Senate 2003, 22).[53]

Behaving more like a supermarket with an aisle devoted to greeting cards than an elite firm, KPMG "maintained an inventory of over 500 'active tax products' designed to be offered to multiple clients for a fee" (U.S. Senate 2003, 3).

Also prominent in the Senate's exposé was alarm at how multiple elements from across the Income Defense Industry had become integrated. The report merits quoting at length because the passage offers a concise summary not only of the network involved in this criminal activity, but also how many of them are household names with a global presence. "The Subcommittee investigation found that BLIPS, OPIS, FLIP, and SC2 could not have been executed without the active and willing participation of the law firms, banks, investment advisory firms, and charitable organizations that made these products work." Each played a different role. In addition, because the parties to these activities

---

[52] The re-naming of SC2 was comical. "Early in its development," the Senate writes, "KPMG tax professionals referred to SC2 as 'S-CAEPS,' pronounced 'escapes.' The name was changed after a senior tax official pointed out: 'I think the last thing we or a client would want is a letter in the files regarding a tax planning strategy for which the acronym when pronounced sounds like we are saying 'escapes'" (U.S. Senate 2003, 6).

[53] The issue of cold calls was mentioned repeatedly by the Senate. "KPMG maintains an extensive marketing infrastructure to sell its tax products, including a market research department, a Sales Opportunity Center that works on tax product 'marketing strategies,' and even a full-fledged telemarketing center staffed with people trained to make cold calls to find buyers for specific tax products," according to the 2003 report. "When investigating SC2, the Subcommittee discovered that KPMG used its telemarketing center in Fort Wayne, Indiana, to contact literally thousands of S-corporations across the country and help elevate SC2 to one of KPMG's top ten revenue-producing tax products" (U.S. Senate 2003, 8). Not all the clients recruited using these techniques were on the discount end of the market. A senior manager at KPMG explained how he attended a meeting in 1999 at the Dallas Airport for training in how to cold-call market BLIPS. "The training at that meeting and on other occasions included a PowerPoint presentation which was to be shown to taxpayers. During and after that meeting I was told which high net worth individuals to approach as potential BLIPS clients. Generally they were individuals who had over $20 million in capital gains or taxable income for the tax year" (U.S. District Court 2006).

know they risk prosecution, the services and schemes are deliberately compartmentalized. Johnston (2006) reports that the tax schemes "rely on complexity,
secrecy, and compartmentalizing information so that advisers can claim they
had no idea that the overall transaction was a fraud."

> In the case of BLIPS, OPIS, and FLIP, law firms and investment advisory
> firms helped draft complex transactional documents. Major banks, such as
> Deutsche Bank, HVB, UBS, and NatWest, provided purported loans for tens
> of millions of dollars essential to the orchestrated transactions. Wachovia
> Bank initially provided client referrals to KPMG for FLIP sales, then later
> began its own efforts to sell FLIP to clients. Two investment advisory firms,
> Quellos Group LLC ("Quellos") and Presidio Advisory Services ("Presidio"),
> participated directly in the FLIP, OPIS, or BLIPS transactions, even entering
> into partnerships with the clients. In the case of SC2, several pension funds
> agreed to accept corporate stock donations and sign redemption agreements
> to "sell" back the stock to the corporation after a specified period of time. In
> all four cases, Sidley Austin Brown & Wood agreed to provide a legal opinion
> letter attesting to the validity of the relevant tax product (U.S. Senate 2003, 9).

None of these elements was new. Identical services had been provided to oligarchs in a less organized – and less prominent – manner for decades. The
difference is that the industry was evolving and becoming rationalized. Left
unchecked, the political consequences could be devastating for oligarchs and
for their enablers in government who had been actively ignoring the crimes and
the tax losses for years.

The KPMG tax shelters functioned as "loss generators" for oligarchs. They
created "phony paper losses for taxpayers, using a series of complex, orches-
trated transactions involving shell corporations, structured finance, purported
multi-million dollar loans, and deliberately obscure investments." The shelters
were provided to 350 clients between 1997 and 2001. Fake losses claimed
on tax returns by these oligarchs totaled about $8.4 billion, or $24 million
per client. Applied against their incomes, these losses reduced the taxes of
each oligarch by an average of $8.3 million. For the group, this amounted to
$2.9 billion in income defense.[54] For its services, KPMG earned more than
$124 million in fees, or roughly $350,000 for each tax shelter.[55] Not only
did all the firms and banks conspiring on behalf of these 350 oligarchs know
that the "investments" they were concocting "had no reasonable potential
for profit,"[56] but KPMG calculated that even if they were fined for failing to

---

[54] Author's calculations from audit data in the U.S. Senate (2003, 3) report.
[55] It is impossible to estimate the total cost of each tax shelter because the Senate report does not
provide data on fees paid to Presidio, Sidley Austin, and the various banks participating in the
conspiracy to defraud the U.S. government. Based only on KPMG receipts, oligarchs defended
$68 in income for every $1 paid in fees.
[56] According to the Senate: "The banks and investment advisory firms knew that the BLIPS loan
structure and investment restrictions made little economic sense apart from the client's tax
objectives, which consisted primarily of generating huge paper losses for KPMG clients who
then used those losses to offset other income and shelter it from taxation" (U.S. Senate 2003,
10).

disclose the shelters to the IRS as required by law, they would still make far more in fees. "Based upon our analysis of the applicable penalty sections," internal KPMG documents stated, "we conclude that the penalties would be no greater than $14,000 per $100,000 in KPMG fees. For example, our average [OPIS] deal would result in KPMG fees of $360,000 with a maximum penalty exposure of only $31,000" (U.S. Senate 2003, 5, 13).

Profits for KPMG should not obscure the bedrock oligarchic intent at the core of these arrangements. The motive force at the root of this entangled conspiracy is the determination of extremely wealthy individuals to defend their incomes. Each oligarch was able and willing to deploy substantial sums to ensure that they could add to their fortunes at a much faster rate than the published tax structure would permit. Pooled together, oligarchic resources for wealth defense formed a succulent market that seeded and then sustained "an armada of professionals" who devised the means through which oligarchs could "hide assets, shift income offshore, or use offshore entities to circumvent U.S. laws" (U.S. Senate 2006, 2). A hit man murders only because he is paid to do so. The buyer is equally guilty of contracting a murder whether he actively searches for an assassin, or one shows up and says, "I hear you want someone killed."

Fortunately for oligarchs, things work differently when they are caught using shelters for criminal tax evasion. In the Senate documents, oligarchs are repeatedly portrayed (and in lawsuits portray themselves) as innocent victims of zealous income defense providers. Ungrateful that they got away with settlements with the IRS rather than criminal proceedings, many oligarchs angrily sued firms like KPMG and Sidley Austin for the taxes and penalties they had to pay. The basis of the suits is that the firms, which are paid handsomely to be masters of the tax code morass, bungled their job of creating tax shelters that would generate phony losses for oligarchs, evade taxes, but be structured with such elegance and complexity that the legal risks to oligarchs were almost zero. This is tantamount to suing one's hit man for a sloppy murder. "Over a dozen taxpayers penalized by the IRS for using these tax products," the Senate writes approvingly, "have subsequently filed suit against KPMG for selling them an illegal tax shelter" (U.S. Senate 2003, 5).

Reserving all opprobrium for the industry and saying almost nothing about the criminality of wealthy tax cheats – whom Johnston (2003) notes also constitutes a significant part of the political "donor class" – the Senate attacks the tax shelter industry for tempting oligarchs to buy shelters they "might otherwise have been unable, unlikely, or unwilling to employ." The industry is guilty of actively "developing new products, marketing dubious tax shelters to numerous individuals and corporations, and continuing to wrongfully deny the U.S. Treasury billions of dollars in revenues, leaving average U.S. taxpayers to make up the difference" (U.S. Senate 2003, 4, 3). Burman (2003, 4) concurs that "tax evasion simply reallocates tax burdens from noncompliant to compliant taxpayers." Missing from Senate criticisms of the wealth defense industry is the recognition that this fraudulent industry exists only because oligarchs supply the resources to sustain it. Not one of the thirty-three findings and twenty-seven recommendations spanning three U.S. Senate reports (2003, 2005, 2006) on the KPMG case and tax shelters more generally focuses on the criminality or culpability of oligarchs.

Instead of devising new means for tracking oligarchs and their money, or proposing harsh prison sentences on them for increasing the tax burdens on others less able to pay, the focus has remained on entities like KPMG, which was fined $456 million for the four tax shelters it provided to 350 clients.[57] Criminal suits were brought against KPMG partners and senior staff, thirteen of which were dismissed when a judge ruled that prosecutors had infringed on their rights of due process by pressuring KPMG not to pay their legal fees.[58] Although many of the oligarchs involved paid the taxes they had evaded, plus penalties and interest, they continue to employ other law firms within the Income Defense Industry to recoup these expenses from KPMG and the other parties to the conspiracy.[59]

Jai Chandrasekhar, an attorney at Bernstein Litowitz Berger & Grossmann LLP, was involved in a class-action suit in 2008 on behalf of oligarchs upset over the quality of the KPMG tax shelters they bought. He defended the notion that his wealthy clients were innocent victims and maintained that the complexity of the tax code and the structured shelters absolved them of culpability.[60] Chandrasekhar was asked: "Isn't it fair to ask – given the borderline nature of the paper transactions involved and the amount of money at stake in tax savings and fees – whether the wealthy taxpayers had the duty to hire a specialist to review the tax shelter and advise on its legality?"

Chandrasekhar replied that the "very lucid and transparent" Senate explanation of the shelters "was after many months of investigation by many staffers, and with the benefit of having subpoenaed thousands of internal documents showing how even people inside KPMG discussed the aggressive and frankly iffy nature of the tax products they marketed as legitimate. This was far less clear to the members of our class action. Although several are businessmen, many are not accountants or tax lawyers, and they accepted the assurances being given to them by KPMG, one of the country's leading accountancy firms,

---

[57] In addition to the fine paid by KPMG, the big-four accounting firms – KPMG, Ernst and Young, PricewaterhouseCoopers, and Deloitte – were pressured to implement minor reforms. "The big four have now set up a body to regulate themselves called the International Accounting Standards Board (IASB)," observes Daniel Finn (2009). "Not only do the accountancy firms appoint representatives to the IASB's committees, they actually fund it themselves – through a foundation registered in a tax haven."

[58] On this logic, senior KPMG personnel not only have a right to a fair trial, but apparently a right to have their employer pay for their defense.

[59] David Saperstein, portraying himself as a victim who was unaware that the $20 million in taxes he saved in 2000 using a BLIPS shelter constituted evasion, sued one of the banks working with KPMG for taxes, penalties, and interest totaling $37 million. Bloomberg reports that Saperstein's attorneys argued in his complaint that "the goal 'was to defraud people like Saperstein into participating in BLIPS and other strategies in order to generate fees and other income,' adding that he was never told the underlying transactions were fraudulent" (Glovin 2010).

[60] Telephone interview with Jai Chandrasekhar, May 19, 2008.

and by Brown & Wood, one of the oldest and most distinguished Wall Street law firms, that the tax products would pass IRS scrutiny." Chandrasekhar added that "one of the very first things you learn in law school classes on taxes is a quote from a famous Supreme Court ruling that states, and I'm paraphrasing, that you are required only to pay the taxes you legally owe, not the maximum amount of taxes possible."[61]

The very structure of the relationship between oligarchs and the Income Defense Industry, principals and agents, not only obscures the daily and potent expression of oligarchic material power in the political realm, but it also shields oligarchs from punishment and blame. This exchange with Chandrasekhar helps explain why.

> Winters: Why is the IRS so reluctant to go after wealthy tax evaders criminally?
>
> Chandrasekhar: Proving criminal tax fraud is a lot harder than winning unpaid taxes and penalties in a civil action by the IRS. To prevail in a criminal action, the government would not only have to prove that the taxpayer engaged in a transaction that in effect was tax evasion, but also that it was the willful intent of the taxpayer to do so. This is very hard to do when you have highly respected and reputable partners of a leading firm like KPMG admitting in Senate testimony and in guilty pleas that they produced tax products they knew were illegal and yet aggressively marketed them to wealthy taxpayers as legal, and backed the claim up with tax opinion letters from one of the most august law firms in New York.

It is not that proving willful criminal intent is so difficult. It is that it would be costly in both time and money to win given the resources oligarchs can bring to a court battle. As Korpi's (1985) "power resources" theory predicts, the potency of wealth as a power resource is expressed in the IRS's calculation of the costs and hazards of litigation. It is enough to anticipate the use of an oligarch's formidable financial resources for defense to get the IRS to compromise or retreat.[62] Meanwhile, oligarchs engage in the use of tax shelters already

---

[61] The actual quote from *Gregory v. Helvering*, 293 U.S. 465 (1935) is: "The legal right of a taxpayer to decrease the amount of what otherwise would be his taxes, or altogether avoid them, by means which the law permits, cannot be doubted. [...] But the question for determination is whether what was done, apart from the tax motive, was the thing which the statute intended."

[62] Korpi (1985, 32) argues for an "intentional mode of explanation" in analyses of power. Intentional explanations "take account of the capacity of human beings for strategic action in the pursuit of goals." The intentional mode suggests that "we should reverse the behavioral approach and begin the study of power with power resources rather than with the exercise of power. By starting the analysis with power resources and their characteristics, we can facilitate the understanding of the rational motives for the differing uses and consequences of power." This explains why a prosecutor's assessment of oligarchic capacities for defense can reduce or block charges, especially criminal ones, before they are even filed. "The difference in power resources affects the evaluation of the means available to the actors as well as their expectations about the actions of the other party, and a rational actor will take this difference into consideration before he activates his pressure resources" (Korpi 1985, 35). It is commonplace for actions and inactions, or compliance and violations, to be based on these bidirectional assessments of power resources (including misperceptions and efforts to deceive), and yet these "nonuse" expressions of power leave no tracks and are impossible to tabulate.

calculating that the IRS, the Department of Justice, and state prosecutors are pre-intimidated.

The KPMG manager trained at the Dallas Airport to make PowerPoint presentations to rich clients admits (U.S. District Court 2006) that both parties were fully aware of the minuet they were dancing. After a presentation, taxpayers signed a representation letter that "contained materially false statements including a statement to the effect that the taxpayer was engaging in the transaction for investment reasons." The manager continues: "The real purpose for the transactions was to generate a phony tax loss which the taxpayer later claimed on their returns." The oligarchs knew why the shelters were being supplied. "I assisted some of the taxpayers in preparing the tax returns," the KPMG manager states. "I signed at least one return for a client that contained losses generated by a transaction which he had entered into solely to generate a phony tax loss. I knew that the losses should not have been claimed on the tax returns and that the taxpayers were claiming the losses to keep the money for themselves instead of paying taxes they owed."[63]

Income Defense and Effective Tax Rates. Because the federal income tax began as a tax only on the wealthy, government data from 1913 until the late 1930s make it possible to analyze oligarchs and the struggles unfolding within the wealthiest strata over who would shoulder the burden. However, once the income tax became a mass tax, data on the richest taxpayers became obscured. Common government reporting of incomes and taxes paid was by deciles, which is useful for producing blunt measurements like the Gini index, but reveals nothing about oligarchs, who constitute a fraction of the top 1 percent. Tax data separating how much is paid by the top 1 percent is available as far back as 1980. However, given that the top 1 percent ranges from oligarchs in the top 1/10th down to the mass affluent (the top 1 percent started at incomes of $400,000 per household in 2007), this aggregated data continued to make it impossible to track how effectively oligarchs were defending income. Certain limited insights became possible once the IRS released tax data on the top 400 taxpayers dating back to 1992 (and accidentally for the single year 1961)[64] and on the top 1/10th of 1 percent covering the years since 2001.

Income defense by oligarchs is multifaceted. Lowering the published tax rates is a key element, as is pushing down bracket thresholds so that those

---

[63] Despite the dismissal of charges against most of KPMG defendants, prosecutors pursued four executives all the way to jury verdicts. The results were a disappointing mixture of convictions and acquittals. According to *CFO Magazine* (Harris 2008), Doug Whitney, a partner with the firm of McDermott Will & Emery, referred to the "long and tortured history of the [KPMG] case," and argued that the acquittals "send the government a strong signal that the criminal courtroom is not the place to define the illusive contours of the economic substance of tax shelters." Whitney added that "reasonable minds will differ on where to draw the lines about what constitutes sufficient economic substance." Prosecutors may have "learned through the last five or six years that trying to criminalize acts on either side of the lines is just too difficult to justify."

[64] Johnston (2010a); Internal Revenue Service (2009).

earning $300,000 and $300 million pay the same marginal rate, and, as much as possible, getting the government to tax income from capital gains at a separate and dramatically lowered rate. Given the progressive and oligarch-focused nature of the income tax in 1913, the compression of progressivity from World War II forward, and the shift away from taxing oligarchs and increasing the burdens on the mass affluent and the middle class, the successes have been significant. The points at which oligarchs have consistently experienced setbacks have been during crises – the economic crises of 1893 setting the stage for the first peacetime income tax a year later, rate increases during World War I, and again during the Great Depression and World War II – although by that point the tax effort was being directed increasingly downward in society and oligarchs could worry less about marginal rates as taxes on capital income fell.[65] It is between the crises, during the politics of the ordinary, that oligarchs and the gnawing political influence they and those struggling on their behalf exert is at its most potent. The best indicator of this potency is the Income Defense Spread, which measures the gap between the published tax rates on oligarchs in any given period and how much of it they actually pay.

Figure 5.4 shows the reduction of the oligarchic tax burden from 1992 to 2007, including the single year of 1961, for the 400 wealthiest taxpayers. This does not represent the success of every oligarch in the top 1/10th of 1 percent, but instead offers a glimpse of how the most materially empowered oligarchs with the most to gain in absolute terms from income defense fared. The levels shown, from a high of 85 percent to slightly more than 45 percent, are actual or effective taxes paid as a percentage of the highest marginal rate. The downward-sloping line means the ultra-rich are doing a better job over time of keeping more of their incomes.

This is only half of the story. As in other periods examined in the twentieth century, oligarchs are not just offloading tax burdens to those below them in society, but the mass affluent, represented in the top 1 percent of incomes, are significantly less successful in reducing their tax burdens than oligarchs.

Figure 5.5 separates the wealthy into three groups – the top 400 incomes, the top 1/10th of 1 percent (visible separately after 2000), and the top 1 percent of incomes. It shows levels of taxes actually paid by each group. Tax cuts on the wealthy reduced the effective tax burden on the mass affluent by a few percentage points. The richest oligarchs won far larger reductions.

Lobbying victories to keep capital gains taxes low explain a significant part of the downward trend in effective tax rates on oligarchs, but not all of it. There have been major changes since the 1960s in the other dimensions of income defense, especially in defending not just capital income but also salary

---

[65] Indeed, during the second half of the twentieth century, federal taxes on income, at least in the public and visible sense, were increasingly defined by the kind of incomes average people earned.

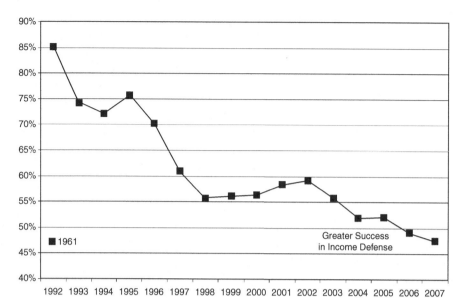

FIGURE 5.4. Reduction of Oligarchic Tax Burden: Actual Income Tax Paid as Percent of "Published" Tax Rate for the Top 400 U.S. Incomes.
Sources: Data on effective tax rates on the top 400 incomes are from Internal Revenue Service (2009); the single year 1961 is from Johnston (2010a, 2010b); nominal (published) tax rates on the highest earners are from the Tax Foundation (2009b); computations by the author.

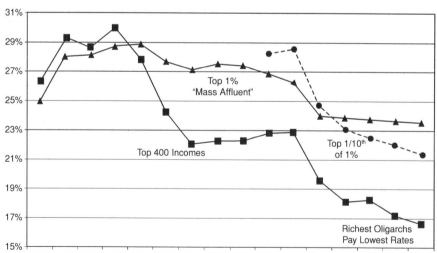

FIGURE 5.5. Effective Federal Tax Rates on Highest U.S. Incomes.
Sources: Data on effective tax rates on top 400 incomes are from Internal Revenue Service (2009); data on effective tax rates on the top 1 percent and 1/10th of 1 percent are from Tax Foundation (2009a); starting in 2001 the IRS reported the top 1/10th of 1 percent separately, and the data shown for the top 1 percent from 2001 forward is exclusive of the top 1/10th of 1 percent; computations by the author.

TABLE 5.4. *Changing Composition of Salary and Capital Income for the Top 400 U.S. Taxpayers Including Changing Marginal and Capital Gains Rates*

	Salary Income	Capital Income	Marginal Rate	Capital Gains Rate	Predicted Effective Tax	Actual Effective Tax	Predicted Tax Minus Actual
1961	22.3	77.7	91	25	39.7	42.4	− 2.7
1992	47.4	52.6	31	28	29.4	26.4	3.0
2007	34.4	65.6	35	15	21.9	16.6	5.3

Source: From Piketty and Saez (2003, including 2007 updates), "data Fig4new," "Top 0.1% of Income Share and Composition, 1916–2007"; Internal Revenue Service (2009); Tax Foundation (2009a); and computations by the author.

and other compensation, from being taken as taxes. Table 5.4 shows that the Income Defense Industry, still in its infancy in the 1960s, did a relatively poor job of reducing tax burdens on the ultra-rich. Too much of their income was being taxed at the 91 percent rate and not enough at the capital gains rate, leading to overpaying their taxes by 2.7 percentage points. Figure 5.6 controls for the effect of changes in tax rates on capital gains. In 1961, actual

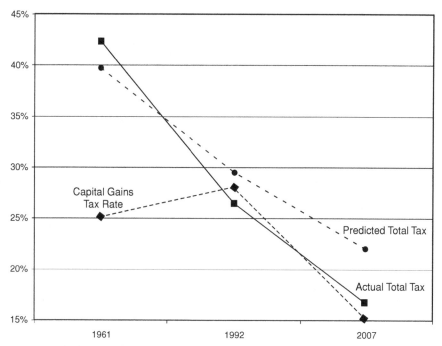

FIGURE 5.6. Oligarchic Success Defending Salary Incomes Effective Income Taxes Paid by the Top 400 U.S. Oligarchs, Controlling for Capital Gains Tax Effects.
Source: From Piketty and Saez (2003, including 2007 updates), "data Fig4new," "Top 0.1 percent of Income Share and Composition, 1916–2007"; Internal Revenue Service (2009); and Tax Foundation (2009a); and computations by the author.

total taxes paid were higher than predicted total taxes, suggesting the Income Defense Industry was underperforming. However, Figure 5.6 also shows that by 1992 a reversal had taken place and was accelerating. Actual taxes paid were three percentage points lower than predicted levels of combined capital gains and compensation income taxes.

By 2007, a far more aggressive pursuit of tax evasion and avoidance had widened the gap to 5.3 percent. For these 400 top oligarchs, earning an average of $345 million per year, this was an additional boost of more than $18 million each in defended income in 2007, and a combined reduction in taxes paid to the U.S. Treasury of $7.3 billion. These are taxes successfully avoided only on reported income. These billions retained by oligarchs are in addition to the nearly $70 billion in lost taxes on income and assets hidden in offshore havens reported by Senator Levin.

Johnston (2009) argues that the tax system has been "recalibrated to take from the poor, the middle class, and even the affluent and give to large corporations and the very richest of the rich." Kenworthy (2009a) notes that data on the top .01 percent of households (about 10,000 families) show that this segment's average inflation-adjusted pretax income "soared from $7 million in 1979 to $35 million in 2005, but the share of that income they paid in taxes didn't increase." Indeed, a tax system that is flat or slightly progressive for the bulk of taxpayers from the 99th percentile downward becomes strongly regressive as one travels up the rungs of the top 1 percent. Johnston's (2009) research shows, for instance, that in 2000, "people making between $50,000 and $75,000 paid the same share of their income to the federal government as those making more than $87 million, and that those making between $100,000 and $200,000 were taxed more heavily than those making $10 million." He continues:

> The marginal tax rate for cops and teachers is more than 40 percent – 25 percent for income taxes and another 15 percent for Social Security and Medicare taxes. The marginal rate for some hedge fund managers, five of whom earned more than $1 billion in 2007, has been zero. That's because many of these speculators have been able to avoid taxes by operating through offshore partnerships under rules that let them defer income taxes. Executives, entertainers, and athletes also have been able to amass vast untaxed fortunes: For example, Roberto C. Goizueta, the CEO of Coca-Cola in the 80s and 90s, built a nest egg of more than $1 billion, but was able to defer taxes on most of it until he died.

Social Security and Medicare taxes are the most regressive on the books because they benefit not only oligarchs, but even the top 1 percent comprising the mass affluent. The Medicare tax is regressive because it is a flat 2.9 percent on incomes at any level. It does not place higher burdens on those more able to pay.

Kenworthy (2009b, 31) points out that the U.S. tax system as a whole is "essentially flat, rather than progressive. Individuals and households throughout the income distribution pay approximately the same share of their market incomes...in taxes." Progressive nominal income tax rates are "offset by regressive payroll and consumption taxes." The Social Security tax is by far the most regressive tax in the United States. It is designed as an exact inversion of the original income tax of 1913. Instead of a threshold that exempts everyone below the ultra-rich from the tax, there is a ceiling that exempts everyone above a certain income from any further taxes. In 2010, the Social Security tax was 12.4 percent on the first $106,800 in earnings. The Social Security tax on someone earning $100,000 and $100 million is $12,400 and $13,240, respectively. The tax burden on the former is 12.4 percent and on the latter about 1/100th of 1 percent.

If the Social Security tax ceiling were eliminated and the richest Americans had to pay the same rate on the salary portions of their incomes that poor citizens pay, the total additional revenues from the top 1 percent of Americans would be $90 billion per year, split evenly between the top 1/10th of 1 percent paying $45 billion and the next 9/10ths of a percent paying the rest. Of this amount, $6 billion would be paid by the top 400 – who would each see an extra $15 million withheld from their salary income (which on average is around $120 million in compensation income out of $345 million in total earnings). By removing the regressive ceiling and applying the Social Security tax to the entire matchable part of the average oligarchic income, each would be forced to pay an extra $300,000 per year. The mass affluent would each pay an extra $30,000 in Social Security taxes per year. The mechanism for collecting these additional billions is already in place because it is a withholding tax on salaries (and taxes on the first $106,800 for the top 1 percent of earners are already being paid). Increasing the tax burden on the top 1 percent of earners would be accomplished simply by eliminating the ceiling. Ninety billion dollars is enough to give a tax rebate of $1,000 to each household in the bottom 90 percent of the population, whose average income was $32,421 in 2007. The obvious political question is how in a democracy does such a tiny slice of the voting population manage to avoid having the ceiling removed?[66]

The Donor Class. The evidence is strong that wealth plays a significant role in shaping policy outcomes in the United States (Phillips 2002; Hacker and Pierson 2010). Larry Bartels (2005, 2008) and Martin Gilens (2005) show that wealthier constituents exert far more influence over government decisions than Americans of modest means, and that the effects of undifferentiated public opinion on decision makers are almost zero.[67] These studies were designed to

---

[66] The findings in this chapter predict, however, that the mass affluent would likely pay all of the extra $30,000 burden, as would some high net worth individuals. However, oligarchs facing tax increases in the millions have the power resources to engage income defense professionals to convert larger portions of their incomes into nonsalary streams to evade paying the added Social Security levy. Higher capacities for income defense at the top of the system would ensure that the actual burdens were deflected downward.

[67] The picture that emerges is even more grim than these findings suggest. Achen and Bartels (2004) show that American citizens not only lack the competence to choose leaders who will advance their material welfare, but they also fail even at "retrospective voting" – punishing those who have undermined their financial welfare during the previous term in office. The theory of retrospective voting on "pocketbook issues" was supposed to "rescue voters from the charge that they are too uninformed or too disengaged to play a meaningful role in the democratic process," Achen and Bartels write (p. 4). "Our view is that they do no such thing.

TABLE 5.5. *Individual Donations of $200 or More to All 2008 U.S. Federal Campaigns*

Range	Number of Donors	Total Donated (million)	Average Donated	% Share of Adult Population	% Share of All Donations
$206,998 and over	100	$23.6	$235,900	.000045	0.9
$95,000 to $206,997	838	$81.3	$97,017	.000376	3.1
$10,000 to $94,999	36,388	$973.7	$26,759	.00163	37.0
$2,300 to $9,999	244,781	$835.8	$3,414	.1098	31.7
$200 to $2,299	1,075,540	$719.1	$669	.482	27.3
TOTALS/AVERAGES	1,357,647	$2,633.5	$1,940	.6089	100.0

Source: Center for Responsive Politics (2010a, 2010b).

measure the broad effects of having higher incomes rather than the potency of concentrated material power held by oligarchs and how it is uniquely exerted.[68] Those focusing on campaign finance reform attempt to probe the nexus between money and political influence by arguing that a small fraction of wealthy Americans constitute a powerful political donor class that provides the vast majority of funds for candidates. They argue that long before ordinary citizens get to vote on a slate of candidates for either party, the choices are reduced to politicians deemed acceptable to the richest Americans via a "wealth primary" in which early campaign funding is unavailable to candidates straying outside a narrow political agenda (Raskin and Bonifaz 1993; Raskin 1994; Overton 2002, 2004). Only candidates who are personally wealthy can escape the constraints of the wealth primary.

The Center for Responsive Politics (2008) reports that historically less than 4 percent of Americans make contributions to political campaigns. The rate increased modestly during the 2008 presidential election. However, despite Obama's success in getting small donations through the Internet in 2008 – rising to 6 percent of Americans donating online from 2 percent in 2004 (Rainie and Smith 2008) – the proportion of all federal election costs financed by large donations totaling $200 or more actually increased from 46.1 percent in 2004 to 49.8 percent in 2008 (Center for Responsive Politics 2010a). Table 5.5 presents data on the largest donors.

Rather, they forget most of their previous experience and vote solely on the basis of how they feel about what has happened lately" (p. 6). The authors conclude that "citizens cannot perform sensible retrospective judgments at election time" (p. 36).

[68] Separating citizens into three broad income groups, Bartels (2005, 4) finds that senators were "vastly more responsive to the views of affluent constituents than to constituents of modest means." His data show that "the views of constituents in the upper third of the income distribution received about 50% more weight than those in the middle third (with even larger disparities on specific salient roll call votes), while the views of constituents in the bottom third of the income distribution received no weight at all in the voting decisions of their senators."

The average contribution for all Americans captured in these data was $1,940. However, the average donation from the top 100 contributors was almost $235,000, and the highest single contributor gave more than $424,000. "For all their influence at the polls, guys like Joe the Plumber aren't typically campaign contributors," notes Sheila Krumholz, executive director of the Center for Responsive Politics (2008). "You're more likely to see John the Bond Trader bankrolling these campaigns." Of the roughly 1.4 million citizens contributing at least $200 to the 2008 elections, three-fourths of the contributions came from one-fifth of the donors, who in turn comprised 1/10th of 1 percent of American adults.

This fraction overlaps with the number used as a rough approximation of the American oligarchy based on incomes. It is likely that the intersection between private (and corporate) wealth and campaign financing makes Democrats and Republicans far more receptive to the interests and complaints of the ultra-rich.[69] This would account for part of the success in compressing the tax structure and shifting burdens off oligarchs. However, it does not mean that campaign finance is the primary or even most effective means through which oligarchic power is expressed, nor that campaign finance reform – even socializing the costs of all elections – would result in policies dramatically less favorable to oligarchs (although it would unburden the wealthy of having to finance campaigns). Spectacular wealth defense victories have been won by oligarchs despite campaign finance playing a minor role in shaping the outcomes.

The Estate Tax Battle. Graetz and Shapiro (2005, 239–41) provide an important example in the battle over the estate tax. The movement that succeeded in phasing out the "death" tax from 2001 to 2010 was indeed fueled by "money, money, money" – even though many of the players swept into the mobilization to repeal the estate tax were not oligarchs. However, the main influence of wealth on the process was not through campaign finance. Graetz and Shapiro emphasize that "the flow of cash did not affect the legislative result in the way that people who fret over money's role in politics usually complain of. Campaign contributions, soft money, spending limits for political candidates, and the like have become controversial issues," they admit, "but they mattered relatively little in the estate tax fight." It was the deployment of material resources by oligarchs to fund a movement whose leaders were drawn from operators on the periphery of the Income Defense Industry – actors from outside the industry's epicenter on K Street in Washington, DC – that accounts for the victory. "The most obvious link between money and the repeal," write Graetz and Shapiro, "came from the ultra wealthy. They stood to gain the most from full repeal, and they got what they wanted."

The struggle over repealing the estate tax is also indicative of oligarchic power in that the middle and lower strata of wealthy Americans, believing

---

[69] According to Avi-Yonah (2002, 1406), "the political power of the rich stems not just from their actual donations or their ability to finance runs for political office, but, more importantly, from politicians knowing that they have the excess funds to donate."

a change in the exemption threshold could be made more permanent than a repeal, favored reforming the estate tax by pushing up the exemption (which for the merely wealthy would be a tantamount to a repeal). In return, they were willing to support higher rates on the oligarchs above the threshold, but once again the oligarchs won. Graetz and Shapiro argue that "in the contest between repeal and reform, the interests of the ultra-rich, who stood to gain little from an increase of $5 million or even $10 million in the exemption, prevailed over those of the merely rich, for whom an extra few million dollars was the whole ball game." Working though lawyers, lobbyists, and other professionals, activist oligarchs funding the battle were careful to avoid public attention. "Though the ultra-rich very much wanted to promote the cause," Graetz and Shapiro argue, "they were mindful that success depended on repeal's retaining its populist hue, so they stayed in the background."[70]

A different kind of background effort shaped the broader setting in which taxes on the rich were framed. "Money mattered more fundamentally in shifting the tectonic plates underlying American tax debates," Graetz and Shapiro suggest. "This reconstruction of the politics of tax policy has been a long-term affair." Oligarchs have realized "a significant return on their three decades of investments in activist, conservative think tanks." These actors blaze the ideological path along which drones in the Income Defense Industry, who do not need to be significant conceptualizers, can follow. Graetz and Shapiro write that the think tanks "have spawned teams of smart, energetic researcher-activists for whom the supply-side hostility to all taxes on capital is second nature." These activists at institutions like the Heritage Foundation "supply legitimacy and ideological ammunition to the lobbyists and interest groups... who work relentlessly, day in and day out, to keep up the tax-cutting pressure on the Hill."

The struggle over the estate tax also brings the discussion full circle about the important interplay between threats and uncertainty in creating and sustaining an Income Defense Industry capable of both concentrating and refracting oligarchic power in civil oligarchies. The political mechanism involving principals and agents that ultimately achieves income defense for oligarchs sometimes operates in ways that are counterintuitive. The permanent elimination of the estate tax would reduce the threats and uncertainties oligarchs face. An industry operating purely as an instrument of oligarchs would pursue this agenda. Indeed, some marginal elements of the Income Defense Industry played a key role in championing precisely this outcome.

---

[70] "All this money from the ultra-rich supporters was crucial to funding the repeal effort. Given the billions of dollars at stake for these wealthy families, this was a tiny investment that will pay an enormous dividend if repeal becomes permanent" (Graetz and Shapiro 2005, 240). Oligarchic successes over decades in reducing their effective tax burdens has, perversely, stoked popular anger against the tax system in general, which was then directed against the estate tax. "Joe Sixpack no longer believes he is getting a fair shake," Graetz (2002, 279) argues. "Joe believes that wealthy people and large corporations have tax advisers – lawyers, accountants, investment bankers, magicians, and alchemists – to help them arrange their affairs to duck the taxes they should be paying, thereby avoiding their fair share of the tax burden" – which has "diminished popular support for the income tax."

However, the Income Defense Industry as a whole, and especially the core players huddled in Washington, DC, do not behave as simple instruments. Threats against the material interests of oligarchs, combined with enough uncertainty and complexity in the tax system for those threats to be overcome, are the lifeblood of the political trade in which the industry serves as a vital agent. This explains why powerful elements in the Income Defense Industry have fought to keep the estate tax. Their efforts are fundamentally propelled by the material power of oligarchs to pay to defend income and wealth. Having no estate tax would save an estimated $75 billion per year for oligarchs between 2014 and 2024 (Birnbaum and Weisman 2005). As long as certain basic tax threats remain in place, even if rates get lowered, the interests of the industry and those who finance it are aligned. Their interests diverge on permanently ending tax threats.

In 2009, as Democrats controlling Congress tried to revive the estate tax, it happened that they had "an important K Street ally: The life insurance companies that peddle estate-planning products" (Carney 2009). The industry's goal was to keep the threat against oligarchs in place while also reminding them that, for fees far below what the tax would cost, they alone could provide the skilled specialists to evade the tax through complex instruments and arrangements. "Proponents of the estate tax point out that very few people actually pay it," Carney writes, "but that doesn't mean many people aren't burdened by it." Permanently repealing the tax would eliminate the burden, "but one man's burden is another man's profit. Enter the life insurance industry." Carney reports that in 2005 the life insurance industry made between $12 and $15 billion in fees from estate planning alone.[71] This was fully 10 percent of life insurance receipts that year (Carney 2007). Pitted against these lobbyists was not an array of organizations and specialists arguing on behalf of the mass affluent and the masses below to decrease their tax burdens by increasing taxes on the richest households.

Once again, the most contested battle was largely within the wealthiest strata. "The very rich and the merely rich are fighting over the fate of the estate tax," Birnbaum and Weisman (2005) noted. Ordinarily, the superior material power resources of the ultra-rich and the income defense forces they could engage would tend to overwhelm the merely rich, a far larger constituency but with weaker material resources individually. However, the highly public battle over extending the Bush-era tax cuts late in 2010 undercut the ability of oligarchs to get their preferred result.

The rich were in broad agreement that Congress should act by the end of 2010 to prevent the estate tax from reverting in 2011 to its pre-2001 rate of 55 percent and a $1 million exemption. However, the ultra-rich rejected this high

---

[71] Powerful entities in the Income Defense Industry, who lobbied in favor of the estate tax so that they could profit by defending against its effects, include the American Council of Life Insurers (which spent $20 million on lobbying for the tax in 2005 and 2006) and the Association for Advanced Life Underwriting.

rate while the less wealthy rejected the low exemption. Oligarchs supported a $3.5 million exemption but demanded a 15 percent rate.[72]

It was decisive for those with smaller fortunes that they were represented in the conflict by the National Federation of Independent Business (NFIB), which has 600,000 members. Its lobbyists insisted on a $5 million exemption ($10 million for couples) and a rate of 35 percent. This formula, passed by Congress in December 2010, allows nearly all NFIB members to avoid the tax.[73]

The efforts at income defense on the part of oligarchs in the American civil oligarchy have unfolded under conditions both of the high rule of law and of participatory democracy. The oligarchic and democratic elements of the system have coexisted far more than clashed. This suggests that there is nothing inherently incompatible about civil oligarchy and liberal democracy as long as oligarchic property and incomes are threatened only by episodic rather than sustained class legislation of the sort attempted in 1894 and 1913. During the long periods between episodes of mass-mobilizational and occasional national crises of war and economic collapse, oligarchs have waged and won a steady battle to defend their incomes. Income defense by oligarchs has necessarily meant pushing the costs of government onto less wealthy strata. That political struggle has been waged by oligarchs – directly and through their agents – as much against the mass affluent as against the remainder of society. Attention now turns to the comparative case of civil oligarchy under the nondemocratic government of Singapore.

Singapore

Singapore shares the status of civil oligarchy with the United States. It is uncommon for these two countries to be compared on almost any dimension except perhaps high gross domestic product (GDP) per capita – Singapore having pulled ahead of the United States for the first time on this measure in 2007 (Heston, Summers, and Aten 2009).[74] The city-state has an unusually large number of wealthy citizens. However, a tremendous amount of wealth is concentrated in the hands of a few thousand oligarchs at the top. The fifty richest Singaporeans, which include eleven billionaires in a population of only 4.8 million in 2009, have an average net worth of $977 million and a combined fortune of $49 billion. They represent 1/1,000th of 1 percent of the population but own

---

[72] "To me, the most important factor is the rate," said Seattle Times Publisher Frank A. Blethen, who is part of a coalition of very rich people who oppose the tax. "I'd like the exemption as high as possible but not if it sacrifices the rate" (Birnbaum and Weisman 2005). At the end of 2009, Republicans blocked estate tax legislation because it did not contain the 15 percent rate oligarchs wanted. The Obama administration agreed with the $3.5 million exemption but proposed a 45 percent rate.

[73] This rate and exemption apply for two years, at which time Congress must revisit the estate tax struggle.

[74] At Purchasing Power Parity (PPP), Singapore surpassed the United States in real terms by all four methods of adjustment available in the 2009 Penn World Table.

5 percent of all wealth.[75] Wealth at the top of Singaporean society is six times more concentrated than in the United States.

In addition to the top fifty, Singapore has about 880 UHNWIs each with at least $30 million in nonhome investable assets. The country has nearly 100,000 millionaires (more than a fifth of whom are Indonesians) each with an average of $4.5 million in nonhome net worth. They make up 2 percent of the population, the thickest layer of millionaires in the world, and own about 47 percent of the nation's private wealth. If the top fifty are included, Singapore's millionaires make up 52 percent of the nation's wealth. The median income in Singapore was $40,400 in 2008 and the average income for the top 10 percent of the population was $188,000. The net worth of the average millionaire in Singapore is about 110 times the income of the median citizen. The net worth of the average member of the fifty richest is about 24,000 times the median income. Despite the broad stratum of millionaires in Singapore, material power is highly stratified and densely concentrated at the very top.

If the absence of democracy were a key determining factor in categorizing oligarchies, Singapore might have been more logically examined in the previous chapter focusing on the Philippines under Marcos and Suharto's Indonesia. However, despite being nondemocratic, Singapore has almost nothing in common with the sultanistic oligarchies under these dictators, and even less with the electoral ruling oligarchies that replaced them in 1986 and 1998. Instead, Singapore meets all of the same defining criteria for civil oligarchy present in the United States. Oligarchs in Singapore are fully disarmed and property is secured by an impersonal state which oligarchs influence but do not rule directly. Singapore's system of laws and enforcement is stronger than its oligarchs (with one insignificant exception addressed at the end of this section), and they also engage in income defense, making extensive use of complex shelters and offshore havens (with Singapore itself serving as an important haven for oligarchs from elsewhere).

As in other chapters, comparative case material is introduced here for purposes of broadening the analytical scope of oligarchic theory.[76] Rather than focus on Singapore's Income Defense Industry, attention is devoted instead to the problem of founding a civil oligarchy – which is to say taming oligarchs through an impersonal system of laws. Singapore is illuminating as a twentieth-century example of how and why the high rule of law was put in place, and how this crucial political-economic transformation resulted in law without democracy, or authoritarian legalism.[77]

---

[75] For these statistics on wealth and incomes in Singapore, see *Forbes* Asia (2010), Capgemini World Wealth Report (2008 to 2010); Singapore Department of Statistics (2010), and Boston Consulting Group (2010).

[76] For important interpretations of Singapore's political economy, see Rodan (1989, 2006), Jayasuriya (1999), and Rodan and Jayasuriya (2009).

[77] Authoritarian legalism (Jayasuriya 2000) and the pioneering work of Fraenkel (1941) on the rise of the "dual state" in Germany are discussed in greater depth later. The most puzzling

An important implication of this case and others like it is that high-growth capitalist development is tightly linked to secure property and tamed oligarchs, but has almost nothing to do with electoral democracy. Growth was unusually high for decades, for instance, when oligarchs were secured and tamed under Suharto's sultanistic oligarchy and also under civil oligarchy in non-democratic Singapore. It is not that democracy is a hindrance. Growth can occur with or without it. Neither, as the Suharto period demonstrates, is the rule of law absolutely essential. What matters is that the core political demands of oligarchs regarding wealth defense, particularly property defense, are satisfied. Conversely, investment and growth are inhibited when oligarchs are wild rather than tamed – that is, when they are compelled to expend significant resources on defense, coercion, and direct rule to secure their property, and yet still fail to manage threats effectively.

There are several ways to achieve a tamed oligarchy. Depending on how they are organized, ruling oligarchs can operate collectively to tame themselves. Likewise, a sultanistic oligarch has the potential to secure oligarchs against threats from below while also protecting them and their property from each other. However, the most effective and durable form of wealth and property defense exists under civil oligarchy, in which oligarchs are both defended and tamed through laws enforced by an impersonal bureaucratic state – democratic or otherwise. Civil oligarchy is the only form in which oligarchs are by definition tamed. The key lies in the intersection of law, the locus of coercion and enforcement, and property. A legal order that fails to provide property defense will also eventually fail to tame oligarchs (who will attempt to re-arm in response to the threats); and a legal system that fails to tame oligarchs cannot effectively secure property (because oligarchs will threaten each other laterally). Warring, ruling, and sultanistic oligarchies are alternative solutions to wealth defense in the absence of a paramount legal regime.

The argument in brief regarding Singapore begins with deep political dangers and instabilities in the period leading up to and immediately following independence in 1965. Oligarchs and elites were weakly tamed and faced a range of threats – casting serious doubts on the city-state's future and viability. There was nothing inevitable about Singapore's material success over the next several decades. It could easily have gone the way of drug-, gambling-, and Triad-infested Macao. Instead, a strong system of legal constraints was erected that secured oligarchs materially as it subdued them institutionally. The irony is that this impersonal system of adjudication and enforcement was put in place by an autocrat who just as easily could have imposed a personalistic dictatorship in which he was, like Suharto, the embodiment of the law. Constraining this option was Singapore's extreme combination of external threats and dependence. The result was an almost pure-form civil oligarchy fused not to democracy, but rather to a strangely bifurcated legal system that receives

aspect of Singapore for international observers remains, according to Nicholas Kristof (2000), "how it could simultaneously be so modern economically and so medieval politically."

universally high marks for its fairness in the defense of all aspects of property and public order, but equally low marks for its treatment of opposition political figures and civil liberties. The same legal system of courts, prosecutors, police, and judges ends up being simultaneously fair and repressive.

This anomalous situation is poorly explained by democratic theories that do not separate the rule of law into its material and political components. Olson (1993, 574), for instance, asserts that democracies "have the extraordinary virtue that the same emphasis on individual rights that is necessary to lasting democracy is also necessary for secure rights to both property and the enforcement of contracts." He adds that "the *same* court system, independent judiciary, and respect for law and individual rights that are needed for a lasting democracy are also required for security of property and contract rights" (1993, 572, emphasis in original). However, in Singapore, the law protects property and contracts. It provides fairness and predictability for oligarchs while providing daily security and order for ordinary citizens. It is a highly functioning system of law that makes judgments in these areas on the merits and thus stands as a veritable gold standard of "good governance," and yet it does not protect liberal freedoms.

The yawning gap between law and freedom goes far beyond "quality of democracy" debates. It is better explained by a theory of civil oligarchy that emphasizes the degree to which the legal regime renders oligarchs materially secure and behaviorally constrained, and treats democracy as a separate and separable realm of law and justice. There are many cases proving that legal systems with strong property rights and tamed oligarchs are often accompanied by pluralist democracy. However, the case of Singapore spanning half a century confirms that there is no necessary association between the two, and that the struggles for one can overlap with or remain distinct from progress toward the other.[78]

Uncertain Beginning. Singapore has the unusual distinction of having gained full national independence by ejection. Prime Minister Lee Kuan Yew famously wept on live national television the night the island nation was voted out of the Federation of Malaysia in 1965. It was the most unhappy independence day on record. "For me it is a moment of anguish," the Prime Minister said before losing his composure and walking off camera. The problems were racial, ethnic, religious, and economic. The majority Chinese population on the island skewed the numbers for all of Malaysia in a way that made Malay leaders nervous. Lee Kuan Yew espoused a fair-sounding level economic playing field for Malaysia which ethnic Chinese entrepreneurs happened to be strongest. Kuala Lumpur wanted affirmative action for Malaysia's poor majority of *bumiputera*, or "native sons," who, compared to the Chinese, had endured centuries of colonial disfavor by the British and Dutch in the region. Religious riots had flared up in Singapore in 1964 when Malay and Chinese youths clashed during

---

[78] Singapore's prime minister, Mr. Lee Hsien Loong, rejects as a "simplistic approach" the notion that "if you develop, you will need democracy" (Low 2009).

a Muslim procession celebrating the Prophet Muhammad's birthday. Twenty-three people were killed and hundreds injured.

On the eve of the separation, as word circulated that Kuala Lumpur was poised to sever ties, Lee remarked that Singapore as an independent nation "is a political, economic, and geopolitical absurdity. . . . Our chances of survival are ten times higher if we form part of a Greater Malaysia than if we stay on our own." Lee fought hard against independence for a nation he was certain to lead, and his view that Singapore was unviable on its own was widely shared. Singapore was born against its will in a state of alarm and paranoia about its security. "We faced tremendous odds," Lee Kuan Yew (2000, 3) wrote in his memoir, "with an improbable chance of survival." This backdrop is important because the transformations that occurred in the formative years of independent Singapore are inexplicable without an appreciation of the siege mentality that gripped the country's leadership from the beginning and never dissipated in the decades that followed. It was an extreme example of what Woo (1991) refers to in the South Korean context as "defensive industrialization" by a "security state." External threats not only shaped and propelled developmental motivations and policies. They changed the forces of internal discipline so that powerful oligarchs or elites who skim and steal to the point of debilitating the state and economy are seen not merely as immoral criminals, but as unpatriotic menaces to national survival.[79]

Taming oligarchs through sultanism is relatively easy as long as an autocrat has sufficient means of coercion and other patronage resources. However, taming them by building a strong legal regime is vastly more challenging because it involves creating institutions and then somehow empowering them rapidly. The gradual empowerment of institutions over oligarchs is a different process when it results from decades or centuries of struggle, as in Western Europe and the United States. Doing so as a deliberate act by a leader who confers authority by a transfusion of power to institutions, and then allows them to

---

[79] Woo argues that an external threat like that posed by North Korea (or by China for Taiwan) transforms economic development and industrialization from vague motives about progress and prosperity into matters of national survival. Rapid development becomes a vital means for avoiding being overrun and occupied. Five months after President Nixon announced he would visit China – interpreted by Seoul as an end to guarantees that the United States would go to war a second time on the peninsula – Park Chung Hee declared in his 1972 New Year's address that "the North Koreans are of one mind, obsessed with making guns, mortars, and tanks." Having to fend for themselves, "South Korea became of one mind, like their brethren," Woo (1991, 147) writes, "concentrating on building basic industries that were indispensable for defense." The Korean state allocated massive resources to build major Korean conglomerates. However, officials demanded performance and restraint. "The state was munificent," Woo (1991, 165) argues, "but also a harsh disciplinarian." Firms that did not meet aggressive targets for production and exports were cut off. There was corruption. However, it was never tolerated on a scale that subverted the goals of national defense or threatened to sap the economy of its momentum. Sucking the country dry, as oligarchs and elites have done since independence in the Philippines and Indonesia, would probably have been met in South Korea at the height of the threat from the North with firing squads broadcast on national television.

function consistently against influential actors across the system, is exceedingly rare. It makes more sense and is easier to use emergency executive powers to confront immediate threats and build a regime of personal rule than to invest in institutions and laws. It was Singapore's extreme external dependence, especially for investment capital and markets, which greatly narrowed the range of options for a leader like Lee Kuan Yew and militated against easy personalistic remedies. Singapore is a pure global price-taker. It has no hinterland, no natural resources, no peasantry, and a tiny domestic market.

These pressures and constraints are an important antidote to the perspective that key policies adopted in Singapore, particularly to tame oligarchs by enforcing the supremacy of law, were the result of "great man" theories or that leaders sometimes simply possess sufficient "political will."[80] Few national leaders are genuinely convinced that national survival hangs in the balance when they attempt to confront and subdue oligarchs and elites. Indeed, shocking challenges to those in power can precipitate a crisis much faster than the slow-drip "crisis" of national decline. The evidence suggests that taming oligarchs in Singapore was not an abstract matter of will. It was one of extreme urgency and fear. Lee Kuan Yew believed that if he did not establish an impersonal system of enforcement that restrained oligarchs and elites, guaranteed property, and enforced contracts, Singapore would be unable to attract capital and serve as a hub of production and commerce. Failing to do this risked triggering a process of national demise.

Compared to what one citizen described in 2003 as "the orderly and secure haven we have today," the situation in Singapore in the early 1960s was dire (Lee 2003). The nation had been beset with chronic corruption at the highest levels dating back to the British and Japanese periods. There were problems of gambling, drugs, organized crime, violent street gangs, kidnappings, and murder in the streets (*Time* 1958, 1959a, 1959b, 1960). Under the leadership of "tiger generals," Singapore's Triads consisted of at least 10,000 youths organized into 360 gangs that clashed using knives and clubs. Their main business was extortion and their monthly revenues exceeded $350,000. The Triads were "making life miserable for Singapore's 100-odd Chinese millionaires," *Time* magazine reported. Six oligarchs and several of their children had been kidnapped in 1960 alone and held for ransoms ranging from $20,000 to $170,000.[81] The threat was not just to oligarchic fortunes, but to their lives. Those who resisted or refused to pay were butchered. "Singapore business has

---

[80] Quah (1982, 176) argues, for instance, that "what is lacking in the Philippines' anti-corruption effort is not adequate measures but rather the political will to implement such measures and apprehend those found guilty of corruption regardless of their status or position in society." The problem in Indonesia and Thailand, meanwhile, is that political leaders "are not really committed to the goal of eradicating corruption because they or their families are not free from direct or indirect involvement in corrupt behaviour." Such views are ahistorical and fail to grasp the interplay among power, threats, and political will.

[81] Prominent oligarchs who were kidnapped included Chia Yee Soh, rubber magnate Eng Hong Soon, and Ong Cheng Siang, the chairman of a bus company, who was pulled from his Mercedes

been greatly affected," one oligarch complained. "We do not have the peace of mind to concentrate on our affairs."

Before focusing on taming Singapore's oligarchs and elites, Lee worked initially on establishing a firmer grip on society at the street level. Within three weeks of becoming prime minister, he began "cracking down on Singapore's boisterous seamy side" (*Time* 1959a).[82] The "low" rule of law improved significantly during the next decade. Meantime, the civil service and bureaucracy Lee inherited from the British was highly corrupt. Theft by officials was rampant under the British, increased during the Japanese occupation, and worsened after the war. According to Quah (1999, 490), a report in 1950 by the Commissioner of Police revealed that "graft was rife in government departments in Singapore." The expulsion from Malaysia in 1965 compounded these pathologies. Unemployment increased from 13.5 percent in 1966 to 15 percent in 1967, and exports plunged by 20 percent as an angry Malaysia erected trade barriers after the separation. Singapore also depended on its former partner for fresh water and raw materials. The island's greatest vulnerability was its reliance for security on a British naval base that was scheduled to be closed. It housed 50,000 British troops and serviced a fleet of 70 naval vessels. The base employed 40,000 locals and accounted for one-third of Singapore's GNP (*Time* 1965).

The tiny enclave of Singapore had six ethnic Chinese for every one Malay Muslim in 1965. Its biggest problem is that it is sandwiched between Malaysia and Indonesia, both with ethnic Chinese minorities and the two largest Islamic populations in Southeast Asia. Both countries were hostile to Singapore in the mid-1960s, and a strong local Communist movement was organizing to take over the government by electoral victory.[83] It was this dangerous combination of circumstances that explains Lee Kuan Yew's odd determination to seek safe harbor for Singapore by becoming part of the Malaysian Federation. Being the junior partner of Kuala Lumpur was better than being invaded, and the chances that Indonesia would bully Singapore were lower if Malaysia provided cover. Independence greatly complicated the task of securing the nation. In his memoir Lee (2000, 6) writes that his primary concern at independence was "to defend this piece of real estate." He continues:

> We had no army. Our two battalions were under the command of a Malaysian brigadier. How were we to build up some defense forces quickly, however rudimentary? We had to deter and, if need be, prevent any wild move by the

Benz on his way home. After the ransom was paid, Ong "was dumped out, hands bound and eyes taped, on a lonely country road."

[82] Singapore's limited police force "cleared the newsstands of pornography, padlocked eight girlie-magazine publishers and swooped through bars, sending B-girls home," and also targeted the country's "notorious gangsterism." There was a brief reprieve. "The immediate, unexpected result: for the first time in memory, a full week went by without a kidnapping, extortion, or gangland rumble reported" (*Time* 1959b).

[83] Defense Minister Goh Keng Swee argued in 1966 that if Singapore could not quickly reverse its economic decline by attracting investment and switching to industrial production, "it's a certain deduction that the Communists will eventually win power by free elections" (*Time* 1966).

Malay Ultras (extremists) in Kuala Lumpur (KL) to instigate a coup by the Malaysian forces in Singapore and reverse the independence we had acquired. Many Malay leaders in KL believed that Singapore should never have been allowed to leave Malaysia, but should have been clobbered into submission.

This was the beginning of Singapore's siege mentality and the defense impulse that informed, motivated, and justified a host of policies adopted to ensure survival.[84] The same commitments propelled and sustained the drive to tame Singapore's oligarchs through laws.

Only the most security-obsessed countries have anything remotely like Singapore's "Total Defense" program and the annual rituals of "Total Defense Day." Working closely with the armed forces, but based at the Ministry of Education, the Total Defense initiative evolved over a period of two decades and was finally launched formally in 1984. To give her neighbors pause, Singapore needed to persuade them that invaders would not just face the army and air force, but the resistance of the whole people, even children in elementary school. The task was partly motivational, and Singapore was assisted immediately after independence by Israeli advisors, who also trained the nation's intelligence and special forces. "People must admire military valor," Lee (2000, 18) explains. "Persuasion alone was not enough. We needed institutions, well organized, well staffed, and well directed to follow up the exhortations and stirring speeches. The prime responsibility was that of the ministry of education."

"Total Defense" was part of Singapore's preparation for "total war." As the education ministry explains:

> Singapore is a small country. It has a small population base and no natural resources. It is a multi-racial and multi-religious society, a young country whose roots are still being planted. All these make Singapore vulnerable not only to military attacks, but also to exploitation of our economic, social, political, or psychological weaknesses by those who may wish to do us harm.

The responses to these dangers consist of five dimensions: psychological, social, economic, civil, and military defense. On Total Defense Day, students in Singapore perform skits and practice eating nutritional crackers and other emergency rations.[85]

---

[84] See Uslaner (2008). The emergence in the 1990s of movements like Jemaah Islamiyah, which is determined to establish a caliphate that would swallow up Singapore in a sprawling unitary state that extends from Malaysia to the southern Philippines, has reinforced the view among Singapore's leaders that the choice is between constant vigilance or certain oblivion. In 2001, two months before the September 11 attacks, I was invited by then Senior Minister Lee to his office for an exchange of interpretations about politicized Islam in Indonesia and Malaysia. He recorded the discussion to be played later for Prime Minister Goh Chok Tong. It was evident that Lee's biggest concern was not illegal Islam, but a takeover in Malaysia and Indonesia by legal movements determined to impose *shari'a* law. This would exacerbate Singapore's security concerns.

[85] Total Defense Day falls on February 15 to coincide with the fall of "fortress Singapore" to the Japanese in 1942. Since the 1960s it has grown into something closer to Total Defense week.

The mindset at the time of independence was that economic strength was the linchpin of national resilience. Apart from accounting for the source of the resolve to tame oligarchs and elites through a civil rather than a sultanistic oligarchy, what the Singaporean case demonstrates most clearly is that the nuts and bolts of making the institutions of law stronger than the most powerful actors in the system is accomplished in the doing – by sending consistent signals to empowered players that the rules would not be bent for expediency, nor would they accommodate those who have money or are especially well connected. A legal regime is partially empowered when it stands up to some among the powerful, and fully empowered when it stands up to all of them. One of the earliest tests of Singapore's augmented commitment to the rule of law, ironically, involved an ominous foreign element. In 1964, two Indonesian commandos had bombed the Hongkong & Shanghai Bank on Orchard Road, killing three Singaporeans. President Suharto dispatched a personal envoy, a brigadier general, to pressure Lee to commute the death sentences of the commandos to life imprisonment. Lee (2000, 21) sent an important signal in resisting Singapore's massive and powerful neighbor:

> We were small and weak. If we yielded, then the rule of law not only within Singapore but between our neighbors and Singapore would become meaningless as we would always be open to pressure. If we were afraid to enforce the law while British forces were still in Singapore, even though they had announced that they would be withdrawing by 1971, then our neighbors, whether Indonesia or Malaysia, could walk over us with impunity after 1971. So we decided not to abort the due process of law by acceding to the petition. The two men were hanged on 17 October [1968].

To rattle the Singaporeans, the Indonesian armed forces immediately announced naval maneuvers in the waters close to Singapore. An Indonesian commander threatened "he would personally lead a task force to invade Singapore" (Lee 2000, 21). Lee's signal of resolve was even more significant given that Singapore's exports had been hurt by Malaysia's hostile posture and the island was desperately trying to revive more than $500 million in trade with Indonesia that had been disrupted during Sukarno's "Crush Malaysia" campaign (*Time* 1966). Although the matter with the commandos was criminal rather than material-oligarchic, the simple message that power would not trump legal findings on the merits had been reinforced.

Corrupt Practices Investigation Bureau. Taming oligarchs and powerful government elites required a targeted effort and an equally targeted institutional apparatus – the Corrupt Practices Investigation Bureau (CPIB). The task, as Quah (1999, 491) explains, was to convert corruption in Singapore from being "a low-risk, high-reward" activity to "a high-risk, low-reward" activity. Power in the form of material resources was being used by oligarchs

The "five aspects" of Total Defense are available at the Ministry of Education's Web site at www.ne.edu.sg/fiveaspects.htm and www.totaldefence.org.sg.

to defend and advance their wealth and business interests, including bribing government officials. In addition to the threats manifested in kidnappings, this behavior injected a menacing uncertainty into property claims and contracts for oligarchs. Even if local players had adapted to this game, it was a significant impediment to attracting desperately needed infusions of new capital from abroad. To ensure that Singapore had genuine property rights supported by law, rather than contingent property claims defended by competing and clashing oligarchs, Lee began a frontal assault on the predatory behaviors of rogue oligarchs and elites as early as 1960. The attack gained momentum and urgency after the trauma of independence.

The CPIB was established by the British in 1952. It occupied a few rooms in the Supreme Court building and had a staff of thirteen investigators, some of whom were borrowed from the corrupt police force. It was originally designed to pursue petty officials – "the police, hawker inspectors, and land bailiffs who had to take action against the many who broke the law by occupying public roads for illegal hawking, or state land for building their squatter huts" (Lee 2000, 159). To have any hope of taming oligarchs and the powerful players in government they influenced with material resources, the CPIB had to be aimed at the top of the system rather than the bottom. "We decided to concentrate on the big takers in the higher echelons," Lee explains, "and directed the CPIB on our priorities." The useless anti-corruption law of 1937 bequeathed from the British was replaced in 1960 with a far more aggressive Prevention of Corruption Act (POCA). The definition of an improper gratuity was widened to include "anything of value" given to officials.

The budget of the CPIB was increased and in 1961 it was moved into its own three-story building. The POCA was amended to give investigators the power to make arrests, search bank accounts (including of family members and close associates), and the rules of evidence were changed to facilitate enforcement and convictions. "The most effective change we made in 1960," Lee (2000, 159) notes, "was to allow the courts to treat proof that an accused was living beyond his or her means or had property his or her income could not explain as corroborating evidence that the accused had accepted or obtained a bribe." This was a dramatic shift in the burden of proof. Instead of investigators and prosecutors having to prove the act of corruption, they only needed to show its results.

The power of the CPIB was further elevated by making it an extension of the prime minister's office and authority. "With a keen nose to the ground and the power to investigate every officer and every minister," Lee argues, "the director of the CPIB, working from the Prime Minister's Office, developed a justly formidable reputation for sniffing out those betraying the public trust." Over the years, the powers of the CPIB and its investigative capacities were enhanced. It could compel witnesses to appear for interrogation, and those caught lying to CPIB investigators were jailed for the offense.

Such reforms are fairly easy and can even be politically expedient. However, they pose no serious challenge to oligarchs as a whole as long as bodies like the CPIB remain dysfunctional. Some of the most chronically corrupt countries have some of the highest-profile agencies supposedly fighting corruption. Uslaner (2008, 212) points out that anti-corruption efforts are often "disguised campaigns to purge political opponents ... or pure shams." Lee (2000, 163) understood that fundamentally altering the equation in the 1960s meant producing consistent results, and hitting targets at the highest levels in Singapore in the most uncompromising manner possible. "It is easy to start off with high moral standards, strong convictions, and determination to beat down corruption," he states. "But it is difficult to live up to these good intentions unless the leaders are strong and determined enough to deal with all transgressors, and without exceptions. CPIB officers must be supported without fear or favor to enforce the rules." Most significantly, a direct connection was made between predatory behavior by oligarchs and political elites, and the survival of Singapore as a nation. "We had established a climate of opinion," Lee writes, "that looked upon corruption in public office as a threat to society."

The CPIB engaged in the relentless pursuit of those who used their massive material resources or elite position in government to distort the system and its laws. A Special Investigation Team (SIT) was set up to handle "the more complex and major cases."[86] A dizzying series of oligarchs and high officials, including sitting cabinet ministers, were prosecuted and punished. Some of the most spectacular cases, and the ones that were vital in laying a legal foundation for civil oligarchy in Singapore, involved figures who were not only prominent in Lee's Political Action Party (PAP), but were close personal associates of the prime minister – sometimes going back decades. If this kind of proximity provided no reliable security from prison, everyone else faced tremendous risks if they engaged their power resources to violate the law. Four cases merit specific mention because they lend new meaning to notions of the "impersonal" enforcement of the law.[87]

"There is no way a Minister can avoid investigations and a trial if there is evidence to support one." This 1987 statement by Prime Minister Lee is featured prominently on the CPIB's Web site. "The Government's anti-corruption stand is clear," the CPIB continues. "It will not hesitate to bring whoever is corrupt to court, irrespective of his rank or status." There is compelling evidence that this was no idle threat. The first major case to make a lasting impression on powerful Singaporeans involved Mr. Tan Kia Gan, the Minister for National Development. Lee had personally placed Tan on the corporate board of Malaysia Airways. In 1966, he was investigated for trying to steer the purchase of Boeing aircraft through a friend in exchange for a large bribe. "We were close colleagues from the early 1950s when he was the leader of the Malayan Airways engineers' union," Lee (2000, 160–1) recalls, "and I was its legal advisor." The effort to prosecute Tan was frustrated by the unwillingness of the bribing oligarchs to testify against him, but Lee acted against his old

---

[86] CPIB Web site: www.cpib.gov.sg.
[87] Others can be found in Lee (2000, 157–71) and on the CPIB Web site: www.cpib.gov.sg.

friend anyway. "Unpleasant and painful as the decision was," Lee writes, "I removed him from the board and from all his other appointments." In stripping Tan of his governmental posts, Lee adds: "I was sad but there was no other course I could have taken."

In 1975, it was Mr. Wee Toon Boon, the Minister of State for Environment and another personal associate of Lee, who was investigated for massive corruption by the CPIB. "It was painful to confront him and hear his unconvincing protestations of innocence," Lee (2000, 161) reflects. With all eyes on the case, the prime minister once again stepped aside and let justice take its course. Wee was prosecuted and punished.

The 1979 case of Mr. Phey Yew Kok is especially instructive because it involved intervention by a trusted intermediary, which is an important method of protection among members of powerful networks. Phey was a member of parliament from Lee's PAP and the president of the National Trade Unions Congress (NTUC), Singapore's sole labor federation. When Phey was caught in corrupt practices, fellow PAP leaders and especially actors inside the NTUC tried to intervene on his behalf, insisting he was innocent and asking that the CPIB "review" the case. "I did not agree," Lee (2000, 161) writes, "because I had seen the investigation reports and had allowed the CPIB to proceed." Over lunch with a personal friend, Lee listened as the intermediary "spoke vehemently" on Phey's behalf. The prime minister phoned the director of the CPIB and instructed him to allow the PAP associate (who was also secretary general of the NTUC) a glimpse of the evidence against Phey immediately after the lunch. Overwhelmed by the facts, the intermediary retreated and the case moved forward. Phey jumped bail and escaped to Thailand "eking out a miserable existence as a fugitive, subject to blackmail by immigration and police authorities" (Lee 2000, 162).

None of these cases compares with the dramatic downfall in 1986 of Mr. Teh Cheang Wan, the Minister for National Development. The CPIB had investigated the minister for two bribes from oligarchs in the early 1980s worth a million Singapore dollars. Lee writes that Teh had denied the charges and "tried to bargain with the senior assistant director of the CPIB" to get the case stopped. "The cabinet secretary reported this and said Teh had asked to see me," Lee (2000, 162) recounts. "I replied that I could not until the investigations were over." Fully aware that he would end up in prison, Minister Teh committed suicide and left a personal note for his boss:

> Prime Minister: I have been feeling very sad and depressed for the last two weeks. I feel responsible for the occurrence of this unfortunate incident and I feel I should accept full responsibility. As an honourable oriental gentleman I feel it is only right that I should pay the highest penalty for my mistake. Yours faithfully, Teh Cheang Wan (Lee 2000, 162).

The determined pursuit of the procedural over the personal did not end there. Lee visited Teh's widow and viewed the body of his cabinet minister lying in his bed. The widow pleaded that the death not be treated as suspicious, thereby avoiding a coroner's inquiry and glaring headlines. Standing over the corpse of the honorable Oriental gentleman, the prime minister refused the request and it soon became public that Teh had died of suicide by a drug overdose. When the opposition, which held only two seats out of seventy-nine, called for a parliamentary commission of inquiry, Lee granted that as well. In an unsentimental account of the ordeal, Lee (2000, 163) reports that Teh's anguished wife and daughter "left Singapore and never returned."[88]

Civil Oligarchy without Civil Rights. This tenacious campaign resulted in a judiciary and a broader system of enforcement that was more powerful than Singapore's oligarchs and elites. As the city-state's oligarchs were tamed and as property was impersonally regulated and secured, civil oligarchy was firmly established under an expanding high rule of law. The establishment of law in the material realm – where oligarchs and the state meet and coexist – was no small feat, even if everyone else in society was left out of the struggle and its direct benefits. What Singapore achieved was the material rule of law without the political rule of law. Oligarchs care deeply about the former and are amenable to the latter. In addition, although both are enforced by a single judiciary, they are not the same thing, and there is no necessary reason from the perspective of oligarchic theory for laws establishing property rights also to create political freedom.

Singapore is useful because it brings into sharper focus the problem of civil oligarchy without civil rights. It is neither a new nor unique phenomenon. Indeed, modern democracy originated with civil oligarchies that were later pushed and expanded through popular movements beyond their founding struggles and scope. The achievement of civil oligarchy without civil rights results in what Jayasuriya (1996, 2000, 2001, 2002) terms authoritarian legalism, drawing on Fraenkel's (1941) work on the dual state in Nazi Germany.[89] The bifurcation of the German political-legal order into one part Fraenkel called "Normative" and the other designated "Prerogative" corresponded to the rigid and predictable defense of oligarchic property by the first combined with the capricious use of authority in all other spheres by the second.

Fraenkel (1941, 186) saw the Normative legal structure defending property as primary and dominant, whereas the Prerogative side was an "indirectly supporting power." The reasons for this were historical. The landed nobility in Germany assented to absolutist rule on two conditions: first, "that those actions

---

[88] In places like Indonesia or the Philippines, this kind of gory exposure is normal fare for one's political enemies or against once-powerful actors who have become politically exposed, or are suddenly useful as an occasional gesture to sow public confusion about whether oligarchs and elites really do face the same consequences as everyone else. However, it is never done against one's own party members, ministers, and long-time personal or business associates. Singapore was taming the nation's most powerful actors by an exaggerated negation of the politics of proximity. The deliberate signal was that nothing, including the overwhelming power of money, could bend the criminal realities or deflect the legal consequences.

[89] Authoritarian legalism is something of a cottage industry among scholars working on Asia. Jayasuriya's analyses remain the best on the subject, especially in tracing the concept to Fraenkel's pioneering work. Also see Pereira (2003) on authoritarian legalism in Brazil, Argentina, and Chile.

which are relevant to its economic situation be regulated in accordance with laws which they consider satisfactory," meaning private wealth was secure; and second, "that the subordinate classes, after having been deprived of the protection of the law, be economically disarmed" (Fraenkel 1941, 154). The absolute monarchs succeeded in destroying the feudal power of the German nobility in the seventeenth and eighteenth centuries, but the "renunciation of political power by the estates could only be obtained in return for other social privileges." An absolute guarantee of property rights was the most important of all. "Only in exchange for such important concessions would the landed nobility renounce its political power and allow the institutions of the *miles perpetuus* [standing armies] to be established" (Fraenkel 1941, 157).

Fraenkel (quoted in Jayasuriya 2001, 119) adds that capitalism "will accommodate itself to any substantial irrationality if only the necessary prerequisites for its technically rational order are preserved" – which is to say that a legal-rational system securing property and markets can adapt to an almost infinite variety of political systems. Elaborating the essence of authoritarian legalism, Jayasuriya (2001, 119–20) argues that "at the core of the dual state is the parallel existence of both an economic order regulated by law and a political sphere unbounded by any legal parameters; in a dual state economic liberalism is enjoined to political illiberalism." The theory of civil oligarchy advanced in this study would add to this only that political illiberalism is a common but hardly necessary feature of legal regimes that strongly defend property for oligarchs. Civil oligarchy is a form of wealth defense, not a form of the polity along an authoritarian-democratic continuum.

The fact that some countries have managed to combine civil oligarchy with democracy and a respect for human rights has led some analysts to insist that legal systems that only defend property and the propertied, no matter how effectively and impersonally, lack "judicial independence." Such arguments fail to appreciate that historically there has been no necessary fusion between genuine judicial independence for matters of concern to oligarchs and those of vital importance to everyone else. Legal systems dating back to Athens and Rome, for instance, have repeatedly been independent and fair for male citizens but not for slaves or women. A sophisticated critique would disentangle the different spheres and kinds of power that are reflected and regulated in the laws in each instance.

Human rights critiques of Singapore have failed to do this and are in serious disarray (Bryan 2007). On the one hand, the International Bar Association acknowledges that Singapore "ranks highly in international recognition of its economic competitiveness, liberal trade policies, property rights, legal efficiency, and business standards." Moreover, in judicial and legal system rankings by investors and those focused on "governance," Singapore's performance is considered exemplary (IBA 2008, 6; Quek 2009).[90] Such high rankings apply

---

[90] Before arguing that Singapore's judiciary lacked independence, the IBA (2008, 21) first cited the abundant evidence that everyone with significant property interests had the exact opposite opinion. "For the 13th year in a row, Singapore has been ranked second (after Hong Kong) of

exclusively around the globe to civil oligarchies where oligarchs are tamed by impersonal systems of law.

Despite these glowing findings, the IBA (2008, 7–8, 21) maintains that Singapore's judicial system lacks "objective and subjective independence" because "its rankings are very low regarding its recognition and implementation of human rights and democracy." World Bank Governance Indicators give Singapore low marks on "voice and accountability, which measures the degree to which citizens are able to participate in selecting their government and enjoy free expression, freedom of association, and a free media." The IBA also notes that the 2007 Worldwide Press Freedom Index published by Reporters without Borders ranked Singapore 141st out of 169 nations, while the Freedom of the World 2007 rankings rated the country as "partly free." The IBA (2008, 7) also points out that PAP officials have "initiated a series of defamation suits that have been won against opposition figures," and that "no PAP leader has ever lost a defamation suit against an opposition figure in court."

In the face of this daunting contradiction – a single legal infrastructure that is somehow both independent and prostrate – the international human rights lawyers drafting the 2008 IBA report pursue two avenues of critique. The first is to try to solve the contradiction through redefining the problem. For the rule of law to be "strong and robust," the IBA (2008, 12) contends, it requires "respect for and protection of democracy, human rights – including freedom of expression and freedom of assembly – and an independent and impartial judiciary." This is simply a denial that there are different realms of judicial impartiality, and that the fair treatment of oligarchic property under the law has always existed apart from other rights and freedoms.

The second tack is to sow fear among oligarchs by emphasizing that there are "clear inconsistencies" in the legal system, that conditions are worse than they seem for those with concentrated wealth, and that the contradictions could pose risks in the longer term. "The judiciary in Singapore has a good international

157 countries in the Heritage Foundation's 2007 Index of Economic Freedom. This is judged on ten criteria, including trade policy, government intervention, monetary policy, foreign investment, and property rights. Singapore was ranked first out of 178 economies for 'ease of doing business' in the World Bank's Doing Business 2008 report and third of 61 countries in the International Institute for Management Development's (IMD) 2006 World Competitiveness Yearbook, receiving the second highest score for 'ease of doing business.' The Singapore Government considers that these rankings evidence its strong support for the rule of law. In judicial and legal system rankings, Singapore has also performed well in international assessments. In Transparency International's Corruptions Perceptions Index 2006, which measures the degree to which corruption is perceived to exist among public officials and politicians, Singapore ranked fifth in the world. Similarly, in an Asian-only based report, the Political & Economic Risk Consultancy's Asian Intelligence Report 2006, strong commendation of Singapore's judicial system was made, stating: 'Within Asia Hong Kong and Singapore are the only two systems with judiciaries that rate on a par with those in developed Western societies ...' Under the World Bank's Governance Indicators, Singapore also ranks very highly in areas such as the rule of law and control of corruption, with most rankings currently being at the very top ranking (90–100 percent)."

reputation for the integrity of their judgments when adjudicating commercial cases that do not involve the interests of PAP members or their associates," the IBA writes. However, in cases involving the PAP, "there are concerns about an actual or apparent lack of impartiality and/or independence, which casts doubt on the decisions made in such cases." The report cited strictly political cases involving defamation suits, but mentioned nothing regarding property or contracts that would worry Singaporean oligarchs or international investors. Identical concerns had been raised two decades earlier by the New York City Bar Association, also without evidence.[91] In addition, as if to acknowledge the charge was weak, the IBA report immediately backtracks. "Although this may not go so far as claimed by some nongovernmental organisations, which allege that the judiciary is entirely controlled by the will of the executive, there are sufficient reasons to worry about the influence of the executive over judicial decision making," the IBA (2008, 70) writes. "Regardless of any actual interference, the reasonable suspicion of interference is sufficient."

The suspicion was not sufficient enough to prevent the International Bar Association from holding its 2007 annual meeting in Singapore. Founded in 1947 and representing 30,000 lawyers and more than 190 Bar Associations from around the globe, the IBA offered a decidedly positive image of Singapore in its publicity for the October 2007 gathering. "Singapore is a unique and dynamic city, filled with culture and brimming with energy and finesse," the IBA (2007a) said. "It is where urban meets traditional offering the modern and cosmopolitan whilst retaining its local flavour. Voted 5th best business meeting city, it offers the perfect opportunity for both business and pleasure." For the first time in its history, and to deflect published criticisms, the IBA's management board also "decided that at the end of the IBA's 2007 Conference in Singapore an entire day will be devoted to discussing the essential nature of the Rule of Law" (IBA 2007b; Macan-Markar 2007).

The almost perfect separation of law and liberty in Singapore is deeply troubling to advocates of democracy and human rights. The problem is not just ideological and philosophical, but also analytical. The IBA's liberal critique is ill equipped to theorize how or why a legal system responds narrowly – even exclusively – and yet impartially to the power of concentrated wealth and property. Authoritarian legalism becomes incomprehensible. Claims that Singapore has a broken judiciary end up sounding strangely detached from the

---

[91] "What emerges," according to the New York Bar fact-finding mission, "is a government that has been willing to decimate the rule of law for the benefit of its political interests. Lawyers have been cowed to passivity, judges are kept on a short leash, and the law has been manipulated so that gaping holes exist in the system of restraints on government action toward the individual. [...] Any U.S. venture contemplating business in Singapore or with a Singapore company is likely to encounter a wide variety of enterprises in which the government has an economic interest. If a dispute arises with such an enterprise, the U.S. company faces the prospect of a lawsuit before Singapore's judiciary. The same forces which have led that judiciary to be sensitive to the PAP government's political interests would lead it to take account of its economic interests" (Frank, Markowitz, McKay, and Roth 1991).

routine operations of the nation's courts adjudicating the fundamental material realm of the social formation. "The judiciary is efficient and constitutionally independent," according to the U.S. Department of State (2004), but "there is a general perception that it reflects the views of the ruling party in politically sensitive cases." The U.S. charge that government leaders use "court proceedings, in particular defamation suits, against political opponents and critics" troubles no one going to court on material matters of contract and property (U.S. Department of State 2010). The response of Singaporean oligarchs and the international business community to this reality is not merely a collective shrug. They actually flock to Singapore to engage the services of its international arbitration facilities – the most vibrant in Asia.[92] The human rights challenge in Singapore lies not in denying judicial independence, but in recognizing its strength with regard to property and contracts and building movements to expand it.

Returning to the comparisons with the United States, a major divide separates the two cases on judicial independence for political rights. However, nothing separates their judicial systems with respect to the impersonal and independent defense of property and contracts for oligarchs. Thus they are both civil oligarchies – one democratic, one not. This is an important reminder that the Aristotelian fusion of oligarchy and democracy rests on the fusion of laws defending property and speech. The historical record shows that the defense of the former, demanded by oligarchs exercising material power, is not only prior but primary, while the defense of the latter, gained through mobilization power, is separate, subsequent, and contingent. As long as the hierarchy of property over speech is maintained, the fusion is stable. However, the first never needs the second to be viable in the way that the second needs the first when democracy coexists with extreme material stratification.

Coda on an Insignificant Exception. Those familiar with Singapore's history since 1965 might argue that the Hotel Properties Limited (HPL) case arising in the 1990s disproves the claim that oligarchs had been tamed because the system faltered in its treatment of Prime Minister Lee Kuan Yew and his family.

---

[92] Although Singapore is one of the few countries that has yet to ratify the International Covenant on Civil and Political Rights (ICCPR) under the United Nations, it is a vigorous supporter of UNCITRAL – the United Nations Commission on International Trade Law. This agreement (United Nations 1976) sets forth the globally accepted rules of binding arbitration. Many investors entering into agreements in more risky locations across Southeast Asia write arbitration clauses into their contracts and investments and insist that they be handled in Singapore. Housed in the refurbished Maxwell Chambers (www.maxwell-chambers.com/about-profile.html), the International Arbitration Centre (www.siac.org.sg) boasts "14 custom-designed and fully equipped hearing rooms and 12 preparation rooms," and "a full suite of supporting services." Arbitration awards are "final and binding, and have extra-territorial enforceability in over 120 countries under the New York Convention." See Huang (2008) for an analysis of the similarly indispensable role Hong Kong plays as a property-defending legal platform for China – especially the phenomenon of "round trip" foreign investment that originates in China, but first goes "abroad" to Hong Kong to register under the highly secure legal regime entrenched there, before returning as "foreign" capital to China.

Francis Seow (2006), the former solicitor general of Singapore, has written the definitive study of the HPL matter. It is a meticulously researched book and it is unnecessary to repeat the details of the case here. Instead, only two questions are raised. First, did the institutional apparatus of investigation and enforcement established in the 1960s by the prime minister ensnare even Mr. Lee? The answer is: yes and no. Second, does the case undermine the claim that oligarchs in Singapore have been thoroughly tamed within a civil oligarchy? The answer is: not at all.

The story, in brief, is that in 1995 during a boom in the property market, several members of the Lee family – including Lee Kuan Yew, who at the time was Senior Minister, and his son, Deputy Prime Minister Lee Hsien Loong – bought luxury condominiums at a discount during a "soft launch." They did so not only before the prized properties were available on the open market, but before HPL shareholders, legally at the front of the queue, had a chance to buy. Profits on the purchases were immediate and significant. Lee Suan Yew, the brother of the former prime minister, was on the board of HPL and played a role in arranging the purchases. The first noteworthy point is that these transactions became public because a key part of the regulatory apparatus designed to safeguard shareholders – the Securities Exchange of Singapore (SES) – functioned according to the law. HPL was a publicly listed property development company, and the regulations stated that shareholders must approve pre-market discount purchases of condos in advance. The sales to the Lees had not been approved in advance. Disgruntled HPL shareholders complained to the SES that they had missed out on quick gains in the heated property market. SES regulators followed the law and promptly issued a public censure knowing that the senior minister and the deputy prime minister were involved. This sequence of events is unimaginable in a ruling oligarchy such as the Philippines or Indonesia, even in their current electoral-democratic forms.

The SES censure did not name the Lees, but the father and son called a press conference themselves the next day and revealed that their purchases had triggered the regulatory action. They insisted that nothing improper had occurred, and they later donated the value of their discounts to charity. In the months following the SES censure, the press reported on the matter extensively, an investigation was conducted, and its findings were presented at a session of Parliament overseen by Prime Minister Goh Chok Tong. In his memoir, Lee (2000, 171) writes that he had "asked the prime minister to take the matter to Parliament for a thorough airing of the issue." He adds:

> In the debate, opposition MPs, including two lawyers, one of them the leader of the opposition, said that in their experience the giving of such discounts was standard marketing practice and there was nothing improper in our purchases. This open and complete disclosure of a perceived unfair advantage made it a non-issue in the general election a year later. As I told the House, the fact that the system I had set in place could investigate and report upon my conduct proved that it was impersonal and effective, and that no one was above the law.

The central problem with this statement concerns what is meant by the "system" that Lee had set in place to investigate allegations of corruption. The core of that system has long been the CPIB. However, the HPL case was handled instead by the Finance Minister and the Monetary Authority of Singapore (MAS) rather than the CPIB. Neither could match the CPIB's expertise in investigating fraud. In a 1996 interview in a Hong Kong weekly circulated widely in Singapore, Tang Liang Hong, a critic of the PAP, was asked to comment on the HPL case and its resolution. He stated:

> Why wasn't this matter handed over to the professional body like the Commercial Affairs Department of the Corrupt Practices Investigation Bureau? They are government departments not only rich in experience, but also well known for being "iron-faced without selfishness" [an idiom meaning firm and impartial]. They would be more detached and their reports would have been more convincing to the people. Koh Beng Seng [of MAS] and Finance Minister Richard Hu are after all not experts in this field (quoted in Seow 2006, 30–1).

Tang raised the obvious question. Since the days of Minister Tan in 1966 and the suicidal Mr. Teh in 1986, the CPIB had played the lead role in handling major cases. However, Senior Minister Lee interpreted Tang's quite reasonable question as an attack on his personal integrity, the legitimacy of the system he had helped build, and the validity of his exoneration. Tang was hit with a barrage of bankrupting defamation suits, lost all of the cases brought against him, and fled with his wife into exile.

At the beginning of this section on Singapore, it was stated that the country's system of laws and enforcement is stronger than its oligarchs – "with one insignificant exception." Through the SES, that system triggered an investigation of the Lees. No one can say if the outcome would have been different had the CPIB conducted the investigation. However, the deeper point is that Singapore's oligarchs were no less tamed before or after the HPL case. Even if, *arguendo*, the system lost its nerve in the HPL matter, the case is insignificant compared to the overwhelming evidence showing that oligarchs are convinced that their property is secure and that their material power will not protect them if they are adjudicated in a Singaporean court. For there to be civil oligarchy, the law need only be enforced consistently and reliably against oligarchs, not flawlessly.

Conclusions

The cases in this chapter on civil oligarchy raise a number of important arguments in oligarchic theory. Three are especially prominent. The first centers on how oligarchs pursue their material interests under conditions of externally defended property rights. The U.S. case provides a clear illustration of wealth defense by oligarchs and traces how their material power is expressed through the mechanism of the Income Defense Industry, which assists them in retaining billions of dollars in income annually. This expression of minority power operates within a liberal democratic framework, but almost entirely off the national radar screen and through means that cannot be understood by representation, voting, or pluralist politics. It is a story not of polyarchy, but of oligarchy alloyed with polyarchy. The U.S. case illuminates how disarmed oligarchs who do not rule can secure their vital interests in a context that is materially stratified and politically democratic.

The second argument centers on how one state founded a civil oligarchy in the twentieth century by enforcing the impersonal rule of law over oligarchs and elites. Singapore is one of the few postcolonial societies to have done this, and the circumstances that favored this outcome are not widely shared in other nations. The Singaporean case extends the discussion about the rule of law begun in the Indonesian and Philippine contexts. A key point in these nations was how the challenges of the rule of law are often not really systemic (although sometimes legal regimes are thoroughly dysfunctional from top to bottom), but instead focused more narrowly on establishing dominance over oligarchs and other powerful actors at the top of society. The historical trade-off is that oligarchs only submit to legal regimes that fulfill the wealth defense objective of secure property. Laws apply fairly routinely to average citizens in Indonesia and the Philippines, but far less reliably to oligarchs – who still use money or violence to influence judicial and political outcomes.

The bifurcation cuts differently in the Singaporean case. There the rule of law applies equally to oligarchs and commoners, but falters in its treatment of political opponents of the government, who wield mobilizational rather than oligarchic power resources. This raises the third argument, centering on the contingent relationship between establishing the high rule of law over oligarchs and creating a democratic polity. Indonesia and the Philippines do not tame their ruling oligarchs through laws, and yet have electoral-democratic governments in place (that oligarchs thoroughly dominate). Singapore tames its oligarchs through impersonal laws and yet does not have a functioning electoral democracy. It is oligarchic theory, which emphasizes the distinction between the material-property dimensions of legal guarantees and the democratic-freedom aspects, which helps make sense of these patterns.

The theory advanced here about civil oligarchy also has implications for the New Institutional Economics (NIE) literature. Its central line of inquiry is focused narrowly on how oligarchs negotiated their relationships with rising states that could provide property defense in exchange for a part of the economic surplus (thus setting up an ongoing income defense game of cat-and-mouse even as property defense became a settled matter). Such an approach addresses one part of the much larger issue of oligarchs and wealth defense over the millennia. That is, the NIE literature is obsessed only with the birth of civil oligarchy and the inevitable predations of the state, but has nothing meaningful to say about warring, ruling, or sultanistic oligarchies – which happen to cover the bulk of human history and probably the lion's share of existing states in the early twenty-first century.

NIE approaches are focused on the arbitrary exercise of state power, which is a threat that arises for oligarchs only under certain forms of organized coercion. It largely ignores situations in which oligarchs themselves are at the heart of the institutions of organized coercion (collective ruling oligarchies), or when such institutions are absent (warring oligarchies), or exist only as the organized instrument of personalistic rule (sultanistic oligarchies). Thus the literature encompasses an admittedly important part of a far larger story of material stratification and the politics of its defense and adaptation, but leaves other important questions poorly theorized. This point is revisited in the concluding chapter.

6

Conclusions

Oligarchic theory starts from the notion that minority power assumes different forms, and that the basis of that power matters for understanding the exaggerated influence small numbers of people have over much larger groups or communities. That oligarchs are few in number is only incidental. Those who govern societies or dominate complex organizations are always few in number – a general point argued convincingly by Mosca and especially Michels. However, oligarchs are something much more specific. It is the extreme concentration of wealth, a power resource, which defines oligarchs and makes them worthy of study as a special class of social actors. This is what Michels failed to emphasize in his misnamed "iron law of oligarchy," which is more accurately a law of elitism. The antidote to elitism is wider and more substantive participation by members of a community.

Perhaps nothing underscores the fundamental difference between elitism and oligarchy better than the fact that expanded and meaningful participation has no necessary or deep impact on oligarchy. Oligarchs feared what the emergence of democracy and then universal suffrage would portend, but history proved the fears to be exaggerated. The reason is that participation by itself strikes at the heart of elitism, but poses only a *potential* threat to oligarchs and the distinct basis of their power. It is only when participation challenges material stratification specifically – when extreme wealth held by oligarchs is dispersed as a democratic outcome – that oligarchy and participatory democracy finally clash.

This book has shown that democratic threats to great riches are just one among many worries for oligarchs, and hardly the most dangerous. Oligarchic theory rests on several premises: that wealth stratification is inherently conflictual, that coercion underlies all property claims and rights (especially when a few hold enormous fortunes while everyone else survives on much less), and that concentrated wealth has the unique characteristic of being a self-sustaining power resource. As one moves up the wealth scale, wealth plays an increasingly vital role as an instrument in its own defense. These elements shape the politics of wealth defense – the core political motive and objective of all oligarchs. The materialist reinterpretation of oligarchic theory presented in Chapter 1 is not new. It was an excavation of the dominant approach to oligarchs and oligarchy that became obscured with the rise of elite theory at the end of the nineteenth century. However, a focus on wealth defense as the central political project of oligarchs is new, as is the related typology of four kinds of oligarchy elaborated in the middle chapters of the book.

The common thread for all oligarchs across history is that wealth defines them, empowers them, and inherently exposes them to a range of threats. What varies across history is the nature of the threats and how oligarchs respond to defend their wealth. These variations yield the types of oligarchy examined here. The dangers can arise from the poor below, laterally from other oligarchs, or from a state or ruler above. Oligarchs can respond to these threats directly or indirectly, they can be armed or disarmed, and they can act individually or collectively. Also, they can rule directly to defend their property, or this role can be provided externally by a sultanistic ruler or an armed impersonal state. Different combinations of these factors yield warring, ruling, sultanistic, and civil oligarchies. Each constitutes a distinct mode of managing threats and pursuing wealth defense. Like all ideal types, these modes are useful for analysis but rarely exist in pure form.

The story of oligarchic rule and power examined in the cases is neither static nor linear. The nature of oligarchy changes as threats to oligarchs change and sometimes as relations among cooperating oligarchs break down or a single powerful oligarch seizes control or is deposed. Changing strategies for wealth defense are important in all the cases examined, and the locus and role of coercion to defend property plays a vital role in these dynamics. In almost every case covered, a change occurred from one kind of oligarchy to another. The causes of these transformations were tracked closely, but no attempt was made to offer a grand theory of oligarchic transitions (and it is not even clear one is possible given an oligarchic history spanning millennia).

Although the organization of the chapters was from warring oligarchy (the form in which oligarchs are fully armed and rule most personally and directly) to civil oligarchy (the one in which they are fully disarmed and are unburdened of the need to rule), there is no implied progression or teleology. Achieving a civil oligarchy in which oligarchs are nonviolent and submit to laws is arguably a benefit to everyone else in society. It was the last form of oligarchy to appear, and the political and economic stability associated with it supports the highly productive system of market capitalism. Civil oligarchy is also the form most amenable to democratic participation.[1] This book showed in the American case that oligarchy undergoes profound transformations when oligarchs disarm and submit to property-defending legal regimes, but it is not eliminated. Moreover,

---

[1] Ancient Athens, Indonesia, and the Philippines showed that ruling oligarchies can also be electoral democracies.

when states fail to defend property rights, reversions to armed oligarchy and direct rule are not only possible, but have occurred repeatedly.

Other Cases and Comparisons

The number of oligarchies that have existed throughout history is far too large to list or cover adequately in a single book. Some persisted through adaptations over centuries. Others collapsed because of internal crises or were destroyed by invading forces. In the modern era, major states that made the holding of large private fortunes impossible – such as the Soviet Union, China, Vietnam, North Korea, or Cuba – were dominated for decades by elites but in the absence of oligarchs. Åslund (2007, 241) notes that in the Soviet Union, for instance, "only a minimum of personal property was allowed, and little legislation existed for the defense of private property rights." The Russian case is an especially important one and would have been included in this book if the literature on the USSR and Russian Federation, both scholarly and journalistic, were not among the most excellent materialist interpretations of oligarchs and oligarchy (Goldman 2003; Hoffman 2003; Gel'man 2004; Guriev and Rachinsky 2005; Åslund 2007; Zhuravskaya 2007; Braguinsky 2009).

The collapse of the Soviet Union and the explosive emergence of a new stratum of ultra-wealthy Russians forced analysts from the outset to emphasize the material foundations of oligarchy in Russia. The Russian case is important for at least four reasons. First, the Russian Revolution provides a major modern example of oligarchs sustaining a devastating attack on the material basis of their power. Desperate and violent efforts at wealth defense failed and Russia's oligarchs were destroyed and oligarchy ceased to exist for decades. Second, with oligarchs eliminated from the mix, and lacking private property and large personal fortunes, the country was dominated for decades during the Soviet era exclusively by elites. Third, the collapse of the Soviet Union suddenly created new opportunities for the reemergence of oligarchs. The rise of multi-millionaires and billionaires was shockingly rapid and unfolded under conditions of damaged rather than strong and stable institutions of law. Fourth, Russia's new oligarchs faced immediate and chronic problems of wealth defense while the Russian state struggled with how to manage these powerful actors. The new oligarchs did not rule, but neither were they effectively tamed until Putin began imposing a decidedly sultanistic solution.

The birth of this new oligarchy has been a turbulent feature of Russia's political economy for more than two decades, and is very different from the creation of a new stratum of oligarchs under Suharto. Defending wealth was particularly difficult for Russian oligarchs in the chaotic and violent period after the USSR collapsed. Confronted with a state that was incapable of securing property, oligarchs used their material resources to hire their own coercive forces for defense – a process well predicted by the theory of oligarchy advanced in this study. "Institutions that protect property rights are crucial for economic growth and particularly for investment," Åslund (2007, 242–4) writes, "but the question was how to create them. A new legal system had to be built, but that was possibly the most complicated task of postcommunism."

Mafia protection rackets stepped in to fill the void, but they were as much a threat to securing property as a solution. In classic fashion, Russian oligarchs pursued wealth defense by deploying part of their resources to acquire coercive capacities so that they could secure their property claims directly in the absence of state-enforced property rights. Åslund describes the response:

> New big businesspeople, oligarchs, thought the fees of the protection rackets were too high – originally 20 percent of turnover, falling toward 10 percent of turnover over the years. Instead the oligarchs set up their own security forces. By the mid-1990s, 8 percent of the employees in a typical oligarchic corporation were occupied with security, both guards and counterintelligence, finding out what their enemies were doing. The top oligarchs hired a deputy minister of interior to run their security and a deputy chairman of the KGB to manage their counterintelligence.

When oligarchs began flexing their financial muscle and intervening visibly at the highest level of the nation's politics, Putin began to engage the state's reconstituted security apparatus to constrain their behavior. It could be decades before Russia is able to tame its oligarchs and political elites through impersonal and impartial laws. As the work of Hendley (2006, 2009, 2010) and Gans-Morse (2010) shows, the Russian case continues to provide an unusually rich context for theorizing many aspects of oligarchic power, wealth defense, and the challenges to creating strong legal institutions even in highly advanced states that once enjoyed super power status in the twentieth century.

Fabulously wealthy oligarchs are also emerging rapidly in newly capitalist China, but under conditions of much stronger state and party institutions than existed in Russia when its oligarchs began to appear.[2] The Hurun Report (2010) tracks changes in the composition of China's wealthiest citizens. Its 2010 data show China had 875,000 people in 2009 with a net worth of $1.5 million or more, and 55,000 with more than $15 million. The richest 1,363 Chinese, who represent 1/10,000th of 1 percent of the country's population, had financial assets of at least $150 million. Their combined wealth was $787 billion, which is roughly equal to 20 percent of China's 2009 GDP.

Another set of comparisons not included in this book focuses on European cases where welfare states are extensive and tax rates on the rich are relatively high. These cases, especially in Scandinavia, are widely viewed as an example of how democratic politics and participation can greatly diminish the scale of oligarchic wealth and power. In fact, they support the opposite conclusion: even where democratic politics have intervened most deeply into the material and economic sphere of society, as in Northern Europe, wealth defense strategies on the part of oligarchs have ensured that they remain intact and

---

[2] Many books comparing China and the USSR (Russia) have been written, but the potentially illuminating divergences in their oligarchic trajectories have yet to be studied.

largely unburdened by the high costs of the welfare states. As in the U.S. case, oligarchs in Europe have deployed their power resources to deflect the burdens of taxation and government transfers onto the strata below them. The big difference in the European cases lies in how the costs of welfare policies have been spread much more widely across the population than in the United States.

The Scandinavian countries have less income inequality than the United States or the United Kingdom. Their total tax bills as a percentage of GDP are significantly higher than in the United States, and government transfers play a far greater role in reducing economic inequality and improving the nations' Gini coefficients, an extremely blunt measurement of income inequality. However, this progress in improving conditions for people at the bottom of society does not alter the fact that the Scandinavian countries continue to have thriving oligarchs (MDRC 2008). Kenworthy (2009b, 29) points out that "high-tax countries such as Sweden, Denmark, and Finland rely heavily on consumption taxes, the burden of which is shared broadly across the citizenry rather than concentrated on firms and affluent individuals."[3]

Although they do not show up in studies using Gini indexes or income data that lump the rich together in the top 1 percent, there is clear evidence oligarchs are alive and well in the Scandinavian countries. In a revealing comparison between the United States and Finland, Karhunen and Keloharju (2001, 209) report that the top 0.5 percent of the population in the United States (Gini coefficient 45) owned 41.4 percent of all investment wealth in the capital market, while the same 0.5 percent of the population in Finland (Gini coefficient 30) owned 71.6 percent of the capital market. They found to their surprise that "shareowner wealth appears to be much more concentrated in Finland than in the U.S. although, for instance, income is much more concentrated in the U.S. than in Finland."[4] Although society is far more equal in Finland than in the United States when making broad Gini comparisons of large swaths of population at the top and bottom, wealth is at least as concentrated in the hands of a fraction of the top 1 percent in Finland as in the United States, and perhaps much more so.

---

[3] "On average across the rich countries," Kenworthy (2009c, 80) adds, "taxes on income and profits total 15 percent of the gross domestic product (GDP), compared to 20 percent for taxes on payroll and consumption. Redistribution, then, is accomplished mainly, and in some countries entirely, via government transfers." Ideally these transfers would continue to be used to address inequality in the future, with the greatest tax burdens shifted to the wealthiest citizens. "But capital mobility has made this more difficult," Kenworthy (2009c, 82) admits. Those most able to pay are also the ones with the strongest capacities to engage in income defense. Evidence presented in Chapter 5 showed that because of higher domestic threats to income (and sometimes property), oligarchs in Europe and Latin America were more likely to use tax havens and the defensive relocation of their wealth offshore than their American counterparts.

[4] The authors note that the more concentrated shareownership in Finland is only partly explained by the fact that the 0.5 percent of the population refers to individuals in Finland and households in the United States. Even at the 0.1 percent level in Finland, the proportion of shareownership was 52.1 percent, which is still dramatically higher than the U.S. figure of 41.4 percent at the 0.5 percent level.

TABLE 6.1. *Evidence of High Wealth Concentration among Scandinavian Oligarchs*

	Gini Index	Billionaires/ Million Citizens	Citizens/Millionaire
United States	45	1.18	103
Finland	30	0.70	126
Denmark	29	0.56	97
Norway	29	0.87	46
Germany	27	0.64	100
Sweden	23	1.00	112

Sources: Gini coefficients and population estimates are from the CIA Factbook. Number of billionaires is from *Forbes* (2010). Number of millionaires is from MDRC (2008). Computations by the author.

There is other evidence that Gini coefficients paint a misleading picture about wealth concentration at the top of Scandinavian society. Table 6.1 compares Gini coefficients against other indicators more likely to reveal the relative significance of millionaires and billionaires in society. With a Gini index of 45, the United States is the most unequal rich industrial country.

Although Sweden's Gini index of 23 is roughly half that of the United States, the number of billionaires per million citizens for the two countries is comparable (1.00 and 1.18, respectively), as is the number of citizens per millionaire (103 and 112, respectively).[5] Norway has almost the same proportion of billionaires as Sweden and the United States, but it has far more dollar millionaires for its size than any other country in the world – one millionaire for every forty-six citizens.

Whatever else democracy and political struggles against inequality have achieved in the Scandinavian countries, they have neither diluted nor eliminated the nations' oligarchs. These findings suggest that when inequality within societies is reduced and Gini coefficients fall because of government transfers, it is due to redistributions within society that leave oligarchs and their fortunes at the top undisturbed. This happens because oligarchs fund robust Income Defense Industries in all of these states to pursue their wealth defense objectives.

Oligarchy and Other Debates

Several arguments were advanced in the first chapter and in the case chapters that followed, each of which highlighted key points in their introductions and conclusions. Building on these arguments, this chapter will close with a brief

---

[5] Högfeldt (2004, 61) argues that in Sweden, "the heavy politicized system has redistributed incomes but not property rights and wealth. The result is an ageing economy with an unusually large proportion of very old and very large firms with well-defined owners in control."

discussion of how the study of oligarchy intersects with other important themes and literatures in the social sciences. A good starting point is Mark Mizruchi's (2004, 603) reference to the "ferocious debate" among social scientists that raged on from the 1950s into the 1980s and centered on the concentration of political power in the United States. Elite theorists argued that power was "concentrated among a unified, self-perpetuating group whose members were unaccountable to the majority."

Pluralists responded that elites did indeed exist, that they governed, but that this did not constitute elite rule. Not only do elites have multiple bases for their status, but they have competing interests, are often divided, and constantly get replaced through elections and other circulating forces in society. Pluralists conceded that elites probably rule in the sense of governing – indeed becoming a political leader or decision maker makes someone by definition an elite. However, the point was deemed a banal criticism of democracy because no coherent elite agenda existed that was opposed to or harmed nonelites. On the contrary, insofar as some elites rose to positions of influence on merit, their net contribution to the democratic management of society could be seen as positive.

Oligarchic theory shifts the terms of this debate over minority power and influence radically. At stake in the arguments over elites is whether they dominate society for themselves without accountability to everyone else (Wedel 2009). Thus, whether there is direct rule and whether societies are dominated matters. Pluralists argued effectively against elite theorists that without these pathologies there is no issue. In the shift to a focus on oligarchs, what matters is not rule, but rather how concentrated wealth is defended and economic stratification in society is maintained. This book has demonstrated that ruling might be vital to oligarchs or it might be irrelevant. In examining oligarchs and oligarchy, the key normative issue and the source of societal conflict lies not in the form of government or in whether a strong minority is accountable, but rather in the phenomenon of concentrated economic resources. The social and political tension associated with extreme material stratification is the sole issue at stake. It is what bonds oligarchs together even if they never meet, and sets in motion the complex dynamics of wealth defense. Although these tensions are never entirely independent of the form of government, they are certainly prior to it.

These observations help account for several important findings that arose in the course of this study. First is the claim that there is no inherent conflict between democracy and oligarchy. The expectation that democracy somehow crowds out oligarchy (or the reverse) arises from the tendency to view oligarchs through the lens of elite theory. Oligarchy is a material project, not a method of rule or system of government. Thus, the far more relevant question is how oligarchs pursue wealth defense within different forms of the polity, of which democracy is only one example.

We saw that partially disarmed oligarchs ruled collectively in ancient Athens and Rome under conditions of limited or nonexistent suffrage, but also ruled collectively under conditions of universal suffrage in modern Philippines. Fully disarmed oligarchs in Indonesia pursued the defense of their wealth under the taming aegis of a sultanistic oligarch until 1998, after which they ruled collectively through an electoral democracy with universal suffrage, but untamed by a legal system they could easily distort with money. Oligarchs in the United States and Singapore are fully disarmed, do not rule, and enjoy strong security of property within civil oligarchies. In both countries oligarchs are well tamed by impersonal systems of law. However, one is an electoral democracy with universal suffrage while the other is anti-democratic. Aristotle was correct in arguing that democracy and oligarchy could be durably fused as long as the many poor did not threaten the few rich through representative institutions, and the few rich did not concentrate wealth to the point that the many poor became politically explosive.

A second observation has deep implications for literatures focused on the relationship of law to democracy, property, and the economy (especially markets). In this study, the treatment of the rule of law was not as a systemic matter. The approach was instead from the perspective of individual capacities of citizens to intimidate or distort the law. The low rule of law exists when the great majority of citizens routinely submit to the legal system because they lack the power resources to deflect police investigations and prosecutions or distort the decisions of judges. Whatever problems there may be with the legal system are technical in nature and can be improved through training, spending on infrastructure, and other common developmental projects focused on the rule of law.

The high rule of law pertains more narrowly to oligarchs and certain extremely powerful elites. On this view, the rule of law problem plaguing dozens of postcolonial societies is a much narrower matter than generally thought, focused at the apex of society, and not at all amenable to technical solutions. Achieving the rule of law is a titanic battle with oligarchs that involves overpowering them. As the Singapore case demonstrated, this is a power contest before it is anything else. Technical investments and institutional reforms play a supporting role, but they are not the essence of the struggle. Thus, for example, the innovation of placing the Corrupt Practices Investigation Bureau directly under the Prime Minister mattered only because Lee Kuan Yew and his coalition in the PAP were determined to exert the full power of his office to tame Singapore's oligarchs and elites through law enforcement.

The intersection of property, law, and especially of coercion figures prominently in the theory of oligarchs and oligarchy advanced here, but not in the manner these are commonly treated in political economy literatures – especially writings in the New Institutional Economics (NIE) tradition (North 1981, 1990, 1994, 2005; North and Weingast 1989). The differences are important analytically. The NIE literature grapples with how property is secured by focusing on the emergence of impersonal institutions that ultimately allow communities to reap the benefits of impersonal transactions. A number of basic flaws in this body of work have been raised (Hodgson 1998). However, the oligarchic approach developed in this book – and especially the emphasis on wealth defense, coercion, and material power – highlights additional analytical problems.

NIE theorists join the discussion of wealth and property defense at a very late stage in the story; their imprecise language blurs the role of powerful propertied actors by referring to them interchangeably as "citizens," "constituents," "subjects," or "entrepreneurs"; they deal almost exclusively with predatory threats from states or rulers; and their treatment of power and coercion is limited mostly to how constraints can be placed on states or rulers so that commitments to property claims can become credible (that is, become property rights).[6] The great bulk of NIE analysis is devoted to the intersection of states, institutions, law, property, and the behaviors of economic actors.

Such an approach yields useful insights into the important transformations that produced the modern nation-state, markets, and representative government. From the perspective of oligarchic theory, however, the entire NIE framework is limited to the historical moment marked by the rise of civil oligarchy, which happens to encompass only a small part of a much larger politics of wealth defense. A theory designed only to explain how property-securing constraints came to be placed on confiscatory states or rulers can shed little light on problems associated with securing property and wealth in warring and ruling oligarchies. In both instances, the actors most concerned with securing property *are* the state or exclusively populate it – assuming one actually exists.

The NIE approach has an extremely weak interpretation of power and coercion. It is fundamentally focused on utility-maximizing choices by voluntary actors engaging in transactions that have transaction costs associated with them. Over time, and through repeated interactions and learning, efficient outcomes are both predicted and achieved. Consider, for instance, North's (1994, 363) idyllic explanation of how tribes became institutionalized polities.

> As tribes evolved in different physical environments, they developed different languages and, with different experiences, different mental models to explain the world around them. The languages and mental models formed the informal constraints that defined the institutional framework of the tribe and were passed down intergenerationally as customs, taboos, and myths that provided cultural continuity.

Tribes were not dangerous zones of conflict in which warring chiefs who died young (and, Earle reminds us, rarely in bed), struggled to elevate themselves from mere warlords to oligarchs, sometimes building institutions along

---

[6] For work arising out of the NIE tradition that deals more explicitly with coercion and enforcement, see Greif (2005, 2006, 2008); Greif, Milgrom, and Weingast (1994); Bates, Greif, and Singh (2002). North, Wallis, and Weingast (2006) also place violence and coercion at the center of their analysis. However, even Greif (2006, 91) in his work on merchant guilds and credible commitments is concerned with "securing property rights from the grabbing hand of the state."

the way. Rather, the image is one of institutional frameworks as the embodiment of informal constraints rooted in mental models and language. North
continues:

> With growing specialization and division of labor, the tribes evolved into poli-
> ties and economies; the diversity of experience and learning produced increas-
> ingly different societies and civilizations with different degrees of success in
> solving the fundamental economic problems of scarcity. The reason is that as
> the complexity of the environment increased as human beings became increas-
> ingly interdependent, more complex institutional structures were necessary to
> capture the potential gains from trade.

Thanks to learning, specialization, cooperation, interdependence, and culture, tribes "evolved into polities and economies." The institutions of private
property in land evolved not through what Moore (1966, 20) argues was a
gradual but violent "destruction of the peasantry" in England, but instead
as an "efficient" response to rising demographic pressures (Chambers 1953;
North and Thomas 1973; North 1981). Theorists writing in the NIE tradition
rarely have to contend with violence, exploitation, and hierarchy between the
rich and the poor (and the difficult challenges this creates for the rich) because
the theory is focused almost exclusively on propertied actors who are usually
struggling to transform property claims into property rights – a fact obscured
by references to them as subjects, citizens, and constituents.

Violence and coercion are not omnipresent in the history of oligarchy, but
neither are they ever absent. This is because the foundation of oligarchy is
the extreme stratification of wealth, which is impossible without enforcement.
During periods of peace, marked by economic and political institutions that
structure transactions and clearly embody elements of cooperation and trust,
the credible threat of violence is what bounds and informs behaviors. The state
has a known capacity and willingness to act coercively to defend property
rights. Highly unequal systems of wealth cannot function as civil oligarchies
if this vital element breaks down or is absent. By downplaying material stratification and hierarchy, and especially the violence that sustains it, the NIE
literature is ill prepared to address broad eras of human history and a good
deal of contemporary political economy.

The last theme concerns the normative dimensions of oligarchy. Oligarchy
describes how a small number of very privileged individuals throughout history have used their exaggerated power to defend their fantastic wealth, often
among populations that are poor. In asking what is to be done, the answers
arising out of the evidence and arguments presented in this study are troubling. It is clear that oligarchy coexists remarkably easily with democracy.
This means that achieving democracy, especially if this only means implanting
the democratic method, is not a solution to the oligarchy problem. There is
nothing automatic about ending oligarchy through the adoption of free and
participatory forms of government. This is because who makes decisions or
how the decisions are made for a society is not the source of oligarchy. This

study leads to a quite different conclusion: ending oligarchy is impossible unless the power resource that defines oligarchs – concentrated wealth – is dispersed. This has happened many times in history as a consequence of war, conquest, or revolution. However, it has never been successfully attempted as a democratic decision.

What of taming? This is the process of imposing constraints on oligarchic behaviors without challenging oligarchy itself. Warring oligarchs have tamed themselves for brief periods through stalemates and shifting alliances; ruling oligarchs have tamed themselves for longer periods through collective arrangements that include regulations they impose on themselves; and sultanistic oligarchs have tamed oligarchs sometimes for decades through concentrated powers of coercion and patronage. This leaves civil oligarchy, which by definition means oligarchs are disarmed, do not rule, and are individually less powerful than a society's system of impersonal laws.

Taming oligarchs through laws does not eliminate them. On the contrary, it keeps this empowered minority intact and places few limits on their capacities to use their wealth to defend their material interests. A campaign to tame oligarchs is a struggle that is unlikely to fire the spirits of those outraged by profound injustices between rich and poor. However, to those enduring the economic and political burdens of living among wild oligarchs, it is an achievement that can improve the absolute welfare of average citizens, even if the relative gap between them and oligarchs widens rather than narrows. Whatever its limitations, taming oligarchs through laws is better than allowing the societal hardships and pathologies of wild oligarchy to continue unchecked.

The material power gap within a political community also matters. One thing that was apparent in the comparisons of Athens and Rome is that the concentration of wealth in the two ruling oligarchies was very different. Although a highly stratified society, Athens exhibited a much smaller material gap between oligarchs and the median citizen than was evident in Rome. This means that oligarchic "intensity" can vary greatly and that addressing oligarchy through decreasing that intensity is not only possible, but a worthwhile project as humanity struggles to develop the political means for addressing the extreme injustices of wealth more fully and permanently. Building a democracy and taming oligarchs through laws – two quite different achievements – are vital first steps along the path toward reaching that goal.

Bibliography

Aaron, Henry J., Leonard E. Burman and C. Eugene Steuerle. 2007. *Taxing Capital Income*. Washington, DC: Urban Institute Press.

Achen, Christopher H. and Larry M. Bartels. 2004. "Musical Chairs: Pocketbook Voting and the Limits of Democratic Accountability." Working Paper. Princeton University. www.princeton.edu/~bartels/chairs.pdf.

Adams, Charles Francis. 1875. *Familiar Letters of John Adams and His Wife Abigail, during the Revolution, with a Memoire of Mrs. Adams*. Boston and New York: Houghton Mifflin Company.

Adams, John. 1854 [1776]. "Letter to James Sullivan." May 26. In *The Works of John Adams, Second President of the United States, with a Life of the Author, Vol. 9.* Charles Francis Adams, ed. Boston: Charles C. Little and James Brown. Text of letter available at: www.britannica.com/presidents/article-9116850.

Agence France-Presse. 2009. "RP Ranking Improves in Asian Corruption Survey." *Agence France-Presse*. April 8.

Alföldy, Géza. 1988 [1975]. *The Social History of Rome*. Revised edition. Translated by David Braund and Frank Pollock. London: Routledge.

Allen, Danielle S. 1997. "Imprisonment in Classical Athens." *Classical Quarterly*, New Series 47(1): 121–135. www.jstor.org/stable/639603.

Allen, Danielle S. 2000. *The World of Prometheus: The Politics of Punishment in Democratic Athens*. Princeton, NJ: Princeton University Press.

Ambler, C. H. 1949. "Review: *The Hatfields and the McCoys* by Virgil Carrington Jones." *Mississippi Valley Historical Review* 35(4): 697–699. www.jstor.org/stable/1892693.

American Political Science Association (APSA). 2004. "American Democracy in an Age of Rising Inequality." Report by the Task Force on Inequality and American Democracy. www.apsanet.org/imgtest/taskforcereport.pdf.

Anderson, Benedict. 1972. *Java in a Time of Revolution*. Ithaca: Cornell University Press.

Anderson, Benedict. 1988. "Cacique Democracy in the Philippines: Origins and Dreams." *New Left Review* 169: 3–33.

Anderson, Benedict. 2008. "Exit Suharto: Obituary for a Mediocre Tyrant." *New Left Review* 50: 27–59.

Anderson, Perry. 1974a. *Passages from Antiquity to Feudalism*. London: Verso Press.

Anderson, Perry. 1974b. *Lineages of the Absolutist State*. London: Verso Press.

Apel, Jan. 2001. *Daggers, Knowledge, and Power: The Social Aspects of Flint-Dagger Technology in Scandinavia 2350–1500 cal BC*. Doctoral dissertation. Uppsala: Department of Archaeology and Ancient History, Uppsala University.

Appian, of Alexandria. 1912–1913. *Appian's Roman History*. Translated by Horace White. Loeb Classical Library. London: Heinemann; New York: Macmillan. penelope.uchicago.edu/Thayer/E/Roman/Texts/Appian/home.html.

Aristotle. 1996. *The Politics and The Constitution of Athens*. Edited by Stephen Everson (original translation by Benjamin Jowett). Cambridge: Cambridge University Press.

Arlacchi, Pino. 1986. *Mafia Business: The Mafia Ethic and the Spirit of Capitalism*. London: Verso.

Aron, Raymond. 1950. "Social Structure and the Ruling Class: Part 1." *British Journal of Sociology* 1(1): 1–16; and Part 2, 1(2): 126–143.

Åslund, Anders. 2007. *How Capitalism Was Built: The Transformation of Central and Eastern Europe, Russia, and Central Asia*. Cambridge: Cambridge University Press.

Aspinall, Edward. 2005. *Opposing Suharto: Compromise, Resistance, and Regime Change in Indonesia*. Palo Alto: Stanford University Press.

Avi-Yonah, Reuven S. 2000. "Globalization, Tax Competition, and the Fiscal Crisis of the Welfare State." *Harvard Law Review* 113. papers.ssrn.com/sol3/papers.cfm?abstract_id=208748.

Avi-Yonah, Reuven S. 2002. "Why Tax the Rich? Efficiency, Equity, and Progressive Taxation." *Yale Law Journal* 111(6): 1391–1416.

Bachrach, Peter and Morton Baratz. 1962. "The Two Faces of Power." *American Political Science Review* 56(4): 947–52.

Baehr, Peter R. 1997. *Caesar and the Fading of the Roman World: A Study in Republicanism and Caesarism*. New Brunswick, NJ: Transaction Press.

Bain, David. 2010. "IMF Finds 'Trillions' in Undeclared Wealth." *Wealth Bulletin*. March 15. www.wealth-bulletin.com/portfolio/tax-trust-and-legal/content/4058538961/.

Bankoff, Greg. 1996. *Crime, Society, and the State in Nineteenth-Century Philippines*. Manila: Ateneo de Manila University Press.

Bartels, Larry M. 2005. "Economic Inequality and Political Representation." Paper presented at the APSA Annual Meeting, Boston, August 29–September 1. (Revised August 2005). www.princeton.edu/~bartels/economic.pdf.

Bartels, Larry M. 2008. *Unequal Democracy: The Political Economy of the New Gilded Age*. Princeton, NJ: Princeton University Press.

Bates, Robert, Avner Greif, and Smita Singh. 2002. "Organizing Violence." *Journal of Conflict Resolution* 46(5): 599–628. www.jstor.org/stable/3176194.

Beesly, Augustus. H. 1877. *The Gracchi, Marius, and Sulla*. London: Longmans, Green and Co. books.google.com/books?id=GsE-AAAAYAAJ&dq=beesly+gracchi&source=gbs_navlinks_s.

Benitez, Conrado, Ramona S. Tirona, and Leon Gatmaytan. 1937. *Philippine Social Life and Progress*. Boston and New York: Ginn and Company.

Bentham, Jeremy. 1978 [1843]. "Security and Equality of Property." In *Property: Mainstream and Critical Positions*. C. B. MacPherson, ed., 39–58. Toronto: University of Toronto Press.

Berent, Moshe. 2000. "Anthropology and the Classics: War, Violence, and the State-less *Polis.*" *Classical Quarterly*, New Series 50(1): 257–289. www.jstor.org/stable/1558951.

Berle, Adolf A. Jr. 1959. *Power without Property: A New Development in American Political Economy.* New York: Harcourt, Brace & World.

Birnbaum, Jeffrey H. and Jonathan Weisman. 2005. "The 1% Split Over Estate Taxes." *Washington Post.* August 12. www.washingtonpost.com/wp-dyn/content/article/2005/08/11/AR2005081102013.html.

Blee, Kathleen M. and Dwight B. Billings. 1996. "Violence and Local State Formation: A Longitudinal Case Study of Appalachian Feuding." *Law & Society Review* 30(4): 671–705. www.jstor.org/stable/3054114.

Blee, Kathleen M. and Dwight B. Billings 2000. "Where 'Bloodshed is a Pastime': Mountain Feuds and Appalachian Stereotyping." In *Back Talk from Appalachia: Confronting Stereotypes.* Dwight B. Billings, Gurney Norman, and Katherine Ledford, eds., 119–137. Lexington: University Press of Kentucky.

Blomley, Nicholas. 2003. "Law, Property, and the Geography of Violence: The Frontier, the Survey, and the Grid." *Annals of the Association of American Geographers* 93(1): 121–141. www.jstor.org/stable/1515327.

Bloomquist, Kim M. 2003. "Trends as Changes in Variance: The Case of Tax Noncompliance." Presented at the 2003 IRS Research Conference. www.irs.ustreas.gov/pub/irs-soi/bloomquist.pdf.

Blum, Jack A. 2009. "Testimony of Jack A. Blum, Esq., before The United States Senate Committee on Homeland Security and Governmental Affairs on S.569, the Incorporation Transparency and Law Enforcement Assistance Act." United States Senate. November 5. hsgac.senate.gov/public/index.cfm?FuseAction=Files.View&FileStore_id=995d74b8–15ca-4152-bd25–6e9289bd304e.

Bonanno, Joseph. 2003. *A Man of Honor: The Autobiography of Joseph Bonanno.* New York: St. Martin's Press.

Boston Consulting Group. 2010. "Regaining Lost Ground: Resurgent Markets and New Opportunities." Global Wealth 2010. June. www.bcg.com.

Bottomore, T. B. 1964. *Elites and Society.* Baltimore: Penguin Books.

Bowman, Alan K. 1994. *Life and Letters on the Roman Frontier: Vindolanda and Its People.* London: British Museum Publications.

Bowsky, William M. 1962. "The Buon Governo of Siena (1287–1355): A Medieval Italian Oligarchy." *Speculum* 37(3): 368–381. links.jstor.org/sici?sici=0038–713428196207%2937%3A3%3C368%3ATBGOS%28%3E2.O.CO%3B2-G.

Bowsky, William M. 1972. "The Anatomy of Rebellion in Fourteenth-Century Siena: From Commune to Signory?" In *Violence and Civil Disorder in Italian Cities, 1200–1500.* Lauro Martines, ed., 229–272. Berkeley: University of California Press.

Braguinsky, Serguey. 2009. "Postcommunist Oligarchs in Russia: Quantitative Analysis." *Journal of Law and Economics* 52(2): 307–349.

Brunt, Peter A. 1962. "The Army and the Land in the Roman Revolution." *Journal of Roman Studies* 52(1-2): 69–86. www.jstor.org/stable/297878.

Bryan, Kelley. 2007. "Rule of Law in Singapore: Independence of the Judiciary and Legal Profession." Lawyers' Rights Watch Canada. NGO in Special Consultative Status with the Economic and Social Council of the United Nations. www.lrwc.org/documents/LRWC.Rule.of.Law.in.Singapore.17.Oct.07.pdf.

Bueno de Mesquita, Bruce, Alastair Smith, Randolph Siverson, and James Morrow. 2004. *The Logic of Political Survival.* Cambridge: MIT Press.

Burman, Leonard E. 2003. "On Waste, Fraud, and Abuse in Federal Mandatory Programs." Statement before The Committee on the Budget. United States House of Representatives. July 9. www.urban.org/url.cfm?ID=900641&renderforprint=1.

Burton, Michael G. and John Higley. 1987. "Elite Settlements." *American Sociological Review* 52(3): 295–307. links.jstor.org/sici?sici=0003-1224%28 198706%2952% 3A3%3C295%3AES%3E2.0.CO%3B2-0.

Cammack, Paul. 1990. "A Critical Assessment of the New Elite Paradigm." *American Sociological Review* 55(3): 415–420.

Capgemini. 2008 to 2010. "World Wealth Report." Capgemini and Merrill Lynch, Inc. www.us.capgemini.com/worldwealthreport08/WWR08_StateWorldsWealth.asp.

Carlton, Eric. 1996. *The Few and the Many: A Typology of Elites*. Aldershot, England: Scolar Press.

Carney, Timothy P. 2007. "Death Tax Is a Lifeline for Insurance Industry." *Washington Examiner*. November 16.

Carney, Timothy P. 2009. "Life Insurers Lobby to Save the Death Tax." Washington Examiner. December 11. www.washingtonexaminer.com/opinion/columns/ Life-insurers-lobby-to-save-the-death-tax-8648320-78996407.html.

Cassinelli, C. W. 1953. "The Law of Oligarchy." *American Political Science Review* 47(3): 773–784. links.jstor.org/sici?sici=0003–0554%2189 5309%2947%3A3% 3C773%3ATL00%3E2.O.C0%3B2.

Catanzaro, Raimondo. 1992. *Men of Respect: A Social History of the Sicilian Mafia*. New York: The Free Press.

CCH. 2010. "Standard Federal Tax Reporter." Commerce Clearing House. A Wolters Kluwer Business. tax.cchgroup.com.

Center for Responsive Politics. 2008. "U.S. Election Will Cost $5.3 Billion, Center for Responsive Politics Predicts." October 22. www.opensecrets.org/news/2008/ 10/us-election-will-cost-53-billi.html.

Center for Responsive Politics. 2010a. "Donor Demographics." www.opensecrets.org/ bigpicture/DonorDemographics.php?cycle=2008.

Center for Responsive Politics. 2010b. "Top Individual Contributors." www. opensecrets.org/bigpicture/topindivs.php?cycle=2008.

Center for Responsive Politics. 2010c. "Tracking the Payback." www.opensecrets.org/ payback.

Chambers, Johnathan D. 1953. "Enclosure and Labour Supply in the Industrial Revolution." *Economic History Review* 3: 319–343.

Chehabi, H. E. and Juan J. Linz. 1998. *Sultanistic Regimes*. Baltimore and London: The Johns Hopkins University Press.

Chen, Katherine K. 2008. "Oligarchy." *Encyclopedia of Social Problems*. Vincent N. Parrillo, ed., 637–638. Thousand Oaks, CA: Sage Publications Inc.

Christensen, John. 2006. "Follow the Money: How Tax Havens Facilitate Dirty Money Flows and Distort Global Markets." RGS-IBG Conference. Economic Geography Research Group – Geographies of Corruption. September 1. www.taxjustice.net/ cms/upload/pdf/Follow_the_Money_-_RGS-IBG_final_31-AUG-2006.pdf.

Clark, Thomas D. 1948. "Review: *The Hatfields and the McCoys* by Virgil Carrington Jones." *Journal of Southern History* 14(3): 427–428. www.jstor.org/stable/2197893.

Clastres, Pierre. 1999. *Archéologie de la violence: La guerre dans les sociétés primitives*. La Tour d'Aigues: Éditions de l'Aube.

Collier, David and Steven Levitsky. 1997. "Research Note: Democracy with Adjectives: Conceptual Innovation in Comparative Research." *World Politics* 49(3): 430–451.

Critchley, John S. 1978. *Feudalism*. London: Allen & Unwin.

Crouch, Harold. 1988. *The Army and Politics in Indonesia*. Revised Edition. Ithaca, NY: Cornell University Press.

D'Altroy, Terence and Christine Hastorf, eds. 2001. *Empire and Domestic Economy*. New York: Kluwer Academic/Plenum Publishers.

Dahl, Robert A. 1958. "A Critique of the Ruling Elite Model." *American Political Science Review* 52(2): 463–469.

Dahl, Robert A. 1985. *A Preface to Economic Democracy*. Berkeley: University of California Press.

Davies, John K. 1971. *Athenian Propertied Families 600–300 B.C.* Oxford: Clarendon Press.

Davis, William Stearns. 1910. *The Influence of Wealth in Imperial Rome*. New York: Macmillan Company.

de Laveleye, Emile. 1878. *Primitive Property*. Translated from French by G. R. L. Marriott, with an Introduction by T. E. Cliffe Leslie. London: Macmillan and Co. socserv.mcmaster.ca/econ/ugcm/3ll3/laveleye/contents.html.

de Montesquieu, C. B. S. 1748. *Spirit of the Laws*. Book 11, Chapter 6. press-pubs .uchicago.edu/founders/documents/v1ch17s9.html.

de Ste. Croix, Geoffrey E. M. 1989. *The Class Struggle in the Ancient Greek World*. Ithaca: Cornell University Press.

de Tocqueville, Alexis. 2007 [1838]. *Democracy in America*. Translated by Henry Reeve. Stillwell, KS: Digireads.com Publishing. books.google.com/books?id= OyiLOES54YgC&printsec=frontcover&dq=%22democracy + in + America%22& hl=en&ei=4XNITMnmJY6TnQfs-MDUDQ&sa=X&oi=book_result&ct=result& resnum=8&ved=0CFcQ6AEwBzgK#v=onepage&q&f=false.

Del Col, Mark, Andrew Hogan, and Thomas Roughan. 2004. "Transforming the Wealth Management Industry." *Journal of Financial Transformation*. Capco Institute. Capco Inc. www.capco.com/files/pdf/75/04_FINANCIAL/04_Transforming %20the%20wealth%20management%20industry.pdf.

Dhakidae, Daniel. 1991. "The State, the Rise of Capital, and the Fall of Political Journalism: Political Economy of Indonesia News Industry." Doctoral Dissertation. Cornell University.

Diamond, Jared. 1999. *Guns, Germs, and Steel: The Fates of Human Societies*. New York and London: W. W. Norton & Company.

Dietz, Mary G. 2007. "Between Polis and Empire: Aristotle's Politics." Prepared for Political Theory Colloquium, University of Michigan, Ann Arbor. April 20. theory .polisci.lsa.umich.edu/colloquium/dietz_paper.pdf.

Dogan, Mattei and John Higley, eds. 1998. *Elites, Crises, and the Origins of Regimes*. Lanham, MD: Rowman and Littlefield Publishers.

Doggart, Caroline. 1997. *Tax Havens and Their Uses*. London: Economist Intelligence Unit.

Domhoff, G. William. 1990. *The Power Elite and the State*. New York: Aldine.

Domhoff, G. William. 2002. "The Power Elite, Public Policy, and Public Opinion." In *Navigating Public Opinion: Polls, Policy, and the Future of American Democracy*. Jeff Manza, Fay Lomax Cook, and Benjamin I. Page, eds. New York: Oxford University Press.

Domhoff, G. William. 2006. *Who Rules America? Power, Politics, and Social Change*. 5th ed. New York: McGraw Hill.

Domhoff, G. William and Hoyt B. Ballard. 1968. *C. Wright Mills and the Power Elite*. Boston: Beacon Press.

Duggan, Christopher. 1984. *A Concise History of Italy*. Cambridge: Cambridge University Press.

Earle, Timothy. 1997. *How Chiefs Come to Power: The Political Economy in Prehistory*. Stanford, CA: Stanford University Press.

Echols, Edward. 1958. "The Roman City Police: Origin and Development." *Classical Journal* 53(8): 377–385. www.jstor.org/stable/3295085.

Ellickson, Robert C. 1993. "Property in Land." *Yale Law Journal* 102(6): 1315–1400. www.jstor.org/stable/796972.

Ellis, Eric. 2010. "Singapore Wishes Indonesian Investigation into Corruption Wasn't Happening." *Sydney Morning Herald*. May 6.

Emmerson, Donald K. 1983. "Understanding the New Order: Bureaucratic Pluralism in Indonesia." *Asian Survey* 23(11): 1220–1241. links.jstor.org/sici?sici= 0004–4687%21898311%2923%3A11%3C1220%3AUTNOBP%3E2.0.CO% 3B2-2.

Encyclopedia Britannica. 2009. "Spurius Cassius Vecellinus." Encyclopedia Britannica Online. www.britannica.com/EBchecked/topic/98296/Spurius-Cassius-Vecellinus.

Engen, Darel. 2004. "The Economy of Ancient Greece." *EH.Net Encyclopedia*. Robert Whaples, ed. July 31. eh.net/encyclopedia/article/engen.greece.

Epstein, Stephan R. 2000a. *Freedom and Growth: The Rise of States and Markets in Europe, 1300–1750*. New York: Routledge.

Epstein, Stephan R. 2000b. "The Rise and Fall of Italian City-States." In Mogens Herman Hansen, ed. *A Comparative Study of Thirty City-State Cultures: An Investigation*. Kongelige Danske Videnskabernes Selskab.

Erlanger, Steven. 1990. "For Suharto, His Heirs Are Key to Life After '93." *New York Times*. November 11. www.nytimes.com/1990/11/11/world/for-suharto-his-heirs-are-key-to-life-after-93.html?pagewanted=all.

Etzioni-Halevy, Eva. 1997. *Classes and Elites in Democracy and Democratization*. New York and London: Garland Publishing.

Federal Bureau of Investigations. 2009. "Italian Organized Crime." Federal Bureau of Investigations Web site. www.fbi.gov/hq/cid/orgcrime/lcnindex.htm.

Ferguson, Yale H. and Richard W. Mansbach. 1996. *Polities: Authority, Identities, and Change*. Columbia, SC: University of South Carolina Press.

Ferraro, Joanne. 1988. "Oligarchs, Protesters, and the Republic of Venice: The 'Revolution of the Discontents' in Brescia, 1644–1645." *Journal of Modern History* 60(4): 627–653. links.jstor.org/sici?sici=0022–280128198812%2960%3A4%3C627%3 AOPATRO%3E2.0.CO%3B2-A.

Field, G. Lowell and John Higley. 1980. *Elitism*. London and Boston: Routledge & Kegan Paul.

Finn, Daniel. 2009. "Short Cuts." *London Review of Books* 31(13): 20.

Fisher, Nick. 1996. "Review: *Policing Athens: Social Control in the Attic Lawsuits, 420–320 B.C.* by V. J. Hunter." *Journal of Hellenic Studies* 116: 218–219. www.jstor .org/stable/632004.

Flynn, Daniel and Antonella Cinelli. 2009. "Crisis Hands Crime Groups Chance to Extend Grip: U.N." *Reuters*. May 28. www.reuters.com/article/idUSTRE54R4H 720090528.

Forbes. 2010. "The World's Billionaires." March 10. www.forbes.com/lists/2010/10/ billionaires-2010_The-Worlds-Billionaires_Rank.html.

Forbes Asia. 2010. "Singapore's 40 Richest." July 28. www.forbes.com/lists/2010/79/ singapore-10_Singapores-40-Richest_Rank.html.

Foucault, Michel. 1980. *Power/Knowledge: Selected Interviews & Other Writings 1972–1977.* Colin Gordon, ed. New York: Pantheon Books.

Fraenkel, Ernst. 1941. *The Dual State: A Contribution to the Theory of Dictatorship.* Translated from the German by E. A. Shils, in collaboration with Edith Lowenstein and Klaus Knorr. New York: Oxford University Press. Available in Lawbooks Exchange version at www.lawbooksexchange.com. The Lawbook Exchange, Ltd. NJ: 2006.

Franchetti, L. 1974 [1876] "Condizioni politiche ed amministrative della Sicilia." In L. Franchetti and S. Sonnino. *Inchiesta in Sicilia, vol. 1. Florence*: Vallecchi.

Frank, Beatrice S., Joseph C. Markowitz, Robert B. McKay, and Kenneth Roth. 1991. "The Decline in the Rule of Law in Malaysia and Singapore: Part II – Singapore, a Report of the Committee on International Human Rights." January/February. *Record of the Association of the Bar of the City of New York* 46(1): 7–85. dlib.nyu.edu/findingaids/html/archives/mckay_content.html.

Frank, Thomas. 2006. "Thus Spake Zinsmeister." *New York Times.* Op-ed, August 25, p. A23.

Fraser, Steve and Gary Gerstle, eds. 2005. *Ruling America: A History of Wealth and Power in a Democracy.* Cambridge, MA: Harvard University Press.

Freedom House. 2009. "Freedom in the World 2009." www.freedomhouse.org.

Freeman, Jo. 1975. "Political Organization in the Feminist Movement." *Acta Sociologica* 18(2–3): 222–44.

Freeman, Jo. 1984. "The Tyranny of Structurelessness." In *Untying the Knot: Feminism, Anarchism & Organisation.* Jo Freeman and Cathy Levine. London: Dark Star and Rebel Press.

Friedrich, Carl J. 1937. "Oligarchy." *Encyclopedia of the Social Sciences* 11: 462–65. New York: Macmillan.

Friend, Theodore. 2003 *Indonesian Destinies.* Cambridge, MA: Harvard University Press.

Gambetta, Diego. 1993. *The Sicilian Mafia: The Business of Private Protection.* Cambridge, MA: Harvard University Press.

Gambetta, Diego. 2000. "Mafia: The Price of Distrust." In *Trust: Making and Breaking Cooperative Relations.* Diego Gambetta, ed., 158–175. Electronic edition, Department of Sociology, University of Oxford. www.sociology.ox.ac.uk/papers/gambetta158–175.pdf.

Gans-Morse, Jordan. 2010. "The Evolution of Russian Business Conflicts and the Development of Legal Institutions." Presented at the Annual Meeting of the Midwest Political Science Association. Chicago, IL. April 22–25.

Gel'man, Vladimir. 2004. "The Unrule of Law in the Making: The Politics of Informal Institution Building in Russia." *Europe-Asia Studies* 56(7): 1021–1040. www.jstor.org/pss/4147495.

Gelzer, Matthias. 1969 [1912]. *The Roman Nobility. Die Nobilität der römischen Republik.* English trans. by R. Seager. Oxford: Oxford University Press.

Gilens, Martin. 2005. "Inequality and Democratic Responsiveness." *Public Opinion Quarterly* 69(5): 778–96.

Glovin, David. 2010. "HVB Is Sued by Ex-Client Saperstein over Tax Shelters." *Bloomberg News.* March 31. www.bloomberg.com/apps/news?pid=20601127&sid=aHQZAzi71458.

Goldman, Marshall I. 2003. *The Piratization of Russia: Russian Reform Goes Awry.* London and New York: Routledge.

Goldsmith, Raymond W. 1984. "An Estimate of the Size and Structure of the National Product of the Early Roman Empire." *Review of Income & Wealth* 30(3): 263–288.

Goodin, Robert and John Dryzek. 1980. "Rational Participation: The Politics of Relative Power British." *Journal of Political Science* 10: 273–292.

Graetz, Michael J. 2002. "100 Million Unnecessary Returns: A Fresh Start for the U.S. Tax System." *Yale Law Journal* 112(2): 261–310. www.jstor.org/stable/1562240.

Graetz, Michael J. and Ian Shapiro. 2005. *Death by a Thousand Cuts: The Fight Over Taxing Inherited Wealth*. Princeton: Princeton University Press.

Greif, Avner. 2005. "Commitment, Coercion, and Markets: The Nature and Dynamics of Institutions Supporting Exchange." In *Handbook of New Institutional Economics*. C. Ménard and M. Shirley, eds. Norwell, MA: Kluwer Academic Publishers.

Greif, Avner. 2006. *Institutions and the Path to the Modern Economy*. Cambridge: Cambridge University Press.

Greif, Avner. 2008. "Coercion and Exchange: How Did Markets Evolve?" Available at ssrn.com/abstract=1304204.

Grief, Avner, Paul Milgrom, and Barry Weingast. 1994. "Commitment, Coordination, and Enforcement: The Case of the Merchant Guilds." *Journal of Political Economy* 102: 745–776.

Guerin, Bill. 2003. "Indonesia's First Family of Corruption." *Asia Times*. October 31. www.atimes.com/atimes/Southeast_Asia/EJ31Ae03.html.

Guilaine, Jean and Jean Zammit. 2001. *The Origins of War: Violence in Prehistory*. Malden: Blackwell Publishing.

Guriev, Sergei and Andrei Rachinsky. 2005. "The Role of Oligarchs in Russian Capitalism." *Journal of Economic Perspectives* 19(1): 131–150. www.jstor.org/stable/4134996.

Guttentag, Joseph and Reuven Avi-Yonah. 2006. "Closing the International Tax Gap." In *Bridging the Tax Gap: Addressing the Crisis in Federal Tax Administration*. Max B. Sawicky, ed. Washington, DC: Economic Policy Institute.

Hacker, Jacob S. and Paul Pierson. 2010. *Winner-Take-All Politics: How Washington Made the Rich Richer – And Turned Its Back on the Middle Class*. New York: Simon & Schuster.

Harrington, James. 1656. *The Commonwealth of Oceana*. The Constitution Society. www.constitution.org/jh/oceana.htm.

Harris, Roy. 2008. "KPMG Tax-Shelter Case Is Mixed Win for U.S." *CFO Magazine* (online). December 18. www.cfo.com/article.cfm/12832380/c_12833296?f=home_todayinfinance.

Harris, William V. 1980. "Towards a Study of the Roman Slave Trade." *Memoirs of the American Academy in Rome* 36: 117–140. The Seaborne Commerce of Ancient Rome: Studies in Archaeology and History. www.jstor.org/stable/4238700.

Hendley, Kathryn. 2006. "Assessing the Rule of Law in Russia." *Cardozo Journal of International and Comparative Law* 14(2): 347–391. www.law.wisc.edu/m/ytdxn/assessing_rol.pdf.

Hendley, Kathryn. 2009. "'Telephone Law' and the 'Rule of Law': The Russian Case." *Hague Journal on the Rule of Law* 1(2): 241–264.

Hendley, Kathryn. 2010. "Coping with Uncertainty: The Role of Contracts in Russian Industry During the Transition to the Market." *Northwestern Journal of International Law and Business* 30(2): 25–45.

Herber, Bernard P. 1981. "Personal Income Tax Reform and the Interaction Between Budgetary Goals: A UK and USA Comparison." In *Reforms of Tax Systems*. Karl W. Roskamp and Francesco Forte, eds. Detroit: Wayne State University Press.

Herber, Bernard P. 1988. "Federal Income Tax Reform in the United States: How Did It Happen? What Did It Do? Where Do We Go from Here?" *American Journal of Economics and Sociology* 47(4): 391–408. www.jstor.org/stable/3486550.

Herlihy, David. 1972. "Some Psychological and Social Roots of Violence in the Tuscan Cities." In Lauro Martines, ed. *Violence and Civil Disorder in Italian Cities, 1200–1500*. Berkeley: University of California Press, pp. 129–154.

Hertzberg, Hendrik. 2009. "Biggus Buckus." *New Yorker*. November 9: 27–28.

Hess, Henner. 1973. *Mafia and Mafiosi: The Structure of Power*. Farnborough: Saxon House.

Heston, Alan, Robert Summers, and Bettina Aten. 2009. "Penn World Table Version 6.3." Center for International Comparisons of Production, Income and Prices at the University of Pennsylvania. August. pwt.econ.upenn.edu/php_site/pwt63/pwt63_form.php.

Hetherington, Kregg. 2009. "Privatizing the Private in Rural Paraguay: Precarious Lots and the Materiality of Rights." *American Ethnologist* 36(2): 224–241.

Higley, John, Michael G. Burton, and G. Lowell Field. 1990. "In Defense of Elite Theory: A Reply to Cammack." *American Sociological Review* 55(3): 421–426.

Higley, John and Richard Gunther, eds. 1992. *Elites and Democratic Consolidation in Latin America and Southern Europe*. Cambridge: Cambridge University Press.

Higley, John, Ursula Hoffmann-Lange, Charles Kadushin, and Gwen Moore. 1991. "Elite Integration in Stable Democracies: A Reconsideration." *European Sociological Review* 7(1): 35–53.

Hodgson, Geoffrey M. 1998. "The Approach of Institutional Economics." *Journal of Economic Literature* 36(1): 166–192. www.jstor.org/stable/2564954.

Hoffman, David E. 2003. *The Oligarchs: Wealth and Power in the New Russia*. New York: PublicAffairs.

Högfeldt, Peter. 2004. "The History and Politics of Corporate Ownership in Sweden." NBER Working Paper No. W10641. July. ssrn.com/abstract=579788.

Hommon, Robert J. 1995. "Social Complex Adaptive Systems: Some Hawaiian Examples." Working Paper. Santa Fe Institute. www.santafe.edu/media/workingpapers/95-07-066.pdf.

Huang, Yasheng. 2008. *Capitalism with Chinese Characteristics: Entrepreneurship and the State*. Cambridge: Cambridge University Press.

Hurun Report. 2010. "The Richest People in China 2010." The Hurun Rich List. Shanghai, China. www.hurun.net/listreleaseen512.aspx.

Hutchcroft, Paul D. 1991. "Oligarchs and Cronies in the Philippine State: The Politics of Patrimonial Plunder." *World Politics* 43: 414–450.

Hutchcroft, Paul D. 1998. *Booty Capitalism: The Politics of Banking in the Philippines*. Ithaca: Cornell University Press.

Hutchcroft, Paul D. 2000. "Colonial Masters, National Politicos, and Provincial Lords: Central Authority and Local Autonomy in the American Philippines, 1900–1913." *Journal of Asian Studies* 59(2): 277–306.

Hutchcroft, Paul D. 2008. "The Arroyo Imbroglio in the Philippines." *Journal of Democracy* 19(1): 141–155.

IBA. 2007a. "International Bar Association Annual Conference: Singapore 2007." Singapore. October 14–19. www.int-bar.org/conferences/singapore2007/.

IBA. 2007b. "Rule of Law Symposium." International Bar Association Annual Conference. Singapore. October 19. Suntec Singapore, International Convention & Exhibition Centre. www.int-bar.org/conferences/Rule_of_Law_Symposium_Singapore/binary/Rule%20of%20law%20symposium%20flyer.pdf.

IBA. 2008. "Prosperity Versus Individual Rights? Human Rights, Democracy, and the Rule of Law in Singapore." An International Bar Association Human Rights Institute Report. July. www.world-rights.org/singapore/07_2008_July_Report_Singapore-Prosperity_versus_individual_rights.pdf.

Indridason, Indridi H. 2008. "Oligarchy." *International Encyclopedia of the Social Sciences*. William A. Darity, Jr. Vol. 6. 2nd ed.: 36–37. Detroit: Macmillan Reference USA.

Internal Revenue Manual. 2010. "Review of Doubt as to Liability Offers: Legal Basis for Compromise." Part 33, Chapter 3, Section 2. Internal Revenue Service. www.irs.gov/irm/part33/irm_33-003-002.html.

Internal Revenue Service. 2009. "The 400 Individual Income Tax Returns Reporting the Highest Adjusted Gross Incomes Each Year, 1992–2007." United States Department of Treasury. www.irs.gov/pub/irs-soi/07intop400.pdf.

International Crisis Group. 2009. *The Philippines: After the Maguindanao Massacre*. Asia Briefing No. 98, December 21. www.crisisgroup.org/library/documents/asia/south_east_asia/b98_the_philippines___after_the_maguindanao_massacre.pdf.

Isaac, Jeffrey C. 1987. "Beyond the Three Faces of Power: A Realist Critique." *Polity* 20(1): 4–31.

Isaac, Jeffrey C. 1988. "Republicanism vs. Liberalism?: A Reconsideration." *History of Political Thought* 9(2): 349–77.

Jackson, Paul. 2003. "Warlords as Alternative Forms of Governance." *Small Wars and Insurgencies* 14(2): 131–150.

Jaczynowska, Maria. 1962. "The Economic Differentiation of the Roman Nobility at the End of the Republic." *Historia: Zeitschrift für Alte Geschichte* 11(4): 486–499. www.jstor.org/stable/4434765.

Jakarta Post. 2004. "Court Tells Kito, Akbar to Settle Out of Court." *Jakarta Post*. April 16.

Jakarta Post. 2009. "Golkar's Younger Members Demand Leadership Roles." *Jakarta Post*. July 15.

Jayasuriya, Kanishka. 1996. "The Rule of Law and Capitalism in East Asia." *Pacific Review* 9(3): 367–388.

Jayasuriya, Kanishka. 1999. "Corporatism and Judicial Independence within Statist Legal Institutions in East Asia." In *Law, Capitalism, and Power in Asia*. Kanishka Jayasuriya, ed., 173–204. London: Routledge, pp. 173–204.

Jayasuriya, Kanishka. 2000. "*The Rule of Law and Regimes of Exception in East Asia*." Working Paper No. 96. Asia Research Centre, Murdoch University. July. wwwarc.murdoch.edu.au/wp/wp96.pdf.

Jayasuriya, Kanishka. 2001. "The Exception Becomes the Norm: Law and Regimes of Exception in East Asia." *Asian-Pacific Law & Policy Journal* 2(1): 108–124. www.hawaii.edu/aplpj/articles/APLPJ_02.1_jayasuriya.pdf.

Jayasuriya, Kanishka. 2002. "The Rule of Law and Governance in East Asia." In *Reconfiguring East Asia: Regional Institutions and Organisations after the Crisis*. Mark Beeson, ed., 99–116. New York: Routledge Curzon.

Jefferson, Thomas. 1950 [1785]. "Thomas Jefferson to James Madison. 28 Oct. 1785." In Julian P. Boyd, et al. *The Papers of Thomas Jefferson*. Papers 8: 681–82. Volume 1, chapter 15, document 32, p. 539. Princeton: Princeton University Press.

Johnson, David G. 1977. *The Medieval Chinese Oligarchy*. Boulder: Westview Press.

Johnston, David Cay. 2003. *Perfectly Legal: The Covert Campaign to Rig Our Tax System to Benefit the Super Rich – and Cheat Everybody Else*. New York: Portfolio Publishing.

Johnston, David Cay. 2006. "Tax Cheats Called Out of Control." *New York Times*. August 1. query.nytimes.com/gst/fullpage.html?res=990CE5DE103FF932A3575BC 0A9609C8B63&sec=&spon=&pagewanted=1.

Johnston, David Cay. 2009. "Fiscal Therapy." *Mother Jones*. January/February. motherjones.com/politics/2009/01/fiscal-therapy.

Johnston, David Cay. 2010a. "Is Our Tax System Helping Us Create Wealth?" *Tax Analysts*. January 29. www.tax.com/taxcom/features.nsf/Articles/313FDACA 4356CFEE8525769C0079A989?OpenDocument.

Johnston, David Cay. 2010b. "Tax Rates for Top 400 Earners Fall as Income Soars, IRS Data." *Tax Analysts*. February 17. www.tax.com/taxcom/features.nsf/Articles/ 0DEC0EAA7E4D7A2B852576CD00714692?OpenDocument.

Jones, A. H. M. 1955. "The Social Structure of Athens in the Fourth Century." *Economic History Review*, New Series 8(2): 141–155. www.jstor.org/stable/2590983.

Jones, A. H. M. 1958. *Athenian Democracy*. New York: Frederick A. Praeger Publishers.

Judson, Bruce. 2009. "Economic Inequality: The Wall Street Journal is Just Wrong." It Could Happen Here. Blog. September 14. itcouldhappenhere.com/blog/wsjiswrong/.

Kapur, Ajay, Niall Macleod, and Narendra Singh. 2005. "Plutonomy: Buying Luxury, Explaining Global Imbalances." *Industry Note*. Citigroup Investment Research. Citigroup Global Markets, Inc. October 16. www.scribd.com/doc/ 6674234/Citigroup-Oct-16–2005-Plutonomy-Report-Part-1.

Kar, Dev and Devon Cartwright-Smith. 2006. "Illicit Financial Flows from Developing Countries, 2002–2006." Global Financial Integrity. Center for International Policy. www.gfip.org/storage/gfip/executive%20-%20final%20version%201-5-09.pdf.

Karhunen, Jussi and Matti Keloharju. 2001. "Shareownership in Finland 2000." *Liiketaloudellinen Aikakauskirja*. *Finnish Journal of Business Economics* 2(1): 188–226. lta.hse.fi/2001/2/lta_2001_02_a2.pdf.

Kenworthy, Lane. 2009a. "Reducing Inequality: What to Do about the Top 1%." *CrookedTimber*. April 17. crookedtimber.org/2009/04/17/reducing-inequality-what-to-do-about-the-top-1/.

Kenworthy, Lane. 2009b. "Tax Myths." *Contexts* 8(3): 28–32. contexts.org/articles/ summer-2009/tax-myths/.

Kenworthy, Lane 2009c. "The High-Employment Route to Low Inequality." *Challenge* 52(5): 77–99. econpapers.repec.org/article/meschalle/v_3a52_3ay_3a2009_3ai_3a5_ 3ap_3a77–99.htm.

Khalik, Abdul. 2004. "Golkar's Internal Fight Heats Up As Polls Near." *Jakarta Post*. March 30.

Kleber, John E. 1992. *The Kentucky Encyclopedia*. Lexington: University Press of Kentucky.

Koh, Joyce. 2010. "Credit Suisse Targets Indonesia Rich as Yudhoyono Beats Karaoke." *Bloomberg News*. January 4. www.bloomberg.com/apps/news?pid=newsarchive& sid=aZDrfo4aQOa8.

Kolb, Michael J. and Boyd Dixon. 2002. "Landscapes of War: Rules and Conventions of Conflict in Ancient Hawai'i (And Elsewhere)." *American Antiquity* 67(3): 514–534. www.jstor.org/stable/1593824.

Korpi, Walter. 1985. "Developments in the Theory of Power and Exchange." *Sociological Theory* 3(2): 31–45.

Kotlikoff, Laurence J. and David Rapson. 2006. "Comparing Average and Marginal Tax Rates under the Fair Tax and the Current System of Federal Taxation." Mimeo. October. www.econ.ucdavis.edu/faculty/dsrapson/FairTax_1006.pdf.

Kristiansen, Kristian. 1999. "The Emergence of Warrior Aristocracies in Later European Prehistory and Their Long-Term History." In John Carman and Anthony Harding, eds. *Ancient Warfare*. Stroud: Sutton Publishing.

Kristof, Nicholas D. 2000. "Big Brother." *New York Times*. November 5. www .nytimes.com/2000/11/05/books/big-brother.html.

Lachmann, Richard. 2000. *Capitalists in Spite of Themselves: Elite Conflict and Economic Transitions in Early Modern Europe*. New York: Oxford University Press.

Lachmann, Richard. 2003. "Elite Self-Interest and Economic Decline in Early Modern Europe." *American Sociological Review* 68(3): 346–372.

Lane, Frederic. 1973. *Venice: A Maritime Republic*. Baltimore, MD: Johns Hopkins University Press.

Lane, Max. 2008. *Unfinished Nation: Indonesia Before and After Suharto*. London and New York: Verso.

Larkin, John A. 1982. "Philippine History Reconsidered: A Socioeconomic Perspective." *American Historical Review* 87(3): 595–628. www.jstor.org/stable/1864158.

Larkin, John A. 1993. *Sugar and the Origins of Modern Philippine Society*. Berkeley: University of California Press.

Leach, Darcy K. 2005. "The Iron Law of What Again? Conceptualizing Oligarchy across Organizational Forms." *Sociological Theory* 23(3): 312–337.

Lee, Kuan Yew. 2000. *From Third World to First: The Singapore Story, 1965–2000*. New York: HarperCollins.

Lee, Philip. 2003. "Had LKY Not Been Tough Then." *Straits Times* (Singapore). September 20: 27.

Lenardon, Robert J. 1974. "Review: *Athenian Propertied Families 600–300 B.C.* by John K. Davies." *Classical Journal* 69(4): 379–380.

Lev, Daniel S. 1965. "The Politics of Judicial Development in Indonesia." *Comparative Studies in Society and History* 7(2): 173–199.

Lev, Daniel S. 1985. "Colonial Law and the Genesis of the Indonesian State." *Indonesia* 40: 57–74. www.jstor.org/stable/3350875.

Lev, Daniel S. 2000. *Legal Evolution and Political Authority in Indonesia: Selected Essays*. The Hague, Netherlands: Kluwer Law International.

Lev, Daniel S. 2007. "The State and Law Reform in Indonesia." In *Law Reform in Developing and Transitional States*. Tim Lindsey, ed. New York: Routledge.

Levin, Carl. 2010. "Closing Tax Loopholes." *Website of Senator Carl Levin*. levin .senate.gov/issues/index.cfm?MainIssue=BudgetTaxesandtheEconomy&SubIssue= ClosingTaxLoopholes.

Lewis, D. M. 1980. "Politics in the Greek City." Review: *Untersuchungen zu Staat und Politik in Griechenland vom 7–4 Jh. v. Chr* by Eberhard Ruschenbusch. *Classical Review*, New Series 30(1): 77–78.

Liddle, R. William. 1985. "Soeharto's Indonesia: Personal Rule and Political Institutions." *Pacific Affairs* 58(1): 68–90. links.jstor.org/sici?sici=0030-851X% 28198521%2958%3A1%3C68%3ASIPRAP%3E2.0.CO%3B2-Y.

Linz, Juan J. 1975. "Totalitarian and Authoritarian Regimes." In *Handbook of Political Science*, vol. 3. Nelson Polsby and Fred Greenstein, eds. Reading, MA: Addison-Wesley.

Low, Aaron. 2009. "Ideal Govt 'A Balance between Quality Leadership and Free Play.'" *Straits Times*. July 23. www.pmo.gov.sg/News/Transcripts/Prime+Minister/Ideal+govt+a+balance+between+quality+leadership+and+free+play+PM+Lee.htm.

Low, Polly. 2008. *The Athenian Empire*. Edinburgh: University of Edinburgh Press.

Lukes, Steven. 1974. *Power: A Radical View*. London: Macmillan.

Lyttkens, Carl Hampus. 1994. "A Predatory Democracy? An Essay on Taxation in Classical Athens." *Explorations in Economic History* 31: 62–90.

Macan-Markar, Marwaan. 2007. "S'pore – Venue for Int'l Bar Association Meet?" *Inter Press Service*. February 24. www.ipsnews.net/news.asp?idnews=36715.

MacClintock, S. S. 1901. "The Kentucky Mountains and Their Feuds II: The Causes of Feuds." *American Journal of Sociology* 7(2): 171–187.

MacDougall, John M. 2008. "Prison *cum* Hostel?" *Inside Indonesia* 93: Aug–Oct.

Machiavelli, Niccolò. 1958 [1519–20]. "A Discourse on Remodeling the Government of Florence." In Machiavelli: *The Chief Works and Others*, Vol. I. Allan Gilbert, trans. and ed., 101–15. Durham, NC: Duke University Press.

MacKenzie, Donald C. 1983. "Pay Differentials in the Early Empire." *Classical World* 76(5): 267–273. www.jstor.org/stable/4349469.

Madison, James. 1787. "The Federalist No. 10: The Utility of the Union as a Safeguard against Domestic Faction and Insurrection (continued)." The Constitution Society. www.constitution.org/fed/federa10.htm.

Magnuson, Ed. 2001. "Hitting the Mafia." *Time Magazine*. June 24. www.time.com/time/nation/article/0,8599,145082,00.html.

Mangunwijaya, Y. B. 1998. "Wawancara Y. B. Mangunwijaya. Cuma Satu: Soeharto Harus Turun." ["Interview with Y. B. Mangunwijaya. Just One Thing: Suharto Must Step Down."]. *AJInews* Edisi 5 Maret. www.hamline.edu/apakabar/basisdata/1998/03/05/0061.html.

Mann, Michael. 1986. *The Sources of Social Power: A History of Power from the Beginning to A.D. 1760 (Volume I)*. Cambridge: Cambridge University Press.

Marten, Kimberly. 2007. "Warlordism in Comparative Perspective." *International Security* 31(3): 41–73.

Martines, Lauro, ed. 1972. *Violence and Civil Disorder in Italian Cities, 1200–1500*. Berkeley: University of California Press.

Marx, Karl. 1978 [1844]. "On 'The Jewish Question.'" In *The Marx-Engels Reader*, second edition. Robert C. Tucker, ed., 26–52. New York: W. W. Norton & Company.

McArthur, Todd Y., Julio A. Castro, Anna-Liza Harris, and Tamara W. Ashford. 2010. "Recent U.S. Tax Bills Target Offshore Tax Abuse." *In the News*. Dewey & LeBoeuf. www.deweyleboeuf.com/~/media/Files/inthenews/2010/20100413_Recent USTaxBillsTargetOffshoreTaxAbuse.ashx.

McClellan, George B. 1904. *The Oligarchy of Venice*. Boston and New York: Houghton, Mifflin and Company.

McCormick, John P. 2006. "Contain the Wealthy and Patrol the Magistrates: Restoring Elite Accountability to Popular Government." *American Political Science Review* 100(2): 147–163.

McCoy, Alfred W., ed. 2009. *An Anarchy of Families: State and Family in the Philippines*. Madison: University of Wisconsin Press.

MDRC. 2008. "European High Net Worth 2008." Research Brief. Market Dynamics Research & Consulting Ltd. February. mdrc-global.com/page25/page31/files/dimensions-of-european-wealth-2008.pdf.

Meisel, James H. 1958. *The Myth of the Ruling Class: Gaetano Mosca and the "Elite."* Ann Arbor: University of Michigan Press.

Merriam, Charles E. 1938. "The Assumptions of Aristocracy." *American Journal of Sociology* 43(6): 857–877.

Michels, Robert. 2001 [1911]. *Political Parties: A Sociological Study of the Oligarchical Tendencies of Modern Democracy*. Kitchener, Ontario: Batoche Books. 209.85.215 .104/search?q=cache:UVLR_mRNh9sJ:upol.ff.cuni.cz/vyuka/sylaby/znoj_michels .pdf + batoche + robert + michels&hl=en&ct=clnk&cd=1&gl=us Originally published as *Zur Soziologie der Parteiwesens in der modernen Demokratie* (Leipzig, 1911).

Milanovic, Branko, Peter H. Lindert, and Jeffrey G. Williamson. 2007. "Measuring Ancient Inequality." *NBER Working Paper Series* No. 13550. www.nber.org/papers/ w13550.

Mills, C. Wright. 1956. *The Power Elite*. New York: Oxford University Press.

Mizruchi, Mark A. 2004. "Berle and Means Revisited: The Governance and Power of Large U.S. Corporations." *Theory and Society* 33(5): 579–617. www.jstor.org/ stable/4144886.

Moldenhauer, David T. 2007. "Tax Opinions." *Social Science Research Network*. ssrn.com/abstract=964082.

Molho, Anthony, Kurt Raaflaub, and Julia Emlen, eds. 1991. *City-States in Classical Antiquity and Medieval Italy*. Ann Arbor, MI: University of Michigan Press.

Mommsen, Theodor. 2006 [1855]. *The History of Rome, Book III: From the Union of Italy to the Subjugation of Carthage and the Greek States*. London: Hard Press.

Monoson, Sara. 2000. *Plato's Democratic Entanglements: Athenian Politics and the Practice of Philosophy*. Princeton: Princeton University Press.

Monsivais, Pablo and Adam Drewnowski. 2007. "The Rising Cost of Low-Energy-Density Foods." *Journal of the American Dietetic Association* 107(12): 2071–2076.

Moore, Barrington Jr. 1966. *Social Origins of Dictatorship and Democracy: Lord and Peasant in the Making of the Modern World*. Boston: Beacon Press.

Mosca, Gaetano. 1939. *The Ruling Class*. Ed. and rev. Arthur Livingston. Trans. Hannah D. Kahn. New York and London: McGraw-Hill Book Company. [Orig. pub. as *Elementi di scienza politica*. Roma: Bocca, 1896].

Myers, Henry A. 1982. *Medieval Kingship*. Chicago: Nelson Hall.

Nam, Suzanne. 2009. "Indonesia's 40 Richest." *Forbes*. December 2. www.forbes.com/ 2009/12/02/indonesia-richest-tycoons-indonesia-billionaires-09-southeast-asia-wealth-intro.html.

Nederman, Cary J. 1987. "Sovereignty, War, and the Corporation: Hegel on the Medieval Foundations of the Modern State." *Journal of Politics* 49(2): 500–520. www.jstor.org/stable/2131311.

New York Times. 1894. "Mr. Cockran's Final Effort." January 31. query.nytimes.com/ mem/archive-free/pdf?_r=1&res=9907E7D81638E233A25752C3A9679C94659 ED7CF.

New York Times. 1986. "The Commission's Origins." November 20. www.nytimes .com/1986/11/20/nyregion/the-commission-s-origins.html.

Nippel, Wilfried. 1984. "Policing Rome." *Journal of Roman Studies* 74: 20–29. www.jstor.org/stable/299004.

North, Douglass C. 1981. *Structure and Change in Economic History*. New York: W. W. Norton & Company.

North, Douglass C. 1990. *Institutions, Institutional Change, and Economic Performance*. Cambridge: Cambridge University Press.

North, Douglass C. 1994. "Economic Performance through Time." *American Economic Review* 84(3): 359–368. www.jstor.org/stable/2118057.

North, Douglass C. 2005. *Understanding the Process of Economic Change*. Princeton: Princeton University Press.

North, Douglass C. and Robert Paul Thomas. 1973. *The Rise of the Western World: A New Economic History*. Cambridge: Cambridge University Press.

North, Douglass C. and Barry R. Weingast. 1989. "Constitutions and Commitment: The Evolution of Institutions Governing Public Choice in 17th Century England." *Journal of Economic History* 49: 803–32.

North, Douglass C., John Joseph Wallis, and Barry R. Weingast. 2006. "A Conceptual Framework for Interpreting Recorded Human History." NBER Working Paper Series. Working Paper 12795. www.nber.org/papers/w12795.

Obama, Barack H. 2009. "Remarks by the President on International Tax Policy Reform." Office of the Press Secretary. The White House. May 4.

Ober, Josiah. 1993. *Mass and Elite Democratic Athens: Rhetoric, Ideology, and the Power of the People*. Princeton, NJ: Princeton University Press.

Ober, Josiah. 2007. "'I Besieged That Man': Democracy's Revolutionary Start." In *The Origins of Democracy in Ancient Greece*. Kurt A. Raaflaub, Josiah Ober, and Robert W. Wallace, eds., 83–104. Berkeley: University of California Press.

O'Donnell, Guillermo. 2004. "Why the Rule of Law Matters." *Journal of Democracy* 15(4): 32–46.

O'Donnell, Guillermo, Jorge Vargas Cullell, and Osvaldo M. Iazzetta, eds. 2004. *The Quality of Democracy: Theory and Applications*. South Bend: University of Notre Dame Press.

Olson, Mancur. 1993. "Dictatorship, Democracy, and Development." *American Political Science Review* 87(3): 567–576. www.jstor.org/stable/2938736.

Onishi, Norimitsu. 2010. "Filipinos Rely on Armies of Their Own for Influence." *New York Times*, February 21.

Otto, Ton, Henrik Thrane, and Helle Vandkilde, eds. 2006. *Warfare and Society: Archaeological and Social Anthropological Perspectives*. Aarhus: Aarhus Universitet.

Overton, Spencer A. 2002. "But Some are More Equal: Race, Exclusion, and Campaign Finance." *Texas Law Review* 80(5). ssrn.com/abstract=309701.

Overton, Spencer A. 2004. "The Donor Class: Campaign Finance, Democracy, and Participation." *University of Pennsylvania Law Review* 152. ssrn.com/abstract=569021.

Palan, Ronen. 2002. "Tax Havens and the Commercialization of State Sovereignty." *International Organization* 56(1): 151–176. links.jstor.org/sici?sici=0020-8183%28200224%2956%3A1%3C151%3ATHATCO%3E2.0.CO%3B2-N.

Palan, Ronen, Richard Murphy, and Christian Chavagneux. 2009. *Tax Havens: How Globalization Really Works*. Ithaca: Cornell University Press.

Paoli, Letizia. 2003. *Mafia Brotherhoods: Organized Crime, Italian Style*. New York: Oxford University Press.

Pareto, Vilfredo. 1935. *The Mind and Society: A Treatise on General Sociology [Trattato di Sociologia generale, 1916]*. Ed., Arthur Livingston and Trans., Andrew Bongiorno, Arthur Livingston, and James Harvey Rogers. New York: Harcourt, Brace and Company.

Pareto, Vilfredo. 1968 [1901]. *The Rise and Fall of the Elites: An Application of Theoretical Sociology*. Totowa, NJ: Bedminster Press. [Originally published as *Un'applicazione di teorie sociologiche*.]

Parker, Paul P. 1950. "The Roach-Belcher Feud." *California Historical Society* 29(1): 19–28.

Payne, James L. 1968. "The Oligarchy Muddle." *World Politics*, 20(3): April, pp. 439–453.

Pepinsky, Thomas B. 2009. *Economic Crises and the Breakdown of Authoritarian Regimes: Indonesia and Malaysia in Comparative Perspective.* Cambridge: Cambridge University Press.

Pereira, Anthony W. 2003. "Explaining Judicial Reform Outcomes in New Democracies: The Importance of Authoritarian Legalism in Argentina, Brazil, and Chile." *Human Rights Review* 4(3): April.

Perlez, Jane. 2004. "Indonesian Court Overturns Conviction of Party Leader." *New York Times.* February 13. www.nytimes.com/2004/02/13/world/indonesian-court-overturns-politician-s-corruption-conviction.html?ref=wiranto.

Phillips, Kevin. 2002. *Wealth and Democracy: A Political History of the American Rich.* New York: Broadway Press.

Phillips-Fein, Kim. 2009. *Invisible Hands: The Making of the Conservative Movement from the New Deal to Reagan.* New York and London: W. W. Norton & Company.

Piketty, Thomas and Emmanuel Saez. 2003. "Income Inequality in the United States, 1913–1998." *Quarterly Journal of Economics* 118(1): 1–39. elsa.berkeley.edu/~saez/pikettyqje.pdf.

Piven, Frances and Richard C. Cloward. 1978. *Poor People's Movements: Why They Succeed, How They Fail.* New York: Random House.

Piven, Frances and Richard C. Cloward. 2000. *Why Americans Still Don't Vote: And Why Politicians Want It That Way.* Boston: Beacon Press.

PERC. 2010. "Political and Economic Risk Consultancy." Hong Kong. asiarisk.com.

Polanyi, Karl. 2001 [1944]. *The Great Transformation: The Political and Economic Origins of Our Time.* Boston: Beacon Press.

Poly, Jean-Pierre and Eric Bournazel. 1990. *The Feudal Transformation, 900-1200.* Trans. by Caroline Higgitt. New York: Holmes & Meier.

Pompe, Sebastiaan. 2005. *The Indonesian Supreme Court: A Study of Institutional Collapse.* Ithaca: Cornell Southeast Asia Publications.

Poor, Jeff. 2009. "Media Deride Tax Haven 'Cheats' and 'Loopholes;' Ignore Benefits." Business & Media Institute. May 6. www.businessandmedia.org/articles/2009/20090506130056.aspx.

Quah, Jon S. T. 1982. "Bureaucratic Corruption in the ASEAN Countries: A Comparative Analysis of Their Anti-Corruption Strategies." *Journal of Southeast Asian Studies* 13(1): 153–177. www.jstor.org/stable/20070476.

Quah, Jon S. T. 1999. "Corruption in Asian Countries: Can It Be Minimized?" *Public Administration Review* 59(6): 483–494. www.jstor.org/stable/3110297.

Quek, Tracy. 2009. "S'pore Ranked World's 3rd Least-Corrupt Country." *Straits Times* (Singapore). November 18.

Quimpo, Nathan Gilbert. 2005. "Oligarchic Patrimonialism, Bossism, Electoral Clientelism, and Contested Democracy in the Philippines." *Comparative Politics* 37(2): 229–250. www.jstor.org/stable/20072884.

Rainie, Lee and Aaron Smith. 2008. "The Internet and the 2008 Election." Pew Research Center. June 15. www.pewinternet.org/Reports/2008/The-Internet-and-the-2008-Election.aspx.

Raskin, Jamin B. and John Bonifaz. 1993. "Equal Protection and the Wealth Primary." *Yale Law and Policy Review* 11(4): 273–332.

Raskin, Jamin B. 1994. "The Constitutional Imperative and Practical Superiority of Democratically Financed Elections." *Columbia Law Review* 94(4): 1160–203.

Rayda, Nivell. 2009. "The Shadowy World of Indonesia's Case Brokers." *Jakarta Globe*. December 13. www.thejakartaglobe.com/home/the-shadowy-world-of-indonesias-case-brokers/347256.

Reed, Adolph L. Jr. 2007. "Sitting This One Out." *The Progressive*. November. www.progressive.org/mag_reed1107.

Reno, William. 1998. *Warlord Politics and African States*. Boulder, CO: Lynne Rienner.

Reno, William. 2002. "Mafiya Troubles, Warlord Crises." In *Beyond State Crisis? Postcolonial Africa and Post-Soviet Eurasia in Comparative Perspective*. Mark R. Beissinger and Crawford Young, eds. Baltimore, MD: Johns Hopkins University Press.

Research and Markets. 2010. "Trends That Will Shake Up the Wealth Management Industry in 2010." *Research and Markets*. Dublin, Ireland. www.researchandmarkets.com/reports/1124707/trends_that_will_shake_up_the_wealth.pdf.

Richardson, Darrell C. 1986. *Mountain Rising*. Oneida, KY: Mountaineer Press.

Ricklefs, M. C. 2008. *A History of Modern Indonesia Since c. 1200*. 4th edition. Stanford: Stanford University Press.

Riedinger, Jeffrey M. 1995. *Agrarian Reform in the Philippines: Democratic Transitions and Redistributive Reform*. Palo Alto: Stanford University Press.

Robinson, Jeffrey. 1995. *The Laundrymen: Inside Money Laundering, the World's Third Largest Business*. London: Pocket Books.

Robison, Richard and Vedi Hadiz. 2004. *Reorganising Power in Indonesia: The Politics of Oligarchy in an Age of Markets*. London: Routledge Curzon.

Robison, Richard. 2008 [1986]. *Indonesia: The Rise of Capital*. Singapore: Equinox Publishing.

Rodan, Garry. 1989. *The Political Economy of Singapore's Industrialization: National State and International Capital*. Basingstoke: Macmillan.

Rodan, Garry. 2006. "Singapore: Globalisation, the State, and Politics." In *The Political Economy of South-East Asia: Markets, Power and Contestation*. Garry Rodan, Kevin Hewison, and Richard Robison, eds., 137–169. Melbourne: Oxford University Press.

Rodan, Garry and Kanishka Jayasuriya. 2009. "Capitalist Development, Regime Transitions, and New Forms of Authoritarianism in Asia." *Pacific Review* 22(1): 23–47.

Roosevelt, Theodore. 1910. "The New Nationalism." Presidential speech. August 31. www.presidentialrhetoric.com/historicspeeches/roosevelt_theodore/newnationalism.html.

Roosa, John. 2006. *Pretext for Mass Murder: The September 30th Movement and Suharto's Coup d'État in Indonesia*. Madison, WI: University of Wisconsin Press.

Roston, Aram. 2010. "Bloomberg's Offshore Millions." *Observer*. April 20. www.observer.com/2010/politics/bloomberg%E2%80%99s-offshore-millions.

Runciman, W. G. 1982. "Origins of States: The Case of Archaic Greece." *Comparative Studies in Society and History* 24(3): 351–377. www.jstor.org/stable/178506.

Runciman, W. G. 1983. "Capitalism without Classes: The Case of Classical Rome." *British Journal of Sociology* 34(2): 157–181. www.jstor.org/stable/590734.

Rustow, Dankwart A. 1966. "The Study of Elites: Who's Who, When, and How." *World Politics* 18(4): 690–717.

Ryter, Loren. 2009. "Their Moment in the Sun: The New Indonesian Parliamentarians from the Old OKP." In *State of Authority: The State in Society in Indonesia*. Gerry van Klinken and Joshua Barker, eds. Ithaca, NY: Cornell University Southeast Asia Program.

Samons, Loren J. 1998. "Mass, Elite, and Hoplite-Farmer in Greek History." A review and discussion of J. Ober, *The Athenian Revolution*, and V. Hanson, *The Other Greeks. Arion*, Third Series, 5(3): 99–123. www.jstor.org/stable/20163692.

Santino, Umberto. 2003. "Mafia and Mafia-Type Organizations in Italy." In *Organized Crime: World Perspectives*. J. A. Albanese, D. K. Das, and A. Verma, eds., 82–100. Prentice-Hall. www.centroimpastato.it/publ/online/mafia-in-italy.htm.

Sarauw, Torben. 2007. "Male Symbols or Warrior Identities? The 'Archery Burials' of the Danish Bell Beaker Culture." *Journal of Anthropological Archaeology* 26(1): 65–87.

Sastre, Inés. 2008. "Community, Identity, and Conflict: Iron Age Warfare in the Iberian Northwest." *Current Anthropology* 49(6): 1021–1051.

Scheidel, Walter. 2005. "Human Mobility in Roman Italy, II: The Slave Population." *Journal of Roman Studies* 95: 64–79. www.jstor.org/stable/20066817.

Schmidt, Alvin J. 1973. *Oligarchy in Fraternal Organizations: A Study in Organizational Leadership*. Detroit: Gale Research Company.

Schneider, Jane T. and Peter T. Schneider. 2003. *Reversible Destiny: Mafia, Antimafia, and the Struggle for Palermo*. Berkeley: University of California Press.

Schryer, Frans J. 1986. "Peasants and the Law: A History of Land Tenure and Conflict in the Huasteca." *Journal of Latin American Studies* 18(2): 283–311. www.jstor.org/stable/157107.

Schumpeter, Joseph A. 1975 [1942]. *Capitalism, Socialism, and Democracy*. New York: Harper Perennial.

Schwarz, Adam. 2000. *A Nation in Waiting: Indonesia's Search for Stability*. Boulder: Westview Press.

Seager, Robin. 1987. "Proscription." A Review of F. Hinard, *Les Proscriptions de la Rome républicaine. Classical Review* 37(2): 248–250. www.jstor.org/stable/3064133.

Seow, Francis T. 2006. *Beyond Suspicion: The Singapore Judiciary*. Monograph 55. New Haven: Yale Southeast Asian Studies.

Shelton, Jo-Ann. 1988. *As the Romans Did: A Source Book in Roman Social History*. Oxford: Oxford University Press.

Sherwin-White, Adrian. N. 1956. "Violence in Roman Politics." *Journal of Roman Studies* 46(1–2): 1–9. www.jstor.org/stable/297959.

Sidel, John T. 1998. "Macet Total: Logics of Circulation and Accumulation in the Demise of Indonesia's New Order." *Indonesia* 66: 158–195. links.jstor.org/sici?sici= 0019-7289%2189 981 0%2966%3C1 58%3AMTLOCA%3E2.O.CO%3B2-W.

Sidel, John T. 1999. *Capital, Coercion, and Crime: Bossism in the Philippines*. Palo Alto: Stanford University Press.

Sidel, John T. 2004. "Bossism and Democracy in the Philippines, Thailand, and Indonesia: Towards an Alternative Framework for the Study of 'Local Strongmen.'" In *Politicising Democracy: The New Local Politics of Democratisation*. John Harriss, Kristin Stokke, and Olle Tornquist, eds., 51–74. Basingstoke, UK: Palgrave Macmillan.

Sidel, John T. 2009. "Walking in the Shadow of the Big Man: Justiniano Montano and Failed Dynasty Building in Cavite, 1935–1972." In *An Anarchy of Families: State and Family in the Philippines*. Alfred W. McCoy, ed., 109–162. Madison: University of Wisconsin Press.

Simbulan, Dante C. 2006. *The Modern Principalia: The Historical Evolution of the Philippine Ruling Oligarchy*. Honolulu: University of Hawaii Press.

Simkhovitch, Vladimir G. 1916. "Rome's Fall Reconsidered." *Political Science Quarterly* 31(2): 201–243. www.jstor.org/stable/2141560.

Simpson, Bradley. 2009. *Economists with Guns: Authoritarian Development and U.S.-Indonesian Relations, 1960–1968.* Stanford: Stanford Univerity Press.

Simpson, Glenn. 2008. "U.S. to Seek Client Names from UBS in Tax Case." *Wall Street Journal.* May 15.

Singapore Department of Statistics. 2010. "Key Household Income Trends, 2009." Occasional Paper on Income Statistics. February. www.singstat.gov.sg/pubn/papers/economy/op-s16.pdf.

Smiley, Gene and Richard H. Keehn. 1995. "Federal Personal Income Tax Policy in the 1920s." *Journal of Economic History* 55(2): 285–303. links.jstor.org/sici?sici=0022–0507%28199506%2955%3A2%3C285%3AFPITPI%3E2.0.CO%3B2-J.

Smith, Adam. 1776. *An Inquiry into the Nature and Causes of the Wealth of Nations.* Library of Economics and Liberty. www.econlib.org/library/Smith/smWN.html.

Smith, Vernon L. 1993. "Humankind in Prehistory: Economy, Ecology, and Institutions." In *The Political Economy of Customs and Culture: Informal Solutions to the Commons Problem.* Terry L. Anderson and Randy T. Simmons, ed. Lanham, MD: Rowman & Littlefield.

Soemitro and Ramadhan K. H. 1994. *Soemitro: Dari Pangdam Mulawarman Sampai Pangkopkamtib. Petikan dari Memoar: 1965–1976.* Jakarta: Pustaka Sinar Harapan.

Solt, Frederick. 2008. "Economic Inequality and Democratic Political Engagement." *American Journal of Political Science* 52(1): 48–60.

Sonnichsen, C. L. 1949. "Review: *The Hatfields and the McCoys* by Virgil Carrington Jones." *Western Folklore* 8(1): 83–85. www.jstor.org/stable/1497184.

Spengler, Joseph J. 1953. "Changes in Income Distribution and Social Stratification: A Note." *American Journal of Sociology* 59(3): 247–259. links.jstor.org/sici?sici=0002–960228 1953 11%2959%3A3%3C247%3ACIIDAS%3E2.0.CO%3B2-A.

Spruyt, Hendrik. 1994. *The Sovereign State and Its Competitors: An Analysis of Systems Change.* Princeton: Princeton University Press.

Sri Saraswati, Muninggar. 2004. "Court Opens New Case against Akbar." *Jakarta Post.* April 13.

Staggenborg, Suzanne. 1988. "The Consequences of Professionalization and Formalization in the Pro-Choice Movement." *American Sociological Review* 53(4): 585–605.

Stalley, Richard. F. 1995. *Politics.* By Aristotle. Trans. by Ernest Barker. Revised with an Introduction and Notes by Richard. F. Stalley. Oxford: Oxford University Press.

Steen, Jennifer A. 2006. *Self-Financed Candidates in Congressional Elections.* Ann Arbor: University of Michigan Press.

Stephenson, Andrew. 1891. *Public Lands and Agrarian Laws of the Roman Republic.* Baltimore: Johns Hopkins University Press.

Syme, Ronald. 1939. *The Roman Revolution.* Oxford: Oxford University Press.

Tarrow, Sidney. 2004. "From Comparative Historical Analysis to 'Local Theory': The Italian City-State Route to the Modern State." *Theory and Society* 33(3/4): 443–471. www.jstor.org/stable/4144880.

Tax Foundation. 2009a. "Summary of Latest Federal Individual Income Tax Data, 1980–2007." Tax Data. July 30. www.taxfoundation.org/taxdata/show/23408.html.

Tax Foundation. 2009b. "U.S. Federal Individual Income Tax Rates History, 1913–2010." Tax Data. December 31. www.taxfoundation.org/publications/show/ 151.html.

Tax Justice Network. 2005. "The Price of Offshore." Briefing Paper. www.taxjustice .net/cms/upload/pdf/Price_of_Offshore.pdf.

Tax Justice Network. 2009. "Financial Secrecy Index." 2009 Results. www.financial secrecyindex.com/2009results.html.

Tax Justice Network. 2010. "Magnitudes: Dirty Money, Lost Taxes, and Offshore." Magnitudes and Measurements. www.taxjustice.net/cms/front_content.php?idcat= 103.

Taylor, Martha C. 2002. "Implicating the Demos: A Reading of Thucydides on the Rise of the Four Hundred." *Journal of Hellenic Studies* 122: 91–108. links.jstor.org/ sici?sici=0075-4269%282002%29122%3C91%3AITDARO%3E2.0.CO%3B2-0.

Tempo. 2004. "Protected by Presidential Order?" *Tempo* 23(4). February 10–16. mbm2.tempointeraktif.com/id/arsip/2004/02/10/LU/mbm.20040210.LU109501.id .html.

Tempo. 2010. "Mafia at the Gates." *Tempo* 28(10). March 10–16. www.tempo.co.id/ majalah/arsip/10th/edition28/index-uk.html.

Thayer, William. R. 1904. "The Oligarchy of Venice: An Essay." *American Historical Review* 9(4): 784–785. links.jstor.org/sici?sici=0002–8762%21890407%299% 3A4%3C784%3ATOOVAE%3E2.0.C0%3B2-H.

Thompson, Mark R. 1995. *The Anti-Marcos Struggle: Personalistic Rule and Democratic Transition in the Philippines.* New Haven: Yale University Press.

Thomson, George. 1949. *Studies in Ancient Greek Society: The Prehistoric Aegean.* London: Lyle Stuart.

Tiberius Sempronius Gracchus. *Encyclopædia Britannica.* 2009. Encyclopædia Britannica Online. October 16, 2009. www.britannica.com/EBchecked/topic/240427/ Tiberius-Sempronius-Gracchus.

Tilly, Charles. 1992. *Coercion, Capital, and the European State: AD 990–1992.* Cambridge, MA: Blackwell.

Time. 1958. "Singapore: Far East Story." *Time* Magazine. September 8. www.time.com/ time/magazine/article/0,9171,868802,00.html.

Time. 1959a. "Singapore: Chophouse Chopin." *Time* Magazine. June 29. www .time.com/time/magazine/article/0,9171,864665,00.html.

Time. 1959b. "Singapore: Triad in Trouble." *Time* Magazine. November 16. www .time.com/time/magazine/article/0,9171,811441,00.html.

Time. 1960. "Singapore: How to Catch a Millionaire." *Time* Magazine. August 15. www.time.com/time/magazine/article/0,9171,939750,00.html.

Time. 1965. "Malaysia: One of Our Islands Is Missing." *Time* Magazine. August 20. www.time.com/time/magazine/article/0,9171,841964,00.html.

Time. 1966. "Singapore: The Boom That Went Bust." *Time* Magazine. January 7. www.time.com/time/magazine/article/0,9171,834961,00.html.

Todd, S. C. 1995. "Policing Athens." Review: *Policing Athens: Social Control in the Attic Lawsuits, 420–320 B.C.* by V. J. Hunter. *Classical Review*, New Series 45(1): 89–91. www.jstor.org/stable/710362.

Transparency International. 2009. "Corruption Perceptions Index 2009." www .transparency.org/policy_research/surveys_indices/cpi/2009/cpi_2009_table.

Tronto, Joan C. 2007. "American Oligarchy?" Presented at the annual meeting of the American Political Science Association, Chicago, IL. August 31–September 2.

Turner, Ralph E. 1948. "Economic Discontent in Medieval Western Europe." *Journal of Economic History* 8, Supplement, pp. 85–100. www.jstor.org/stable/2113566.

United Nations. 1976. "UNCITRAL: United Nations Commission on International Trade Law, 1976." Arbitration rules. www.uncitral.org/uncitral/en/uncitral_texts/arbitration/1976Arbitration_rules.html.

Uslaner, Eric M. 2008. *Corruption, Inequality, and the Rule of Law.* Cambridge: Cambridge University Press.

U.S. Department of Defense. 2009. "Military Pay Tables – Basic Pay Effective January 1, 2009." Defense Finance and Accounting Service. www.dfas.mil/militarypay/militarypaytables/2009MilitaryPayTables.doc.

U.S. Department of State. 2004. "Singapore: County Report on Human Rights Practices." Bureau of Democracy, Human Rights, and Labor. Office of the Under Secretary for Democracy and Global Affairs. Released: February 28, 2005. www.state.gov/g/drl/rls/hrrpt/2004/41659.htm.

U.S. Department of State. 2010. "Background Note: Singapore." Bureau of East Asian and Pacific Affairs. April 1. www.state.gov/r/pa/ei/bgn/2798.htm#political.

U.S. District Court. 2006. *United States of America v. David Rifkin.* Plea in the United States District Court, Southern District of New York, before the Hon. Lewis A Kaplan, District Judge. March 27.

U.S. Senate. 2003. "U.S. Tax Shelter Industry: The Role of Accountants, Lawyers, and Financial Professionals – Four KPMG Case Studies: FLIP, OPIS, BLIPS, and SC2." Report Prepared by the Minority Staff of the Permanent Subcommittee on Investigations of the Committee on Governmental Affairs. United States Senate. Released in Conjunction with the Permanent Subcommittee on Investigations' Hearings on November 18 and 20, 2003. Washington, DC: GPO.

U.S. Senate. 2005. "The Role of Professional Firms in the U.S. Tax Shelter Industry." Report Prepared by the Permanent Subcommittee on Investigations of the Committee on Homeland Security and Governmental Affairs. United States Senate. April 13.

U.S. Senate. 2006. "Tax Haven Abuses: The Enablers, the Tools and Secrecy." Minority & Majority Staff Report, Permanent Subcommittee on Investigations. United States Senate. Committee on Homeland Security and Governmental Affairs. Norm Coleman, Chairman; Carl Levin, Ranking Minority Member. Released in Conjunction with the Permanent Subcommittee on Investigations August 1, 2006 Hearing.

Vandenbosch, Amry. 1930. "A Problem in Java: The Chinese in the Dutch East Indies." *Pacific Affairs* 3(11): 1001–1017. www.jstor.org/stable/2750073.

Verba, Sidney, Kay Lehman Schlozman, and Henry E. Brady. 1995. *Voice and Equality: Civic Voluntarism in American Politics.* Cambridge: Harvard University Press.

Waller, Altina. 1988. *Feud: Hatfields, McCoys, and Social Change in Appalachia, 1860–1900.* Chapel Hill: University of North Carolina Press.

Wedel, Janine R. 2009. *Shadow Elite: How the World's New Power Brokers Undermine Democracy, Government, and the Free Market.* New York: Basic Books.

Wantchekon, Leonard. 2004. "The Paradox of 'Warlord' Democracy." *American Political Science Review* 98(1): 17–34.

Whibley, Leonard. 1896. *Greek Oligarchies: Their Character and Organisation.* London: Methuen & Co.

Whitte, John F. 1986. *The Politics and Development of the Federal Income Tax.* Madison: University of Wisconsin Press.

Williams, John A. 1976. *West Virginia: A Bicentennial History*. New York: Norton Publishing Co.

Winters, Jeffrey A. 1988. *"Indonesia: The Rise of Capital, A Review Essay."* Indonesia 45: 109–28.

Winters, Jeffrey A. 1996. *Power in Motion: Capital Mobility and the Indonesian State*. Ithaca: Cornell University Press.

Winters, Jeffrey A. 1999. "The Determinants of Financial Crisis in Asia." In T. J. Pempel, ed. *The Politics of the Asian Economic Crisis*. Ithaca: Cornell University Press.

Winters, Jeffrey A. 2000. "The Financial Crisis in Southeast Asia." In Richard Robison, Mark Beeson, Kanishka Jayasuriya, and Hyuk-Rae Kim, eds. *Politics and Markets in the Wake of the Asian Crisis*. London and New York: Routledge.

Winters, Jeffrey A. and Benjamin I. Page. 2009. "Oligarchy in the United States?" *Perspectives on Politics* 7(4): 731–751.

Wiranto. 2003. *Witness in the Storm: A Memoir of an Army General*. Jakarta: Delta Pustaka Express; and The Centre for Globalisation and Social Studies.

Wolff, Edward N. 2007. "Recent Trends in Household Wealth in the United States: Rising Debt and the Middle-Class Squeeze." Working Paper No. 502. The Levy Economics Institute of Bard College. June. www.levyinstitute.org/pubs/wp_502.pdf.

Woo, Jung-en. 1991. *Race to the Swift*. New York: Columbia University Press.

Wood, Ellen Meiksins. 1989. "Oligarchic 'Democracy.'" *Monthly Review* 41: 1–7.

Yarros, Victor S. 1917. "Representation and Leadership in Democracies." *American Journal of Sociology* 23(3): 390–402.

Zhuravskaya, Ekaterina. 2007. "Whither Russia? A Review of Andrei Shleifer's *A Normal Country*." *Journal of Economic Literature* 45(1): 127–146. www.aeaweb.org/articles.php?doi=10.1257/jel.45.1.127.

Index

Made in the USA
Columbia, SC
20 November 2017